Robert Frost

The American Critical Tradition

M. Thomas Inge
General Editor

Theodore Dreiser: The Critical Reception
Edited by Jack Salzman
Long Island University

Thomas Wolfe: The Critical Reception
Edited by Pascal Reeves
University of Georgia

Ernest Hemingway: The Critical Reception
Edited by Robert O. Stephens
University of North Carolina

William Faulkner: The Critical Reception
Edited by M. Thomas Inge
Virginia Commonwealth University

Robert Frost: The Critical Reception
Edited by Linda W. Wagner
Michigan State University

Robert Frost

The Critical Reception

Edited with an Introduction by
Linda W. Wagner

Burt Franklin & Co., Inc.

Library of Congress Cataloging in Publication Data

Main entry under title:
Robert Frost: the critical reception.
(The American critical tradition)
Includes index.
1. Frost, Robert, 1874-1963—Criticism
and interpretation—Addresses, essays, lectures.
I. Wagner, Linda Welshimer.
PS3511.R94Z9185   811'.5'2   77-21719
ISBN 0-89102-064-0 (cloth)
0-89102-096-9 (paper)

Acknowledgments and permissions
are listed on pp. xxiii-xxv,
which constitute an extension of the
copyright page for the purposes
of notice.

For
Evelyn, Margaret, Maye

General Editor's Preface

When we speak of a writer's reputation in critical terms, we should recognize that he actually has two: the response of book reviewers and critics during his own lifetime to each of his works as it was published, and the retrospective evaluation of his achievement by literary historians and academic critics in the decades after his career is concluded. The primary concern of modern scholarship has been the latter, on the assumption that the passage of time is essential before a writer's achievement can be objectively viewed and assessed. The purpose of the volumes in the American Critical Tradition series, however, is to provide overviews of the critical reputations earned by major American authors in their own times. Such overviews are necessary before the full impact of a writer's influence can be properly evaluated and an understanding of how he related to his contemporary cultural milieu achieved.

The few efforts hitherto made in summarizing a writer's contemporary critical standing have usually been based on a reading of sample reviews or vague impressions retained by veterans of the era. Seldom have literary historians gone back to locate and read all or most of the comment elicited by a career in progress. In the present volumes, the editors have sought to unearth every known review of each book in the contemporary newspapers, journals, and periodicals, and to demonstrate the critical response chronologically through reprint, excerpt, or summary. Exhaustive checklists of reviews not included in the text are appended to each chapter, and the editor has provided an introduction summarizing the major trends observable in the criticism. The results not only elucidate the writer's career, but they reveal as well intellectual patterns in book reviewing and the reception of serious writing by the American reading public. Each volume is, therefore, a combined literary chronicle and reference work of a type previously unavailable.

M. Thomas Inge
General Editor

Contents

Introduction   xi

Acknowledgments   xxiii

A Boy's Will (1913)   1

North of Boston (1914)   11

Mountain Interval (1916)   43

New Hampshire: A Poem with Notes and Grace
    Notes (1923)   55

West-Running Brook (1928)   69

Collected Poems (1930)   83

A Further Range (1936)   113

Collected Poems of Robert Frost (1939)   151

A Witness Tree (1942)   169

A Masque of Reason (1945)   185

Steeple Bush (1947)   207

A Masque of Mercy (1947)   221

Complete Poems of Robert Frost (1949)   227

In the Clearing (1962)   241

Appendix   275

Index   277

Introduction

Robert Frost made no attempt to find a publisher for a first book of poems until he was thirty-nine. Even though he had written poetry since he was in high school, and did try to publish it in magazines, he had collected his work only in the small gift booklets that he gave to his future wife Elinor White *(Twilight)* in 1894 and to his friend Susan Hayes Ward (editor of *The Independent*) in 1911. Frost considered himself a serious writer but he was also a cautious person and, as Lawrance Thompson depicts in the Frost biography, an easily discouraged one. Failing to sell his poems to magazines probably kept him from pursuing higher aspirations.

It was only with the 1912 move to England that Frost grew bolder and collected some of his poems into the manuscript *A Boy's Will*. On October 26, 1912, the firm of David Nutt—the first publisher Frost had approached—accepted the manuscript. The beginning of his career was hardly typical, especially when one considers that forty publishers had rejected the manuscript of James Joyce's *Dubliners* before Ezra Pound finally placed the short-story collection for him, and that William Carlos Williams—and many other modernist poets—paid to have several early books of poetry printed.

Atypical, too, was the pattern of critical reaction to Frost's poetry. Not only was Frost the only poet to win four Pulitzer prizes for poetry, he also was one of the few modern writers whose work received generally favorable reviews. From the 1913 publication of *A Boy's Will*, critics praised his poetry for its subject matter, craft, natural sentence rhythms, and imagery. In a literary world vehemently divided by controversies over the appropriateness of free verse and common ("antipoetic") subjects, the consistency of favorable response to Frost's work was surprising—even inexplicable. The *Dial* reviewer compared his poems with those of A. E. Housman, remarking on their "simple phrasing and patent sincerity" (September 16, 1913). The *Academy* found Frost important because his poems combined "with a rare sufficiency, the essential qualities of inevitability and surprise." (The poems also were free from "any new and twisted theory of art.") Like W. S.

Braithwaite who placed Frost "in the very front rank of contemporary American poets" (*Boston Evening Transcript,* April 28, 1915), the *Academy* reviewer labeled him "a true poet," adding,

> We have not the slightest idea who Mr. Robert Frost may be, but we welcome him unhesitatingly to the ranks of poets born, and are convinced that if this is a true sample of his parts he should presently give us work far worthier of honour than much which passes for front-rank poetry at the present time (September 20, 1913).

Even the few less-enthusiastic comments—those of the *Athenaeum* (April 5, 1913) and *Times Literary Supplement* (April 10)— acknowledged Frost's poetic abilities, objecting only to the simplicity of his diction and phrasing. This simplicity was, ironically, the trait which avant-garde poets like Ezra Pound and F. S. Flint most admired.

Frost benefited greatly by having relatively well-known modern writers like Pound, Flint, Norman Douglas, Amy Lowell, and Ford Madox Ford among his champions. Pound's May 1913 review in *Poetry* magazine gave Frost acceptance among the many younger poets who were excited by the new freedoms of the Chicago school, the French symbolistes, and Imagists like H. D., William Carlos Williams, and Pound himself. (In 1914 Pound also reviewed *North of Boston* and later claimed credit for "discovering" Frost; the younger poet knew the value of his patronage.) Emphasizing Frost's use of "the thing, the thing as he sees it," and his natural speech rhythms, Pound pointed to the essential modernity in Frost—his focus on the concrete image or scene, and his firmly realized concepts of rhythm (the "sound of sense," as he was later to describe his prosody). F. S. Flint's review in *Poetry and Drama* (June 13, 1913) praised Frost's "spontaneity, subtlety in the evocation of moods, humour, an ear for silences." Flint found Frost's importance to lie in his innovations in both technique and attitude, with a pervasive skepticism balanced against the poet's more charitable impulses.

In Frost's writing, the latter seemed to be most often directed toward the personae of his poems. In *North of Boston* Frost's empathy with his rural characters—the farm wives, the various servants, old Silas—was an important strength. Originally titled *Farm Servants, and Other People,* Frost's second collection was dominated by his interest in the colorful (and sometimes painfully colorless) characters and the dramatic scenario he used to convey those characterizations. It also—for better or worse—established him as the poet of New England. Several critics commented on Frost's need to have his characters interact through dialogue. *The Nation* (London, June 13, 1914) called the poems "psychological idylls"; Edward Thomas termed the book "a collection of dramatic narratives in verse" *(English Review*, August 1914). Most critics saw Frost's use of scenario accurately, as an effective means of allowing the personae to speak in natural sentence patterns. In fact, George H. Browne's essay, "Robert Frost, A Poet of Speech," explains the appeal of Frost's poetry in terms of these natural rhythms:

> American readers have discovered that they can understand and enjoy poetry which deals veraciously with the life and the people they know—poetry which is written in a language they can understand and enjoy, because it is the language they speak, vibrant with the feeling and force and form of the familiar spoken sentence *(The Independent,* May 22, 1916).

Frost himself often commented on the "sentence sense" of a poem's rhythms, explaining that the center of his prosody was the tension between line end and sentence end: "if one is to be a poet he must learn to get cadences by skillfully breaking the sounds of sense with all their irregularity of accent across the regular beat of the metre" (Frost to John Bartlett, July 4, 1913, cited in Margarett Bartlett Anderson, *Robert Frost: The Record of a Friendship* [New York: Holt, Rinehart and Winston, 1963], p. 54). The sentence also kept the dominant rhythm moving through the poem and was therefore an "emotional indicator" of tone and mood.

Along with some perceptive analyses of the early poems, critics also began formulating the various Frost legends. Ezra Pound (erroneously) presented him as an artist at odds with commercial American publishing, and Frost's concern over this image is reflected in his letter to Sidney Cox ("It was not in anger that I came to England," *Letters,* p. 148). Despite his California birthplace and childhood, Frost had already been firmly locked into his New England identity. And the *Review of Reviews'* inclusion of a photo of the pensive poet, his hair even then thatched and unruly, initiated the creation of the personal myth. So pervasive did these views of Frost and his poetry become that by the publication of his last collection, *In the Clearing* (1962), many reviewers sounded as if they were writing summaries of the earliest reviews.

These early reviews also show that, whatever their technical prowess, Frost's poems appealed to readers at least partly because of subject matter and themes. "Mending Wall," "Home Burial," "The Wood Pile," "The Mountain," "After Apple-Picking," "A Servant to Servants," "The Road Not Taken," "The Death of the Hired Man"—many of the best-known poems were published in the first two collections. Frost's choice of commonplace men and women, who find their understanding of life through immediate—and apparently real—experience, reflected the trend of modern artists to write about unpretentious, lifelike characters. What Dreiser's Sister Carrie was to Antigone, Frost's hill wife was to Browning's last duchess. Whether the poet himself or some other character was the focus of the poem, Frost managed to convey a psychological reality that was convincing to many readers.

Perhaps more important than his focus on believable characters was Frost's comparative ambivalence toward his subjects. As Frank Lentricchia points out in his 1975 study, *Robert Frost: Modern Poetics and the Landscapes of Self* (Durham, N.C.: Duke University Press), one of Frost's most contemporary attitudes was reflected in his mixture of a realistic, even ironic comprehension of the world and a softer Kantian view. Placing Frost in line from William James and George Santayana, Lentricchia finds the evidences of Frost's own often hard-won "balance" to be an effective means of reaching the modern reader, whether that balance was expressed through humor, suggestion, or paradox. Frost's view of life was seldom "easy." The platitudes that he occasionally quoted in his poems ("Good fences make good neighbors," for example) were often treated ironically and were usually answered by a maxim of the poet's own devising (as, "Something there is that doesn't love a wall,/That wants it down"). Although one would hesitate to label Frost "confessional," he was one of the first modern poets to let his readers sense the private contradictions that underlay his world view.

Lentriccia's recent arguments for considering Frost a modern poet rather than a post-Georgian are timely because one of the recurring issues in Frost criticism has been chronological categorizing. Many readers place Frost at the end of the nineteenth century rather than at the opening of the twentieth. Because Frost did frequently write in regular stanzas instead of free forms, readers tended to consider him a "traditional" poet (with some unpleasant connotations of stodginess and turgidity). And because of his tendency to use nature imagery, the pastoral label was also readily affixed—hence, the relation to the British Georgian poets. While such a designation in Frost's case may not be entirely misleading, it was often used pejoratively. Innovation, the search for the new, became the twentieth-century *modus operandi*. Despite T. S. Eliot's attempt to explain the new poet's use of past conventions (in his essay, "Tradition and the Individual Talent"), the literary community respected the dramatically inventive rather than the subtle kind of experimentation that suffused Frost's poetry.

So far as Frost's individual concepts of prosody were concerned, few poets achieved as distinctive a voice so quickly. From *A Boy's Will*,

Frost wrote effectively in his sound-of-sense metier. In the midst of the interminable battle over *vers libre,* free verse, quantitative verse, and organic form, Frost firmly followed his own direction, modifying accent patterns and varying regular meters whenever necessary to achieve his approximation of natural voice rhythms.

Just as important as subject matter, attitude, and prosody may have been Frost's use of the extended image to give his poems their distinctive impact. Throughout his writing, he seldom used a rigidly developed series of images; rather, his tactic was to employ a "spun-out" structure in which oblique parts of the central image joined the main and then disappeared, recurring in an almost stream-of-consciousness pattern, as in "Birches" or "Mending Wall." In part, this associative image organization may have succeeded because of the poem's pervasive and unifying rhythms.

With Frost's third collection, the 1916 *Mountain Interval,* critics praised his versatility. The frequent blank-verse narratives in *North of Boston* had been replaced by generally shorter lyrics. "The Hill Wife" and "Birches" were singled out for special mention, and Padriac Colum made the point that Frost was more interested in a "spiritual history" than in social commentary, that Frost's fascination lay with mood, not with the physical trappings of the culture (*New Republic,* December 23, 1916).

A seven-year pause before the appearance of *New Hampshire* in 1923 gave critics the chance to stabilize their generally favorable opinions. In 1922, although it had been six years since *Mountain Interval,* Frost tied with James Branch Cabell for fifth place in a "most important American writer" poll, conducted among American writers by the *Literary Digest.* Joseph Hergesheimer led the balloting, followed by Eugene O'Neill, Sherwood Anderson, and Willa Cather; then Frost and Cabell. Few readers shared Edmund Wilson's opinion of Frost as "excessively dull . . . he certainly writes very poor verse. He is, in my opinion, the most generally overrated of all [the current] group of poets" (*The Shores of Light* [New York: Farrar, Straus and Young, 1952], p. 111). Indeed, it is with *New Hampshire* that John Farrar proclaimed Frost "one of the few great poets America has ever produced (*Literary Digest International Book Review,* November 1923), and Louis Untermeyer began his long career writing in support of Frost's poetry. In *Bookman* (January 23, 1924), Untermeyer emphasized Frost's increasing whimsicality, the growing humor that underlies even the structure of *New Hampshire,* with its "notes" and "gracenotes." But he also reassured the reader that the humane and skillful Frost remained:

Nothing, really, has changed. The idiom is clearer, the convictions have deepened—the essential things, the point of view, the tone of voice, remain the same.

Only the reviews of *West-Running Brook* (1928), Frost's fifth collection, show in retrospect that 1923 was the peak of Frost's critical reception. In that year, praise for *New Hampshire* had been uniform, culminating in Frost's being awarded his first Pulitzer prize for poetry. Even though some critics stressed the similarities between *New Hampshire* and Frost's earlier books, while others emphasized the differences, their intention was singular: to prove that Frost was writing better poetry. In 1928, however, this tendency reversed itself. *West-Running Brook* disappointed at least some of Frost's critics. Like others, Babette Deutsche complained about the volume's slimness and its inclusion of some "unworthy" poems (*Bookman*, December 1928). Frederick Pierce (*Yale Review*, December) questioned the value of the poet's limiting his scope to "a little walled-in nook" instead of taking a wider life-view. The reasons for this fault-finding are, in many ways, of less interest than the fact that the fault-finding did exist: that the time had come to detract from Frost's growing reputation. With the more chary stance of these reviewers, however, came some perceptive critical comment, i.e., Mark Van Doren's description of the most effective poems, "poems which represent Mr. Frost in the act of standing and looking at some very definite thing—a pool in the spring woods, a chimney smoking under the new moon . . . standing and looking at it and talking about it in such a way that it suddenly and weirdly becomes a world" (*Nation*, January 23, 1929).

"The World of Robert Frost" was precisely the title of Granville Hicks' favorable review of Frost's first *Collected Poems* (*New Republic*, December 3, 1930). Hicks found the source of Frost's "intense," "sustained" poetic power to lie in his creation of a coherent, believable world when so many other modern artists were content to reflect the chaos of twentieth-century life. Richard Church similarly described Frost as a "*complete* poet; that is, a man who interprets the whole of himself" (*Spectator*, February 21, 1931); just as Virginia Moore appraises Frost as "personality," albeit with limitations ("There are moods beyond which he cannot go," *Yale Review*, March 1931). For James Southall Wilson, the primary quality in Frost's writing is "humanity" (*Virginia Quarterly Review*, April 1931), and because of that quality, Wilson concludes: "To my judgment no richer volume of poetry has been produced in America since Poe's volume of 1845." In this opinion, both American and English critics concurred. Geoffrey Grigson, writing in *Saturday Review* said that, "Taking this book in all, I think it the most important poet's collection which has appeared for several years. It is rare to find three hundred and fifty pages of verse so consistently good" (London, April 4, 1931). Frost's first *Collected Poems* won him his second Pulitzer prize for poetry.

Many of the titles Frost chose for his books helped set the tone of their reviews. With the choice of *A Further Range* for his 1936 collection, Frost implied that his concerns were broader than the New England corner he was usually allowed. "In 'A Further Range' Robert Frost Advances" and "Mr. Frost Ranges Further" were representative titles as reviewers seemed eager to erase the major limitation of Frost's appeal.

A Further Range was the most widely reviewed of any of Frost's books, partly because it was a Book-of-the-Month Club selection, partly because it was published during a period of national literary self-consciousness. The years of the Great Depression fostered discontent with writing that had little social import; so-called Marxist critics tended to dislike much literature because its social stand was either wrong or absent. Rolfe Humphries, who found Frost's work definitely minor, titled his review "A Further Shrinking" (*New Masses*, August 11, 1936). Morton D. Zabel found Frost's attitude disappointing, one of "complacent mock-innocence" (*Southern Review*, 1936-37).

R. P. Blackmur, however, focused the issue more precisely when he noted that Frost's "political" or social poems are not very well realized, are, in fact, often "dull verse" (*Nation*, June 24, 1936). Horace Gregory (*New Republic*, June) concurs, adding that when Frost becomes political, "his wisdom may be compared to that of Calvin Coolidge." Coming under attack most often are Frost's epigrams ("He is not a wit," writes Leonard Feeney in *America*, July 4, 1936) and the long poem "Build Soil." As Dudley Fitts concludes about the latter,

> the diction is faded, the expression imprecise, and the tone extraordinarily tired and uneasy.... It is not that his social attitude suggests nothing new.... The trouble is that it suggests nothing at all so much as a man who wishes he had never brought up the subject in the first place (*New England Quarterly*, September 1936).

For the more characteristic poems in the collection, however, critics had only praise, and it was the affirmative vote that brought Frost his third Pulitzer prize.

Uncongenial as the role of poet-economist/poet-propagandizer seems to have been for Frost, it was a role he followed conscientiously, if sporadically. During the next decade, his writing included *A Masque of Reason* (1945) and *A Masque of Mercy* (1945), both products of the

"Build Soil" kind of impulse (Frost as institution, as voice of a people's conscience); and the tendencies that Fitts describes so well surface frequently in *A Witness Tree* (1942) and *Steeple Bush* (1947).

But first, in 1939, another *Collected Poems* appeared. A few critics (e.g., Louise Bogan in the March 4 *New Yorker*) found fault with the "curiously static" tone and the late-expressed "conservatism"; and Muriel Rukeyser challenged Frost to prove that his "rigid preconception of life" and self was "enough" for a poetics (*Poetry,* July 1939). More critics, however, were happy simply to describe Frost's career since the 1913 publication of *A Boy's Will,* culminating with his acknowledged position in modern American literature.

A Witness Tree (1942) was met with nearly uniform praise. Stephen Vincent Benét described the collection as "a beautiful book, serene, observing, and passionate . . . a book to read, a book to remember, and a book that will be part of our inheritance" (*Saturday Review of Literature,* April 25, 1942). *A Witness Tree* brought Frost his fourth Pultizer prize, and enthusiasm continued with the 1945 *A Masque of Reason,* Frost's wry treatment of an extension of the Book of Job, although Mark Van Doren finally took the responsibility—in the midst of a positive review—for assaying the weaknesses of the masque:

> there is also the danger that a man who *has* a voice will decline into a man who *is* one. . . . To be a Voice is not to be enviable, for it means taking whatever you say as valuable merely because you hear yourself saying it (*New York Herald Tribune,* March 25, 1945).

In a harsher vein, Anne Fremantle called it a "volume of verse" (*Commonweal,* March 30, 1945) and Conrad Aiken described the pattern as "unrewardingly blank . . . there are times when the cracker-barrel wisecrack grates a little, and when the texture and text alike become too thin" (*New Republic,* April 16, 1945).

Whether critics were bewildered by Frost's shift in subject and approach, or embarrassed by their own ambivalence toward the first masque, Frost's second such attempt—the 1947 *A Masque of Mercy*—received very few reviews. Lawrence McMillin found the second masque more cohesive, more powerful than the first, but both he and William Carlos Williams were troubled because of the commonplace diction (*Hudson Review,* Spring 1948; *Poetry,* April 1948).

In 1947, reviewers' attention was given instead to *Steeple Bush,* Frost's penultimate collection of single poems. Leonard Bacon praised it in *Saturday Review* (May 31, 1947), because "there is no falling off. There is no resting on oars or on laurels." Although Randall Jarrell thought otherwise, he continued to puff Frost's lifetime achievement, recaptured here in poems like "Directive":

> Frost is one of the subtlest and saddest of poets; and no other living poet has written so well about the actions of ordinary men (*New York Times Book Review,* June 1, 1947).

With reviews of the 1949 *Complete Poems,* Frost's last book before *In the Clearing,* summaries, affirmations, and eulogies were the order. The "Dean of American poetry," Frost could hardly do wrong. One of the most provocative reviews came from Rolfe Humphries, as he hypothesized about the "frightful and fascinating interest that he [Frost] almost dared to follow . . ."

> there are other poems which show where he has turned off the woodland trail, briefly, toward the heart of some deeper forest, jungle, sinister tarn—Fire and Ice, The Bonfire, The Lockless Door, Bereft, The Lovely Shall Be Choosers, with its cadences broken, out of dreams, and here and there very frightening, Desert Places, The Rabbit Hunter, The Night Light, Design. Reading such poems as these, one cannot escape the impression that they are much more truly the essence of the poet than the plain New Hampshire farmer is, or Meliboeus the potato man, or whoever; one wishes he had been a little less fearful of evil tidings, less scared of his own desert places. . . . It is this night side of life and nature that Frost's art has, I think, scamped reporting, and not because he does not know it; no American poet in our time, no American poet, nor Poe in his stories, has come closer to Baudelaire (*Nation,* July 23, 1949).

Humphries' view was anticipatory of Lionel Trilling's praise of Frost as a "poet of terror" some twelve years later, at the poet's eighty-fifth birthday party. Controversial as the incident was—and John Ciardi recalls the furor in his *Saturday Review* essay for March 24, 1962—it points to the impasse in Frost criticism: somehow, suggesting that Frost was a complex and perhaps even disturbing person rather than a relic of early Americana undermined his position as poet. As Ciardi phrased it, however,

> If he is half radiance he is also half brimstone, and praise be. His best poems will endure precisely because they are terrible—and holy.

Philip Booth's *New York Times* essay on *In the Clearing* also characterized Frost as "the darkly ulterior poet who has become confirmed,
lightly, as a great public figure" (March 25, 1962). Booth found that
Frost's great poems stemmed from this sense of paradox and pain that
shaped and colored Frost's own life. Richard Wilbur also acknowledged
this current, but spoke more interestingly about the spirit of adventure
in these late poems—"sweepingly assertive" in tone. He noted, too, that
the word *venture* dominates the collection (*New York Herald Tribune,*
March 25, 1962). Many critics commented on "Kitty Hawk," the major
poem in the book, with its themes of exploration both scientific and
personal—all integral to helping man establish his place in the universe.

The result of a wide range of laudatory reviews is the image of Frost
as pioneer, experimenter—in life and art—continuing even into his
eighty-ninth year. As John Holmes wrote so sagely of the poet persona
in this last collection:

> There are all the other Frosts in this book, the rural Frost we
> fondly think is the only one; the topical Frost we are less accus-
> tomed to but find deep and shrewd; the later political Frost, still
> wise and earthy; the mischievous, epigrammatic Frost; and the
> magical, the fabulous Frost that invents timeless tales; the
> direct-descriptive Frost; the ironic-tragic; and the Frost of the
> classical and American perspective in a responsible world-view
> (*Christian Science Monitor,* March 29, 1962).

As these last reviews suggest, the marvel of Frost the poet was not
entirely distinct from the marvel of Frost the man. The range of emotion and empathy, the idiosyncratic postures, the fierce pride (directed
most consistently toward his poetry, and his own position as poet)—
these qualities had characterized Frost from the days of *A Boy's Will;*
and critics often quoted the closing couplet of "Into My Own," the opening poem from that early book:

> They would not find me changed from him they knew—
> Only more sure of all I thought was true.

These lines assuredly emphasize Frost's consistency. Perhaps a better
epigraph—to capture that sense of adventure, that spirit so dominant
in Frost's best poems—would be from "A Fountain, a Bottle, a Donkey's Ears and Some Books":

> We made a day of it out in the world,
> Ascending to descend to reascend . . .

There seems little question that today, 1977, reader response to Frost's work remains high; whether critical interest has already peaked is doubtful. This compilation is intended to provide interested readers and scholars with still another source of useful information, so that subsequent work on Frost's poems can move to higher levels of competence. Without two recent books, Peter Van Egmond's *The Critical Reception of Robert Frost* (Boston: G. K. Hall, 1974) and Donald Greiner's *Robert Frost, The Poet and His Critics* (Chicago: American Library Association, 1974), this book would have been much more difficult. Doubtlessly, other reviews of Frost's work are still to be discovered; the general editor and I will appreciate and happily acknowledge any reviews brought to our notice.

Since the volumes in the American Critical Tradition series are intended to show American reaction to literary works, only a few British reviews are included. (Because Frost's first two collections appeared initially in England, there is somewhat more reason to include a sampling of British opinion.) Reviews of only the major poetry collections are included, the various volumes of selected poems being omitted except when reviewers combined their notices.* Because there were many issues of selected poems, and only two books entitled *Collected Poems,* it seemed of greater importance, critically, to include the 1930 and 1939 collections, and the 1949 *Complete Poems,* in addition to separate volumes from the 1913 *A Boy's Will* to the 1962 *In the Clearing.* The arrangement is chronological.

I have also tried to avoid reprinting only reviews that appeared in major newspapers, but the nature of poetry reviewing poses several problems. First, many newspapers do not review poetry volumes at all—and when they do, their standards for judging quality are likely to be aberrant. Second, the places in which one might review a book of poems—little magazines, for example, or obscure quarterlies—are often not indexed systematically, if at all: such magazines are notoriously short-lived, and their coverage, whimsical.

To avoid repetition, quoted poems and comments on tables of contents have sometimes been deleted; such omissions are noted by ellipses. Three kinds of silent changes have been made: the deletion of publishing information; the deletion of section headings in newspaper reviews; and the correction of obvious typographical errors. For the most

---

*See Appendix for list of reviews of books not included in this volume.

part, brief notices have not been included, and the checklist does not list all of the appearances of syndicated reviews. Finally, it should be noted that many fine essays on Frost's work are cumulative, are not limited to comments on single collections of his poems, and therefore have been omitted from this collection.

Thanks to many colleagues and libraries, particularly that at Michigan State University, Interlibrary Loan Division, and Special Collections. Without the help of the Radcliffe Institute facilities, this project would have taken much longer than it has. Personal thanks, as well, to M. Thomas Inge, Alan Hollingsworth, Frederick Eckman, Howard O. Brogan, and Kathryn Gibbs Harris.

Linda W. Wagner
East Lansing, Michigan
July 1977

Acknowledgments

Acknowledgment is made to the following newspapers, journals and individuals for permission to reprint reviews: reviews by Leonard Feeney, Alfred Barrett, and William A. Donaghy from *America*, reprinted with permission of *America*, 1936, 1939, 1942, © by America Press. Louis Untermeyer's "Robert Frost: Revisionist," permission of *American Mercury*, Box 1306, Torrance, California. Peter Davison, review of *In the Clearing*, permission of the author and the Atlantic Monthly Company; other reviews by Mark Schorer, Donald Stauffer, Edward Garnett, and Peter Viereck from *The Atlantic Monthly*, permission of journal. *Canadian Forum* reviews, both by Malcolm Ross and unsigned, permission of journal, June 1931 and November 1947. Elva Bascom's review in *Among Our Books*, reprinted courtesy of Carnegie Library of Pittsburgh. Reviews by Katherine Brégy and M.K.B., reprinted with permission from *Catholic World*; reviews by Marion Strobel, Walter Harding, and Louis Untermeyer, reprinted from *Chicago Tribune* and *Chicago Evening Post*, respectively. Reviews by E. Merrill Root and unsigned, © 1929, 1931, 1936, Christian Century Foundation; reprinted by permission from *The Christian Century*. Reviews by Esther W. Bates and John Holmes © 1947 and 1975, 1962, The Christian Science Publishing Society, reprinted with permission of *The Christian Science Monitor*. Robert S. Newdick's review, permission of *Columbus Dispatch*. With permission of *Commonweal*: reviews by Legarde S. Doughty, Anne Fremantle, J. H. Johnston, and Rosemary Deen. L. W. Payne, Jr., review, reprinted with permission of *The Dallas Morning News*; review by B. C., permission of *Denver Post*; Edgar C. Knowlton's "Poems by Robert Frost," *South Atlantic Quarterly*, 1936, reprinted with permission of Duke University Press. Arthur H. Nethercot review, permission of *Evanston Daily News-Index*. Permission of *The Guardian*, Richard Kell's "Veteran Verse"; of Harper's Magazine Company, W. D. Howells' review, reprinted from the September, 1915 issue of *Harper's* by special permission; © 1915 by *Harper's Magazine*. Lawrence McMillin's review, permission of *The Hudson Review*. Reviews by Frances A. Boyle and Burton A. Robie appear courtesy of *Library Journal* (March 1, 1945; April 15, 1962), pub-

lican, for Elspeth Bragdon's 1936 review. Reviews from *Time,* reprinted by permission from *TIME*, The Weekly Newsmagazine; Copyright Time Inc. June 8, 1936; May 15, 1939; May 18, 1942; May 7, 1945; June 27, 1949. Permission of *Times Literary Supplement,* Times Newspapers Limited, London, "Prose and Poetry," 1923; "Robert Frost," 1931; "Harvest of Poetry," 1939; "Life and Nature," 1943; "The Old Masters," 1962. *Virginia Quarterly Review,* reviews by James Southall Wilson (1931, 1939) and Louis Untermeyer (1928); *Wisconsin Library Bulletin,* permission for review by R. S., 1962; *Yale Review,* permission for reviews by Frederick E. Pierce, Virginia Moore, James M. Dabbs, and George Whicher.

A BOY'S WILL

BY
ROBERT FROST
AUTHOR OF "NORTH OF BOSTON"

NEW YORK
HENRY HOLT AND COMPANY
1915

A Boy's Will

"Notices of New Books."
Athenaeum, No. 4458
(April 5, 1913),
379.

These poems are intended by the author to possess a certain sequence, and to depict the various stages in the evolution of a young man's outlook upon life. The author is only half successful in this, possibly because many of his verses do not rise above the ordinary, though here and there a happy line or phrase lingers gratefully in the memory.

*Times Literary
Supplement,*
April 10, 1913,
p. 155.

There is an agreeable individuality about these pieces; the writer is not afraid to avoid the simplest of his thoughts and fancies, and these, springing from a capacity for complete absorption in the influences of nature and the open air, are often naively engaging. Sometimes too, in a vein of reflection, he makes one stop and think, though the thought may be feebly or obscurely expressed (as in the last stanza of a poem, otherwise striking, called "The Trial by Existence.")

Ezra Pound.
"A Boy's Will."
Poetry, 2
(May 1913),
72-74.

I had withdrawn in forest, and my
    song
Was swallowed up in leaves.

There is another personality in the realm of verse another American, found, as usual, on this side of the water, by an English publisher long known as a lover of good letters. David Nutt publishes at his own expense *A Boy's Will*, by Robert Frost, the latter having been long scorned by the "great American editors." It is the old story.

Mr. Frost's book is a little raw, and has in it a number of infelicities; underneath them it has the tang of the New Hampshire woods, and it has just this utter sincerity. It is not post-Miltonic or post-Swinburnian or post-Kiplonian. This man has the good sense to speak naturally and to paint the thing, the thing as he sees it. And to do this is a very different matter from gunning about for the circumplectious polysyllable.

1

It is almost on this account that it is a difficult book to quote from.

She's glad her simple worsted gray
Is silver now with clinging mist—

does not catch your attention. The lady is praising the autumn rain, and he ends the poem, letting her talk.

Not yesterday I learned to know
  The love of bare November days,
Before the coming of the snow;
  But it were vain to tell her so,
And they are better for her praise.

Or again:

There was never a sound beside
  the wood but one,
And that was my long scythe
  whispering to the ground.
. . . .
My long scythe whispered and
  left the hay to make.

I remember that I was once canoeing and thirsty and I put in to a shanty for water and found a man there who had no water and gave me cold coffee instead. And he didn't understand it, he was from a minor city and he "just set there watchin' the river" and didn't "seem to want to go back," and he didn't much care for anything else. And so I presume he entered into Anunda. And I remember Joseph Campbell telling me of meeting a man on a desolate waste of bogs, and he said to him, "It's rather dull here;" and the man said, "Faith, ye can sit on a middan and dream stars."

And that is the essence of folk poetry with distinction between America and Ireland. And Frost's book reminded me of these things.

There is perhaps as much of Frost's

personal tone in the following little catch, which is short enough to quote, as in anything else. It is to his wife, written when his grandfather and his uncle had disinherited him of a comfortable fortune and left him in poverty because he was a useless poet instead of a money-getter.

IN NEGLECT

They leave us so to the way we took,
  As two in whom they were
    proved mistaken,
That we sit sometimes in a
    wayside nook,
With mischievous, vagrant,
    seraphic look,
  And *try* if we cannot feel forsaken.

There are graver things, but they suffer too much by making excerpts. One reads the book for the "tone," which is homely, by intent, and pleasing, never doubting that it comes direct from his own life, and that no two lives are the same.

He has now and then such a swift and bold expression as

The whimper of hawks beside the
  sun.

He has now and then a beautiful simile, well used, but he is for the most part as simple as the lines I have quoted in opening or as in the poem of mowing. He is without sham and without affectation.

[Norman Douglas]. "Poetry." *The English Review,* 14 (June 1913), 505.

. . . it does one good to glance awhile into the simple woodland philosophy of Mr. Frost. Nowhere on earth, we fancy, is there more outrageous nonsense printed under the name of poetry than in America; and our author, we are told, is an American. All the more credit to him for breaking away from this tradition—if such it can be called—and giving us not derivative, hypersensuous drivel, but an image of things really heard and seen. There is a wild, racy flavour in his poems; they sound that *inevitable* response to nature which is the hallmark of true lyric feeling.

F. S. F[lint]. *"A Boy's Will." Poetry and Drama,* 1 (June 1913), 250.

Mr. Robert Frost's poetry is so much a part of his life that to tell his life would be to explain his poetry. I wish I were authorised to tell it, because the one is as moving as the other—a constant struggle against circumambient stupidity for the right of expression. Be it said, however, that Mr. Frost has escaped from America, and that his first book, *A Boy's Will,* has found an English publisher. So much

information, extrinsic to the poems, is necessary. Their intrinsic merits are great, despite faults of diction here and there, occasional inversions, and lapses, where he has not been strong enough to bear his own simplicity of utterance. It is this simplicity which is the great charm of his book; and it is a simplicity that proceeds from a candid heart:

MY NOVEMBER GUEST

My Sorrow, when she's here with
  me,
  Thinks these dark days of
  autumn rain
Are beautiful as days can be;
She loves the bare, the withered
  tree;
  She walks the sodden pasture
  lane.

Her pleasure will not let me stay.
  She talks, and I am fain to list:
She's glad the birds are gone away,
She's glad her simple worsted grey
  Is silver now with clinging mist.

The desolate, deserted trees,
  The faded earth, the heavy sky,
The beauties she so truly sees,
She thinks I have no eye for these,
  And vexes me for reason why.

Not yesterday I learned to know
  The love of bare November days
Before the coming of the snow;
But it were vain to tell her so,
  And they are better for her praise.

Other poems almost or quite as perfect as the one above are: "A Late Walk," "To the Thawing Wind," "Mowing," "Going for Water," "Reluctance." Each poem is the complete expression of one mood, one emotion, one idea. I have tried to find in these poems what is most characteristic of Mr. Frost's poetry, and I think it is this: direct observation of the object and immediate correlation with the emotion—spontaneity, subtlety in the evocation of moods, humour, an ear for silence. But behind all is the heart and life of a man, and the more you ponder his poems the more convinced you become that the heart is pure and the life not lived in vain.

William Morton Payne. *The Dial,* 55 (September 16, 1913), 211-12.

A dream world of elusive shapes and tremulous imaginings is half revealed to our vision by the subdued lyrics which Mr. Robert Frost entitles "A Boy's Will." It is a world in which passion has been stilled and the soul grown quiet—a world not explored with curious interest, but apprehended by the passive recipient. The sun does not shine, but the pale grey of twilight enfolds nature with a more gracious charm. The song called "Flower-Gathering" offers an exquisite example of the wistful and appealing quality of the author's strain.

"I left you in the morning,
And in the morning glow,
You walked away beside me
To make me sad to go.
Do you know me in the gloaming,
Gaunt and dusty grey with roaming?
Are you dumb because you know me
    not,
Or dumb because you know?

"All for me?   And not a question

For the faded flowers gay
That could take me from beside you
For the ages of a day?
They are yours, and be the measure
Of their worth for you to treasure,
The measure of the little while
That I've been long away."

The desire of the solitary soul for companionship has rarely found such beautiful expression as it receives in this quotation:

"We make ourselves a place apart
    Behind light words that tease
    and flout,
But oh, the agitated heart
    Till someone find us really out."

"Reluctance" is the poem that closes the collection—a lyric of lassitude with just a faint flicker of the spent fire of life.

"But through the fields and the
    woods
    And over the walls I have wended;
I have climbed the hills of view
    And looked at the world, and
    descended;
I have come by the highway home,
    And lo, it is ended.

"The leaves are all dead on the
    ground,
    Save those that the oak is keeping
To ravel them one by one
    And let them go scraping and
    creeping
Out over the crusted snow,
    When others are sleeping.

"And the dead leaves lie huddled
    and still,
    No longer blown hither and
    thither;
The last lone aster is gone,

The flowers of the witch-hazel
  wither
The heart is still aching to seek,
  But the feet question 'Whither?'

"Ah, when to the heart of a man
  Was it ever less than a treason
To go with the drift of things
  To yield with a grace to reason,
And bow and accept the end
  Of a love or a season?

If Mr. Frost's verses show the cast of melancholy, there is at least nothing morbid about it. In their simple phrasing and patent sincerity, his songs give us the sort of pleasure that we have in those of the "Shropshire Lad" of Mr. Housman.

"Procession of the Muses."
The Academy, 85 (September 20, 1913), 360.

We wish we could fitly express the difference which marks off *A Boy's Will* from all the other books here noticed. Perhaps it is best hinted by stating that the poems combine, with a rare sufficiency, the essential qualities of inevitability and surprise. We have read every line with that amazement and delight which are too seldom evoked by books of modern verse. Without need of qualification or a trimming of epithets, it is undoubtedly the work of a true poet. We do not need to be told that the poet is a young man: the dew and the ecstasy—the audacity, too—of pristine vision are here. At the same time, it is extraordinarily free from a young man's extravagances; there is no insistent obtrusion of self-strain after super-things. Neither does it belong to any modern "school," nor go in harness to any new and twisted theory of art. It is so simple, lucid, and experimental that, reading a poem, one can see clearly with the poet's own swift eye, and follow the trail of his glancing thought. One feels that this man has *seen* and *felt;* seen with a revelatory, a creative vision; felt personally and intensely; and he simply writes down, without confusion or affectation, the results thereof. Rarely today is it our fortune to fall in with a new poet expressing himself in so pure a vein. No one who really cares for poetry should miss this little book. . . . We have not the slightest idea who Mr. Robert Frost may be, but we welcome him unhesitatingly to the ranks of the poets born, and are convinced that if this is a true sample of his parts he should presently give us work far worthier of honour than much which passes for front-rank poetry at the present time.

W. S. B[raithwaite]. "A Poet of New England."
The Boston Evening Transcript April 28, 1915, Section 3, p. 4.

Under the surface of New England art is New England life, and this life has been adumbrated in the best poetry wherever it has been created throughout the country during the last forty years. A localized New England art, I am speaking now of verse, really ceased more than a generation ago. Half a century of the famous New England poets never did more than scratch the surface of this life. Emerson went a little deeper than his contemporaries, but he brought up water instead of soil; Whitman went wider in all directions from the centre but he never fertilized the ground for anything better than a staple poetic crop. In all matters of expression these poets kept pretty closely to the traditional methods of the English poets, and achieving the ordinary they let the best of the unique material which lay about them go by without getting into their verse. It took the generation of novelists and storytellers succeeding them to show what New England life and character really was like. Hawthorne in their midst really saw and knew New England life and character, but he took it in its invisible and not visible aspects and left us with a sense of light rather than substance. But Howells and James, Sarah Orne Jewett, Mary E. Wilkins and Alice Brown gave us the fabric of New England, with all its qualities of inner and outer existence, moral and social, individually and collectively.

The natural expression of New England, however, is a poetic expression. And poetry is coming back to New England as its natural voice. Since 1870 there can be no doubt that Aldrich was the most considerable poet with the New England substance in his work. But he was a perfect craftsman rather than an illuminating perceptor of life. One came after him much later who is today our foremost poet in whom the very fundamental substance of New England life burns with extraordinary inten-

sity. This poet is Edwin Arlington Robinson, who has localized the New England environment in the mythical Tilbury Town of his poems, and the essence of the New England spirit in those strange characters that make up the masculine gallery of his work. There comes now another poet to help Robinson uphold the poetic supremacy of New England: one in whose veins as in Robinson's flows generations of New England blood, and who like him has evoked from the New England tradition an art that is once native and new, and through whose individual expression we get an entirely new value of the homely dramatic, psychologic and simply human sense of this life. This poet is Robert Frost.

Mr. Frost's first book, "A Boy's Will," appeared in England in 1913. Last year his second book, "North of Boston," was also brought out in England, and was immediately acclaimed by all the authoritative English critics as an achievement "much finer, much more near the ground and much more national, in the true sense, than anything that Whitman gave the world." It must be remembered that Mr. Frost had no influence to attract the critical attention except what the work itself commanded. He has accomplished what no other American poet of his generation has accomplished, and that is, unheralded, unintroduced, untrumpeted, he has won the acceptance of an English publisher on his own terms, and the unqualified approbation of a voluntary English criticism. . . .

Though Mr. Frost's two books were published in consecutive years, they represent a more divergent period of development. The earlier book expresses an individuality, the later interprets a community. Completely as "A Boy's Will" performs its nature in the lyrical demonstration of an individual who attempts to account for himself and emotional experiences in a social scheme he tries to understand and define, its greatest spiritual and human value is a preparation for the more wonderful analysis of the objective experience of life which the poet limns in "North of Boston." As is shown, the two books really represent two points of view, and between the two there is a very startling contrast in both method and substance. What the first essentially represents is shown in the first book in a piece called "Mowing":

There was never a sound
    beside the wood but one,
And that was my long scythe
    whispering to the ground.
What was it it whispered?
    I knew not well myself;
Perhaps it was something
    about the heat of the sun,
Something, perhaps, about the
    lack of sound—
And that was why it whispered
    and did not speak.
It was no dream of the gift
    of idle hours,
Or easy gold at the hand
    of fay or elf:
Anything more than the truth
    would have seemed too weak
To the earnest love that
    laid the swale in rows,
Not without feeble-pointed
    spikes of flowers
(Pale orchises), and scared
    a bright green snake.
The fact is the sweetest dream
    that labor knows.
My long scythe whispered and
    left the hay to make.

But he had come to realize a different philosophy which is indicated in the opening poem called "Mending Wall," in "North of Boston." It was a philosophy rather of art than of substance; the substance would include too many terms that make up the quality of life as it touched the rural community and farm life of New England to be reduced to a word. . . .

For all his hard substance of human circumstance in these narratives, Mr. Frost is an idyllist. The poems are always in the form of dialogue or soliloquy, and the rendering in its significance is always psychological. The very spirit of Theocritus for the first time pervades through Mr. Frost our New England forms and meadows. The atmosphere of the bucolic life has never been so delicately transported into literature by an American poet before. In spite of all the other qualities which make Mr. Frost's poems remarkable, it is this natural delicacy of vision which gives a tone to the atmosphere which envelops the undertone of his subjects. Take the passage from "The Generations of Men," that delightful idyl of the gathering of the descendants of the Stark families in reunion at the home of the original Stark, when two members hitherto unknown to each other fall in love. . . .

Though this poem is a favorite of mine, it is only a lighter and fairer toned idyl among the others of this book. Such a one as "The Death of the Hired Man," grimly realistic as it is, has been highly praised but "A Hundred Dollars," in which the humor of the man learning sharing the same bedroom with a garrulous newspaper agent makes a delightful comedy, "Home Burial," in which the callousness of a father burying his only child brings out the poignant difference in the sensibility of the father and mother and the feeling of bitter antagonism killing the love of the wife for the husband, "Blueberries," an exquisitely rhymed pastoral of a family living on the foraged bounty of the fields, "A Servant to Servants," in which an overburdened farmer's wife talks until she suggests to the reader that her life is lived under the shadow of inherited lunacy, and other such poems as "The Housekeeper," "The Bear," "The Self-Seeker," all prove that not only is there still an inexhaustible store of material in New England life, but that Mr. Frost is the first poet for half a century to express it completely with a fresh, original and appealing way of his own. By it he places himself with almost a single achievement in the very front rank of contemporary American poets.

O. W. Firkins. "Poets of the Day." *The Nation,* 101 (August 18, 1915), 228.

In Mr. Frost's "A Boy's Will" criticism detects three elements: first, vigorous landscapes sketched, or scooped out, with a bold, free hand; second, feeling of a certain trenchancy and distinction; and, third, superadded interpretations. Of these three constituents the last seems wholly perfunctory. Mr. Frost is a poet by endowment; he is a symbolist only by trade. The meaning he personally attaches to landscape seems quite unrelated to the meaning by which he hopes to enlist the sympathies of his readers. His

philosophy, in a word, is propitiatory; it is Mr. Frost's apologetic bow to a supposedly intellectual public, and I am uncourtly enough to wish that the obeisance had been withheld. When Mr. Frost's intellectual revenues come in his verse will profit by the circumstance, but I doubt if it profits in the least by his anticipation of his income.

One point of detail unrelated to Mr. Frost's essential claims deserves a passing comment. Under the title of each poem in the table of contents a few words indicative of its purpose are set, and these phrases, read seriatim, make up a single coherent paragraph. This is an artifice, no doubt, but, in my opinion, a pardonable and commendable artifice; if poets will be locksmiths, they should furnish keys. I object personally to researches into obscure poetic meanings, not merely from the healthy human disinclination to overwork, but from a sense that the faculties which the assessing of probabilities and the summing up of evidence call into play are destructive of the moods in which poetry is absorbed and enjoyed. To extract, and so to separate, the soul from the body is surely the wrong way of approaching an art whose basis is the idea that the two are inseparable. Mr. Frost's expedient impresses me as sensible and considerate.

The real value of these poems lies in the quality of their emotion. Their tone is sombre, but it is that youthful sombreness which is little more than a play of hide-and-seek with cheerfulness. The definition of the feeling is not always sharp, but, even in its vagueness, it exhibits a savor, a saltiness, a reaching and penetrating quality which augurs well for this young writer's future. I regret that

Mr. Frost should think it desirable to exhibit in many places a crabbed syntax and a jolting metre. I am not consoled for these asperities by the probability that they are intentional, for I do not subscribe to the theory that in our day, when the Muses are lethargic, they must be jostled before they can be made to dance. I content myself with this gentle and modest imprecation: May Mr. Frost mount high on the slopes of Parnassus in a wagon without springs!

NORTH OF BOSTON

BY

ROBERT FROST

NEW YORK

HENRY HOLT AND COMPANY

North of Boston

[Lascelles Abercrombie.]
"A New Voice."
The Nation, 15 [London]
(June 13, 1914),
423-24.

Poetry *per se* is one of the most troublesome things in the world to discuss exactly. Like Goodness and Personal Identity, it is a thing which everyone is aware of, but a thing which, when you try to lay hold of it, proves a ghost that will scarcely be cornered. For, like those famous apparitions in philosophy again, poetry does not come into actual experience as the spectre of its own essence; we know it as the spirit that selects for its embodiment, informs and impregnates, a mass of things derived from racial environment, habits of language, and personal peculiarities. The temptation therefore is to discuss all this material embodiment, these accidents that hold the essence, in the hope that the discussion will turn out to be, by implication, a discussion of the poetry itself—a hope that does not always succeed. But, in the case of Mr. Robert Frost, the temptation is peculiarly irresistible, not only because the enclosing substance of idiosyncrasy, linguistic manners, and circumstantial traits and characteristics, is very interesting and attractive, but perhaps still more because the poetic spirit inhabiting all this is exceptionally shy and elusive; so much so that the most analytically disposed reader must often be wondering whether even a notional existence can be contrived here for poetic impulse apart from expressive substance. That, of course, may be a great compliment; it may mean that poetic impulse has made the exactly appropriate selection of expressive material, and has fused itself into this so completely as to be inextricable. On the contrary, it may also mean that notional existence of poetry, apart from material, cannot be alleged for the same reason that you cannot conceive the notional existence of the heat of a bar of iron when the bar is not perceptibly hot. In the case of Mr. Frost, it seems to us that the explanation is sometimes the one and sometimes the other. His method—we cannot quarrel with it, because in its final result it nearly always accomplishes something remarkable—is to invite us to assist, first, at his careful and deliberate laying of the material for a poetic bonfire; the skill is interesting, and the stuff is evidently combustible; and suddenly, we do not quite know when, while we were intent on these structural preliminaries, we find that a match has been put to the pile. It burns out, as a rule, rather quickly; but while it is burning, substance and fire are completely at one, and at the

11

end we are not left with embers, but with the sense of a swift and memorable experience.

First, however, for the stuff which the fire lays hold of—the personal and circumstantial characteristics of Mr. Frost's poetry. To start with, Mr. Frost is an American poet who noticeably stands out against tradition. That is what one might expect of an American poet; notoriously, it is just what American poetry proves most incapable of doing. In consequence, American poetry has not often been concerned with America; and the first and most obvious novelty in Mr. Frost's poems is their determination to deal unequivocally with everyday life in New England—"North of Boston." It is not, perhaps, quite what one might have anticipated, this New England life that Mr. Frost takes as his beloved material; certainly, not what we have come to think of as typical of the United States. Most of Mr. Frost's subjects are in some way connected with farming; the few that touch anything urban have the atmosphere of country towns—nothing in the book, at any rate, suggests in the least a nation of dwellers in vast, roaring, hurly-burlying cities. These specimens of New England life are not greatly different from the corresponding life of the old England; yet there *is* an unmistakable difference, on which it would not be easy to lay one's finger. American democracy contributes to the difference, but is certainly not the most important element in it. The life seems harder and lonelier, and it also seems, oddly enough, more reflective and philosophic. Here, for instance, is a man who has been injured in a saw-mill, talking with his friend:—

Everything goes the same
    without me there.
You can hear the small buzz saws
    whine, the big saw
Caterwaul to the hills
    around the village
As they both bite the wood.
    It's all our music.
One ought as a good villager
    to like it.
No doubt it has a sort of
    prosperous sound,
And it's our life.

    "Yes, when it's not
    our death."
"You make that sound as if
    it wasn't so
With everything. What we live by
    we die by."

The sentiment is not extraordinary, but it seems deeply characteristic. The same sort of reflectiveness sounds through most of these dialogues and soliloquies. It is life that has, on the whole, a pretty hard time of it, though a queer, dry, yet cordial, humor seldom fails it; but it is life that has time to look at itself as well as to look about itself. How much of this is due to Mr. Frost's interpretation of New England we, on this side of the Atlantic, can hardly say; but, if internal evidence goes for anything, life has seldom been made into literature with as little manipulation as in this book.

To say that a poet stands out against tradition is not to accuse him of being a rebel. He may be, as Mr. Frost certainly is, one of those in whom the continual re-adjustment of poetry to life is taking place. When that re-adjustment comes, manner must inevitably be obedient to matter. And so we find very little of the traditional manner of poetry in Mr. Frost's work; scarcely anything, indeed, save a peculiar adaptation, as his usual form, of the pattern of blank verse. It is poetry which is not much more careful than good prose is to stress and extract the inmost values and suggestive force of words; it elaborates simile and metaphor scarcely more than good conversation does. But it is apt to treat the familiar images and acts of ordinary life much as poetry is usually inclined to treat words—to put them, that is to say, into such positions of relationship that some unexpected virtue comes out of them; it is, in fact, poetry composed, as far as possible, in a language of *things*. The similes, when they do appear, are usually striking, because of the concrete familiarity of the experiences they employ. Thus, a man's recollection of his own boyhood is a vision of

> "a little, little boy,
> As pale and dim as a match flame
> in the sun."

The same sort of simile occurs in the following passage, which is quoted, however, as a more general type of Mr. Frost's habit of composing in things:—

> "A lantern light from deeper
> in the barn
> Shone on a man and woman in the
> door,
> And threw their lurching shadows
> on a house
> Near by, all dark in every
> glossy window.
> A horse's hoof pawed once
> the hollow floor,
> And the back of the gig
> they stood beside

> Moved in a little. The man
> grasped a wheel,
> The woman spoke out sharply,
> 'Whoa, stand still!'
> 'I saw it just as plain as a white
> plate,'
> She said, 'as the light of
> the dashboard ran
> Along the bushes at the roadside—
> a man's face.' "

Language *quâ* language does very little here; the selection and arrangement of the substance do practically everything. So, at least, it seems at first. But poetry, after all, is an affair of specialized language; and if Mr. Frost's verse be read with some attention, it will soon appear that his verses are built with language specialized for a purpose beyond close, faithful service to concrete imagery. We have heard a good deal lately of the desirability of getting poetry back again into touch with the living vigors of speech. This usually means matters of vocabulary and idiom; and Mr. Frost certainly makes a racy use of New England vernacular. But he goes further; he seems trying to capture and hold within metrical patterns the very tones of speech—the rise and fall, the stressed pauses and little hurries, of spoken language. The kind of metrical modulation to which we are most accustomed—the modulations intended for decoration or purely aesthetic expressiveness—will scarcely be found in his verses. But, instead, we have some novel inflections of metre which can only be designed to reproduce in verse form the actual shape of the sound of whole sentences. As a matter of technique, the attempt is extraordinarily interesting. Sometimes the metrical form goes to pieces; at other times the verse is, however much we try to hear a voice in it, a little monotonous, which may be due to the fact that it is extremely hard to indicate by a verse-movement such an elusive thing as the intonation of speech—supposing that intonation is as constant as accent. But often enough the intention is clear, and the result decidedly exciting. The intention itself is not a new thing in poetry; but such complete reliance on it as the chief element of technique, though it holds Mr. Frost's expression rather tight, is rewarded by some new and very suggestive effects.

Naturally, this technical preoccupation bears strongly on the general form of Mr. Frost's poetry. He uses almost entirely dialogue or soliloquy; he must have somebody talking. We might call these poems psychological idylls. Within their downright knowledge, their vivid observation, and (more important) their rich enjoyment of all kinds of practical life, within their careful rendering into metre of customary speech, the impulse is always psychological—to set up, in some significant attitude, a character or a conflict of characters. The ability to do this can turn a situation which is not very interesting at first into something attractive, as when a rather protracted discourse of two distant relations on genealogy gradually merges into a shy, charming conversation of lovers; or, in a more striking instance, when the rambling speech of an over-tasked farmer's wife works up into a dreadful suggestion of inherited lunacy. If, as we have said, we cannot quarrel with this deliberate method of exposition, it can scarcely be questioned that Mr. Frost is at his best when he can dispense with these structural preliminaries, as in the admirable soliloquy of the old philosopher of a farmer mending his wall, or in the exquisite comedy of the professor sharing a bedroom with the talkative newspaper-agent, or in the stark, formidable tragedy called "Home Burial." Though it is difficult to state absolutely the essential quality of Mr. Frost's poetry, it is not difficult to suggest a comparison. When poetry changes by development rather than by rebellion, it is likely to return on itself. Poetry in Mr. Frost exhibits almost the identical desires and impulses we see in the "bucolic" poems of Theocritus. Nothing so futile as a comparison of personal talents is meant by this; but for general motives, the comparison is true and very suggestive. Poetry, in this book, seems determined, once more, just as it was in Alexandria, to invigorate itself by utilizing the traits and necessities of common life, the habits of common speech, the minds and hearts of common folk. And the impulse of Mr. Frost's poetry is not an isolated phenomenon to-day—therein is its significance; he is doing for New England life, in his own unique and entirely original way, what Mr. Wilfrid Gibson is so splendidly doing for the life of modern England.

Edward Thomas. "Poetry." *English Review,* 18 (August 1914), 142-43.

This is a collection of dramatic narratives in verse. Some are almost entirely written in dialogue: in only three is the poet a chief character, telling a story, for the most part, in his own words. Thus he has got free from the habit of personal lyric as was, perhaps, foretold by his first book, "A Boy's Will." Already there he had refused the "glory of words" which is the modern poet's embarrassing heritage, yet succeeded in being plain though not mean, in reminding us of poetry without being "poetical." The new volume marks more than the beginning of an experiment like Wordsworth's, but with this difference, that Mr. Frost knows the life of which he writes rather as Dorothy Wordsworth did. That is to say, he sympathises where Wordsworth contemplates. The result is a unique type of eclogue, homely, racy, and touched by a spirit that might, under other circumstances, have made pure lyric on the one hand or drama on the other. Within the space of a hundred lines or so of blank verse it would be hard to compress more rural character and relevant scenery; impossible, perhaps, to do so with less sense of compression and more lightness, unity, and breadth. The language ranges from a never vulgar colloquialism to brief moments of heightened and intense simplicity. There are moments when the plain language and lack of violence make the unaffected verses look like prose, except that the sentences, if spoken aloud, are most felicitously true in rhythm to the emotion. Only at the end of the best pieces, such as "The Death of the Hired Man," "Home Burial," "The Black Cottage," and "The Wood Pile," do we realise that they are masterpieces of deep and mysterious tenderness.

Harold Munro. "New Books." *Poetry and Drama,* 14 (September 1914), 297.

From Robert Frost's *North of Boston* I have selected for quotation one long poem in a blank verse altogether remarkable for its originality and emotional qualities. Mr. Frost appears to have studied the subtle cadences of colloquial speech with some peculiar and unusual apprehension. The jerky irregularity of his verse is due to the fact that the laws of emotional value have evidently overmastered the rules of prosody. Through some acute process of psychological analysis he casts up all the hidden details of a superficially simple tale into stark prominence. The rhythm of his verse escapes the usual monotonies of stress; its current follows the stresses of what it relates; it is like an indicator passing along some continuous fluctuating line, or it has the sound of a swift and excited voice. All the poems in this book are good reading.

Ezra Pound. "Modern Georgics." *Poetry,* 5 (December 1914), 127-30.

It is a sinister thing that so American, I might even say so parochial, a talent as that of Robert Frost should have to be exported before it can find due encouragement and recognition.

Even Emerson had sufficient elasticity of mind to find something in the "yawp." One doesn't need to like a book or a poem or a picture in order to recognize artistic vigor. But the typical American editor of the last twenty years has resolutely shut his mind against serious American writing. I do not exaggerate, I quote exactly, when I say that these gentlemen deliberately write to authors that such and such a matter is "too unfamiliar to our readers."

There was once an American editor who would even print me, so I showed him Frost's *Death of the Hired Man.* He wouldn't have it; he had printed a weak pseudo-Masefieldian poem about a hired man two months before, one written in a stilted pseudo-literary language, with all sorts of floridities and worn-out ornaments.

Mr. Frost is an honest writer, writing from himself, from his own knowledge and emotion; not simply picking up the manner which magazines are accepting at the moment, and applying it to topics in vogue. He is quite consciously and definitely putting New England rural life into verse. He is not using themes that anybody could have cribbed out of Ovid.

There are only two passions in art; there are only love and hate—with endless modifications. Frost has been honestly fond of the New England people, I dare say with spells of irritation. He has given their life honestly and seriously. He has never turned aside to make fun of it. He has taken their tragedy as tragedy, their stubbornness as stubbornness. I know more of farm life than I did before I had read his poems. That means I know more of "Life."

Mr. Frost has dared to write, and

for the most part with success, in the natural speech of New England; in natural spoken speech, which is very different from the "natural" speech of the newspapers, and of many professors. His poetry is a bit slow, but you aren't held up every five minutes by the feeling that you are listening to a fool; so perhaps you read it just as easily and quickly as you might read the verse of some of the sillier and more "vivacious" writers.

A sane man knows that a prose short story can't be much better than the short stories of De Maupassant or of "Steve" Crane. Frost's work is interesting, incidentally, because there has been during the last few years an effort to proceed from the prose short story to the short story in verse. Francis Jammes has done a successful novel in verse, in a third of the space a prose novel would have taken— *Existences* in *La Triomphe de la Vie.* Vildrac and D. H. Lawrence have employed verse successfully for short stories. Masefield is not part of this movement. He has avoided all the difficulties of the immeasurably difficult art of good prose by using a slap-dash, flabby verse which has been accepted in New Zealand. Jammes, Vildrac and Lawrence have lived up to the exigencies of prose and have gained by brevity. This counts with serious artists.

Very well, then, Mr. Frost holds up a mirror to nature, not an oleograph. It is natural and proper that I should have to come abroad to get printed, or that "H. D."—with her clear-cut derivations and her revivifications of Greece—should have to come abroad; or that Fletcher—with his *tic* and his discords and his contrariety and extended knowledge of everything— should have to come abroad. One need not censure the country; it is easier for us to emigrate than for America to change her civilization fast enough to please us. But why, IF there are serious people in America, desiring literature of America, literature accepting present conditions, rendering American life with sober fidelity—why, in heaven's name, is this book of New England eclogues given us under a foreign imprint?

Professors to the contrary notwithstanding, no one expects Jane Austen to be as interesting as Stendhal. A book about a dull, stupid, hemmed-in sort of life, by a person who has lived it, will never be as interesting as the work of some author who has comprehended many men's manners and seen many grades and conditions of existence. But Mr. Frost's people are distinctly real. Their speech is real; he has known them. I don't want much to meet them, but I know that they exist, and what is more, that they exist as he has portrayed them.

Mr. Frost has humor, but he is not its victim. *The Code* has a pervasive humor, the humor of things as they are, not that of an author trying to be funny, or trying to "bring out" the ludicrous phase of some incident or character because he dares not rely on sheer presentation. There is nothing more nauseating to the developed mind than that sort of local buffoonery which the advertisements call "racy"—the village wit presenting some village joke which is worn out everywhere else. It is a great comfort to find someone who tries to give life, the life of the rural district, as a whole, evenly, and not merely as a hook to hang jokes on. The easiest thing to see about a man is an eccentric or worn-out garment, and one is godforsakenly tired of the post-Bret-

Hartian, post-Mark-Twainian humorist.

Mr. Frost's work is not "accomplished," but it is the work of a man who will make neither concessions nor pretences. He will perform no money-tricks. His stuff sticks in your head—not his words, nor his phrases, nor his cadences, but his subject matter. You do not confuse one of his poems with another in your memory. His book is a contribution to American literature, the sort of sound work that will develop into very interesting literature if persevered in.

I don't know that one is called upon to judge between the poems in *North of Boston*. *The Death of the Hired Man* is perhaps the best, or *The Housekeeper*, though here the construction is a bit straggly. There are moments in *Mending Wall*. *The Black Cottage* is very clearly stated.

Amy Lowell. "North of Boston." The New Republic, 2 (February 20, 1915), 81-82.

Some six months ago there appeared in London a modest little green-covered book, entitled "North of Boston." It was by an American living in England, so its publication on the other side of the Atlantic came about quite naturally, and was no reflection on the perspicacity of our publishers at home. To those of us who admire Mr. Frost's book it is no small pleasure to take up this new edition, bearing an American imprint, and feel that the stigma of non-comprehension so often put upon us by expatriated Americans can never be justified in this case.

Indeed, Mr. Frost is only expatriated in a physical sense. Living in England he is, nevertheless, saturated with New England. For not only is his work New England in subject, it is so in technique. No hint of European forms has crept into it. It is certainly the most American volume of poetry which has appeared for some time. I use the word American in the way it is constantly employed by contemporary reviewers, to mean work of a color so local as to be almost photographic. Mr. Frost's book is American in the sense that Whittier is American, and not at all in that subtler sense in which Poe ranks as the greatest American poet.

The thing which makes Mr. Frost's work remarkable is the fact that he has chosen to write it as verse. We have been flooded for twenty years with New England stories in prose. The finest and most discerning are the little masterpieces of Alice Brown. She too is a poet in her descriptions, she too has caught the desolation and "dourness" of lonely New England farms, but unlike Mr. Frost she has a rare sense of humor, and that, too, is of New England, although no hint of it appears in "North of Boston." And just because of the lack of it, just because its place is taken by an irony, sardonic and grim, Mr. Frost's book reveals a disease which is eating into the vitals of our New England life, at least in its rural communities.

What is there in the hard, vigorous climate of these states which plants the seeds of degeneration? Is the violence and ugliness of their religious belief the cause of these twisted and tortured lives? Have the sane, full-

blooded men all been drafted away to the cities, or the West, leaving behind only feeble remainders of a once fine stock? The question again demands an answer after the reading of Mr. Frost's book.

Other countries can rear a sturdy peasantry on the soil, a peasantry which maintains itself for generations, heavy and slow perhaps, but strong and self-replenishing; and this for a length of time beside which our New England civilization is as nothing. We are often told that the telephone has done much to decrease insanity in the farming districts, and doubtless it is true. New England winters are long and isolating. But what about Russian winters, Polish, Swedish, Norwegian? After all, the telephone is a very modern invention, and these countries have been rearing a sturdy peasantry for hundreds of years. It is said that the country people of these nations are less highly organized, less well educated, than are New Englanders, and so better able to stand the loneliness of long winters. But this does not explain the great numbers of people, sprung from old New England stock, but not themselves living in remote country places, who go insane.

It is a question for the psychiatrist to answer, and it would be interesting to ask it with "North of Boston" as a text-book to go by. Mr. Frost has reproduced both people and scenery with a vividness which is extraordinary. Here are the huge hills, undraped by any sympathetic legend, felt as things hard and unyielding, almost sinister, not exactly feared, but regarded as in some sort influences nevertheless. Here are great stretches of blueberry pasture lying in the sun; and again, autumn orchards cracking with fruit which it is almost too much trouble to gather. Heavy thunderstorms drench the lonely roads and spatter on the walls of farm-houses rotting in abandonment; and the modern New England town, with narrow frame houses, visited by drummers alone, is painted in all its ugliness. For Mr. Frost's is not the kindly New England of Whittier, nor the humorous and sensible one of Lowell; it is a latter-day New England, where a civilization is decaying to give place to another and very different one.

Mr. Frost does not deal with the changed population, with the Canadians and Finns who are taking up the deserted farms. His people are left-overs of the old stock, morbid, pursued by phantoms, slowly sinking to insanity. In "The Black Cottage" we have the pathos of the abandoned house, after the death of the stern, narrow woman who had lived in it. In "A Servant to Servants" we have a woman already insane once and drifting there again, with the consciousness that her drab, monotonous life is bringing it upon her. "Home Burial" gives the morbidness of death in these remote places; a woman unable to take up her life again when her only child had died. The charming idyll, "After Apple-picking," is dusted over with something uncanny, and "The Fear" is a horrible revelation of those undercurrents which go on as much in the country as in the city, and with remorse eating away whatever satisfaction the following of desire might have brought. That is also the theme of "The Housekeeper," while "The Generations of Men" shows that foolish pride in a useless race which is so strange a characteristic of these people. It is all here—the book is the epitome of a decaying New England.

And how deftly it is done! Take this picture:

We chanced in passing by
    that afternoon
To catch it in a sort of mental
    picture
Among tar-banded ancient cherry
    trees,
Set well back from the road
    in rank lodged grass,
The little cottage we were
    speaking of.
A front with just a door
    between two windows,
Fresh painted by the shower
    a velvet black.

Or this, of blueberries:

It must be on charcoal they
    fatten their fruit.
I taste in them sometimes
    the flavor of soot.
And after all really they're
    ebony skinned:
The blue's but a mist from the
    breath of the wind,
A tarnish that goes at a touch
    of the hand,
And less than the tan with which
    pickers are tanned.

"The Fear" begins with these lines, and we get not only the picture, but the accompanying noises;

A lantern light from deeper in the
    barn
Shone on a man and woman in the
    door
And threw their lurching shadows
    on a house
Near by, all dark in every glossy
    window.
A horse's hoof pawed once the hollow
    floor,

And the back of the gig they stood
   beside
Moved in a little.

The creak and shift of the wheels is quite plain, although it is not mentioned.

I have said that Mr. Frost's work is almost photographic. The qualification was unnecessary, it is photographic. The pictures, the characters, are reproduced directly from life, they are burnt into his mind as though it were a sensitive plate. He gives out what has been put in unchanged by any personal mental process. His imagination is bounded by what he has seen, he is confined within the limits of his experience (or at least what might have been his experience) and bent all one way like the wind-blown trees of New England hillsides.

In America we are always a little late in following artistic leads. "Les Soirées de Médun," and all Zola's long influence, are passing away in Europe. In England, even such a would-be realist as Masefield lights his stories with bursts of a very rare imagination. No such bursts flame over Mr. Frost's work. He tells you what he has seen *exactly* as he has seen it. And in the word *exactly* lies the half of his talent. The other half is a great and beautiful simplicity of phrase, the inheritance of a race brought up on the English Bible. Mr. Frost's work is not in the least objective. He is not writing of people whom he has met in summer vacations, who strike him as interesting, and whose life he thinks worthy of perpetuation. Mr. Frost writes as a man under the spell of a fixed idea. He is as racial as his own puppets. One of the great interests of the book is the uncompromising New Englander it reveals.

That he could have written half so valuable a book had such not been the case I very much doubt. Art is rooted in the soil, and only the very greatest men can be both cosmopolitan and great. Mr. Frost is as New England as Burns is Scotch, Synge Irish, or Mistral Provençal.

And Mr. Frost has chosen his medium with an unerring sense of fitness. As there is no rare and vivid imaginative force playing over his subjects, so there is no exotic music pulsing through his verse. He has not been seduced into subtleties of expression which would be painfully out of place. His words are simple, straightforward, direct, manly, and there is an elemental quality in all he does which would surely be lost if he chose to pursue niceties of phrase. He writes in classic metres in a way to set the teeth of all the poets of the older schools on edge; and he writes in classic metres, and uses inversions and *clichés* whenever he pleases, those devices so abhorred by the newest generation. He goes his own way, regardless of anyone else's rules, and the result is a book of unusual power and sincerity.

The poems are written for the most part in blank verse, blank verse which does not hesitate to leave out a syllable or put one in, whenever it feels like it. To the classicist such liberties would be unendurable. But the method has its advantages. It suggests the hardness and roughness of New England granite. It is halting and maimed, like the life it portrays, unyielding in substance, and broken in effect.

Mr. Frost has done that remarkable thing, caught a fleeting epoch and stamped it into print. He might have done it as well in prose, but I do not think so, and if the book is not great poetry, it is nevertheless a remarkable achievement.

Sylvester Baxter. "New England's New Poet." *American Review of Reviews* April 1915, pp. 432-34.

A poet star of exceptional magnitude has risen for New England. Yet it was in old England that it emerged from a misty horizon, there to be recognized for what it was. The book which has brought to its author this measure of fame bears the title, as felicitous as significant, "North of Boston."

The poet is Robert Frost, born in San Francisco of a New England father and a Scotch mother, March 26, 1875. The elder Frost was then a newspaper editor in the Pacific metropolis and was prominent in local politics. He went thither from Lawrence in Massachusetts; he died when the boy was eleven years old and the family returned to their old home.

A POET-PSYCHOLOGIST

His secondary schooling over, Robert Frost went to Dartmouth College for a while. Not finding what he felt he wanted, he turned to Harvard, there to be no better satisfied. This breaking away from educational opportunity made the impression among family connections of ne'er-do-well inclinations, correspondingly impairing material prospects that otherwise would have been bright for him. But his was one of the natures that must grow in their own way if they are not to break. His studies away from academic bounds appear to have given him as much as he had gathered within. Altogether, he managed to assimilate what he needed. His bent was towards psychology, and its fruit is discernible in his poetry.

Marriage, farming in northern New Hampshire, and then school-teaching; in these may be summarized the activities which in the main marked his life up to the great departure which proved the crucial point in his career and definitely determined his future. He had qualified in his special study to a degree that led to his appointment to the teaching staff at Derry Academy, in the charming old New Hampshire town of that name. And there he taught psychology with such acceptance that doubtless professorial honors might eventually have become his had he been so inclined.

His urge to poetic expression in verse had been steadily gaining upon him ever since adolescence had turned his thoughts to life's deeper meanings. Fugitive poems occasionally appeared in the magazines, now and then to be treasured in the scrapbooks where so many poets, young and true, find abiding places in human hearts. Doubtless not a few will recall from shadowy nooks of memory the name of Robert Frost as one remotely familiar. But editors' ears are too often unattuned to new notes, preferring the resinging of old songs. One of Frost's youthful lyrics, called "Reluctance," however, so impressed a certain eminent publisher of choice books with its lofty appeal that only just now, in preparing the index for a monumental series which for about a quarter of a

century he has been issuing, he chose
for its motto two significant stanzas
from it. And it now gratifies him to
recall that in correspondence with the
youth,—whom he counselled to seek
wider fields than his own limited
range could offer,—he early recognized the rare quality of his genius.
Again at Derry there was a friendly
minister who predicted to one of the
academy trustees, a newspaper editor
of high station in New England, a
great future for the young poet. The
editor, confessing to little taste for the
poetic, was highly gratified to learn,
only the other day, that it was "that
boy" who as a poet was now coming to
his own.

A SOJOURNER IN OLD ENGLAND

It may have been the friendly publisher's counsel, subliminally linger-
ing, which, about three years ago, impelled Robert Frost to resign his comfortable teaching-berth at Derry, "pull
up stakes,"—and go somewhere. But
it was only two weeks before sailing
that he and his wife decided upon England.

It seems now as if he must have
been irresistibly impelled thither,
obedient to Destiny's silent call. For
some months Frost and his family,—
which included four children,—lived
quietly in a village not far from London. Then came his first book, a small
collection of poems called "A Boy's
Will," issued by Henley's publisher.
For Robert Frost a boy's will had
truly been the wind's will: blowing
where it listeth. These poems make
an intimate record of the gradual un-
folding of a personality,—perhaps too
intimate, the author is inclined to
hold. The book brought quick recognition in the work of a rare nature, and
Frost was promptly drawn out from

his rural retirement to be heartily
welcomed in those choice circles of
London's best intellectual life where
caste distinctions count for nothing
and the sole test is merit. Nowhere is
recognition more genuine; in few
places does it count so fully as a measure of worth.

LONDON'S RESPONSE TO A YANKEE BARD

Early last year "North of Boston"
was brought out by the same publisher. Here the author came fully to
his own. The book brought instant
acclaim, and without reserve Frost
was honored as a poet of high distinction. Perhaps if Walt Whitman himself had chosen England for his ad-
vent and had there dawned unheralded upon the world the effect
would hardly have been more electri-
cal. Judgment as to the poet's quality
was singularly unanimous. The reviews and the great weeklies gave the
book exceptional space; the London
Nation, for instance, devoted three
columns to it. Frost was eagerly
sought on every side; foremost poets
welcomed him as their peer and took
him to their hearts.

Frost liked England immensely and
has won a host of dear friends there.
Beaconsfield, the village where he
lived, was also the home of the two
young poets, Lascelles Abercrombie
and Wilfred Gibson, and he was with
them almost daily. But he was of New
England in every fiber, and through
the dull English winters, bone-
chilling, the ground greasy with mud,
he felt the most intense longing for
the home country, its sparkling and
tonic air, the sturdy New Hampshire
landscape. He felt desperately
homesick, and out of this mood
"North of Boston" was conceived and

wrought. One almost marvels that such a book, so vividly true to New England scenes and character, could have been created across the water. As with a Monet canvas, one feels that the artist must have produced it in the presence of his subjects. But it was this intense home-longing which visualized his themes. A few of these poems had been written in New England, but for much the greater part the work was done in old England.

Meanwhile the home-public had been singularly slow in responding to the British acclaim of the new poet. There were two causes for this: first, there had been no simultaneous American editions of either work. Indeed "A Boy's Will" is still practically unknown on this side. Second, the war broke out soon after, and little attention was given to anything else beyond the Atlantic. A few echoes from England were now and then heard. One of the poems, "The Code," had first appeared in the Chicago magazine, *Poetry*. And last summer the Boston *Transcript*'s accomplished and appreciative "Listener" had found in the London *Nation*'s review material for a charming article. A few copies of "North of Boston" found their way across the ocean and into public libraries and private collections. This public was very limited in number, but its interest was deep, and the inquiry, "Who is Robert Frost?" grew insistent,—waxing in volume with the recent appearance of an American edition, promptly exhausted. This article will doubtless furnish the first answer to the question.

THE RETURN TO AMERICA

With the war, and the national up-heaval, further stay in England became painful, notwithstanding the many good friends there. So one day late in February Robert Frost and his family were happy to touch American soil again. It seemed a good omen to find at a news-stand, the first thing after landing in New York, a copy of a weekly paper with his "Death of the Hired Man" conspicuously reproduced. The American edition of "North of Boston" had appeared a few days before.

The poet is now in Bethlehem, New Hampshire, about to return to farming on his beloved soil. Early in March, stopping over in Lawrence, the home of his youth, he ran in to Boston intending to spend only a few hours in town. But so many people,— leading people in New England letters,—wanted to see him at dinner, luncheon, and otherwise that, although wholly unprepared for such attentions, having with him only the clothes he wore, he found it impossible to get away inside of four days. Frost's recognition in Boston is gratifyingly cordial and bears out the London estimate of his work. Intellectual Boston naturally feels a high satisfaction that, with all the wide development of poetic talent in other sections of the country, New England is still holding her own. Such men as Edwin Arlington Robinson and Robert Frost will maintain the lofty traditions of her Golden Age when Emerson, Longfellow, Lowell, Thoreau, Holmes, Whittier, and the others were active. One eminent woman author, herself ranking with the best interpreters of New England character, says: "Robert Frost's work is the greatest that has ever come out of New England,—and Mary Wilkins is next." Another author says: "In

Frost we have another Masefield,— not a man like Masefield, but one of equally compelling power in his interpretations of life and nature."

THE POET'S PERSONALITY

Frost has a winsome personality, unassuming but not shy; a figure of average height, well built; a finely modeled head, mobile features and sensitive, dark brown hair of youthful abundance, the expressive blue eyes, tinged with a lightness as of summer mist at dawn, suggesting a dash of Celtic blood.

It is interesting to trace the derivations of a new poet. There is a suggestion of Wordsworth in Frost's method; a shade of Whitman in his native flavor and closeness to the home soil, though not the least resemblance in construction; something of Maeterlinck in his sense of lurking mystery, creeping and pervasive; a Hawthorne-like faculty of endowing our familiar New England world, even in its keen every-day reality, with that glamor of romance which Colonel Higginson so felicitously called "penumbra," tracing it back to Arthur Austin; and almost a blood relationship with Edwin Arlington Robinson,—both in the vagueness (so unlike obscurity) which in its blendings with realistic textures confers values and qualities of tone that often lead to exquisite gradations in sensitive shadings; and again in a humor that at times becomes grimly sardonic,—though with Frost as often touched with most delicate charm. To all this Frost has brought an individual quality of compelling force and a sweeping range of dramatic expression. The work is so essentially dramatic, underlaid and interwoven with

keen psychological perceptions, as to lead some who most heartily like it to deny that "North of Boston" is poetry at all. But that is merely a matter of definition,—as when some powerful drama work of unconventional construction is declared to be "not a play." It may have been the last lines of Frost's exquisite picture of "The Woodpile":

"far from a useful fireplace
To warm the frozen swamp
as best it could
With the slow smokeless burning
of decay,"

which inspired some genuine poet to say of "North of Boston" in the London *Times* that "poetry burns up out of it as when a faint wind breathes upon smouldering embers."

Louis Untermeyer. *"North of Boston." Chicago Evening Post,* April 23, 1915, p. 11.

With or without all technical and esthetic considerations, this book of Robert Frost's stirs me tremendously. It stirs me from such a bald statement to even balder superlatives. I have little respect—literary respect—for anyone who can read the shortest of these poems without feeling the skill and power in them. But I have far more respect for the man who can see nothing at all in this volume than for him who, discovering many other things in it, cannot see the poetry in it. For that attitude represents a theory of poetry as false as it is doctrinaire. And also as common. Even some of Mr. Frost's most ardent adherents begin and end their praises by saying, with a more or less deprecatory gesture, "Whether this is poetry or not" . . . or, even more frequently, "While this may not be poetry in the strict sense. . . ." And so on, to less cautious stammerings.

Waiving that nebulous and glib phrase concerning "the strict sense" which screens nothing behind it— pomposity, it is the very misapprehension of an art that misleads the well-meaning and wary. For poetry has more than one function, one manifestation and one standard. The touchstone test applied to poetry is about as satisfactory as measuring a twisting river with an inflexible yardstick. So when one comes with his inched-off and ruled notions of let us say, "glamour," he is very likely to find none of it here. But if he throws away his measuring rod he is apt to find something else in its place: something which I think is a sterner but even more genuine sort of "glamour."

There is, for instance, a lack of "poetic" figures and phrases in this volume: a lack of regard for the outlines and fragility of the medium, a lack of finesse, of nicely rounded rhetoric or raptures. But although these are all the property and perquisites of even the greatest poets, Mr. Frost neglects them—and still writes poetry. I cannot recall a single obviously "poetic" line in "A Hundred Collars" or "The Self-Seeker"—to take two dissimilar poems—and yet the sum total of these two is undeniably poetic. In no particular thing that has been said, but rather in retrospect, the afterglow, is it most apparent. The effect rather than the statement

is poetry; the air is almost electric with it.

Not that Mr. Frost cannot write colorful and sharp images. He can and does. But only when the mood rises to demand them: they are not dragged in by the hair or used as a peg to hang a passage on. Here, for instance, in the midst of "The Death of the Hired Man" (possibly the roundest and most poignant thing in the book) is this bit:

> Part of the moon was falling
>   down the west.
> Dragging the whole sky with it
>   to the hills.
> Its light poured softly in her lap.
>   She saw
> And spread her apron to it.
>   She put out her hand
> Among the harplike morning-glory
>   strings,
> Taut with the dew from garden bed
>   to eaves,
> As if she played unheard the
>   tenderness
> That wrought on him beside her
>   in the night.

There is another thing that poetry can do and that Mr. Frost's work does. And that is to crystallize. Poetry is removed from prose not only because it tells a thing more nobly but more quickly. A disciple of Dr. Jung could never have summed up the force of psycho-analysis in less than a quarto volume: James Oppenheim prophetically snthesizes and reflects it all in eight pages of "The Unborn." You will find most of Professor Whicher's imposing "Faery Myths" in Keats' "Belle Dame sans Merci." The Japanese have some of their most vivid tragedies told in poems of seventeen syllables. . . . And so when Robert Frost tells a story or sketches a character, the use of the poetic line gives it a clarity that is made sharper by its brevity.

This all, as a consideration from the lesser and more craftsmanlike standpoint. Apart from its poetic content, these fifteen poems glow with their honest, first-hand apprehension of life. It is New England life that is here: the atmosphere and idiom of it. The color, and for that matter the absence of color, is as faithfully reproduced as is that of the Arran Islands in the plays of Synge and the racy Paris slang in the ballades of Villon. Behind the persons in these poems one can feel a people. Often this sense of character is keenest when the person is suggested rather than drawn. Now that I think of it, it occurs to me that some of Mr. Frost's finest characterizations do not speak: they do not even appear. The high-hearted adventurer, for instance, in "The Woodpile" (a lesser poet would have bungled the theme; or, more likely, would never have seen it): that unknown, careless rover, continually turning to fresh tasks. Or the tired, incompetent hired man, a mediocrity typical enough to be tragic. Or that positive, tight-lipped old lady in "The Black Cottage."

On the other hand, take, as an example of pure delineative power, the first brief poem. In "Mending Wall" you have, in two pages, the gait, the impress, the very souls of two people. The poem is in the first person and in the alternate whimsy and a something like natural anarchy one gets a full-length portrait of one. The other person has just one line—repeated: but the portrait is no less full. He is drawn as completely as though the artist had put in every wrinkle and trouser-crease.... And it

is after one has put the volume down that the power of these people persists—and becomes something bigger. One feels that one has perceived beneath the opposition of two men the struggle of two forces as primal as Order and Revolution.

All of which is neither as fanciful or as rhetorical as it sounds, and Mr. Frost would be the first to disclaim any vatic intentions. At least I hope he would for his power lies not alone in his directness, but in his avoidance of making his figures and landscapes metaphysical, symbolic or in any way larger than they are. For sheer dramatic feeling I know few scenes tenser than "The Fear," with its vague, suggestive background. Nor do I know many novels disclosing the brooding insanity that springs from the stark and lonely rigors of farm life, as well as "A Servant to Servants." There's humor in Frost, too. "The Code" has a big-shouldered kind of it. And "Blueberries" has a lesser though more genial shade. It is impossible to quote scraps of these poems: it is, owing to the proverbial exigencies of space, equally impossible to quote an entire poem. Besides, these poems should be read in batches and 'out loud. Most poems should, for that matter, but these, particularly, because of their colloquial flow and their conversational give-and-take, call for the tongue. And, incidentally, the nasal twang, if one can manage it.

As the last-paragraph kind of climax, it should be insisted that Mr. Frost's work is indigenous and as American as Whitman's. And, outside of the fact that he is much more local and much less rhapsodic than Whitman, there is, it is true, a decided bond between them. There is the same clear sight, honesty of expression, freedom from pose and old patterns (patterns either of speech or thought) and fidelity to his times.

"The Tragedy of Loneliness."
Independent,
May 31, 1915,
p. 368.

Truly did Boston lose the last opportunity to redeem slipping literary laurels when to the English at second hand, was left the discovery of the best interpreter New England life has had in a generation. English literary "finds," particularly when they are Americans,—despite John Bull's most cherished traditions of conservatism—are to be accepted hesitatingly; they suffer, as a rule, from a tendency toward exaggeration, which renders them peculiarly catching on this side of the Atlantic. But there can be no occasion to quarrel with the judgment in the case of Robert Frost and *North of Boston,* no matter how erroneous at other times it may be. For this "discovery" at least can be accepted, not for what the British have extravagantly said of him, but for the sheer inability of his light to stay hid under a bushel.

The New England that *North of Boston* introduces is the same bleak land that Mary Wilkins Freeman and Alice Brown have made so thoroughly their own in fiction; the bare hill-tops, and cold, harsh winds, where human beings, like the plants, must grapple close with roots deep in the flinty soil, to withstand the struggle for existence. It is a conflict that strips life of non-essentials, that under its bar-

renness locks up molten drama, which is the more portentous for its suppression.

From out the dreariness of life on these rugged farms, the motif that Mr. Frost has chosen is its tragic loneliness. And the pictures he presents are not abstractions, their detail is that of the cameo, their vividness and sympathy drawn from experience. For Mr. Frost, before he felt the literary call that took him across the now submarine-infested seas, tilled New Hampshire's flinty soil. The "Servant of Servants," "Home Burial" and "The Hired Man" are perhaps the most notable poems in the volume. Take, for instance, the picture of the farmer's wife in "The Servant of Servants," who feels herself slowly being driven mad by the monotony of her life; or the woman's sympathy, given in a few bold strokes, with the poor derelict of the Hired Man, who has come back to die:

With nothing to look backward to
    with pride,
And nothing to look forward to
    with hope,
So now, and never any different.

And how, in the opening lines, she seeks to shield the old man from her less sympathetic husband:

Mary sat musing on the lamp-flame
    at the table
Waiting for Warren. When she heard
    his step,
She ran on tip-toe down the
    darkened passage
To meet him in the doorway
    with the news
And put him on his guard.
    "Silas is back."

She pushed him outward with her
   thru the door
And shut it after her.
   "Be kind," she said.

And thus in a sentence is revealed the whole psychology of a woman. The chief charm of these poems—if the word can be employed somewhat loosely—is not in the pithy verse, but in the psychological insight they reveal, in the Browningesque quality of their drama. Indeed, analyzed on the score of verse, the poems would be almost negligible; they suffer all the halting awkwardness which is ever the handicap of *vers libre;* but they are gripping, they are powerful; rime would have spoiled them, robbed them of the homely atmosphere, as it does "Blueberries" and most of the poems of "A Boy's Will," an earlier and unconvincing volume of Mr. Frost's rimed poems which has also just been published.

In the necessity of this atmosphere, it may be believed, that we strike the reason for Mr. Frost's English debut, for we cannot help but be a little piqued at having been passed for our cousins. It is the bond with Masefield, with Housman, and with Wilfrid Gibson, and others of the newer English school, that has given strength and promise to his own work. And very great promise indeed, it is, if *North of Boston* is but the second guide-post.

Edward Garnett. "A New American Poet." *Atlantic Monthly,* 116 (August 1915), 214-24.

A short time ago I found on a London bookstall an odd number of *The Poetry Review,* with examples of and comments on 'Modern American Poets,'—examples which whetted my curiosity. But the few quotations given appeared to me literary bric-à-brac, the fruit of light *liaisons* between American dilettantism and European models. Such poetry, aesthetic or sentimental,—reflections of vagrant influences, lyrical embroideries in the latest designs, with little imaginative insight into life or nature,—abounds in every generation. If sufficiently bizarre its pretensions are cried up in small Bohemian coteries; if sufficiently orthodox in tone and form, it may impress itself on that public which reads poetry as it looks idly at pictures, with sentimental appetite or from a vague respect for 'culture.' Next I turned to some American magazines at hand, and was brought to a pause by discovering some interesting verse by modern American poets, especially by women whose sincerity in the expression of the inner life of love compared well with the ambitious flights of some of their rivals. I learned indeed from a magazine article that the 'New Poetry' was in process of being hatched out by the younger school; and, no doubt, further researches would have yielded a harvest, had not a literary friend chanced to place in my hands a slim green volume, *North* *of Boston,* by Robert Frost.* I read it, and reread it. It seemed to me that this poet was destined to take a permanent place in American literature. I asked myself why this book was issued by an English and not by an American publisher. And to this question I have found no answer. I may add here, in parenthesis, that I know nothing of Mr. Robert Frost save the three or four particulars I gleaned from the English friend who sent me *North of Boston.*

In an illuminating paper on recent American fiction which I hope by and by, with the editor's permission, to discuss along with Mr. Owen Wister's smashing onslaught in the *Atlantic Monthly,* Mr. W. D. Howells remarks, 'By test of the native touch we should not find genuine some of the American writers whom Mr. Garnett accounts so.' No doubt Mr. Howells's stricture is just, and certain American novelists—whom he does not however particularize—have been too affected in spirit by European models. Indeed Frank Norris's early work, *Vandover and the Brute,* is quite continental in tone; and it is arguable that his study of the French Naturalists may have shown beneficial results later, in the breadth of scheme and clarity of *The Pit.*

This point of 'the native touch' raises difficult questions, for the ferment of foreign influence has often marked the point of departure and rise of powerful native writers, such as Pushkin in Russia and Fenimore Cooper in America. Again, if we consider the fiction of Poe and Herman Melville, would it not be difficult to

*I am told, after writing this, that an American edition has been published by Henry Holt & Co.

assess their genuineness by any standard or measure of 'native touch'? But I take it that Mr. Howells would ban as 'not genuine' only those writers whose originality in vision, tone, and style has been patently marred or nullified by their surrender to exotic influences.

So complex may be the interlacing strains that blend in a writer's literary ancestry and determine his style, that the question first to ask seems to me whether a given author is a fresh creative force, an original voice in literature. Such an authentic original force to me speaks from *North of Boston.* Surely a genuine New England voice, whatever be its literary debt to old-world English ancestry. Originality, the point is there,—for we may note that originality of tone and vision is always the stumbling-block to the common taste when the latter is invited to readjust its accepted standards.

On opening *North of Boston* we see the first lines to be stamped with the magic of *style,* of a style that obeys its own laws of grace and beauty and inner harmony.

Something there is that doesn't
    love a wall,
That sends the frozen-ground-swell
    under it,
And spills the upper boulders
    in the sun;
And makes gaps even two
    can pass abreast.
The work of hunters is another
    thing:
I have come after them and
    made repair
Where they have left not
    one stone on stone,
But they would have the
    rabbit out of hiding.

To please the yelping dogs. . . .

Note the clarity of the images, the firm outline. How delicately the unobtrusive opening suggests the countryman's contemplative pleasure in his fields and woods. It seems so very quiet, the modern reader may complain, forgetting Wordsworth; and indeed, had Wordsworth written these lines, I think they must have stood in every English anthology. And when we turn the page, the second poem, 'The Death of the Hired Man,' proves that this American poet has arrived, not indeed to challenge the English poet's possession of his territory, but to show how untrodden, how limitless are the stretching adjacent lands. 'The Death of the Hired Man' is a dramatic dialogue between husband and wife, a dialogue characterized by an exquisite precision of psychological insight. I note that two college professors have lately been taking Mr. Ruckstuhl to task for a new definition of poetry. Let us fly all such debates, following Goethe, who, condemning the 'aesthete who labors to express the nature of poetry and of poets,' exclaimed, 'What do we want with so much definition? A lively feeling of situations and an aptitude to describe them makes the poet.' This definition, though it does not cover the whole ground, is apropos to our purpose.

Mr. Frost possesses a keen feeling for situation. And his fine, sure touch in clarifying our obscure instincts and clashing impulses, and in crystallizing them in sharp, precise images,—for that we cannot be too grateful. Observe the tense, simple dramatic action, foreshadowing conflict, in the opening lines of 'The Death of the Hired Man':

Mary sat musing on the lamp-flame
at the table
Waiting for Warren. When she heard
his step,
She ran on tip-toe down the
darkened passage
To meet him in the doorway
with the news
And put him on his guard.
'Silas is back.'
She pushed him outward with her
through the door
And shut it after her.
'Be kind,' she said.

'It's we who must be good to him now,' she urges. I wish I had space to quote the debate so simple in its homely force, so comprehending in its spiritual veracity; but I must restrict myself to these arresting lines and to the hushed, tragic close:— . . .

Yes, this is poetry, but of what order? the people may question, to whom for some reason poetry connotes the fervor of lyrical passion, the glow of romantic color, or the play of picturesque fancy. But it is precisely its quiet passion and spiritual tenderness that betray this to be poetry of a rare order, 'the poetry of a true real natural vision of life,' which, as Goethe declared, 'demands descriptive power of the highest degree, rendering a poet's pictures so lifelike that they become actualities to every reader.' One may indeed anticipate that the 'honorable minority' will appraise highly the spiritual beauty of the lines above quoted.

But what of his unconventional *genre* pictures, such as 'A Hundred Collars'? Is it necessary to carry the war against the enemy's cardboard fortresses of convention by using Goethe's further declaration:—

'At bottom no subject is unpoetical, if only the poet knows how to treat it aright.' The dictum is explicit: 'A true, real, natural vision of life . . . high descriptive power . . . pictures of life-like actuality . . . a lively feeling of situation'—if a poet possess these qualifications he may treat any theme or situation he pleases. Indeed, the more prosaic appears the vesture of everyday life, the greater is the poet's triumph in seizing and representing the enduring human interest of its familiar features. In the characteristic fact, form, or feature the poet no less than the artist will discover essential lines and aspects of beauty. Nothing is barred to him, if he only have *vision*. Even the most eccentric divagations in human conduct can be exhibited in their true spiritual perspective by the psychologist of insight, as Browning repeatedly demonstrates. One sees no reason why Browning's 'Fra Lippo Lippi' with all its roughcast philosophic speculation should be 'poetry' and Mr. Frost's 'A Hundred Collars' should not; and indeed the purist must keep the gate closed on both or on neither. If I desired indeed to know whether a reader could really detect the genuine poet, when he appears amid the crowd of *dilettanti,* I should ask his judgment on a typical uncompromising passage in 'A Hundred Collars,' such as the following:—

The night clerk led him up three
   flights of stairs
And down a narrow passage full of
   doors,
At the last one of which he knocked
   and entered.

'Lafe, here's a fellow wants to share
   your room.'

'Show him this way. I'm not afraid of
   him.
I'm not so drunk I can't take care of
   myself.'

The night clerk clapped a bedstead
   on the foot.
'This will be yours. Good night,' he
   said, and went.

. . . .

The Doctor looked at Lafe and
   looked away.
A man? A brute. Naked above the
   waist,
He sat there creased and shining in
   the light,
Fumbling the buttons in a
   well-starched shirt.
'I'm moving into a size-larger shirt.
I've felt mean lately; mean's no
   name for it.
I've found just what the matter was
   to-night:
I've been a-choking like a nursery
   tree
When it outgrows the wire band of
   its name-tag.
I blamed it on the hot spell we've
   been having.
'Twas nothing but my foolish
   hanging back,
Not liking to own up I'd grown a
   size.
Number eighteen this is. What size
   do you wear?'
The Doctor caught his throat
   convulsively.
'Oh-ah-fourteen-fourteen.'

The whole colloquy between this tipsy provincial reporter, Lafayette, and the scared doctor, will, at the first blush, seem to be out of court to the ordinary citizen trained from childhood to recognize as 'poetical,' say Bryant's 'Thanatopsis.' The latter is a good example of 'the noble manner,' but the reader who enjoys it does not therefore turn away with a puzzled frown from Holmes's 'The Wonderful One-hoss Shay.'

But is Mr. Frost then a humorist? the reader may inquire, seeing a gleam of light. Humor has its place in his work; that is to say, our author's moods take their rise from his contemplative scrutiny of *character* in men and nature, and he responds equally to a tragic episode or a humorous situation. But, like creators greater in achievement, his humorous perception is inter-woven with many other strands of apprehension, and in his *genre* pictures, sympathy blends with ironical appreciation of grave issues, to endow them with unique temperamental flavor. If one styled 'Mending Wall' and 'A Hundred Collars' idyls of New England life, the reader might remark sarcastically that they do not seem very idyllic; but idyls they are none the less, not in the corrupted sense of pseudo-Arcadian pastorals, but in the original meaning of 'little pictures.' One may contend that 'The Housekeeper' is cast in much the same gossiping style as Theocritus's idyl, 'The Ladies of Syracuse,' with its prattle of provincial ladies over their household affairs and the crush in the Alexandrian streets at the Festival of Adonis. And one may wager that this famous poem shocked the academic taste of the day by its unconventionality, and would not indeed, please modern professors, were it not the work of a Greek poet who lived three hundred years before Christ.

It is not indeed a bad precept for readers who wish to savor the distinctive quality of new original talents to judge them first by the *human interest* of what they present. Were this simple plan followed, a Browning or a Whitman would not be kept waiting so long in the chilling shadow of contemporary disapproval. Regard simply the people in Mr. Frost's dramatic dialogues, their motives and feelings, their intercourse and the clash of their outlooks, and note how these little canvases, painted with quiet, deep understanding of life's incongruous everyday web, begin to glow with subtle color. Observe how the author in 'A Servant to Servants,' picturing the native or local surroundings, makes the *essentials* live and speak in a woman's homely confession of her fear of madness.

But it is best to give an example of Mr. Frost's emotional force, and in quoting a passage from 'Home Burial' I say unhesitatingly that for tragic poignancy this piece stands by itself in American poetry. How dramatic is the action, in this moment of revelation of the tragic rift sundering man and wife!

* * *

I have quoted 'Home Burial' partly from the belief that its dramatic intensity will best level any popular barrier to the recognition of its author's creative originality. But one does not expect that even a sensitive taste will respond so readily to the rare flavor of 'The Mountain' as did the American people to Whittier's 'Snowbound,' fifty years back. The imagery of the Quaker poet's idyl, perfectly suited to its purpose of mirroring with faithful sincerity the wintry landscape and the pursuits and character of a New England farmer's family, is marked by no peculiar delicacy or originality of style. Mr. Frost, on the other hand, may disappoint readers who prefer grandeur and breadth of outline or magical depth of coloring to delicate atmospheric imagery.

But the attentive reader will soon discover that Mr. Frost's cunning impressionism produces a subtle cumulative effect, and that by his use of pauses, digressions, and the crafty envisagement of his subject at fresh angles, he secures a pervading feeling of the mass and movement and elusive force of nature. He is a master of his exacting medium, blank verse,—a new master. The reader must pause and pause again before he can judge him, so unobtrusive and quiet are these 'effects,' so subtle the appeal of the whole. One can, indeed, return to his poems again and again without exhausting their quiet imaginative spell. For instance, the reader will note how the feeling of the mountain's mighty bulk and hanging mass, its vast elbowing flanks, its watching domination of the near fields and scattered farmsteads, begins to grow upon him, till he too is possessed by the idea of exploring its high ravines, its fountain springs and granite terraces. One of the surest tests of fine art is whether our imagination harks back to it, fascinated in after contemplation, or whether our interest is suddenly exhausted both in it and the subject. And 'The Mountain' shows that the poet has known how to seize and present the mysterious force and essence of living nature.

In nearly all Mr. Frost's quiet dramatic dialogues, his record of the present passing scene suggests how much has gone before, how much these people have lived through, what a lengthy chain of feelings and motives and circumstances has shaped their actions and mental attitudes. Thus in 'The Housekeeper," his picture of the stout old woman sitting there in her chair, talking over Estelle, her grown-up daughter, who, weary of her anomalous position in the household, has left John and gone off and married another man, carries with it a rich sensation of the women's sharp criticism of a procrastinating obstinate man. John is too dense in his masculine way to know how much he owes to them. This psychological sketch in its sharp actuality is worthy of Sarah Orne Jewett.

But why put it in poetry and not in prose? The reader may hazard. Well, it comes with greater intensity in rhythm and is more heightened and concentrated in effect thereby. If the reader will examine 'A Servant to Servants,' he will recognize that this narrative of a woman's haunting fear that she has inherited the streak of madness in her family, would lose in distinction and clarity were it told in prose. Yet so extraordinarily close to normal everyday speech is it that I anticipate some academic person may test its metre with a metronome, and declare that the verse is often awkward in its scansion. No doubt. But so also is the blank verse of many a master hard to scan, if the academic footrule be not applied with a nice comprehension of where to give and when to take. In 'A Servant to Servants' the tragic effect of this overdriven woman's unburdening herself of her load of painful memories and gloomy forebodings is to my mind a rare artistic achievement,—one that graves itself on the memory.

And now that we have praised

North of Boston so freely, shall we not make certain stiff, critical reservations? Doubtless one would do so were one not conscious that Mr. Frost's fellow poets, his deserving rivals, will relieve one of the task. May I say to them here that because I believe Mr. Frost in *North of Boston* has found a way for himself, so I believe their roads lie also open before them. These roads are infinite, and will surely yield, now or to-morrow, vital discoveries. A slight defect of Mr. Frost's subtle realistic method, and one does not wish to slur it over, is that it is sometimes difficult to grasp all the implications and bearings of his situations. His language in 'The Self-seeker' is highly figurative, too figurative perhaps for poetry. Again in 'The Generations of Men,' his method as art seems to be both a little casual and long-winded. In several of his poems, his fineness of psychological truth is perhaps in excess of his poetic beauty,—an inevitable defect of cool, fearless realism. And the corollary criticism no doubt will be heard, that from the intensity with which he makes us realize things we should gain a little more pleasure. But here one may add that there is pleasure and pleasure, and that it seems remarkable that this New England poet, so absorbed by the psychological drama of people's temperaments and conduct, should preserve such pure outlines and clear objectivity of style.

Is his talent a pure product of New England soil? I take it that just as Hawthorne owed a debt to English influence, so Mr. Frost owes one also. But his 'native touch' is declared by the subtle blend of outspokenness and reticence, of brooding conscience and grave humor. Speaking under correction, it appears to me that his crea-tive vision, springing from New England soil, and calmly handing on the best and oldest American tradition, may be a little at variance with the cosmopolitan clamor of New York. It would be quaint indeed if Americans who, according to their magazines, are opening their hospitable bosoms to Mr. Rabindranath Tagore's spiritual poems and dramas of Bengal life, should rest oblivious of their own countryman. To certain citizens Mr. Frost's poems of the life of inconspicuous, humble New England folk may seem unattractively homely in comparison with the Eastern poet's lofty, mystical dramas; but by American critics this view will doubtless be characterized as a manifestation of American provincialism. The critics know that a poet who has no 'message' to deliver to the world, whose work is not only bare of prettiness and sentimentality but is isolated and unaffected by this or that 'movement,' is easily set aside. Nothing is easier, since his appeal is neither to the interests nor caprices of the market. Ours indeed is peculiarly the day when everything pure, shy, and independent in art seems at the mercy of whose who beat the big drum and shout their wares through the megaphone. And knowing this, the critic of conscience will take for his watchword *quality*.

'Mr. Frost is a true poet, but not a *poetical* poet,' remarked a listener to whom I read 'A Servant to Servants,' leaving me wondering whether his verdict inclined the scales definitely to praise or blame. Of poetical poets we have so many! of literary poets so many! of drawing-room poets so many!—of academic and dilettanti poets so many! of imitative poets so many! but of original poets how few!

William Dean Howells. "Editor's Easy Chair." *Harper's,* 131 (September 1915), 635.

... Freak for freak, we prefer compressed verse to shredded prose, but because both of these are freak things we will not decide whether Uncle Walt will be more enduring than Mr. Masters. We merely speak here of their respective truth to our human nature and our American mood of it. Prophecy is not our job, or not our present job, but we have a fancy that when it comes to any next book of shredded prose it will not be so eagerly welcomed as some next book of Mr. Robert Frost's or Mr. Dana Burnet's. Mr. Frost's volumes, *A Boy's Will* and *North of Boston*, have already made their public on both sides of the Atlantic, and they merit the favor they have won. They are very genuinely and unaffectedly expressive of rustic New England, and of its deeps as well as its shallows. We should say the earlier book sings rather the most, but youth is apt to sing most, and there is strong, sweet music in them both. Here is no *vers libre,* no shredded prose, but very sweet rhyme and pleasant rhythm, though it does not always keep step (wilfully breaks step at times, we should say), but always remains faithful to the lineage of poetry that danced before it walked. When we say Mr. Frost's work is unaffectedly expressive of New England life, we do not mean that it is unconsciously expressive; we do not much believe in unconscious art, and we rather think that his fine intelligence tingles with a sense of that life and beautifully knows what it is at in dealing with it. If we may imagine the quality of Sarah Orne Jewett and Miss Mary Wilkins and Miss Alice Brown finding metrical utterance, we shall have such pleasure in characterizing Mr. Frost's poetry as comes to us from knowing what things are by knowing what they are like; but this knowledge by no means unlocks the secret of his charm, and it does not adequately suggest the range of his very distinctive power. His manly power is manliest in penetrating to the heart of womanhood in that womanliest phase of it, the New England phase. Dirge, or idyl, or tragedy, or comedy, or burlesque, it is always the skill of the artist born and artist trained which is at play, or call it work, for our delight. Amidst the often striving and straining of the new poetry, here is the old poetry as young as ever; and new only in extending the bounds of sympathy through the recorded to the unrecorded knowledge of humanity. One might have thought there was not much left to say of New England humanity, but here it is as freshly and keenly sensed as if it had not been felt before, and imparted in study and story with a touch as sure and a courage as loyal as if the poet dealt with it merely for the joy of it.

But of course he does not do that. He deals with it because he must master it, must impart it just as he must possess it. . . .

George H. Browne. "Robert Frost, A Poet of Speech."
Independent,
May 22, 1916,
pp. 283-84.

A year ago, Robert Frost was an unfamiliar name in this country. Within a year, however, seven editions of "North of Boston" have been printed! Why? Not because he was "discovered in England" [as a matter of fact, he was "discovered" by The Independent in 1894] but because American readers have discovered that they can understand and enjoy poetry which deals veraciously with the life and the people they know—poetry which is written in a language they can understand and enjoy, because it is the language they speak, vibrant with the feeling and force and form of the familiar spoken sentence. In Frost's poetry, as in all effective writing and in any animated conversation, the sentence does double duty: not only conveys the necessary information, but also records, in an unmistakable tho unwritten notation, the natural tones and inflections which alone give emotional and imaginative vitality to the expression of live thought.

Most people misconceive the real reason why verse of this kind gets its message over so quickly and so effectively. In language, most of us are not used to observing closely (either physically or imaginatively) the really most significant technical elements, namely, the audible tones in which the thought of the sentence-unit is conceived and is to be uttered. The domination of the newspaper, the magazine, and the expository essay—of reading by eye without hearing anything, so that, as a result, our untrained ears cannot even understand most oral reading without seeing the text—has made us content, in poetry as well as in prose, with the dead level of a flat, emotionless, mere algebraic informatory tone. Too much of our so-called poetry is only words fitted to metres—no true tone values, no emotional realities—plenty of melodious rhythm, perhaps, but none of the live tones that infuse with expressiveness even our most ordinary and uninspired conversation. Now, the spoken language is alive with characterizing tones, as nature and the human face are alive with characterizing colors. These tones may be, but seldom caught by ear, reimagined, and fixed on the page, so that the reader will hear and reproduce them exactly.

Verse like Robert Frost's gets its message over, therefore, because in form as well as in substance it is true to life; and no popular verse "gets over" to stay except when it is thus true. Frost is as simple in his diction and imagination as Wordsworth and even more sympathetic with his subjects, whether people or nature. He gets more music and pathos and force out of homely Saxon monosyllables than any other writer, not excepting Lincoln; and he acquired his mastery in quite the same way that Lincoln did: never letting pass any but the best attainable expression of his thought. Frost has more than once brought a letter back from the country post-office and rewritten it, because one sentence in it was not as good as he thought he could make it.

"I recall distinctly the joy with which I had the first satisfaction of getting an adequate expression for my thought," he has said; "it was the second stanza of the little poem on the 'Butterfly,' written in my eighteenth year." That was twenty-five years ago! Thus, tho Frost is a recent candidate for popular American favor, and to that extent is new, he is no novice; few American poets have had a longer or more fruitful training, either in technique or in experience.

Born in San Francisco (1874), he came back in his twelfth year with his widowed Scotch mother to live in Salem, New Hampshire, not far from his father's people in Lawrence, Massachusetts. Up to the time of graduation from the Lawrence High School, young Robert was a docile pupil; but then he declared his intellectual independence, and never again took much interest in tasks not self imposed. He spent a few months at Dartmouth (1892), "acting like an Indian in a college founded for Indians." He left abruptly (but voluntarily), took his mother's school, worked in the mill, engaged in newspaper work, married at twenty-one; and after another futile attempt to conform to the "academics," this time at Harvard, retired again to school-teaching and farming in Derry, New Hampshire (1899). For the next seven years he farmed, thought, and wrote—among shorter lyrics the first of his longer poems in the newer characteristic style: "The Death of the Hired Man," "The Housekeeper," and "The Black Cottage," subsequently incorporated into "North of Boston." In 1906 he began to teach English in the Pinkerton Academy at Derry. His success was so marked that he was invited to the Plymouth Normal School (1911) to teach psychology; but the restrictions of even freer teaching there again became irksome; and only two weeks before he sailed (August, 1912), with wife and four children, he decided upon England as a freer field for poetical composition and the realization of his literary ideals.

The Frosts had neither friends nor letters of introduction. Like migratory birds they flitted into solitary independence at Beaconsfield, about twenty miles from London—almost by accident. The publication in London (1913) of his first book of poems, which he carried over with him, was almost accidental; his first meeting with literary friends was most accidental; but the success of his book and the intensity of concentration in the composition of his second book, "North of Boston" (1914), were far from accidental. It was fortunate for him (and perhaps for us) that his work received immediate and hearty recognition in England; but it is a pity that the force and originality of the New England idylls, written in home-sickness over there, should have diverted attention at home from the merits of the first book, written in rustic isolation over here; for tho more traditional in form, it is hardly less original and forcible. As its name implies, "A Boy's Will" is the lyrical record of a young man's thoughts— "and the thoughts of youth are long, long thoughts." This, on his art, from "Pan with Us":

Pan came out of the woods one
    day—
His skin and his hair and his eyes
    were gray; . . .
He tossed his pipes, too hard to teach
A new-world song, far out of
    reach; . . .
Times were changed from what they
    were;

Such pipes kept less of power to
    stir; . . .
They were pipes of pagan mirth,
And the world had found new terms
    of worth.
He laid him down on the sun-burned
    earth,
And ravelled a flower and looked
    away—
Play? Play?—What should he play?

No longer, was the answer, only
beautiful lyrics, in a variety of traditional meters, lyrics which will maintain an enviable position in any anthology of American verse; but, in a
new and original rapid measure, gripping, dramatic pictures of the places
and the people he was brought up
among—interpretations of New England life and character, displaying a
psychological insight, spiritual veracity, and artistic simplicity, power and
originality, such as no other con-
tributor to American literature has
displayed since Emerson and Whitman.

Frost finds his metrical freedom,
not in *vers libre* like Whitman, but in
decasyllabic, unrimed verses, no two
of which are alike, because of the
tones of living speech in them—the
stressed pauses, the little hurries of
extra-syllabled feet, the preponder-
ance of light and weak endings to the
run-on lines, and fresh metrical inflections, which reproduce in verse the
actual shape of the colloquial sentence. It is a new kind of blank verse,
strange at first sight, from its very
colloquialism; but its strangeness disappears if it is read out loud.

"When I began to teach, and long
after I began to write," he told the
boys in our school, "I didn't know
what the matter was with me and my
writing, and with other people's writ-

ing. . . . I found the basis of all effective linguistic expression to be the
sound in the mouths of men—not
merely words or phrases, but
sentences—living expressions flying
around—the only vital 'parts of
speech.'" And his poems are to be
read most appreciatively, out loud, in
the natural tones of this live speech.
The first poem, "Mending Wall," the
author likes best in "North of Boston," because the verses best catch the
sentence sounds. Can't you see and
hear the old farmer shaking his head,
challenging, threatening, playing and
mistrusting his neighbor across the
old wall in the spring?

Mr. Frost is not a vers librist, or
imagist, or even realist, except that
he agrees with Carlyle that a poet has
not far to seek for his subject. "It all
depends upon what you call 'beauty,'"
says Frost. "Terror is beautiful. A
mob raging down the street may be
made beautiful if you catch the right
tones and rouse the right emotional
reaction by the poetic expression of it.
You can catch the tones only with the
imagination." Mr. Frost, if he is a
realist, is an imaginative realist.

Mr. Frost is not a Socialist nor a
profound moralist, but he is sane
and simple and moral. He is a
philosopher, even if he doesn't preach
and interpret. He is above all a dramatist, for all poetry is to him dramatic. Fortunately for us he is still in
the prime of his creative activity.
Much of his recently written work,
which he has been reading in public
this winter, surpasses the best of his
published verse; and he will soon be
giving us still better.

John Gould Fletcher. "Some Contemporary American Poets." *Chapbook, 2* (May 1920), 5-7.

If Robinson's poetry clearly presents the mind of New England, the poetry of Robert Frost no less clearly presents its heart. Yet Frost is neither temperamentally nor by birth a New Englander. His father found himself so much at variance with his New England neighbours that he not only sympathised with the cause of the South in the Civil War, but gave to his son the name of the great Southern leader, Lee. And the future poet was not only born in San Francisco, but spent the first ten years of his life there. It was only the accident of a return to New England that fixed upon the sensitive plate of Robert Frost's temperament the scenes and characters with which he has made us familiar.

People in Europe generally suffer from a mistaken impression that the West is the wildest part of America. This is not the case. The West, except for one or two "National" Parks, and a few stretches of desert, is decidedly the most cultivated part of the United States. The true region of wildness lies at the threshold of the European visitor arriving in New York. It is in Northern Massachusetts, Maine, Vermont, New Hampshire, the backwoods of New England; the "North of Boston" of Frost's most famous book.

This part of America has the melancholy charm of a country which was once prosperous and cultivated, but which has since fallen into decay. At the time of the Revolution it was a rich agricultural country. Since the opening-out of the West and the development of New England industry it has been gradually emptied of its population, until what remains of the old New England agricultural stock—the true descendants of the *Mayflower* pilgrims—have dwindled in numbers and in prosperity, and have practically given up agriculture, living on stock-raising, apple-growing, and the like. In the last few years many of the deserted and half-overgrown farms have again become populated by Finns, Norwegians, and the like, thanks to the overcrowding of immigrants into the great industrial centres. But is is not with these people that Frost deals, but with the remnant of the original stock—a remnant tough, obstinate, reserved, weakened in fibre through intermarriage, half-crazed in many cases through the combined spiritual and physical loneliness of long winters, few neighbours, the chill isolations of Puritanism. It is with these people, and with the scenes of their daily lives, that Frost has dealt faithfully. In a sense, he has been but an instrument in their hands.

Throughout his work one is faced with the feeling that Robert Frost is only a recording instrument, and one which functions only under compulsion. He is a fastidiously slow worker, and many of the poems in *North of Boston* have developed from a germ which lay latent in his mind for years. In some cases the first idea of a poem was duly committed to paper, to be printed in the *Youths' Companion,* and was taken up later on to be expanded, subtilized, re-cast. I believe that *The Death of the Hired Man* was so treated. Thus the composition of many of his poems, and the gradual evolution of them into their final form, has taken a great number of years. Insatiably he seeks the quintessential features of a vanishing state of society. His is the most carefully weighed, the most mature poetry now being written in America.

In order to render with finality what may be called, without irony, the most completely finished and exhausted aspect of America—the aspect of Northern New England—Frost has evolved a form peculiar to himself, and which even he does not always handle with equal success; the rambling quasi-narrative, conversational, blank-verse poem, of which *The Death of the Hired Man, The Mountain, A Servant to Servants, The Fear, The Woodpile, In the Home Stretch, Birches,* are the most conspicuous examples.

These poems may owe, conceivably, something to Robinson, who essayed the same type less successfully in his *Isaac and Archibald,* which, I believe, dates back to 1902. But to whatever poet Frost may owe the germ of the form that is his, it is certain that he alone has handled it most richly.

This form is based upon commonplace incidents, told as far as possible in the language of common speech. Frost has attempted to revive blank verse by means of restoring the connection, lost since Elizabethan days, between the common tongue and the language of literature. But since the figures with which he is familiar live greyer, more colourless, more confined lives than the Elizabethans, and employ a less rich vocabulary, he employs in the place of dramatic climax a subtler reverbera-tion. His poetry is intended to echo in our hearts, to attract us by a sense of sympathy, rather than to uplift us by a feeling of heroic conflict. It is poetry deliberately written without "purple patches," as the late Edward Thomas, possibly the most sincere follower Frost ever had, long ago recognised. It is poetry filled with a brooding sense of mystical kinship with nature which is almost Celtic (one suspects a Celtic strain in Frost, such as existed in Thomas). And in its deliberate avoidance of definite conclusions about the world, as in its employment of carefully differentiated repetitions of the same thought, it recalls the poetry of the great Chinese poets, familiar to us through Mr. Waley's translations.

For this reason Frost is something more than a New England poet. By his deliberate refusal to employ dialect speech (a wise omission), by his quiet observation that always shines through his scenes and figures, he has raised himself to universal stature. It is only by accident that he has been selected by destiny to render New England, or any part of America. He knows this well enough, and in several more poignant and personal poems he has looked upon New England as having been in a sense a frustration of a higher destiny he might have obtained. These poems, which are, contrary to his usual practice, in rhyme, are by no means the least of his achievements. To read *After Apple-Picking, The Road Not Taken, The Sound of Trees,* and many pieces in *A Boy's Will* is to understand the brooding, sensitive soul of a great poet.

Checklist of Additional Reviews

Times Literary Supplement, May 28, 1914, p. 263.

Ford Madox Heuffer (Ford). "Mr. Robert Frost and 'North of Boston.'" *Outlook* (London), June 27, 1914, pp. 879-80.

Wilfrid Wilson Gibson. "Simplicity and Sophistication." *Bookman*, 46 [London], (July 1914), 183.

"Some Recent Verse." *Times Literary Supplement*, July 2, 1914, p. 316.

Alice Corbin Henderson. "Recent Poetry." *The Dial*, 57 (October 1, 1914), 254.

William Stanley Braithwaite. "The Best Poetry of 1915." *Anthology of Magazine Verse for 1915 and Year Book of American Poetry*. New York: Gomme and Marshall, 1915, pp. 231-32.

Bulletin of the Poetry Society of America, January 1915.

William Aspenwall Bradley. "The New Freedom—In Verse." *Bookman* [London], April 1915, pp. 184-195.

Llewellyn Jones. "Robert Frost." *Chicago Evening Post*, April 23, 1915, p. 11.

Zoë Akins. "In the Shadow of Parnassus." *Reedy's Mirror*, 24 (May 7, 1915), 6-7.

"Current Poetry." *Literary Digest*, 50 (May 15, 1915), 1165.

Jessie B. Rittenhouse. "North of Boston." *New York Times Book Review*, May 16, 1915, p. 189.

[Edmund J. Wheeler.] "Literature and Art." *Current Opinion*, 58 (June 1915), 427-28.

F[ranklin] P[ierce] A[dams]. "The Conning Tower." *New York Tribune*, June 11, 1915, p. 9.

"Short Stories in Verse." *New York Evening Post*, June 11, 1915, p. 14.

MOUNTAIN INTERVAL

BY

ROBERT FROST

Author of " North of Boston "

NEW YORK

HENRY HOLT AND COMPANY

Mountain Interval

William Stanley
Braithwaite.
"Fifteen Important
Volumes of Poems
Published in 1916."
*Anthology of Magazine
Verse for 1916 and Year
Book of American Poetry*.
New York: Laurence J.
Gomme, 1916,
p. 247.

That indescribable magic which Mr. Frost evokes from the plain and severe quality of New England life and character glows again in these pages.

W. A. Bradley.
"Four American Poets."
The Dial, 61
(December 14, 1916),
528-30.

... It is for this purely sensuous quality, as well as for his genuine passion for nature, expressed through such wealth and delicacy of observed detail, that one most legitimately reads and admires Mr. Frost. There are, too,

elements of deep divination in his art, where it touches complex human relations and reactions. But as a dramatic and narrative poet, his method is often unnecessarily cryptic and involved. Thus in "Snow" there is nothing sufficiently remarkable either in the incident itself, or in the resultant revelation and clash of character, to justify its long and elaborate treatment. But in "In the Home Stretch" the poet is singularly successful in suggesting ghostly presences, in creating a veritable haunted atmosphere for the old New England farmhouse, akin to that produced by the English poet, Mr. Walter de la Mare, in "The Listeners." Mr. Frost is the one continuator at present of the "tradition of magic" in American poetry.

Padraic Colum.
"The Poetry of Robert
Frost."
The New Republic, 9
(December 23, 1916),
219-22.

The poetry of American local life, after having been hinted at for long, made a significant appearance last year not from one, but from two quarters—from the Illinois of Edgar

Lee Masters and the New England of Robert Frost. The New England book had less of a shudder, and it shows a readiness of response on the part of the public here that, with the grave and, as one might say, featureless poems in it, it had a success equal to "The Spoon River Anthology," in which, besides the poetic and dramatic appeal, there was the interest of exciting fiction. To go from "The Spoon River Anthology" to "North of Boston" is to go from the court-house into the fields. The fields are usual, and, as we have been in an unusual place, we are not at first impressed. Then we perceive that the fields, the apple-trees, the bounding hill, the frame-house have each a character of their own. We notice that the people—a few of them at all events—have the inaccessible life that Burns's and Wordworth's people have. Such a life belongs to the woman in "A Servant to Servants." Such a life, too, belongs to the man in "The Self-seeker."

Unlike Mr. Masters, Mr. Frost seems to have no notion of satire or of social judgment. This is a terrible background to "A Servant to Servants." A bride has been brought into a house where her husband's mad brother lives as in a den and delights himself by yelling out filthy things in the night. Mr. Masters would have left a social judgment to be inscribed on a tombstone. But Mr. Frost's spirit goes into the current of a life that still moves on. And as that life expresses itself we feel only sympathy with a soul that does not judge and which is beyond our judgments. In "The Self-seeker" we come to know a student and a lover of wild flowers. His legs have been crushed in a mill, and he can never again search out the

flowers he loves so well. He takes five hundred dollars' compensation. There is no satire here. Mr. Frost lets us see the reachings and the reserves of a soul, and he lets us know besides the forms and the hiding places of the wild flowers.

Though there were few people in "North of Boston" and though these people knew of few events, still the book gave the sense of a community. And the brooding of the poet gave life to the inanimate things around. We were made remember the unlived-in Black Cottage and the wood-pile that warms "the frozen swamp as best it could with the slow, smokeless burning of decay"—we were made remember the wall that has some undiscovered enemy; the mountain that crushes the life of the village; the thousands and tens of thousands of gathered apples. In "North of Boston" Mr. Frost's real achievement was not, perhaps, the creation of men and women, but in the hint of mystery that he gave—in the atmosphere that he made surround the inanimate thing— "something there is that does not love a wall" he says, and, as he plods and labors after the explanation we begin to have glimpses and revelations. His very slowness and laboriousness give a hint of this earthy mystery:

"Something there is that does not
     love a wall,
And sends the frozen ground-swell
     under it,
And spills the upper boulders in the
     sun;
And makes gaps even two can pass
     abreast.
The work of hunters is another
     thing;
I have come after them and made
     repair

Where they have left not one stone
    on a stone,
But they would have the rabbit out
    of hiding,
To please the yelping dogs. The gaps
    I mean
No one has seen them made or heard
    them made,
But at spring mending time we find
    them there."

He has made a certain featureless
blank verse his own. Using it, his
men and women, who obviously have
little eloquence in their natures, have
a speech that sometimes lifts into
beauty and tragic eloquence. "I can
repeat the very words you were saying," cries the mother in "Home Burial" to her husband who has buried
their child callously:

"I can repeat the very words you
    were saying.
'Three foggy mornings and one rainy
    day
Will rot the best birch fence a man
    can build.'
Think of it, talk like that at such a
    time!
What had how long it takes a birch
    to rot
To do with what was in the
    darkened parlor.
You couldn't care! The nearest
    friends can go
With any one to death, comes so far
    short
They might as well not try to go at
    all.
No, from the time when one is sick
    to death,
One is alone, and he dies more
    alone.
Friends make pretense of following
    to the grave,

But before one is in it, their minds
    are turned
And making the best of their way
    back to life
And living people, and things they
    understand."

Mr. Frost's recent volume, "Mountain Interval," has more of the personal, less of the communal life. Only
in a few poems does he give us those
detached dramatic pieces that made
the bulk of "North of Boston." The
sense of personal life comes from the
sonnets and from the dramatic sequence that he calls "The Hill Wife." In
these few dramatic lyrics there is a
poetic grace that his featureless blank
verse did not reveal. The poem before
the last one in the sequence, "The
Oft-repeated Dream" has what is rare
in American poetry—the mystery-
suggesting phrase:

"She had no saying dark enough
For the dark pine that kept
Forever trying the window-latch
Of the room where they slept.

The tireless but ineffectual hands
That with every futile pass
Made the great tree seem as a little
    bird
Before the mystery of glass.

It never had been inside the room
And only one of the two
Was afraid in an oft-repeated dream
Of what the tree might do."

The sequence and its title and its
suggestions recalls "James Lee's
Wife," but if it does it matches
Browning's in poignancy. In "The Hill
Wife" Mr. Frost, I think, attains to
the finest expression of the distinctive
thing he brings into literature—the

tremor that comes from many haunting things.

Mr. Frost must be very much aware of this haunting, for does not one of his people cry out "Our very life depends on everything's recurring till we answer from within." For him there are no beginnings. "It would take for ever to recite all that's now new in where we find ourselves," the woman in "The Home Stretch" tells the man. And this being so, it is needful to be aware of the haunting things that try to signal to something within us. What signals to the poet of "Mountain Interval" most persistently are trees—trees by their outline, movement, sound:

"I shall set forth for somewhere,
I shall make the reckless choice
Some day when they are in voice
And tossing so as to scare
The white clouds over them on.
I shall have less to say
But I shall be gone."

Both "North of Boston" and "Mountain Interval" envelop in atmosphere things, which, as it seemed, would never be brought within the domain of poetry—kitchen-sinks, stove-pipes, telegraph-poles. But if another thinks he can create poetry by cataloguing these things he will make a mistake. Mr. Frost is a poet because he knows and because he can show us a spiritual history.

H[arriet] M[onroe]. "Frost and Masters." *Poetry,* 9 (January 1917), 202.

In Kipling's story of primitive men the bard becomes a thing of awe because he can "tell the tale of the tribe," can save the tribe from engulfing oblivion by "making words run up and down in men's hearts"—words that move too grandly to be forgotten. In the final accounting perhaps this is the first function of the bard, even more his office than the setting of dreams to magic measures.

These two poets, Frost and Masters, are telling the tale of the tribe, the varying tales of their separate tribes; and the simultaneous appearance of their latest books tempts one to comparison and contrast. Reading the two books as a whole, without stopping for details, one gets an over-powering impression, not only of two different individuals but of two different crowds. In Frost Puritan New England speaks with a voice as absolute as New Hampshire's granite hills. Whittier wandered there once, singing a few songs, and Emerson from those slopes looked inward and outward for truth. But neither of these felt New England as Frost feels it. . . .

"Yankees are what they always were," sings Mr. Frost. His New England is the same old New England of the pilgrim fathers—a harsh, austere, velvet-coated-granite earth, bringing forth rigid, narrow, heroic men and women, hard but with unexpected softnesses. Their religion has been modified since Cotton Mather, but not their character, at least not the character of those who stay on their farms, resisting the call of the West and the lure of towns. To present this earth, these people, the poet employs usually a blank verse as massive as they, as stript of all apologies and adornments. His poetry is sparing, austere, even a bit crabbed at times; but now and then it lights up with a sudden and intimate beauty, a beauty springing from life-long love and intuition, as in these images of trees from two different poems:

> A resurrected tree,
> A tree that had been down and raised
>   again,
> A barkless spectre—he had halted too,
> As if for fear of treading upon me.
>
> . . . .
>
> She had no saying dark enough
>   For the dark pine that kept
> Forever trying the window-latch
>   Of the room where they slept.

Nature is always thus an integral part of Mr. Frost's human dramas—not a mere background but one of the cast. It is wonderful how he builds up the terrific winter tempest in *Snow,* for example, and does it, not by mere statement, but through the talk of those delicately contrasted characters, the dry skeptical wife, the slower matter-of-fact husband, and the deep-breathing, deep-dreaming evangelist, lover of life and the storm. And "a springtime passion for the earth," with human life—yes, and brute life—as a part of it, burns in such poems as *In the Home Stretch, Putting in the Seed, Birches,* and *The Cow in Apple Time.*

Sidney Cox.
"The Sincerity of Robert Frost."
The New Republic, 12 (August 25, 1917), 109-11.

Mountain Interval, Robert Frost's recent volume, like the two which preceded it, manifests as its fundamental and embracing quality, sincerity—sincerity in perception, sincerity in thought, sincerity in feeling and sincerity in expression. Mr. Frost believes that "A poet must lean hard on facts, so hard, sometimes, that they hurt." And it is because he has that belief that after reading one of his poems the reader feels that he has had an actual experience. Leaning hard on things not only presses them in; it prints them with distinct outline, and makes the salient nubs sink deep. Consequently a poet who leans, so, on experience is able to present segments of life as it is, with every essential detail in just relief. The segments of life in the poems of Mr. Frost all existed first as experiences; none were conceived at the desk. And in so far as setting is concerned they are parochial. Those in North of Boston may be said to have *happened* north of Boston. And, as the new title suggests, these last poems belong to an even more restricted region. The territorial limitation is set because Mr. Frost believes that a poet must utter not what he conjectures but only what he knows.

In the region he knows he has seen much both of nature and of men and women. Like a true lover he is sincere with nature; he never pretends to see what isn't there, but he sees everything, and reveals fresh charms. He doesn't heighten the charms. "We love the things we love for what they are," he says, and we believe him when we read passages like the following from Birches, which I cite to illustrate the marvelous effectiveness of his sincerity in nature description.

Often you must have seen them
Loaded with ice a sunny winter
    morning
After a rain. They click upon
    themselves
As the breeze rises, and turn many
    colored
As the stir cracks and crazes their
    enamel.
Soon the sun's warmth makes them
    shed crystal shells
Shattering and avalanching on the
    snow-crust—
Such heaps of broken glass to sweep
    away
You'd think the inner dome of
    heaven had fallen.

The vividness of that description is secured partly by the sedulous avoidance of pretty words the connotation of which use has dulled. There is not a word in it that fails to elicit attention. And throughout Mr. Frost's poems there prevails the same verbal sincerity.

The extract I have given displays another, and a still more unique aspect of Mr. Frost's veracity. Read aloud, it shows, sentence by sentence, a startling reproduction of the sounds of speech. The author of Mountain Interval has discerned that gesture and inflection are not the only means in conversation of registering subtleties of feeling and shades of meaning supplementary to the sense of the

words. The order of the words in the sentence gives to the whole speech unit a meaning tone. And these sound patterns are things of beauty; writing is alive when it takes those shapes which suggest sentence tones. I may be pardoned for singling out a few specimen sentences in which vital character significance inheres in the tone which the sentence form evokes.

From The Bonfire:
Oh, let's go up the hill and scare
    ourselves,
As reckless as the best of them
    to-night
By setting fire to all the brush we
    piled
With pitchy hands to wait for rain or
    snow.
Oh, let's not wait for rain to make it
    safe

and

Oh, but war's not for children—it's
    for men.

From The Vanishing Red:
Oh, yes, he showed John the wheel
    pit all right.

From Snow:
I could, but what's the sense? The
    rest won't be
So bad.

and again

    Oh, yes you do
You like your fun as well as anyone.

It will be interesting to observe in particular the use of "Oh" in those citations. Each one is pregnant, and no two mean the same. Of that single ejaculation I have discovered twenty-six distinct varieties in Mr. Frost's three books of poems; each would exact from a reader who let himself respond to the subtleties of the piece a particular degree of voice, breath, length, roundness or pitch. All of us have heard each one of them in actual speech. Besides the conditions of mind or emotion more familiar to literature such as apostrophe, alarm and agony, they express indifference, a sudden flash of thought, cajolery, playful coaxing, concession, deprecation, remonstrance, discovery of an unexpected solution, sardonic reflection, disillusionment, scorn, resignation, passionate yearning and tragic protest.

These tones of speech are incomparably more effectual in presenting genuine Yankee conversation than the use of dialect would be. And a further reason why there is such sparing use, in North of Boston and the new book, of barbarous locutions, is that the men and women who live in northern Massachusetts, Vermont and New Hampshire have no uniform set of provincial words and expressions. Nowadays at any rate, one never meets Hosea Bigelow in the flesh. Therefore this sincere poet has no code of dialect.

Not only the language but the souls of Yankee men and women appear as they are upon Mr. Frost's pages. A mere journalist could from the observations of a few vacation trips fabricate a caricature of a Yankee farmer. But even a genius must have shared their lives to describe living individuals with just so much distinctive Yankee character as the real people of the region possess. Working and bargaining and walking and talking with the people would not alone give Mr. Frost that power, of course. He understands people, first, because he has the sincerity and courage to know himself, second, because he likes people, and, third, because he is a searcher after truths; by reason of those qualifications he can put himself almost completely into the emotional and moral vortices in the hollow of which even simple lives are swirled, and can therefore discern the relationships between overt motions and utterances, and inner desires, fears, thoughts, and purposes. Intense, imaginative sympathy suffuses Mr. Frost's poems of people.

There is a sort of intellectual vision of the conflicts and diverse evolutions of the human soul which does not deserve the name of sympathy; it is astute penetration without participation. Mr. Frost is always tender; he always cares. His participation of the feeling saves from being horrible that masterpiece, Out, Out. The setting of that poem is as real as my father's back yard in the country, yet full of the loveliness that touches a sensitive imagination, sometimes, when he snuffs the air and lifts his eyes in one of the New Hampshire intervals. A youth is on the edge of a ghastly accident. Listen to the wistfulness with which the poet presages the catastrophe:

And nothing happened: day was all
    but done.
Call it a day, I wish they might have
    said
To please the boy by giving him the
    half hour
That a boy counts so much when
    saved from work.

That word "wish" is charged with tenderness. But the pathos is restrained, for Mr. Frost believes that "a real man must lean back against his feelings." One must salt his sentiment with stoicism if he is to preserve his mental poise. And therefore the poem closes thus:

> and that ended it.
> No more to build on there. And they, since they
> Were not the one dead, turned to their affairs.

Passion in Mr. Frost's poems is invariably restrained. Yet one would know from Boy's Will that Mr. Frost had known love in its intensity. And Mountain Interval contains some of the most beautiful expressions that could be found of the deep, assured love of man and wife. I suppose that may be the reason why, each time I read it, In the Home Stretch gives me new pleasure. The reader is bound to feel the mysterious oneness of hearts; it doesn't need to be rhapsodically expressed.

Mountain Interval is first of all sincere, I have said. And that sincerity exercises a modulating influence as well upon Mr. Frost's humor as upon his emotion. Even the fun is intrinsic in a real situation, usually provoked, somehow, by character. It is never exaggerated. The poet doesn't make fun; instead he sees and discloses comic facts. Comic in a sense are certain aspects of sober fact, too. There seems a shade of whimsical humor in The Exposed Nest when he raises the troublesome question whether the effort at helpfulness may not injure. If I am right, the joke, there, is at the heart of things, more nearly "down to China" than most of us ever mine for truth.

However, Mr. Frost is devoid of any delusion that he has delved to the center. He sees what he can and de-scribes much; his poems are so sincere that the impressions of life they give us cannot affect us as false fires. For the rest he has no message of ultimate wisdom. But that is no more a defect in him than is the absence in such poems as The Hill Wife of conclusions that leave the mind tranquil. Mr. Frost has put into a poem the reason why he presents no compact message and why some poems seem "not quite finished."

> "You're searching, Joe,
> For things that don't exist; I mean beginnings.
> Ends and beginnings—there are no such things.
> There are only middles"

....

> "It would take me forever to recite
> All that's not new in where we find ourselves.
> New is a word for fools in town who think
> Style upon style in dress and thought at last
> Must get somewhere."

It is very hard indeed to be as sincere as that. It takes courage, and, perhaps, also, what Mr. Frost assuredly has, faith in God.

He is too affectionate and too sensitive to existing beauty to be a pessimist. The closing lines of a poem that has baffled some intelligent readers show that though he doesn't expect mechanical or intellectual inventions to get us anywhere, yet there is joy to be had. I quote from An Encounter:

> Me? I am not off for anywhere at all.
> Sometimes I wander out of beaten ways

Half looking for the orchid Calypso.

"Half looking" instead of anxiously searching because beauty evades systematic or over-earnest search.

Not a pessimist; but not an optimist either. He has sad moods.

It's when I'm weary of
    considerations,
And life is too much like a pathless
    wood
Where your face burns and tickles
    with the cobwebs
Broken across it, and one eye is
    weeping
From a twig's having lashed across
    it open.
I'd like to get away from earth
    awhile.

All sensitive and honest people have felt that way. But Mr. Frost goes on:

And then come back to it and begin
    over.
May no fate wilfully misunderstand
    me
And half grant what I wish and
    snatch me away
Not to return. Earth's the right place
    for love:
I don't know where it's likely to go
    better.

How good and reassuring to know that a man who faces life so squarely would want to come back to it, and that it is attractive because of love!

And now I have indicated that because Mr. Frost really believes

The fact is the sweetest dream that
    labor knows,

he is sincere—in perceiving, in feeling, in thinking and in expressing. And I hope I have not concealed the fact that because his sincerity is so dauntless, so deep-probing, so exacting and so passionate he is in every sense original.

"A New England Poet." *Spectator,* 126 [London] (January 22, 1921), 114.

A few weeks ago, in reviewing the works of another American writer, we said that we hoped to return to the subject of Mr. Robert Frost. He is a poet who in style and outlook stands in sharp contrast to such American writers as Miss Amy Lowell, Mr. Ezra Pound, and Mr. Vachel Lindsay; indeed, it might be said of these three writers that they resemble each other in nothing except their unlikeness to their compatriot.

Every one knows how, if you glance at the faces of two brothers, you are likely, in that brief look, to see a family resemblance which a long scrutiny would persuade you was not there. So it is with comparison in the arts. If you take an "owl's glance" at Mr. Frost's work and then look quickly at Mr. Laurence Binyon's, you will probably realize that they have a good deal in common; there is the same careful writing, the same staidness of thought and expression, a certain power of visualization and quick statement, and the same pleasure in psychological study. For Robert Frost is perhaps the more Wordsworthian of the two; that is to say, he takes pleasure in employing very simple language and in relating very simple occurrences—a man offering three cents each for young spruces for Christmas trees, a colt frightened by the first fall of snow. To English readers the curious flora and fauna and outward circumstances of his poems seem to stamp him with a difference that is only accidental. Incidentally, how much this little strangeness in illustration shows how necessary it is for America to have poets of her own, if to the simple people of her country poetry is ever to have any meaning! It is difficult to imagine a greater bar to the popularity of poetry than the fact that you are familiar with hickory, pumpkins, and corn, while the poet persists in talking about hazel, vegetable marrows, and oats, if the poet will listen to the song of the nightingale when you know of nothing but the "Rachel Jane."

In Mr. Robert Frost's *Mountain Interval* we get poems which taste, queerly under an English tongue—it is something undefinable, in "A Time to Talk," for instance:—

"When a friend calls to me from the
    road
And slows his horse to a meaning
    walk,
I don't stand still and look around
On all the hills I haven't hoed,
And shout from where I am, What is
    it?
No, not as there is a time to talk.
I thrust my hoe in the mellow
    ground,
Blade-end up and five feet tall,
And plod: I go up to the stone wall
For a friendly visit.

In this same book there are one or two narrative poems which are rather Browning-like. . . .

Notes

NEW HAMPSHIRE

A POEM WITH NOTES
AND GRACE NOTES BY
ROBERT FROST
WITH WOODCUTS
BY J. J. LANKES

PUBLISHED BY
HENRY HOLT
& COMPANY : NEW
YORK : MCMXXIII

New Hampshire, A Poem with Notes and Grace Notes

John Farrar.
"The Poet of New England's Hill-men."
Literary Digest International Book Review, 1 (November 1923), 25-26.

When most of us visualize Robert Frost, the poet, we visualize the stern granite hills of New England, we call to mind morbid bits of portraiture like "The Death of a Hired Man," we think of him as a grave and reverend gentleman solemnly driving a plow down some lonely hillside of New Hampshire or Vermont. Frost and his work are quite otherwise. Quaint, genial, humorous, wisely tolerant, he is not only a writer of grim dramatic portraits but of lyrics whose precision and beauty are overpowering, and of bits of Yankee whimsicality that are irresistible because they are both funny and true. As a man he is gentle, humorful and kindly. It is difficult for me to write sanely of Robert Frost; for, in my opinion, he is one of the few great poets America has ever produced.

Mr. Frost, as he appears now, is a sturdy gentleman, with iron-gray hair, cold, clear blue eyes, and features that are clean-cut and rugged. That he was born in San Francisco seems to have made little difference in the fact that he is obviously and thoroughly a New Englander. I have been guilty of the statement that Robert Frost is, first and foremost, the farmer. It is true that he has practically always insisted on having somewhere near him a plot of ground which he can work with his own hands. Even in England, where he lived for some time, where his first volume of verse was published, as a matter of fact, he found his land and cultivated it. The reason for this is that Frost is a man seeking some permanence in a world of change. The soil is a symbol of calmness and fertility. There is the progress of seed to fruit; but it is a change which comes with the repeating rhythm of the spheres. For Robert Frost, as one comes to know him better and better, is a philosopher and poet. Farming is very much an avocation. As I remember him on the hill-farm in South Shaftsbury, he was the same: gentle, ruminative, walking to the village, working quietly in the field, but liking best to sit at the edge of a meadow, looking down over a purpling stretch of land, talking of life and of work, speculating on the whimsies and the fates of mankind.

Last year and the year before, Frost was a visiting professor at Ann Arbor. Now he has returned to Amherst, where he will teach "philosophy" and "English reading." Amherst is near enough to Vermont so that Mr. and Mrs. Frost can visit the farm often, where young Carol Frost insists on living and working the land. Two of Mr. Frost's daughters are learning the trade of bookselling. One of them, Leslie, has shown marked ability in writing; she uses a pseudonym in her desire to be quite independent of her father's fame.

The poetry of Robert Frost is great to me because it interprets the qualities of mankind that are universal. His people are the hill-people of Vermont and New Hampshire; but they are the hill-people of the world also. They are the shepherds of Vergil. They are the peasants of Wordsworth. They are human beings shorn of artificiality. They are true to type—and their type is time-destroying. After reading the poetry of Robert Frost for years, I have come to the conclusion that he is essentially a lyric poet, a nature poet. His philosophical and dramatic poems are, perhaps, more strikingly original than his shorter pieces; but there is a characteristic beauty of form and phrase, with, in his later work, an added ease and grace, that mark him as a superb singer of delicate and deep-ringing songs. You have only to compare any one of the lyrics in his first volume, "A Boy's Will," with any one of those in "New Hampshire" and you will realize the heights to which he has risen in the perfection of his art. There is no repeating of an old melody. It is a new strain sung with added beauty. . . .

Only the other day here in New York he said, "Yes, I suppose I am a Puritan!" Then he went on to define, slowly, and as if he were thinking aloud, what a Puritan was to him. To Frost there is the need of *character* in the world. There must be standards on which to build life. The *family* means much to Frost. He is impatient of modern loosenesses. "A man says to me: '—but everything is change— change is progress—do you stand in the way of change?' " said Frost. "And my reply to him is: 'There are those who prefer the things which change more slowly to those which change swiftly.' This is *form* in art and life— this is what the Greeks had—what all great cultural movements have had!" And a regard for the precisions of life is, after all, beauty, isn't it?—and beauty is, in the final instance, character. This is Puritanism, if you will. This is, to me, the American tradition which we must preserve. Here, firmly rooted, stand Robert Frost and his work.

"I wonder if it helps a young writer to advise him, to work with him on his efforts," Mr. Frost was musing. He has spent much time, as I well know, aiding and advising the ambitious young poets who come to him with their manuscripts. Probably not, was the conclusion.

"I remember one man who really molded all my future by his advice," Frost told me. "I had sent him some of my verses. He returned them to me with his comment, which was that they were written too much in the way people talk. I considered this criticism and decided to try to make my verses even nearer to the qualities of human speech."

This characteristic in Frost's poetry is annoying to some people. The clipt phrase, the occasionally jerky rhythm, the sometimes rather ponderous humor; but it is a part of the whole. It is probably largely on this very quality that the truth and wisdom of the whole depend.

The book, "New Hampshire," is, at root, a whimsical book. Its form is whimsical. (Incidentally its woodcut illustrations are dignified and beautiful.) The book is divided into three parts: Frost calls it a long poem, with notes and grace-notes. The notes, to which we are referred by footnotes in the initial poem, are dramatic portions of New England life. The grace-notes are lyrics. The long poem "New Hampshire" has not appeared elsewhere. Mr. Frost credits its inception to *The Nation*. They had asked him to write one of their series on the various States of the Union. He had grown weary of reading criticisms of States—so one night he decided that he'd like to write a poem in praise of New Hampshire. The idea grew on him. Altho he usually works slowly, this time it was with an almost furious rapidity that the poem progressed. He sat down in the farmhouse at South Shaftsbury, one evening at ten o'clock, and wrote through until ten o'clock the next morning. Later, he added the last line—

At present I am living in Vermont.

This long poem is Robert Frost at his mellowest. It is filled with biting observation, genial fun-poking, and wise tolerance. It has passages of great beauty.

"I paid off a few grudges in that poem!" Frost told me. But if that is his way of paying grudges, it is surely harmless enough. What the poem really is, I think, is evident enough. It is a statement of the philosophy of

Robert Frost, which has not changed one whit since the day he wrote "The Black Cottage," but which has deepened and mellowed. A sensibilitist, he calls himself.

I'm what is called a sensibilitist,
Or otherwise an environmentalist.
I refuse to adapt myself a mite
To any change from hot to cold, from
  wet
To dry, from poor to rich, or back
  again.
I make a virtue of my suffering
From nearly everything that goes on
  round me.
In other words, I know wherever I
  am,
Being the creature of literature I
  am,
I shall not lack for pain to keep me
  awake.

If you wish to read the best poised and wisest diatribe against current literary smartness, read the last two pages of this poem. Frost has called "The Older Generation" (as our literary journalists name them) and "The Younger Generation" (again as our literary journalists name them) by their right names.

Choose you wish you will be—a
  prude, or puke,
Mewling and puking in the public
  arms!

Prude or puke! Not a pretty phrase, perhaps; but how expressive!

Well, if I have to choose one or the
  other,
I choose to be a plain New
  Hampshire farmer
With an income in cash of say a
  thousand

(From say a publisher in New York City).

Of the dramatic lyrics which follow, there is no one, perhaps, quite as striking as "The Death of a Hired Man" or "Home Burial"; but what a new beauty is here—a beauty that comes from long converse with the hills. When Frost first came back to New England, he saw the passion, the stamina, the degeneracy of the dying hill-people; now he sees their wistfulness and their vision, the almost prophetic quality. There is a great and breath-taking irony in "A Star in a Stone-Boat," and almost Celtic fantasy in "Paul's Wife," pathos and tragedy in "The Star-Splitters," a perfect portrait of Yankee reserve in "Maple," terror and drama in "Two Witches," and the most delicate mixture of whimsy and sadness in "A Fountain, a Bottle, A Donkey's Ears and Some Books." Frost still loves the awkward phrase, the idiom that drags the reader suddenly to attention; but he has gained a new grace, both of line and of soul.

Turn to these lyrics and you find half a dozen poems at least that you'll remember forever. "Stopping by Woods on a Snowy Evening" is as simple as nature herself—as inevitable—as beautiful. "To Earthward" has a note of real passion that betokens a new Frost. "Looking for a Sunset Bird in Winter," "A Boundless Moment." They are all perfect in their way. This volume marks so great an advance over his previous work that it should be hailed with any amount of hand-shaking and cheers.

Perhaps this is the perfection of Frost's singing. Perhaps this is the fruit of his ripest powers. It is a book of which America may well be proud, which is quite above cavil and prejudice. . . .

Robert Littell. "Stone Walls and Precious Stones." *The New Republic,* 37 (December 5, 1923), Part 2, pp. 25-26.

Mr. Frost divides this book of verse about his state (he lives in Vermont, and was born in California), into the easy-going, gossipy soliloquy which gives the book its name, and "Notes," and "Grace Notes." These parts are, in their manner and their mood, fairly distinct from each other, and they show Robert Frost with more colors on his palette than we had suspected, an artist with all sorts of distances from his subject, and with many different ways of approaching it.

The title poem is hardly a poem at all—though one soon forgets this, for it is not quite like anything else that was ever written, even by Mr. Frost. More than anything perhaps it resembles a journey across country in the company of a wise, shrewd, humorous person with an uncommon gift of common speech, a journey punctuated with philosophy, anecdotes, reminiscence, scandal, sudden gusts of salty, contented sadness, sudden glimpses of homely, local loveliness, sudden views, through narrow vistas, to the whole wide world. And at the end of the journey—or rather when the horse stops, for there is a lot more to see, we have been across a whole state, and overheard a race of men, and been amused, and informed, and disillusioned, and enchanted. The voice which talks to us does so in an easy, unhurried monotone, never dull, never lifted, never strained; now it ı speaking prose, now doggerel, now verse, now poetry. This Morgan Pegasus sometimes slows his trot to a walk, but he never balks, nor shies, nor takes the bit in his teeth.

The curse of bad poetry as of some that is good is its author's destructive consciousness that what he is writing is "poetry." Those cut flowers flourishing in captive water are not for Mr. Frost, who is careful to leave his growing from the earth. Weeds, grass, daisies, lilies—at any rate they are all alive. How he keeps his grass from turning to hay is his own secret. If any one else wrote about fire insurance, it would be hay, and dry at that. But listen to Mr. Frost:

I knew a man who failing as a
    farmer
Burned down his farmhouse for the
    fire insurance,
And spent the proceeds on a
    telescope
To satisfy a life-long curiosity
About our place among the
    infinities.

Maybe this is not poetry. But does that matter? Or does it matter very much that so many of Mr. Frost's lines sound as if they had been overheard in a telephone booth—

And she has one I don't know what
    to call him
Who comes from Philadelphia every
    year. . . .

It doesn't matter a bit if you are on the other end of the line listening to the whole conversation.

Such lines are only the low spots and gaps in a long stone wall. And "New Hampshire" is just like an old,

wandering stone wall. Made of human hands, it rests in the ground, or is partly buried there; it is never the same height in any two places. . . . So bends and wanders Mr. Frost's pithy, moving, garrulous, and invulnerable poem.

The Notes to "New Hampshire" are shorter pieces, mostly about people, around whom they revolve slowly, toward whose tell-tale secrets they move with a sometimes annoying deliberateness. Yet when the circuitous expedition—full of asides, pauses, details which in any one else would be resented as padding—is completed, there stands clear a singularly real individual, belonging, not to his creator, but to himself. Even the grindstone and the axe-helve are as much characters as the people, and equally with them yield to Mr. Frost their likeness but not their secrets.

If an ordinary conversation between ordinary people were written down, it would sound as if padding had been written into the stuff of life. Yet to those who spoke them, those matter of fact sentences meant something. Whatever Mr. Frost says, he means. Even his most prosaic lines are intended so to be. To ask him to cut them out, or squeeze a little more poetry into them, or build a hotter fire under the whole poem, would be asking him to become another person. His matter of factness in saying just what he means is a part of his virtue of never trying to say more than he means. If he doesn't use as much precious stone as we would like him to, if he uses too many plain ordinary boulders to fill in the chinks, it is because he knows that's the proper way to build his kind of a wall, because he knows that, for the kind of thing he's writing, there aren't enough real jewels to go all the way around. He never stoops to paste.

This restraint, at its worst, verges upon caution; at its best, it produces clear and lovely poetry. Mr. Frost is a perfect example of the difference between reticence and reserve. He never holds back true feeling for fear of giving rein to false. He will tell you how fast his heart is beating, but he will not wear it upon his sleeve. People with less sense of humor would manage to squeeze more poetry out of New Hampshire, and overpaint the portrait of a state for which Mr. Frost has so just an eye:

> She has a touch of gold, New
>   Hampshire gold—
> You may have heard of it. I had a
>   farm
> Offered me not long since up Berlin
>   way
> With a mine on it that was worked
>   for gold;
> But no gold in commercial
>   quantities.
> Just enough gold to make the
>   engagement rings
> And marriage rings of those who
>   owned the farm.

The poetry in these lines is in perfect proportion to the amount of gold in New Hampshire.

All this applies to the Robert Frost of the title poem and the Notes. The Frost of the Grace Notes is a very different matter. Instead of the leisurely conversational pentameter straying over acres of time and country we have a number of delicate, economical, well-rounded poems, in the good old sense, poems with just and inevitable rhyme, with fragile cadences, with quick turns, with swift changes of mood. The stone wall architect has,

in most of these poems, disappeared to give place to a sure and skilful jeweller. It is not so much that in these poems Mr. Frost has turned to another method. He has moved, emotionally, much closer to his subject. He is feeling things in a different way, which requires and inspires a different expression. The author of New Hampshire and the author of Stopping by Woods on a Snowy Evening are the same man, but in the latter case he is expressing emotion and not emotion plus amusement, interest, curiosity all at the same time.

Mark Van Doren. "Robert Frost." *The Nation,* 117 (December 19, 1923), 715-16.

During the seven years since "Mountain Interval" Mr. Frost has not been silent. From time to time poems have appeared in magazines or anthologies, and a good many of them, at least among those readers who like Mr. Frost better than any other poet, have become legends. Now at last these come together and fall naturally into the places which they were born to take in the unique unity of their author's work. And as if to emphasize that unity, Mr. Frost as editor has bound them by footnote and cross-reference to a long poem, New Hampshire, which endeavors to express his attitude in general toward the world.

New Hampshire is full of philosophy and fun. If it can be summarized at all, it is a statement of Mr. Frost's partiality to wildness. He likes

New Hampshire because it is no good to anybody but itself. It is solitary and queer; it has no standard product for the trade.

"Just specimens is all New
    Hampshire has,
One each of everything as in a
    show-case,
Which naturally she doesn't care to
    sell."

All of its people are different, and its many resources are too slight to be exploited.

"One of my children ranging after
    rocks
Lately brought home from Adover or
    Canaan
A specimen of beryl with a trace
Of radium. I know with radium
The trace would have to be the
    merest trace
To be below the threshold of
    commercial,
But trust New Hampshire not to
    have enough
Of radium or anything to sell."

It is not much on education, although—worse luck—there is Dartmouth. Its inhabitants have mastered the fine art of wise living by themselves.

The shorter poems round out a volume which is quite as good as any of Mr. Frost's other three, and which stands up very well with "Selected Poems" (1913-1920). Incidentally, these notes and grace notes make it possible to see wherein the indirectness of their poet's method is effective and wherein it fails. At its worst it is a mannerism, a tour de force of syntax; it puzzles with mere obscurity. At its best it is poetry of the subtlest

sort, because it carries the conviction that there was no other way to communicate the reticence inherent both in the subject and in the poet. Out of A Star in a Stone-Boat, for instance, an idea gradually emerges which Mr. Frost could not and should not have expressed directly. He has paced all the way around the idea, hinting of this or that aspect; the idea itself is left for the reader to get, and if he is the right kind of reader he will get it and rejoice. In a larger sense also the indirectness of Mr. Frost justifies itself. His love of the country is so profound that he will not say in so many words that he loves it. Indeed, one has the illusion that Mr. Frost would rather not talk at all. Now and then he has confessed to being moved by birches, or an occasional lonely house; but countless other things must wait their day, and most of them will wait in vain. To create such an illusion is to be one poet in ten thousand.

The Witch of Coös. was already famous as a ghost story. The Runaway is unsurpassed of its kind. It remains to point out the excellence as narrative of such a poem as The Axe-Helve, the beginning of which slips us so easily and silently—almost alone by means of rhythm—into the situation.

"I've known ere now an interfering
    branch
Of alder catch my lifted axe behind
    me.
But that was in the woods, to hold
    my hand
From striking at another alder's
    roots,
And that was, as I say, an alder
    branch.
This was a man, Baptiste, who stole
    one day

Behind me on the snow in my own
   yard
Where I was working at the
   chopping-block,
And cutting nothing not cut down
   already.
He caught my axe expertly on the
   rise,
When all my strength put forth was
   in his favor,
Held it a moment where it was, to
   calm me,
Then took it from me—and I let him
   take it."

Louis Untermeyer.
"Robert Frost's 'New Hampshire.' "
Bookman (New York), 58 (January 1924), 578-80.

It is somewhat more than seven years since Frost, following "North of Boston" with an equally characteristic though less integrated volume, published "Mountain Interval". The latter work never succeeded to the popularity of its famous forerunner, and for no other reason but its very lack of unity. "North of Boston" presented a pattern—to many a dark and terrible pattern—in its interknit New England monologues; "Mountain Interval" scattered its effects, introduced new inflections, puzzled the admirers of Frost's "grey monotones" by an infusion of bright colors. Yet some of this poet's finest moments are in the lesser known book. Nothing from the more popular collection will last longer than the dramatically suspended "Snow", the idyllic "Birches",

or the intensity of the "Hill Wife" lyrics; even "The Death of the Hired Man" scarcely surpasses the charged pathos of "An Old Man's Winter Night".

And now, after seven years, we have "New Hampshire" which, structurally, is a cross between both its predecessors. With an almost equal division of narratives and lyrics, it seems to recall "Mountain Interval", but the unity of "North of Boston" is achieved by a peculiar and simple device. "New Hampshire" pretends to be nothing but a long poem with notes and grace notes, and the title poem (some fourteen pages long) purports merely to celebrate Frost's favorite state. Very gravely, the rambling tribute to the state that "hasn't much of anything to sell" is starred and dotted with scientific numerals in the manner of the most profound treatise, the references being to poems that look at first as if they were only inserted to reenforce the text. In reality, these explanatory "notes" are some of the richest poems of our time, poems steeped in that extraordinary blend of intellect and emotion which is Frost's particular magic. Thus the tiny numeral after the line:

She has one witch—old style[1]

refers us to [1]"The Witch of Coös", one of the most singularly related ghost stories in poetry. Thus, another strange narrative is introduced in this way:

I met a Californian who would
Talk California—a state so blessed,
He said, in climate none had ever
   died there
A natural death, and Vigilance
   Committees

Had had to organize to stock the
graveyards[2]
And vindicate the state's humanity.
"Just the way Stefansson runs on," I
· murmured,
"About the British Arctic. That's
what comes
Of being in the market with a
climate."
2 Cf. page 51, "Place for a Third."

But is it a different poet that
breaks silence after seven years with
so unusual an arrangement? Will the
admirers of the earlier Frost fail to
find him in this strange composition?
Frost himself might answer with the
words of the first poem in his first
book:

They would not find me changed
from him they knew—
Only more sure of all I thought was
true.

Nothing, really, has changed. The
idiom is clearer, the convictions have
deepened—the essential things, the
point of view, the tone of voice, remain the same. The following imaginative lyric is typical of the later
Frost. It would be easy to point to it
as a proof of Frost's maturer warmth
and show how with the increase of
years his style has grown more
genial—were it not for the fact that
this poem was written at the age of
twenty and published in "The Youth's
Companion" in 1896. As readers of
"New Hampshire" will look for it in
vain, I take the liberty of quoting it
in full:

THE FLOWER-BOAT

The fisherman's swapping a yarn for
a yarn

Under the hand of the village
barber;
And here in the angle of house and
barn
His deep-sea dory has found a
harbor.

At anchor she rides the sunny sod
As full to the gunnel of flowers
growing
As ever she turned her home with
cod
From George's Bank when winds
were blowing.

And I judge from that Elysian
freight
That all they ask is rougher
weather,
And dory and master will sail by
fate
To seek for the Happy Isles together.

And here, in "New Hampshire"—in
exactly the same half playful, half
pathetic accents, in precisely the same
curious pitch—is an exquisite and
similar fantasy:

A BOUNDLESS MOMENT

He halted in the wind, and—what
was that
Far in the maples, pale, but not a
ghost?
He stood there bringing March
against his thought,
And yet too ready to believe the
most.

"Oh, that's the Paradise-in-bloom," I
said;
And truly it was fair enough for
flowers
Had we but in us to assume in
March
Such white luxuriance of May for
ours.

We stood a moment so in a strange
  world,
Myself as one his own pretense
  deceives;
And then I said the truth (and we
  moved on):
A young beech clinging to its last
  year's leaves.

It is this colloquially colored ex-
travagance, this deceptive conversational tone, which is so full of
spiritual implications. It is the picture
first ("The fact is the sweetest dream
that labor knows") but it never remains a purely pictorial representa-
tion. Beneath the light touch of such
a poem, one is conscious of suggested
depths, of a quiet but compelling affirmation, of a faith great enough to
dare to believe too much. "Two Look
at Two" repeats this confidence with a
more personal emotion—again in the
framework of a picture—drenched in
the trembling colors and quivering
tenderness of twilight.

What change there is, is one of emphasis. It seems incredible that most
of the appraisers of Frost's previous
work spoke chiefly of its grimness,
whereas its whimsicality, though less
obvious, was equally pronounced. In
"Mountain Interval", the occasional
quizzical raillery of "North of Boston"
was more apparent, the momentary
descent of the eyelash was perceptibly
prolonged; in "New Hampshire" it declares itself on every page. The very
form of the new book is an extended
piece of badinage; the long title poem
is a broad smile from beginning to
end; the most serious of the narratives sparkle with a slily intimate
banter. This increase in humor, so
rich in its varying timbres, will irritate the literal minded almost as
much as it will delight those to whom

fact and fantasy are not inimical opposites but continually shifting facets
of the same many sided thing. The orthodox Cambridgian (Mass.), for example, will boil over at such an outrageous heresy as:

Her husband was worth millions.
I think he owned some shares in
  Harvard College.

The critics who concluded that
Frost was too overburdened with his
lonely farms and isolated cottages,
who maintained that he could never
be "whimsical or quaint", will
scarcely know what to make of this
volume in which practically every
poem proceeds from a magnified
whimsicality. There will be those
who, granting the charm of this elfin
imagination, may question its use in
such serious themes. Yet what is
poetry but metaphor—what is it but
the establishing of a congruity between apparently unrelated things?
What then is metaphor but the child
of whimsy?

So much has been made of Frost's
factual realism that at the risk of
being redundant I insist that, beneath
the surface naturalism, his work is
distinguished—even impelled—by a
rare and fantastic mind. This side of
Frost's genius has been so under-
emphasized that I may be allowed to
overstress it by directing attention to
the fundamental quaintness of conception of "Paul's Wife", the extraordinarily adroit "An Empty Threat",
"A Star in a Stone-Boat", that lovely
chain of tercets, and "Wild Grapes",
which is a feminine complement to
"Birches".

But it is in the lyrics that Frost's
warmth is most apparent. There are
few circumlocutory asides, few *sotto*

voce murmurs, in these direct communications—only a firm intensity. A great love of the New England countryside, of earth itself, surges from such poems as "Stopping By Woods on a Snowy Evening", "Gathering Leaves", "In a Disused Graveyard", and the brightly ironic "The Need of Being Versed in Country Things". A less physical and almost unearthly passion speaks in the beautiful though troubled lines of "To Earthward", the mystical sonority of "I Will Sing You One-O", and the condensed wisdom of "Fire and Ice". I consider the last, one of the greatest epigrammatic poems in the English language; every line—and there are only nine altogether—seems to have been carved in crystal. Similarly concentrated, though in far lighter accents, is this perfectly balanced composition. It seems so spontaneous and integrated a song that it is interesting to note that the first six lines were composed a score of years ago, Frost having waited twenty years for the last two.

Nature's first green is gold,
Her hardest hue to hold.
Her early leaf's a flower;
But only so an hour.
Then leaf subsides to leaf.
So Eden sank to grief,
So dawn goes down to day.
Nothing gold can stay.

In the very simplicity of these lines we have the unaffected originality of Frost. With absolute freedom from contemporary fashions, technical trickery, or the latest erudite slang, Frost has created a poetry which is at one time full of heat and humor, a poetry that belongs not only to the America of our own day but to the richest records of English verse.

Dorothy Dudley. "The Acid Test." *Poetry,* 23 (March 1924), 328-35.

Once I asked a New York critic of the drama why it was that to the Ziegfeld *Follies*—a prodigious, fascinating, yet not impeccable production—he never gave the same accurate eye that gladly he turned on the so-called high-brow show. His reply was short, "What sells is."

The initial poem, *New Hampshire,* of this new volume (at least in November it was new, now I suppose commercially seasoned) rather intimates that what doesn't sell has a better chance of being. Here Mr. Frost departs from the implicative method of other poems of his, which has sometimes deceived the obtuse into thinking of him as a "New England poet," and plays on themes more common to the market. He "relates himself," as the phrase goes and as he has not had the name of doing, to some of the precious drifts of the day. Though used conversely, this same sales-standard figures at the start:

I met a traveller from Arkansas
Who boasted of his state as beautiful
For diamonds and apples. "Diamonds
  and apples in commercial
  quantities?"
I asked him, on my guard. "Oh yes,"
  he answered,
Off his. The time was evening in the
  Pullman.

"I see the porter's made your bed," I
    told him.

A Californian is in the market with
his climate, and a poet from another
state with a protest against the Vol-
stead Act—"an idea to sell":

It never could have happened in
    New Hampshire.
. . . .
Just specimens is all New
    Hampshire has,
One each of everything as in a
    show-case,
Which naturally she doesn't care to
    sell.
. . . .
She has a touch of gold. New
    Hampshire gold— . .
But not gold in commercial
    quantities.
Just enough gold to make the
    engagement rings
And marriage rings. . . .
. . . .
A specimen of beryl with a trace
Of radium. . . . .
But trust New Hampshire not to
    have enough
Of radium or anything to sell.

You wonder a little which way the
laugh really is—whether at New
Hampshire for having nothing to sell,
or at the others for having nothing
except things to sell. To this the answers are elusive, Frost being a
blend—satirist and poet. . . .
New Hampshire is a kind of non-
chalant overcoat; in the pockets are
poems of a more lonely, absolute
character—*Notes* and *Grace Notes*
which complete the volume. Whether
story or song, or tracery of truth,
paradox, or vanishing moment otherwise lost and the world less made for

us, each of these is a prism of words
existing for and by itself, by reason of
its own intimate logic of incident,
rhyme, color and sound. Art, like science, goes toward intimacy, toward
knowledge, violent and delicate. The
fashion of the day, save where
machinery is in question, goes more
and more away from it toward publi-
city, violent and less delicate. For all
the talk of modernists and editors,
poems inexorable as some of these
seem to be waiting for a more intensely intimate moment in history;
where the fitting of word to word, of
tone to tone, of shape to shape is of
more import than the jolt, the scream,
the rush order. Or else perhaps that
moment is always at hand and always
hidden till afterwards.

One might make a choice of
favorites—*The Census-taker,* ending
on this note of fire:

The melancholy of having to count
    souls
Where they grow fewer and fewer
    every year
Is extreme where they shrink to
    none at all.
It must be I want life to go on living.

Paul's Wife, fable of a woman made
out of a white pine-log in a lumber
camp, which for glint of wildness
matches Greek or Venetian; *Gathering Leaves, Goodbye and Keep Cold, I
Will Sing You One—O, Fire and Ice,
The Aim Was Song.* Or one might
choose *Two Witches, The Grindstone,
Misgiving, Stopping by Woods on a
Snowy Evening, Two Look at Two, A
Star in a Stone-boat.* Choice is difficult among poems which, holding
within them tears, smiles and mysteries, are so many of them facts of
poetry, hard with that quality. Frost

knows how—which, with all the booming of poetry now in the air, you can say of only a few others.

Some may ask, "But what is New Hampshire to us?" forgetting that, when the artist knows how, life at any point is boundless; protoplasm is protoplasm, dirt is dirt, space is space where the stars have room. Some will hint they prefer their New England psycho-analyzed—a D. H. Lawrence turned loose there to uncover what lies beneath. Frost is a poet of voices, postures, appearances. Perhaps that is what the artist should be; the facts then are all of them implicit; the spokes fit and reach the centre. The figure of the witch of Coös, looking in her button-box for the knuckle-bone of a lover she helped murder years before, brings every desperate contrast of youth.

Perhaps Frost is purposely spare with fashionable candors, thinking of them as forced products, not native enough yet. I have heard of Lenin saying he did not make the revolution; the revolution made him. Negro, Jew, and foreigner may in the end change us beyond recognition. But as yet we are about as we were, not really at ease with the more crucial facts of life. We think of them as secrets; scarcely do they show in our eyes—maybe not even in drink. They lurk deep in Frost's poems, which take you along the skilled path of the familiar to the very edge of the unknown—which in turn gives tone.

If in Frost there is any grain of hypocrisy, it is that possibly loneliness and hardship are vanities with him. Yet the prism, the sphere, he makes of such a mood, belies by music its meaning. It is as if he said, "These are my perverse words, but turn the piece around; while revolving you will see it shine." As here you do:

It went many years,
But at last came a knock,
And I thought of the door
With no lock to lock.

I blew out the light,
I tip-toed the floor,
And raised both hands
In prayer to the door.

But the knock came again.
My window was wide;
I climbed on the sill
And descended outside.

Back over the sill
I bade a "Come in"
To whatever the knock
At the door may have been.

So at a knock
I emptied my cage
To hide in the world
And alter with age.

Checklist of Additional Reviews

David Morton. "Poet of the New Hampshire Hills." *Outlook,* 135 (December 19, 1923), 688-89.

"New Hampshire—Robert Frost's New Volume." *Michigan Alumnus,* 30 (January 17, 1924), 429.

WEST-RUNNING BROOK

BY

ROBERT FROST

NEW YORK

HENRY HOLT AND COMPANY

West-Running Brook

Babette Deutsch.
"Poets and Poetasters."
The Bookman, 68 [New York]
(December 1928),
471-72.

The one other poet [in addition to Yeats] who has achieved a similar unity of vision—though how different a one!—is Robert Frost. His latest volume, *West-Running Brook,* is slight, physically speaking, and contains several pieces that are unworthy of inclusion. Such, for example, are several quatrains, and the piece called "Rose Family", which might have been written by Austin Dobson in his sleep. These flaws notwithstanding, the book as a whole has the seriousness and acuteness which marks all of Frost's work, and while it shows no impressive advance upon his previous achievement, that is high enough to make any new collection of his important. There are no narrative pieces. The lyrics are compact of pity and sly humor and hardihood, all expressed in an easy conversational tone, and all characterized by that familiarity with, and devotion to, the—shall we say, domesticated?—natural scene, to which Frost has accustomed us. It is seldom that a line strikes one as particularly fine, a phrase as peculiarly fitting, a whole poem as singularly lyrical, yet almost every piece is wrought of the true gold of poetry. As for the animating spirit of the volume, one finds it clearest, perhaps, in the title-poem, a dialogue in which one fancies the poet to have the final word, when in these terms he speaks of existence:

It flows beside us in this water
    brook,
But it flows over us. It flows between
    us
To separate us for a panic moment.
It flows between us, over us, and
    with us.
And it is time, strength, tone, light,
    life and love—
And even substance lapsing
    unsubstantial;
The universal cataract of death
That spends to nothingness—and
    unresisted,
Save by some strange resistance in
    itself,
Not just a swerving, but a throwing
    back,
As if regret were in it and were
    sacred.
It has this throwing backward on
    itself
So that the fall of most of it is
    always
Raising a little, sending up a
    little. . . .
It is this backward motion toward
    the source,

Against the stream, that most we
    see ourselves in,
The tribute of the current to the
    source.
It is from this in nature we are from.
It is most us.

Among the poems that wear charm like a flower or burn with a special vitality are "Birthplace", "The Bear", "Sand Dunes", "On Looking Up By Chance At The Constellations", "Riders", "Bereft", "Canis Major" and "Once By The Pacific".

Frederick E. Pierce. "Three Poets Against Philistis." *Yale Review,* 18 (December 1928), 365-66.

Robert Frost has loomed large in our poetical world now for some years, and we have grown to expect a good deal of him. His present book arouses mingled admiration and disappointment. Our admiration is for the sincerity and delicate insight with which the theme is handled. Our disappointment is because of the smallness, limitation, almost barrenness, of the theme itself. It may be true that a perfectly carved cameo is a greater work of art than a clumsily constructed pyramid; but it is equally true that the greatest poems lead us out into the vast complexity of life and do not keep us indefinitely in a little walled-in nook, however beautiful. We think of Mephistopheles's proud boast to Goethe's Faust—"The

little world, and then the great, we'll see"; and we turn back to Mr. Frost, I repeat, with mingled disappointment and admiration. It is as if the mountain had travailed and brought forth an elf. That is no severe condemnation, in some ways it is very high praise; yet we are left with a half-satisfied craving. We are also left with the question on our lips whether America is not partly to blame for this, whether Goethe could have written "Faust" in our Main Street world, whether Mr. Frost, like King Albert of Belgium in the World War, is not clinging gallantly to the little fragment of his kingdom which the George F. Babbitts have still left poetical. And, with all its limitations, "West-Running Brook" is a charming piece of work. From the roar and bustle of Wall Street and the overelaborate intellectual life of our educational system, it calls us back to childhood's dreams among the green fields. From the vulgarity and hustle of our cut-throat competition, it brings us into the company of a poet whose true nature shows in his quiet rejection of the blatant and novel, in his quiet insistence on the unostentatious and noble, in his tactful reticence about himself, in the gentle and subdued character of his occasional irony. His poetry does not dazzle, but its spell lingers long.

Edward B. Hall. "Robert Frost as a Significant Poet." *Boston Evening Transcript,* December 15, 1928, Book Section, p. 5.

The poetry of Robert Frost is as indigenous to New England as her own White Mountains. Never once in the course of his lifelong career has this poet turned elsewhere for inspiration. Unlike ordinary mortals to whom distance lends enchantment, he has been able to perceive beauty in his own barnyard and poetic appeal in his immediate neighbors. Of these he has written, and his tremendous and ever-increasing popularity, both here and abroad, definitely confirms the wisdom of his choice. . . .

In "West-Running Brook," in addition to the characteristic charm, intensity, and vigor of expression that is Frost's, there is much that is altogether new. With no less of the thought that his readers have learned to expect from him, Mr. Frost, in this latest collection of poems, becomes more subjective, more personal and purely lyrical. Dramatic character studies and episodical domestic views of his New Hampshire farmer folk have largely given place to lyrics of a self-revelatory nature. He writes in a calm, reminiscent manner, isolating to mould into perfect form and memorable expression such experiences, moods and impressions as might present themselves to the imagination of a man musing at ease before the fireplace on a stormy winter's night. His manner of expression is consistently calm, and unprotesting. There is no satire, no resentment, no whining in his poetry. . . .

Louis Untermeyer. "Still Robert Frost." *Saturday Review of Literature,* 5 (December 22, 1928), 533, 536.

No contemporary poet has been more praised than Robert Frost, and no poet has ever been more praised for the wrong things. The early reviews of "West-Running Brook" have renewed the false emphasis. Most of the critics are surprised that the writer identified with the long monologues in "North of Boston" should turn to lyrics, forgetting that Frost's first volume (written in the 1890's and published twenty years later) was wholly and insistently lyrical. One reviewer, echoing the false platitude concerning New England bleakness, applauds Frost's almost colorless reticence, his "preference for black and white." Another makes the discovery that "where he was formerly content to limn a landscape . . . here the emphasis is primarily on the poet's emotion."

A more careful rereading of Frost's other works should instruct the critics. Were they less anxious to affix labels and establish categories, there would be less confusion—a confusion that leads one otherwise intelligent reviewer to declare that "the poet nearest akin to him (Frost) is A. E. Housman," although, continues the bewildered reviewer, "Housman will admit color at times." . . . Forget for the moment Frost's most famous "North of Boston" and its successor "Mountain Interval"; examine his earliest volume "A Boy's Will," published in 1913, and "New Hampshire," published in 1923. What disappears first is the complaint (if we have heard it made) of colorlessness. Never were volumes less black and white; never were shades of expression more delicate and at the same time more distinct. Equally obvious is the absence of inhibitions. Poems like "Two Look at Two," "To Earthward," "Fire and Ice," "Moving," "The Tuft of Flowers" are anything but reticent; they are profound, ever personal, revelations. Frost has never been "content to limn a landscape." He cannot suggest a character or a countryside without informing the subject with his own philosophy, a philosophy whose bantering accents cannot hide a depth of emotion. Beyond the fact ("the dearest dream that labor knows"), beyond the tone of voice, which is, at least technically, the poet's first concern, there is that intense and unifying radiance which is not only Frost's peculiar quality but his essential spirit.

SAND DUNES

Sea waves are green and wet,
But up from where they die,
Rise others vaster yet,
And those are brown and dry.

They are the sea made land
To come at the fisher town,
And bury in solid sand
The men she could not drown.

She may know cove and cape,
But she does not know mankind
If by any change of shape,
She hopes to cut off mind.

Men left her a ship to sink:
They can leave her a hut as well;
And be but more free to think
For the one more cast off shell.

Here, in his latest work, is a reflection and a restatement of his earliest. This is philosophy in terms of the lyric. But the first as well as the final appeal is neither to the brain nor to the ear; beneath the graceful image there speaks a greatness of soul.

It is this spiritual sustenance which has always strengthened Frost's passionate puritanism. And since, in this so-called mechanistic age, spiritual values are not gauged by popular appraisers, the estimators have dwelt on the tone, the technique, the subject matter, in short on everything but the source of his poetry. This is the more astonishing since Frost, legend to the contrary, reveals himself, actually gives himself away with every raillery, every wisp of metaphor, every conversational aside. Avoiding the analytical, this poetry is a constant search; a search for absolutes. Better still, it is a search for the Absolute—in man, in poetry, in God.

BEREFT

Where had I heard this wind before
Change like this to a deeper roar?
What would it take my standing
        there for,
Holding open a restive door,
Looking down hill to a frothy shore?
Summer was past and day was past.
Sombre clouds in the West were
        massed.
Out in the porch's sagging floor,
Leaves got up in a coil and hissed,
Blindly struck at my knee and
        missed.

Something sinister in the tone
Told me my secret must be known:
Word I was in the house alone
Somehow must have gotten abroad,
Word I was in my life alone,
Word I had no one left but God.

This may be considered a key-note poem. It is, in a sense, a sequel to the extremely early "Trial by Existence"; here, at the end of independence, is only the last courage, the loneliness, the nothingness—"and where there is nothing, there is God." But "West-Running Brook" is not so much a sequel as it is a composite of the early and later Frost. What seems a mellowing and maturing turns out to be the fruit of intuition rather than experience. Thus a student will learn that the recognizably "late" poem entitled "On Going Unnoticed" was written as early as 1901; the poem "Bereft" (already quoted) was composed in about 1893. As for "Once by the Pacific"—let it appear in full.

The shattered water made a misty din.
Great waves looked over others coming in,
And thought of doing something to the shore
That water never did to land before.
The clouds were low and hairy in the skies,
Like locks blown forward in the gleam of eyes.
You could not tell, and yet it looked as if
The shore was lucky in being backed by cliff,
The cliff in being backed by continent;
It looked as if a night of dark intent
Was coming, and not only a night, an age.

Someone had better be prepared for rage.
There would be more than ocean-water broken
Before God's last *Put out the Light* was spoken.

This memory of Frost's childhood on the beach at San Francisco is given in the table of contents "as of about 1880." Here, again, is the same combination of understatement and simplicity, of the trivial and the tremendous, of economic line and prodigal implication. Frost's power of lifting the colloquial to the pitch of poetry has always been apparent (it raises even so broad a bucolic as "Something inspires the only cow of late"); in the new volume he maintains his rôle of half-earnest synecdochist. Here, again, offering the part for the whole, he reestablishes the force of suggestion and reaffirms his conviction: "All that an artist needs is samples." Parsimony is achieved in almost every one of the new poems. It sharpens the fancy of "Fireflies in the Garden"; quickens the meditative accents of "A Passing Glimpse"; points the epigrammatic, "The Peaceful Shepherd"; intensifies the sombre color of "Acquainted with the Night"; repeats, with a wry twist, the poet's protest in "A Minor Bird":

I have wished a bird would fly away,
And not sing by my house all day,

Have clapped my hands at him from the door
When it seemed as if I could bear no more.

The fault must partly have been in me.

The bird was not to blame for his key.

And of course there must be something wrong
In wanting to silence any song.

A certain technical shift may be noticed here and there, a somewhat more rhythmic ease apparent in the slightest of his quatrains. The verse itself has more of the "sound" that Frost cherishes, a talk-flavored tone that has the common vitality of prose without ever ceasing to be poetry. Especially pungent in their concision are the introductory "Spring Pools," the firm epigram, "Hannibal," the exquisite "Tree at My Window," the equally delightful "The Birthplace," and "Riders" with its typical Frostian last line:

We have ideas yet that we haven't tried.

Here, in short, is the metaphysical lyric as no one but Robert Frost could write it. And so it is throughout "West-Running Brook." The ripe repose, the banked emotion, the nicely blended tenderness and humor are everywhere. Growth? Change? A new note? The answers may be found in two lines of one of Frost's first poems, a premonitory couplet written before 1900:

They would not find me changed from him they knew,
Only more sure of all I thought was true.

No reviewer has written, no critic will write, a better summary.

E. Merrill Root. "Encore for the Morning Stars!" *The Christian Century*, 46 (January 3, 1929), 19-20.

Some good fairy named the poet of "West Running Brook" with a wise pun: for he is the Jack Frost of Poetry, etching on the windows of the world his coldly clear pictures with a technique that is a phase of nature. He is an artist in the black-and-white of the cosmos: he has a narrowly world-accepting philosophy, a calmly but pungently life-affirming mood, a grey elfin mysticism. He is (to change the figure) a provincial Virgil of a more sprawling and obtuse empire than the grandeur that was Rome, writing georgics not on Italian marble, but on Yankee granite, and ending with the lyricism of his youth made subtler and lovelier, rather than with a national and cosmic epic of Arms and the Man. His memorable work is, after all, not his excellent dramatic stories of grey rustic characters, but his lovely lyrical eclogues mingled of nature and atmosphere, of a shrewd and half-daemonic philosophy, and, above all, of his own inimitable self—all written in the tang-and-accent of racy essential Yankee speech. He is the poet not of characters, but of his own character—and, beyond himself, of the Yankee blood. His limitation is that he is a *provincial* Virgil: in his long poem, "New Hampshire," he does not show Virgil's spiritual mastery of the surge of empire—he uses a "loveliness and dignity of diction . . . put to the service of . . . a small and anomalous national scheme"—he is sadly inadequate about Russian Revolutions or that fete of dinosaurs with St. Vitus' dance which is industrial America. Nor has he the fierce and flaming challenge of Nietzsche's psychological lightning; nor is he, like Shelley, a Wild West Wind, blowing the clouds of cosmic being. He knows much of New England's green and pleasant, or white and wintry, land; he cares little for Blake's Bow of Burning Gold.

But what he is, he is superbly—a New Hampshire birch, lovely in line and grace and rooted in granite close to "earth's fiery core," a birch on which grows sometimes the rich purple loveliness of wild-grapes. "West Running Brook," not so large as "New Hampshire," is more exquisitely perfect—lovely as spring afternoons when the snow melts, and the trees are lilac haze of Arcady, and the sun is a warm golden dazzle against the blue of old-porcelain skies. Here are poems where the poet has dipped his pen in magic—till we truly see "The colors run, all sorts of wonder follow." The title poem (so fortunate, as always, in its implications!) is a darkly superb piece of mysticism written with Nature's own pen—the wonder and the wild desire of life, like a white swan of foam, seen upon the darkwater of death that drags it down in spite of "That strange resistance in itself, As if regret were in it and were sacred," which is itself "Time, strength, tone, light, life, and love." It is a poem to be remembered as long as American is spoken.

B. C.
"Frost's Poetry Shows Lyricism."
Denver Post,
January 13, 1929,
Section 2, p. 8.

Robert Frost has come to be associated with the kind of dramatic poem that Robert Browning created—substituting perhaps a feeling for the earth in place of Browning's biting characterization. But in this new volume, that familiar mode has disappeared with the exception of the title poem, "West-Running Brook." All the rest is purely lyrical. Mr. Frost's peculiar quality of telling a situation in rhythmic and poetic colloquialisms is not absent, but it is very much diminished because of his restricted medium.

Life has always been depicted in his work as tragic, but beautiful in its kinship to the land. That picture has not necessarily been a personal reaction—very seldom so. Mr. Frost is now preoccupied with his own place in the universe and he injects an element of reiterated loneliness.

I have been one acquainted with the
    night,
I have walked out in rain—and back
    in rain.
I have outwalked the furthest city
    light.

This quotation strikes the keynote of the book. Yet, whatever the keynote, the quality of Mr. Frost's poetry is always such as to move the reader with its steady simplicity. This has not faded—nor those occasional traces of humor as in the last poem of the book, "The Bear." . . .

This mood, though, is not characteristic of the volume as a whole. It is more like a stray pink petal floating with many brown autumn leaves on the stream of Mr. Frost's somber realizations.

Someone has said that there is a quality of sadness in all beauty and paradoxically the reverse is true of Mr. Frost's poetry. Its beauty and melody remain undisturbed by the dark shadows of the author's thoughts.

Mark Van Doren. "North of Eden." *The Nation,* 128 (January 23, 1929), 110.

The best poems in Mr. Frost's new volume will repay a third or a fourth or a fifteenth reading. Certain pages of the book remain for me, after several attempts to find more in them than meets the eye, trivial; and certain others are merely good enough. But at least five poems here have all of their author's unique excellence, which is to say that they are not to be compared with the poems of any other living man, and to say that they give an absolute, almost undiscussable pleasure.

These few do not include, though they come near doing so, any of the several epigrams in which Mr. Frost may be seen taking a swing through universals. I suspect that he cannot afford extreme brevity, any more than he can afford great length; and universals (directly stated) are not for him. Neither do they include the one dialogue of the volume, which inci-

dentally is the title-poem. And certainly they do not include any of the half-dozen pieces which are but conceits, even if these conceits have the pure mark of Mr. Frost's mind upon them. But they do include the poems which represent Mr. Frost in the act of standing and looking at some very definite thing—a pool in the spring woods, a chimney smoking under the new moon, the water coming in off the Pacific, a bird going to bed, or a "winter garden in an alder swamp"—standing and looking at it and talking about it in such a way that it suddenly and weirdly becomes a world.

The thing is done so quietly, and sometimes in lines of such bald, even awkward clarity, that one cannot say how it is done. But it *is* done—in Once by the Pacific, for instance, where the coming of the waves against the shore takes on the ominous importance of all force whatsoever; in the Cocoon, where a poor house smoking silently in the evening haze becomes a creature spinning its anchor to the earth and moon; and in Acceptance, where birds settling after sunset into their dark nests quite sufficiently express the comfort there is in all darkness, and in the need no longer to think.

It is done even better in two poems which, fitly enough, have winter or late spring for their time and the unpeopled woods for their scene. For Mr. Frost is a northerly poet, and his paradise—he is concerned almost wholly with paradise—is a wintry one. Spring Pools shows him by no means comfortable in the certainty that these bits of forest water which

still reflect
The total sky almost without defect

will soon be gone,

And yet not out by any brook or
   river,
But up by roots to bring dark foliage
   on.

That means shade, and therefore
luxuriance, and therefore hiding and
confusion; Mr. Frost so much prefers
the total sky on an uncomplicated
day. And thus in A Winter Eden,
where a simple scene is so delicately
stroked in that it lives even more
truly than the birds and deer who
move across it, he contemplates perfection:

So near to paradise all pairing ends:
Here loveless birds now flock as
   winter friends,
Content with bud-inspecting. They
   presume
To say which buds are leaf and
   which are bloom.

Theodore Spencer. *"West-Running Brook."* New Republic, 58 (February 20, 1929), 24-25.

Mr. Frost holds an eminent and enviable position in American poetry. He
has the gift of stamping on nearly all
he writes a personality that is valuable not only because it is felt as individual, but because it gives voice to
many qualities we consider typically
American. He has used, apparently
naively, but actually with great care,
that homely and partly frustrated
eloquence which is usually associated
with New England, to produce a
number of poems either tragic or de-

lightful, according to the mood that
inspired them. Most of these poems—
one misses one or two personal
favorites—are included in the present
selection of his work [*Selected Poems*
included in this dual review].

It is because of his previous accomplishment that one turns to Mr.
Frost's new book with excitement, and
at the same time feels justified in sub-
jecting it to vigorous criticism. For it
is on the whole disappointing. Not
that it is without its successes;
"Spring Pools" is a fine poem, so is "A
Soldier," and lines such as the description of a tree, "thing next most
diffuse to cloud," are awakening in a
way that only Mr. Frost can manage.
But there is an impression of thinness
gained from this book which Mr.
Frost has not given before. One feels
that he has lost or abandoned a view
of life which was, in its implications,
tragic, and adopted instead an al-
legorizing method which is far less
important. If, for example, one compares "The Death of the Hired Man"
with "West-Running Brook"—the title
poem of the present volume—one misses in the latter any sense of a present reality; Mr. Frost, instead of describing human emotions, points out
the analogy between human life and
the idiosyncracies of a particular
stream; objects unconnected except in
the poet's mind. The point of view, in
other words, is fanciful rather than
imaginative.

It is this allegory-breeding in-
tellectualization (the quality that
makes Spenser only a minor master)
which, reflected in many of the poems
it contains, is chiefly responsible for
turning Mr. Frost's book into a disappointment. It also helps to make such
poems as "Lodged," "The Thatch,"
"Canis Major," seem unnecessarily

trivial. And one wonders, as a result, if Mr. Frost has not already absorbed all that New England can give him (this book is much less local than the others); if his wooing of allegory, which is one of the easiest modes of thought, is not symptomatic of something more than a personal choice. Perhaps it is another and more damning characteristic of the type of American mind which he has already so admirably expressed.

H[arriet] M[onroe].
"A Frugal Master."
Poetry, 33
(March 1929),
333-36.

Mr. Frost is an abstemious poet; he is content with frugal fare at the banquet of the muses. They serve him nuts and berries, salty savory green things, washed down with a homebrew of apple brandy or elderberry wine. And of these he partakes sparingly, bringing out, as the result of such stern nourishment, a thin little volume every five or six years.

West-running Brook, the latest of these, is the most frugal of all. Forty poems, mostly of sonnet length or less—a bare six hundred lines in all—are given thick paper and pictures and blank pages to beguile us into gratitude for a book from this well-beloved hand. And some of those brief entries are marked "very early," or "as of about 1893," as if the poet had looked over forgotten portfolios to fill out the tiny volume and excuse to his conscience what he has himself called his "laziness."

Well, these poems are Frost's own, all right, but none of them may be ranked among Frost's best. They have the tang, the flavor, the keen speech-rhythms, the tart human sympathy—all the curves and angles of style and mood which we have learned to associate with Robert Frost, and which so many other poets have imitated in vain. But there is nothing here to match the tragic beauty of *The Hired Man,* the fragile delicacy of *The Hill Wife,* the spicy humor of *The Code* or *Brown's Descent,* or even of a little thing like that spring-drunken *Cow in Apple Time.* The title-poem dialogue is a slight affair beside *Snow* or *Home Burial,* though an interesting addition to the poet's gallery of couples more or less comfortably, or uncomfortably, married.

Did I say none of Frost's best? Well, there may be one or two which could hold their own among those chosen for the *Selected Poems.* This sententious brief one, *Dust in the Eyes,* is delicious:

If, as they say, some dust thrown in
    my eyes
Will keep my talk from getting
    overwise,
I'm not the one for putting off the
    proof.
Let it be overwhelming, off a roof
And round a corner, blizzard snow
    for dust,
And blind me to a standstill if it
    must.

And this tribute to Ridgely Torrence's *Hesperides* gave me a keen thrill, not only as a poem delicate and beautiful but also as a swift and true characterization of his friend's exquisite book:

I often see flowers from a passing car
That are gone before I can tell what
    they are. . . .

Sarah N. Cleghorn.
"West-Running Brook."
World Tomorrow, 12
(March 1929),
135.

Robert Frost's attention has been gradually turning for years toward the life of the earth itself and, as one may say, toward the thoughts and emotions of earth. In *West-Running Brook* the life of man (of which the poet is never for an instant unconscious) has melted into the life of the earth as a whole, sometimes being itself a background—in the same way that the farmhouse is the background for the powerful personality of the tree, in the third woodcut by Lanke, who has illustrated the volume.

Penetrating into his life of earth, in the lovely poem "Spring Pools," Frost has extracted from his subtle depths of sympathy a line of extraordinary beauty. No one who has read or heard

These flowery waters and these
watery flowers

will ever consent to let his memory be impoverished of it. It will be remembered with Wordworth's "Breaking the silence of the seas," and Keats' "While barréd clouds bloom the soft dying day." It might have been part of Il Penseroso.

The title poem is Frost at his finest. Whatever we have most loved in *North of Boston, New Hampshire,* or *Mountain Interval,* we shall never

read them again without recollecting *West-Running Brook* in somewhat the rôle of an Interpreter. And that is to say, an interpreter of life.

"West-Running Brook."
The Dial, 86
(May 1929),
436.

In the most recent volume of poems Robert Frost has written in a manner that is quite different from that of the poems in North of Boston and Mountain Interval. These are not poems about people; they are, in the main, gnomic verses that read as if the poet had entered a world where words and movement do not matter so much, and where there is "no devotion Greater than being curve to ocean." A few of these poems appear to have been written at an early date, but even these have the gnomic quality. There are two poems in the collection which are probably the most poignant that Robert Frost had written, Acquainted with the Night, and The Thatch.

B. M. K.
Catholic World, 129
(June 1929),
377.

West-Running Brook is stamped with that New England asceticism which has so little of the mystical about it. It offers as frugal fare, a sparse kind of beauty, rain-washed and windswept,—swept but not garnished. The poems are not the offspring of emotion but of thought, the ruminative thought of a man who works while he thinks or who smokes a pipe while he trudges through the woods, pondering as he goes, to distinguish them from the results of Wordsworth's profounder musings.

Checklist of Additional Reviews

Leon Whipple. "Poets Americano." *Survey,* 41 (November 1, 1928), 169.

Babette Deutsch. "Inner Weather." *New York Herald Tribune Books,* November 18, 1928, p. 1.

Percy Hutchinson. "New Poems by Robert Frost in 'West-Running Brook.'" *New York Times Book Review,* November 18, 1928, p. 2.

John Crawford. "Frost's Poems Do Not Waste Away in Pathos." *New York Evening Post,* November 24, 1928, p. 9.

"Robert Frost's Poems and Outlook on Life." *Springfield Union-Republican,* December 30, 1928, p. 7E.

Herschel Brickell. "Four Books of Poetry." *North American Review,* 226 (December 1928), n.p.

"Robert Frost." *Booklist,* 25 (February 1929), 201.

Mary Katherine Reely, ed. "A Selected List of Current Books." *Wisconsin Library Bulletin,* 25 (February 1929), 71.

Notes

COLLECTED POEMS
OF ROBERT FROST

NEW YORK

HENRY HOLT AND COMPANY

Collected Poems

Granville Hicks.
"The World of Robert
Frost."
The New Republic, 65
(December 3, 1930),
77-78.

In one of the poems in his "West Running Brook," Frost says,

> I have been one acquainted with the
>   night.
> I have walked out in rain—and back
>   in rain.
> I have outwalked the furthest city
>   light.

He has known, he would tell us, what the world has to offer of pain and sorrow. He is not unfamiliar with the experiences that make men grieve and despair. If he has kept his sanity, it is not because he has blinded himself to the elements in life that make men mad. But to him as a poet the most important result of his acquaintance with sorrow has been the realization that the exercise of the creative faculties is independent of circumstance—

> And further still at an unearthly
>   height
> One luminary clock against the sky
> Proclaimed the time was neither
>   wrong nor right.
> I have been one acquainted with the
>   night.

This is vigorous doctrine in an age that has been fertile in self-analysis and self-commiseration. Frost's credo, however, runs counter to the consensus of opinion of the critics of all ages as well as to the temper of his own era. Matthew Arnold summarized the verdict of most students of letters when he said, "For the creation of a master work of literature two powers must concur, the power of the man and the power of the moment, and the man is not enough without the moment." Wordsworth said something of the same sort, and perhaps came closer to the difficulties of our own time, when he pointed out that facts and ideas have to become familiar to mankind, have to become part of common human experience, before the poet can use them. The poet cannot accept them until they are "ready to put on, as it were, a form of flesh and blood." So much in modern life has not been assimilated to organized human experience, so many of our acts and thoughts are unrelated to any central purpose or unifying hypothesis, so many obstacles stand in the way of the much-discussed modern synthesis, that the poet must grow desperate who looks for the order of ideas, the intellectual and spiritual atmosphere, that Arnold says he needs. It is no wonder that most poets and critics would say that a time may indeed be either wrong or right and that the present time is decidedly wrong.

So strong is the case for this view of literature that we may omit the task of defending it in detail, and, instead, ask ourselves how it is possible for Frost to hold the contrary opinion. The answer is to be found, of course, not in any critical writings of his but in his poetry. "Collected Poems" shows and shows clearly that Frost has written as fine poetry as any living American and that the proportion of first-rate poetry to the whole is greater than that in the work of any other contemporary. This last point is important, not because quantity matters, but because so many American poets, after a brief productive period, have slipped into silence or mediocrity. The fact that Frost's power is not only intense but also sustained forces us either to accept his theory or find some other explanation of his achievements.

What the other explanation may be is suggested when we realize how compact and unified Frost's work is. Instead of writing about this aspect of our civilization and that, instead of yielding himself to the casual inspirations of unrelated phenomena, he has occupied himself with a limited body of experiences. He has, in short, found, for poetic purposes, a world of his own. In so doing he is not, obviously, alone among contemporary poets: Robinson, Aiken, Eliot, each has his own world. But Frost's world is different from the world of any of these other poets, in that it is related to a real world with definite boundaries in time and space. That is why

his poetry is more substantial than the poetry of any of the others, why his people are three-dimensional, why his figures of speech are always concrete and non-literary. His world is not an artificial, intellectual abstraction from the real world; it is set apart from the rest of the world by geographical and historical facts. Of course his world is not to be completely identified with the rural New Hampshire of the maps and books of statistics; it is, after all, his world. But it is directly related to rural New Hampshire, as Dante's world was directly related to medieval Europe and Shakespeare's to Elizabethan England.

Let us enter Frost's world and examine its advantages for the poet. What we do not find is perhaps more important than what we do. We find, in the first place, nothing of industrialism, and since at present so many of both the demands and the accomplishments of the machine are unrelated to the permanent hopes and impulses of the human heart, the absence of this phenomenon is significant for the poet. In the second place, we look in vain for evidences of the disrupting effect that scientific hypotheses have had on modern thought. The natives may have heard that

"The trouble with the Mid-Victorians
Seems to have been a man named
     John L. Darwin."

But the fundamental problems of conduct and destiny are still considered in terms older and richer in emotional connotations than the phraseologies of Darwinian biology and Einsteinian physics:

"Go 'long," said I to him, he to his
   horse.

Frost, living in that world, can afford
to look with amusement on the bewildered modern—

A baggy figure, equally pathetic
When sedentary and when
   peripatetic.

Finally, to take a third example of the
absence in Frost's world of some of
the less assimilable factors in our
civilization, there is the matter of
Freudianism. He is still free to treat
love in the language of an era before
psychoanalysis was known. When he
is in New York he may be told,

"Choose you which you will be—a
   prude, or puke,
Mewling and puking in the public
   arms."

But he can reply,

"Me for the hills where I don't have
   to choose."

It remains to summarize briefly
some of the things that can be found
in Frost's world. For purposes of his
narrative verse he can find not
merely pathos but also, because there
are certain standards implicit in that
world, something close to tragedy. He
can find subjects for comedy there,
dramatic conflicts, objects of natural
beauty. He can treat abnormality and
yet keep it in its place, or he can find
a theme for as illuminating a commentary on failure as Robinson ever
wrote. In the contemplation of nature
he can, as scores of lyrics show, find
the beginnings of paths that lead
straight to the problems that have pe-

rennially perplexed the mind of man.
He can, in short, find opportunity and
stimulus to exercise to the full the
poetic imagination.

There is one thing, of course, Frost
cannot do: he cannot contribute directly to the unification, in imaginative terms, of our culture. He cannot
give us the sense of belonging in the
industrial, scientific, Freudian world
in which we find ourselves. The very
limitations that are otherwise so ad-
vantageous make it impossible. That
is why no one would think of maintaining that he is one of the great
poets of the ages. To that extent the
time, even though he refuses to lay
the responsibility at its door, is not
right. But, if the time is so completely
wrong as there is reason to suspect,
no poet, however great his genius,
could render that ultimate service of
the imagination. Every poet today is
necessarily a limited poet. Frost's relative greatness lies in the fact that,
endowed with the power, he discovered a way to make the time as favorable for the exercise of that power
as it could possibly be. He told the
story himself when he said of the star
in the stone boat—

Such as it is, it promises the prize
Of the one world complete in any
   size
That I am like to compass, fool or
   wise.

He compassed it, and we should be
considerably the poorer if he had not.

Genevieve Taggard.
"Robert Frost, Poet."
*New York Herald
Tribune Books,*
December 21, 1930,
pp. 1, 6.

The humanists have been trying to pigeonhole Robert Frost. Long, long shall our humanists sit with their rubber bands in their hands ready and waiting to snap them around the quotations they want from his works. The rest of Frost they would undoubtedly discard. Texts from this book laid neatly on four sides of him may serve the two-dimensional critic and the literal-minded reader; but not even his own texts nicely dove-tailed, can box the intelligence expressed here so sure of its goings-out and its comings-in. Frost is too cussedly nonconformist to trust even his own words as texts five minutes after he has uttered them. His mind is too seasoned, too humorous, to relish the owlish solemnity of dicta and dictations. He trusts his poems as poems, as metaphors spread to catch meaning, as words that have become deeds. He has given them speech that suggests not one meaning but many. Any effort, therefore, to strip Frost down to singleness of meaning in the interests of propaganda must be opposed. The wisest and most mature poet of our time should not be hacked at and shaved down to suit a pigeonhole. If, in their text-gathering, the humanists had paid more attention to Frost's behavior with his poems, if they had understood the meaning of tone and intention—if, in other words, they had known how to read poetry and not merely how to collect texts, they would have abandoned the attempt.

If they had not claimed, but rather praised Frost, some similarity might have been noted; for Frost embodies virtues the humanists extol. It is only natural that they should covet the aphorisms—pithy phrases, culled here and there from his work, which would help plead their case.

Those who have read each of Frost's books over a period of fifteen years have observed certain traits of character in his poetry. Frost detests seeing an idea used past its strength, or a metaphor with wobbly knees urged to a gallop. In this he is like a farmer who will not over-tax his beasts, or a good rider who knows his horse's capacity as surely as he knows its management. Frost flogs no emotions up hills too steep. This instinct of delicate judgment about the weight and value, fitness and right use of materials is the sign of a master. The humanists who study masters have found this virtue outstanding. They call it a humanist virtue, and claim Frost because he possesses it. "The Lockless Door" should have given sufficient warning:

It went many years,
But at last came a knock,
And I thought of the door
With no lock to lock.

I blew out the light,
I tiptoed the floor
And raised both hands
In prayer to the door.

But the knock came again.
My widow was wide;
I climbed on the sill
And descended outside.

Back over the sill
I bade a "come in"
To whatever the knock
At the door may have been.

So at a knock
I emptied my cage
To hide in the world
And alter with age.

There is always an empty room and a just-opened window when you knock imperiously on Robert Frost's door.

In this collected edition of his poems we may study, with especial profit, the prevailing meditation which runs, from the first poem written thirty years ago, on and on in, and out and through and under the facts and faiths of our contemporary life, down to the last poems written yesterday. Here is a mind that grows but never changes, that understands, with each poem accomplished, more and more about the mastery of form, storing much observation and illustration from experience, handling actualities with assurance, but a mind, nevertheless, that does not change, because it gives to experience something more spiritual, more creative than the things it takes away. This is a mind that unfolds, but never learns; it is that old phenomenon, the poet's mind, first described by Plato when he said that all knowledge was recollection. "Into My Own," which opens this collection, gives the key to the entire book. With the dark forest of life before him, with the ache for exploring it within him, the poet says, of his return:

They would not find me changed from
    him I knew—
Only more sure of all I thought was
    true.

Experience is merely the test and discipline for intuition and insight. Such inner certainty needs no texts and rules as outer props.

This inner certainty which is akin to Emerson's self-reliance and Thoreau's self-sufficiency, is the mental vantage point for Frost, about which he wrote while he was still a young man:

If tired of trees I seek again mankind,
    Well I know where to hie me—in
    the dawn,
    To a slope where the cattle keep
    the lawn.
There amid lolling juniper reclined,
Myself unseen, I see in white defined
    Far off the homes of men, and
    farther still,
    The graves of men on an opposing
    hill,
Living or dead, whichever are to
    mind.

And if by noon I have too much of
    these,
    I have but to turn on my arm and
    lo,
    The sun-burned hillside sets my
    face aglow.
    My breathing shakes the bluet
    like a breeze,
    I smell the earth, I smell the
    bruised plant,
    I look into the crater of an ant.

This ability to look at man, and then at an ant or a star and then back again, gives Frost a point of view from which he may criticize our life even while he participates in it. He is a thoroughgoing critic of all our thought. His wisdom which is self-made carries him past many of our jumping-off places. He goes on after

we stop. Often Frost seems to be saying to himself: "No, no, that won't
quite do." Examined, this system
works just so far. One more step and
it breaks down. It is plausible,
perhaps; but as a system, it won't do.
The strength of a poem or a metaphor
lies in the fact that it need only be
plausible. A system must be water
tight; it guaranties, it advertises itself
as water tight. Frost disbelieves in
guaranties and systems. He insists,
for instance, that science is merely an
extended metaphor—that is, that science is attempting to describe the unknown in terms of the known. It is
then a kind of poetry, and should be
treated as plausible material—not as
cold fact. When Einstein's theory of
relativity was mentioned in conversation, Frost countered, "Wonderful,
yes, wonderful; but no better as a
metaphor than you or I might make
for ourselves before 4 o'clock" . . .

"Robert Frost."
New Statesman, 36 [London] (December 27, 1930), 365-66.

The mature personality of Robert
Frost represented in these collected
poems is arrestingly attractive. There
is no other poet to whom he can be
compared. Even his English disciple,
Edward Thomas, is different. Frost's
humour is superb; a dignified, subtle
force, probing its ways into life and
finding a form of self-expression that
has to be known to be believed. Ordinary praise misses the mark.

He seems, for one thing, always to
choose the disappearances of life and
nature as symbols to fit his moods.

His is the genius of shyness, and its
abbreviated gestures may be overlooked by the reader who expects to
discover the fine exaggerations so
common in poetry. You have to watch
for the flicker of an eyelid, and even
then it may not come. That failure
would be intentional, and you would
discover afterwards the meaning of it,
and chuckle to yourself with satisfaction and a deep gratitude towards
that deliberately half-articulated wisdom. As for this poet's music, that too
has an intentional flatness and whimsicality, like the whirr of the nightjar,
that sound which can make the common neglected spots become magical
with a sort of drab expectancy.

It is often useful, but probably
restrictive, to quote from a poet
passages which seem to sum up his
character and his method. Every original character has such moments of
self-betrayal, and Mr. Frost's may be
found in these quotations, though
they are not representative of the
highest beauty in his work:

By June our brook's run out of song
    and speed.
Sought for much after that, it will be
    found
Either to have gone groping
    underground
(And taken with it all the Hyla
    breed
That shouted in the mist a month
    ago,
Like ghosts of sleigh-bells in a ghost
    of snow)—
Or flourished and come up in
    jewel-weed,
Weak foliage that is blown upon a
    bent
Even against the way its waters
    went.
Its bed is left a faded paper sheet

Of dead leaves stuck together by the
    heat—
A brook to none but who remember
    long.
This as it will be seen is other far
Than with brooks taken otherwhere
    in song.
We love the things we love for what
    they are.

This brook that just dries up is typical of the people, places and moods that Robert Frost writes about: something gone, but still here: something that perhaps may never have been, yet probably must have been. These powerful and life-veering intangibilities, and the clouds of beauty trailing after them, constitute the interests of this poet's life. Yet with these quaint interests runs a shrewd sense of reality, a sly, farmerlike wisdom, thrown out in asides and hints, full of knowing-kindness and ancient malice. Shrunken, crabbed human nature, toughtened by contact with earth, is good enough for Mr. Frost, and he sings of it in a strange, yet half-familiar strain:

> . . . a singer everyone has
>   heard,
> Loud, a mid-summer and a mid-wood
>   bird,
> Who makes the solid tree-trunks
>   sound again.
> He says that leaves are old and that
>   for flowers
> Midsummer is to spring as one to
>   ten.
> He says the early petal-fall is past
> When pear and cherry bloom went
>   down in showers
> On sunny days a moment overcast;
> And comes that other fall we name
>   the fall.
> He says the highway dust is over all.

The bird would cease and be as other
    birds
But that he knows in singing not to
    sing.
The question that he frames in all
    but words
Is what to make of a diminished
    thing.

Those last three lines are an explanation of this poet's whimsical technique, that seeks out awkwardnesses and makes music from them, a queer sort of music without which the deeps of the man's nature would not be sounded.

C. Henry Warren.
" 'An Original, Ordinary Man.' "
*The Bookman,*79[London] (January 1931), 242-44.

They read a good deal of English poetry in the United States. Scan the publishers' lists, over there, and you will find a fair sprinkling of our poets. It can hardly be said that we, in this country, reciprocate the compliment. Indeed the average Englishman probably thinks there have not been any considerable American poets since Whitman. A publisher is to be the more commended, therefore, when he issues over here the collected poems of a living American poet. Not that Robert Frost is a typical American of to-day. Nor, to be fair, is his poetry quite unknown to us: at least one of his poems (and a good one) has found its way into a number of our anthologies; and, among those people who *do* read modern American poetry, his is the name that would probably spring to the lips when asked who is the best living American poet.

Robert Frost is as near English "as makes no difference." So English is he, in fact, that if one had to name the poet whose work is most like his, one would inevitably instance that most English of all English poets, the late Edward Thomas. The likeness between their poetry is quite extraordinary; and it is no wonder that Frost counted Thomas among his best friends and dedicated to his memory the "Selected Poems" which appeared in America some two years ago. Both loved the same things in life; and (by one of those miracles that unite men over seas and centuries) both found much the same way of expressing in poetry their delight. Coming upon such a poem as that with which the present book opens and finding it unlabelled, the student of modern poetry would find it hard to choose, between the two poets, who was the author:

"I'm going out to clean the pasture
    spring;
I'll only stop to rake the leaves away
(And wait to watch the water clear, I
    may):
I sh'n't be gone long.—You come too.

I'm going out to fetch the little calf
That's standing by the mother. It's so
    young,
It totters when she licks it with her
    tongue.
I sh'n't be gone long.—You come
    too."

After all, the sound of falling snow, or the feel of moss beneath the foot, or the way sunlight hangs on old bricks is much the same all the earth over—if only you have the eyes to see it; and when it comes to appreciating the simple bedrock emotions of men, whether they come from the Old World or the New makes little difference—if you yourself are among the pure in heart. Both Frost and Thomas have that same singleness of heart and eye.

An American critic once spoke of Robert Frost as "an ordinary man—an original, ordinary man." The label is a good one, if any be. He was a schoolmaster and is now (we believe) a lecturer; he has also been a farmer; and if to-morrow should somehow see him President of the United States he would still be that same "original, ordinary man." "The axis of his character," said that same critic, "is unspoiled manliness and humanity." There is the key to his finest qualities: he has never allowed himself *to be improved away*. In a country guided mainly by a mechanistic civilisation that is a rare achievement; but then he has apparently always had the wisdom, in the face of whatever opposition, to trust his deepest intuitions. When he was only seventeen, for instance, he quitted college after a few months, because college seemed to him "a mill for being made into decent boards, and he was going to stay a growing tree." Later, when work took him into a factory, where his job was to look after the electric lights, he stole into out-of-the-way places and read poetry in secret, "because poetry was the thing he cared about, and he couldn't be beguiled into putting success at his bread-and-butter job ahead of it."

He left job after job—shoe-making, teaching, working in a mill, newspaper writing—because he would not let anything "press him out of shape."

Even when he became a New England farmer (removed thither by his grandfather, as the best way of disposing of the family disgrace) he remained first of all a poet. As with himself, so, when the opportunity offered, with his attitude to others: it is reported of him that, as a lecturer, he once told a group of teachers that their first duty was to themselves, their second to their books, and their third to their pupils. In fact we see in him a man safe-guarding his essential "self," that root of pure personality, that stuff of individuality, that quality which alone can give the single heart and eye.

It is because Frost kept undefiled the well of his being, that he is able (as it were) to look down therein and see so clearly those manifold reflections of life which he has transmuted into poetry. There they are, those reflections, shining the brighter for the water that holds them, sharp-edged, clean-coloured, simple. That is his poetry. And sometimes, looking down, he faintly discerns beyond and through the picture, "a something white, uncertain, Something more of the depths": then:

"One drop fell from a fern, and lo! a
    ripple
Shook whatever it was lay there at
    bottom,
Blurred it, blotted it out. What was
    that whiteness?
Truth? A pebble of quartz? . . ."

No matter; whatever it was, he has seen it; and we who read his poetry may see it too.

"Original, ordinary man." Because he is "ordinary" he chooses the most commonplace subjects to write about; but because he is both "original" and "ordinary" he gives those commonplace subjects a brightness, a loveliness, a significance we had not noticed in them before. Not for him do things fade into the light of common day. An incident as usual and trivial as the spilling of a parcel in the road can, for him, become fraught with the utmost significance:

"For every parcel I stoop down to
    seize,
I lose some other off my arms and
    knees,
And the whole pile is slipping,
    bottles, buns,
Extremes too hard to comprehend at
    once,
Yet nothing I should care to leave
    behind.
With all I have to hold with, hand
    and mind
And heart, if need be, I will do my
    best
To keep their building balanced at
    my breast.
I crouch down to prevent them as
    they fall;
Then sit down in the middle of them
    all.
I had to drop the armful in the road
And try to stack them in a better
    load."

Not that he is always as obvious as that in revealing the significance of the incident which has moved him to poetry. Indeed at his best he is usually content to let the picture speak for itself, knowing that the very incantation, and the word, will reveal everything. The poem by which he is best known over here, "Mending Wall," is an admirable instance of this power of objectification. A better one to give as an instance, however, may be "Stopping by Woods on a

Snowy Evening"—a lyric that ought certainly to be included in the ultimate (and brief) perfect anthology of the poetry of to-day:

"Whose woods these are I think I
      know.
His house is in the village though;
He will not see me stopping here
To watch his woods fill up with snow.

"My little horse must think it queer
To stop without a farm-house near
Between the woods and frozen lake
The darkest evening of the year.

"He gives his harness bells a shake
To ask if there is some mistake.
The only other sound's the sweep
Of easy wind and downy flake.

"The woods are lovely, dark and
      deep.
But I have promises to keep,
And miles to go before I sleep,
And miles to go before I sleep."

In that you may see all (or nearly all) of his characteristics perfectly concentrated: rare sensitiveness of perception, easy mastery of technique, and most delicate humour. One of the longer narrative poems would serve even better, because then one could show the additional characteristic of an unusual insight into the finer emotions of common humanity—those brief and quiet flashes born of human contact, so simple that the majority of us miss them altogether, so revealing when pointed out to us by a poet like Frost—or Edward Thomas.

All this he achieves by the use of a prosody apparently so near to prose that the unpractised ear may well be excused for missing the many overtones with which it is loaded. It is as if he were expressing the emotions of an ordinary man in that same ordinary man's simple words—until you come to examine the expression more closely and see with what consummate art that "ease" is contrived.

So, too, with the picturing of the rural scene which is the happy background of these some hundred and fifty poems. It is the tiny things he makes to count: snow slipping off a leaf, fruit ripening on a sunny wall, a bird singing so quietly it seems to know "in singing not to sing." Heart and eye are quick to respond in him to all that "tiny circumstance of peace" which is the very pulse and rhythm of purposeful life. Reading him, we have the thought that here is a man to whom we would delight to introduce our most intimately English scenery and our most natively English traits. He would understand them entirely. That he was born some three thousand miles away would not matter at all. The wonder is the greater, therefore, that we have been so late (the majority of us) in discovering him. Let us make haste to do amends.

F. B.
"Robert Frost, A Collected Edition of the Work of an American Poet."
Boston Evening Transcript, January 10, 1931, Book Section, p. 3.

It would be difficult to persuade true lovers of the verse of this one of the outstanding American poets of today that they have not met him, even if with their bodily eyes they have never beheld him save in counterfeit presentment. For in his poems, and especially in his longer New England poems, the sense of his personality is so strong that it seems at times as if one could hear his voice telling the story to us individually, through lyric, or sonnet, or blank verse. Not the least charm of his austerely beautiful verse lies in this sense of personal contact. New Englander par excellence of all our leading poets today, he epitomizes the dry humor, the emotion concealed under an ironclad reserve, the Hellenic acceptance of fate under the name Calvinism, the introspection as rigid as even Hawthorne knew, engendered by our rock-ribbed land. Personally experienced difficulties met and overcome, or accepted grimly, lie between the lines of many of his poems. Hence the reader's heart is reached and touched more poignantly, difficulty of some kind being the common inheritance of humanity. Not "I also have been in Arcady," is the nature of the reaction, but "I have been one acquainted with the night." Yet Mr. Frost, knowing well the vanity of much of life's effort, always makes that effort bravely and hopefully, and so helps his readers to do the same. To us his verse seems like the measures plucked by the wind from tree-harps, sometimes in summer delicately lovely, stronger if harsher when November takes its turn, and most magnificent when winter ice storms set the key. . . .

L.A.G. Strong.
"A Fine Poet."
The Nation & Athenaeum 48 [London] (January 10, 1931), 486.

There is a popular game which consists of sending a message round a dinner-table. Each person whispers it to his neighbour, till it comes back, more or less recognizable, to its inventor. The long vowels remain, and a whole word here and there; perhaps it even keeps the same number of syllables. It may be adorned, it may be caricatured, it may be merely flattened and made a fool of; but it never returns intact. Poetry, at the best of times, loses in crossing the sea. When it brings us back something we have ourselves exported, we are almost irresistibly reminded of this message game. Thus there is no denying that, to an English ear, the American admirers of Wordsworth's Number Two manner seem to outprattle their master. It would be unfortunate if a new reader were to open Mr. Frost's book on page 69, and read:—

"He saw her from the bottom of the
    stairs
Before she saw him. She was
    starting down,
Looking back over her shoulder at
    some fear.
She took a doubtful step and then
    undid it
To raise herself and look again. He
    spoke,
Advancing toward her: 'What is it
    you see
From up there always—for I want to
    know.' "

He might think, with some excuse,
that the formula was being over-
worked, and the poet only made sure
he was not writing prose by inserting,
every now and then, a stilted phrase.
Finding another page, and churning
in his jaws the slushy sibilants,

"Where wheels have freshly sliced
    the April mire,"

he might think their realism too
dearly bought. But at this point, being a
fairminded man, he will reopen the
volume at the first page, and go
ahead. Almost at once he will see that
this apparently naïf technique can
sound an individual note. At

"The footpath down to the well is
    healed,"

he will put down the book, and stare
into his thoughts for a minute. Re-
suming, he will quicken upon

"O give us pleasure in the orchard
    white
Like nothing else by day, like ghosts
    by night":

and, by the time he has read the last

two stanzas of "My November Guest,"
he has settled down, with a thrill of
grim delight, to make the acquaintance of a fine poet.

While his charm is apparent from
the first, Robert Frost does not yield
himself impetuously to his reader. His
personality is too deep, too cool, too
humorously assured to be in a hurry.
He has written magic poems, but
their magic is subtle, the effect of a
suggestion infinitely delicate: a kind
of poetic innocence. Take the famous
lyric, "Stopping By Woods on a Snowy
Evening," which has stood many
years' acquaintance and lost nothing
of its first fresh quality. It is easy,
almost bare: where does its effect
come from? We can only be sure that
the effect—the cold stillness, the
dark—is there, uncannily held. In the
same way any dozen of Frost's poems
evoke a composite image of the man,
steady, serene, attractive, with very
great reserves of power and sincerity
underlying the sung or spoken words.
He is quiet, and unemphatic: often he
trifles, and smiles at a small joke; but
there is no lack of epigrammatic
power when it is needed. Read "Sand
Dunes":—

"They are the sea made land
To come at the fisher town,
And bury in solid sand
The men she could not drown."

The present writer's approach to
Robert Frost's work was not as grudging or as difficult as the opening of
this notice would suggest. He has admired it for years now: and if the
opening seem graceless, it is only because such work deserves and can
survive the severest approaches on
traditional lines: and because even
the finest poetry suffers in crossing

the water. There are pieces in this volume which have lost their flavour. They seem pointless, not worth writing. Native ears will hear in them what ours miss; for no one, after reading this book, can imagine that its author would write idly. Wordsworth's message has gone round the long table, and New England gives it back in a clear, steady tone, changed, with new life in it, new tolerance, new wisdom, and new beauty. Robert Frost is a notable figure in a great tradition. His work is original. He is like a host, who slowly, kindly, and humorously shows you the places where he lives. You learn to love the places: and, when your stay is over, you are bound by a deep affection to the personality of your host—one of the least obtrusive and most individual in modern literature.

Isdor Schneider. "Robert Frost." *The Nation,* 132 (January 28, 1931), 101-102.

A reading of the "Collected Poems" can leave no doubt of Mr. Frost's importance. They have an appearance of obscurity, but what renders them difficult to first reading renders them also powerful and compact. The simplicity of their subject matter is never betrayed into coarseness or sentimentality. They constitute a body of poetry certain to enter into classic American literature.

However, since current reviews of this volume are all praise and no serious criticism is being attempted, I think it may be of interest to point out the limiting elements in Mr. Frost's work. There is a danger in too complete an acceptance of any man's achievement, a possibility of his influence becoming a catch-all for literary prejudice.

Mr. Frost, for instance, is singularly out of touch with his own time. Indeed, many poets who antedate him are more contemporary in spirit. It has, indeed, been Mr. Frost's wish to keep out of his own age and his own civilization. We may go therefore to his poetry for diversion and relief from our time, but not for illumination. Mr. Frost does not understand our time and will make no effort to understand it. When he essays to speak of it, as in the long poem New Hampshire (one of the poorest in the book and a sort of pudding of irrelevancies), he shows a surprising lack of comprehension. There, to the challenge of contemporary ideas, he replies with know-nothing arrogance, "Me for the hills where I don't have to choose."

In fact, Mr. Frost's work is weakest in ideas. His style is gnomic; it sounds impressively thoughtful and many sentences have the rounded conclusiveness of proverbs. But his thought, disengaged from the style, is often discovered to be no thought at all, or a banality. (I am far from agreeing with Mr. George Moore and other advocates of "pure poetry" that ideas are foreign to the nature of poetry. Shakespeare, Dante, Goethe, Milton, Donne, Lucretius would have to be among the many poets sacrificed, and the purification of poetry would turn out to be its annihilation.) Mr. Frost has casual ambitions to be a philosopher in his poetry; and in these strivings he is not successful.

We may take for example the

beautiful poem A Star in a Stone Boat. The star is a meteorite built into a stone wall. Mr. Frost follows it from its fall to the time a farmer finds it, handles it, puts it into a stone boat, and drags it to the wall he is building. We are given a marvelous sense of its weight and feel in the hands and the puzzled awe with which one looks at it. The concluding lines are perfect:

Such as it is it promises the prize
Of the one world complete in any
    size
That I am like to compass, fool or
    wise.

These lines, summarizing as much of philosophy as the poem comes to, do not contain thought so much as a renunciation of thought. I doubt whether a poet of philosophic imagination could have given us a more satisfying poem. Nevertheless, this piece, so suggestive and so full of possibilities, shows how little the philosophic imagination is developed in Mr. Frost.

It is curious, therefore, that Mr. Frost should be so regularly praised for the thought content of his poetry. But there is a reason for it. The touch of philosophy in his writing is the commonest, most easily understood, most easily applied, most comforting form of thinking—renunciation. Mr. Frost adds to it no subtlety and no depths; when it occurs in his poems it is, despite the graces and novelties of his style, banality.

I dwell upon this because it is the one respect in which Mr. Frost clearly shows himself to be influenced. The influence is New England, the New England of other days. The individuality of his style is one of the valuable effects of this influence, for New England life and tradition have always encouraged intense individualism. But this individualism derives in part from renunciation. What a man renounces he is free from and in freedom he can be himself. Perhaps here lies an explanation of the individuality of Mr. Frost's style. He has made a renunciation of usual poetic subject matter and usual poetic effects, not primarily for originality's sake, but in disdain of literary comforts. He has chosen instead to write of homely and country things, regarding them with his matchlessly keen observation and celebrating them with his almost painfully restrained eloquence. No doubt some deliberate and unnecessarily harsh lines are a further process of this renunciation.

Related to this lack of a developed and original philosophy is another lack. Mr. Frost's narrative poems are frequently poised upon a psychological situation. The satisfaction the poetry and the narrative give the reader often leaves him with the impression that Mr. Frost is an excellent psychologist. Now many poets have been good psychologists, as Freud has shown; but Mr. Frost as a psychologist does not get very far. He can describe sensations perfectly; in fact, such descriptions are among his finest achievements. But he does not reach beyond the sensation; and in a psychological narrative he does not reach beyond the fact. The interesting poem of the man who burned down his house to buy a telescope with the insurance money succeeds only in reporting a curiosity; the poem Maple, which attempts to describe the psychological effects of having an unusual name, stretches out to absurd length in the attempt and succeeds in doing no more than to supply the reader data for his own psychologizing.

No, the distinctions Mr. Frost achieves are not those of a thinker or a prober; nor does he need those. He has rounded out a poetic individuality of exceptional dignity; he has developed his descriptive powers to an accuracy so sensitive that his lines often have an effect of clairvoyance; and the patient, logical fulfilment of his metaphors gives his rhetoric an effectiveness achieved by very few poets besides him.

Mr. Frost's style is one of the most individual in all poetry and certainly the most individual of our time. The consciously aristocratic T. S. Eliot, with his almost selfish obscurities, the dazzlingly inventive E. E. Cummings, with all his inimitable experiments, sound like the generality beside him. It is impossible to describe this individuality because its most conspicuous elements, terseness and the use of plain words and the avoidance of metronomic rhythms, are characteristics of many other poets. One can only say that Mr. Frost writes in a manner wholly his own; and if he has been influenced in it at all, it is only in the individualism urged by the New England tradition.

The descriptive power of Mr. Frost is to me the most wonderful thing in his poetry. A snowfall, a spring thaw, a bending tree, a valley mist, a brook, these are brought not to, but into the experience of the reader. The method is simple and can be analyzed. What he describes is never a spectacle only, but an entire adventure. In Our Singing Strength we follow him disputing with birds a bit of roadway; in A Hillside Thaw we almost see him on his knees trying to feel with his hands the process of snow turning into water. With the sight and the act the emotional response comes naturally. The three fuse together and the experience comes whole to us. It is an effect rare even in the best poetry. This simultaneous description gives the reader almost a sensory instrument with which to share the perception; and since it is natural, anyway, for the reader to identify himself with the author, the result is to bring the reader into closer touch with this aloof poet than with many poets who directly seek such a companionship.

Metaphors as Mr. Frost uses them are more functional than they commonly are in poetry. Many poets have more abundance and more brilliance, but few have used metaphor so justly, so carefully, and so fully. It is worked in naturally and at length, becoming a part of the whole idea, not a mere illuminating flash. The most conspicuous example of this is A Hillside Thaw. The first three lines announce the metaphor,

> To think to know the country and
>   not know
> The hillside on the day the sun lets
>   go
> Ten million silver lizards out of
>   snow!

For most poets this would be sufficient. They would turn to other metaphors. But Mr. Frost continues it for thirty-two lines more, and we have a wonderfully complete sense of the coolness, swiftness, and liquidness of these snow lizards that the night will catch and hold, and the sun will again release in the next daylight.

There remains to make some estimate among the poems themselves. The later sections are much superior to the earlier, where the poems are frequently incomplete, beginning with promises of drama, of discoveries of thought that fail into unresolved and weak endings. This disappears in the later poems which, with the exception of the poem New Hampshire, are sound throughout. On the whole it seems to me that the longer lyrics are the most thoroughly satisfying of his poems. The narratives, although among the best in English poetry, suffer from the incompatibility found in all narrative poetry which attempts to be realistic—the rivalry of the poetic and the colloquial. The attempt to fuse the two seems to me doomed to failure; a noble failure, preferable to easier successes, but a failure nevertheless. It were better for a narrative poem to be written wholly in poetic language, which, being complete and self-sufficient in its own terms, will sound natural, certainly more natural than when colloquialisms are inset and draw attention to their competing naturalness. A few of the very short lyrics in the book are inconsequential and, as in Fireflies in the Garden, tend to become cute. Mr. Frost seems to require space to express himself, for in a few lines his terseness and involution have the look of a mannerism.

In conclusion I wish to say again outright in words what I have already said by implication—Robert Frost is one of the great poets, one whose perceptions are among the most acute and the most personal in the whole range of literature. To this nearly every one of the poems written in his maturity bears witness.

"Robert Frost." *Times Literary Supplement,* January 29, 1931, p. 75.

It is some fifteen years since Mr. Frost's first book of poems, "A Boy's Will," was published, but this volume represents considerably more than the labour of fifteen years, for Mr. Frost had to wait as many years for recognition. Even then it was left to England to recognize this very American poet. He came to this country in 1912, when he was thirty-seven, and soon found a publisher for his first and second books. When he returned to America in 1915 his literary reputation was already established in both countries.

Considering the length of time Mr. Frost must have had in which to shape his talent and select from his output, it is not surprising that his early work shows little of the hesitancies of immaturity. In "A Boy's Will" that whimsical humour which is to become so dominant in his later work is not yet evident, and there is an exuberance—as in the lines "To the Thawing Wind" and "A Line-Storm Song"—which is soon to disappear; but the author of "Mowing" and "October" is already confident of his direction and speaking with his own voice. The idiom of careful simplicity foreshadowed in "A Boy's Will" is fully developed in his second book, "North of Boston," along with most of the qualities by which we recognize his poetry. The long, unrhymed monologues and dialogues which form the bulk of this book, as of Mr. Frost's work as a whole, are written throughout in the colloquial language and manner of casual conversation. It is Mr. Frost's peculiar talent to give to his most delicate utterance the air of a chance remark, never to stress in his verse a note that would not be stressed in the context of ordinary speech. Such a diction has dangers and disadvantages which Mr. Frost has not been able entirely to escape. In the shorter, lyrical poems the narrowness of compass and restriction of rhyme serve to keep a balance between economy and Mr. Frost's natural discursiveness; but the balance is often lost in the longer poems, at the risk of tedium. The characters in the dialogues speak so unvaryingly with Mr. Frost's voice and accent, with such a flat, circumlocutory sameness, that the subtlety of his psychological delineation cannot always save them from monotony. Here and there, too, his simplicity defeats itself and obscures his meaning: such a passage as this from "Maple," though the subject is admittedly involved, needs to be more carefully unravelled than we feel should be necessary:—

It was as personal as he could be
About the way he saw it was with
    you
To say your mother, had she lived,
    would be
As far again as from being born to
    bearing.

But at his best, in the short lyrics, his writing has an exquisite case; the lines come as easily as one speaks, and the beauty which takes shape in them is all the more arresting for its fortuitous air. Consider, for example, the unassuming loveliness of the line which concludes "Our Singing Strength," a poem which describes how the birds in spring were driven by snow from the trees and fields to gather in the road. We quote the ending:—

Well, something for a snowstorm to
    have shown
The country's singing strength thus
    brought together,
That though repressed and moody
    with the weather
Was none the less there ready to be
    freed
And sing the wildflowers up from
    root and seed.

Mr. Frost is essentially a poet of Nature; one feels that urban life is beyond the range of his interest or comprehension. The people in his poems, the country people of New England, live close to the earth, close enough to dread the menace of winter, to welcome the spring with more than poetic gladness. And Mr. Frost looks at Nature with the understanding of the farmer as well as the insight of the poet. As he bids good-bye to the orchard in "Good-Bye and Keep Cold" his affection is quickened by the knowledge

of all that can happen to harm
An orchard away at the end of the
    farm
All winter, cut off by a hill from the
    house.
. . . No orchard's the worse for the
    wintriest storm;
But one thing about it, it mustn't get
    warm.
"How often already you've had to be
    told.
Keep cold, young orchard. Good-bye
    and keep cold. . . ."

And only one who is intimate with country things could tell with such tender precision how

> just as the soil tarnishes with weed,
> The sturdy seedling with arched body comes
> Shouldering its way and shedding the earth crumbs.

Mr. Frost's is always a quiet voice. One is aware of his emotional responses more by implication than by his admission. We have mentioned the lack of exuberance in his mature work; but though his reticence of feeling gives a certain air of moroseness to his poetry it is, we think, due less to the pessimism which has sometimes been ascribed to him than to his scrupulous refusal to falsify or poeticize the essential quality of what has moved him, his reluctance to testify to "anything more than the truth." And if there is a gesture of resignation in his attitude towards life there is still an earnest faith in its courage and ability to endure—all that is implied in the assurance

> that winter death has never tried
> The earth but it has failed,

and a faith in the simple self-sufficiency of love which remains true to the youthful affirmations of "A Boy's Will," achieving with maturity a more perfect expression:—

> On snow and sand and turf, I see
> Where Love has left a printed trace
> With straining in the world's embrace.
> And such is Love and glad to be.

It is his ability to see that "printed trace" of love on the world about him that gives Mr. Frost's subdued utterance an inward warmth and radiance that are rare enough in poetry to-day. His field of vision is perhaps limited, but within it his perception is penetratingly keen.

"Collected Poems." *Christian Century*, 48 (February 18, 1931), 242.

Five previously published volumes of Robert Frost's poems are assembled between one pair of covers. It is wonderful how a man can hold one mood through all the seasons for twenty years or more, and how everything that he has written reflects a single emotional state and seems part of a single picture. One wonders—does he always feel that way, or does he write only when he is in this mood, or does he suppress whatever he writes in any other key? Perhaps it is the dominating quality of his New Hampshire and Vermont hills that imposes upon him that uniformity of tone. There are poems of winter and spring, of summer and fall, of lonely housewives and varied rustic characters, but always it seems late afternoon of a chill November day. Frost is a pensive commentator upon life and nature in upper New England. But within this limited emotional range, he is exquisitely sensitive and searching. There are no false notes, no bathos, no sentiment unsupported by clear and vigorous thought. All of which is to say that Frost is a major poet voluntarily operating under self-imposed limitations in a minor field. His work will be one of the permanent contributions of our time to American literature.

Richard Church.
"Seven From the Forest."
The Spectator (London), 146 (February 21, 1931), 277-78.

Here are the collected poems of Mr. Edmund Blunden and Mr. Robert Frost, two poets who have so mastered the secrets of their localities that their work is universal. Each of these is a *complete* poet; that is, a man who interprets the whole of himself, and of the various life that has come to him, in terms of poetic expression. It is difficult to explain what I want to say; but I may succeed by pointing to those giants whom the world accepts without question as beings possessing this *complete* poetic nature, to whom poetry is synonymous with breathing, a power towards which they give all their responsible vitality. Wordworth and Keats were such men. One does not think of them as amateurs, or dilettanti, of verse. So one feels about Mr. Blunden and Mr. Frost, both poets to whom one can return constantly for further exploration. . . .

Mr. Frost has an even more pronounced personality, as one might expect from an artist who has spent twice as long in the world. His vision is quite unliterary, and his poetry is the result of infinite literary consciousness working out a personal medium from orthodox "poetical" beginnings to a final form of self-expression that is only to be described

by copious examples. His genius is the genius of mirth. Laughter, that serious laughter which holds all tenderness and love, rings through his work, toning down the high lights, and lifting up the shadows, so that its music has an almost laconic monotone, at first strange to the ear, but becoming dearer and more entrancing by familiarity. And with this laughter there trembles a note of passion; deep understanding of the conflict of mind with heart, of man with woman, of humanity with the blind forces of life and death. But I must not let myself go, for there are other poets to consider. I am content that Robert Frost needs no bush. Such a unique artistry, so gradual in growth, so noble and generous in stature, cannot fail to grip the world in its roots, and to fasten itself by a myriad tendrils into immortality. Here is just one leaf from the tree:

> "The rain to the wind said
>   'You push and I'll pelt.'
> They so smote the garden bed
>   That the flowers actually knelt,
> And lay lodged—though not dead.
>   I know how the flowers felt."

Virginia Moore.
"Robert Frost of New Hampshire."
Yale Review, 20 (March 1931), 627-29.

We have tried, but we have not succeeded in making a better definition of poetry than Milton's: "simple, sensuous and passionate." Robert Frost in his "Collected Poems" is simple in a fine New England way; he is sensuous if sensuous means seeing, hearing, smelling, tasting, and touching with pleasure; but it is hard to understand how he could be called passionate, though "Fire and Ice" speaks of the working of fire, and "To Earthward" asks for

. . . the aftermark
Of almost too much love.

Not that he tries for this effect and fails. His eyes are elsewhere. He is looking at life in its simplicity as he lives it and sees it lived. Without embellishment and with probity he records what happened, what he thought at the time, and, by inference, what it means. He is not taken possession of; he does not want to be. Neither his anger, his love, nor his wonder is such that his mind is as if passively swayed by it, as many great poets have been swayed. Probably he feels that he is delivered from the too much emotion which falsifies. He strives, as in "The Armful," to arrange, balance, and carry home unpretentious truths. The results to poetry are, at the least, a personality. A man like no other and of absolute integrity is attested; attested by words very like conversation, with overtones of humor and a basic conviction that life is not futile. This is important; but it does not necessarily prove great poetry. Poetry is a matter of "pitch and intensity"; it must not die with the last word but go on emotionally in the mind of the reader; the proof of its power and excellence is in its effect, soley. Does Frost's poetry meet this test? Does it move profoundly? Does it persist in beauty after the book is closed? Even Burns, I think, that man

of the country, who wrote unpretentiously, of homely realities, like Frost, and, like Frost, used plain speech, would have missed in the bulk of Frost's poetry exultation, the heroic sad act, audacity, the leap without warning, the lift, the total view.

Nevertheless he is one of the outstanding American poets, past and present. At least forty-five among a hundred and sixty-two poems are flawless for what they are, first-rate, amply deserving of the fame they have now and most assuredly will keep: "The Pasture," so whimsical, tender, and casual, "October," "Mending Wall," which transcends locality, "The Death of the Hired Man," quietly like revelation, "The Road Not Taken," "The Oven Bird," "New Hampshire," "Fire and Ice," "Dust of Snow," "The Runaway," "Stopping by Woods on a Snowy Evening," lovely imperishable, "Birches," "To Earthward," too intense to be typical, "Lodged," "Acquainted with the Night," "The Armful," pure Frost, "On Looking up by Chance at the Constellations"—to name only a few. Never a false note; never a breach of taste; never a cheap effect. There are moods beyond which he cannot go. But the man, so far as he goes, goes true.

The Vermont and New Hampshire landscape is familiar not only to his eyes but to his spirit: the little houses, the stock, orchards, roads under changing weather, brooks, fields, birds, stars at night, the hillside in thaw. This sort of place-consciousness breeds song. A particular farm is the world in small. Frost can say without presumption or vanity:

However it is in some other world
I know that this is the way in ours.

He has deliberately cut himself off
from the modern, metropolitan, and
commercial scene, and gained more, I
think, than he has lost.

James Southall Wilson. "Robert Frost: American Poet."
Virginia Quarterly Review, 7 (April 1931), 316-20.

There is a respect in which Robert
Frost is the most fortunate poet in
America. He has never been
exploited: neither by himself nor anyone else. How familiar the spectacle is
of the artist in the United States who
all of a sudden "makes the front
page." He is the subject of essays, the
guest of complimentary dinners, the
starred performer of the lecture
agency—a nine days' wonder for the
social teas. Enthusiasm boils over and
scalds his soberer reputation by its
excesses. Then if he becomes a trifle
drunken with the heady wine of pub-
licity and, like Miss M. in Walter de
la Mare's "Memoirs of a Midget,"
staggers ungracefully before his
exhibitors' eyes, a surge of revulsion
follows and his popularity ebbs out,
leaving a sense of over-adulation and
staleness on the public mind. There is
nothing spectacular about Frost and
there has been nothing spectacular
about the slow growth of his fame.
Now that at last all his published
poems are gathered in one volume,

the first quality that his reader feels
present in them all is his humanity.
There is such a cool, sane, human
interest that one is tempted to feel a
lack of the passionateness that a poet
must have to be a real poet. But if
passion is depth and intensity of feeling, Robert Frost is the most
passionate poet America has ever
produced. It is the genuineness of his
feeling that keeps Frost from ever
striking the false note. His love of nature goes so deep that he is tempted
neither to paint pretty pictures of it
nor to read into it an animism that he
does not find. Yet he sees it all
through the eye of human nature. His
wood-pile with strings of clematis
wound about it suggests to him
"someone who lived in turning to
fresh tasks." His birches make him
feel that "some boy's been swinging
them." His wild grape vine hints at "a
philosophy of hang-and-let-hang," because he knows the way of boys with
wild grapes. Even the oven bird that
raises the question of "what to make
of a diminished thing," though objectively treated as a bird, is seen
through human eyes: the poet too, we
feel, frames in all but words the same
question. The subject he writes about
is never wrenched from the dignity of
its own nature and expressed in
human terms, but it is chosen because
it has some significance to human
eyes besides its picturesqueness.
When the two lovers come face to face
with the buck and his doe in "Two
Look at Two," it is human nature facing deer nature. Such a picture might
be symbolical of how nature and man
reflect each other in Frost's poetry.
Frost, like the buck in the poem,
views things quizzically.

Sometimes there has been read into
certain of Frost's poems a mysticism

which he would not grant he had put there. It is there all the same. That is, it is there for the mind that sees it there. In a poem, humorous in this case, like "The Bear," the poet has chosen in fun to make the bear anthropomorphic. But it is man that is treated in terms of bear rather than bear that is made man: "he almost looks religious but he's not." Frost can find, even for comic purpose, the same values outside of man's experience that he finds in man. He seems to suggest his philosophy mystically by symbols out of nature, by individual incidents about men, but he himself as a poet is not being mystical or using the symbolic method. He simply chose the theme because he sees it is the one case that will serve as the pebble in the water. He throws it in to start the waves of suggestion and they go on rippling and rippling; but it is in your mind that the circles spread. There may be quite another series of circles in another mind, though their relation to the point at which the pebble struck the water will be the same.

In his poems about people it is easier to see both the sane humanity of Frost and the strong reserve power which makes his passion such a controlled passion. "The Code," or the long poem "Snow," would either serve as an example. The strong human feeling of the poet in his dealing with his characters is as taciturn and restrained as his characters, which are for all that so "human" that they are never remembered as imagined but as actual people. In "The Code," the closing line, "Discharge me? No! He knows I did just right," is like the release of a powerfully restrained spring or coil; the smoke of the explosion suddenly puffs in your face. So

with "The Death of the Hired Man," the most popular of Frost's dramatic short-stories in verse. The one phrase of the wife's, "Warren, he has come home to die," is just the release-snap that changes the irony of the situation to tragic pathos. Frost in adopting the conversational tones of the human voice as the basis for his metre, and in tuning his finest musical lines, as well as expressing his most moving human episodes, to the conversational tones, hit upon the very medium for the expression of passion in restraint. The quiet speech of his New Englanders must escape sensationalism as it also makes impossible sentimentalism. Pathos and even tragedy remain human and sound as long as they are spoken in the tones of human intercourse.

If Frost is one of the most philosophic of poets, it is still beside the point to try to formulate his philosophy. His is a philosophy of common-sense. In the combination of the philosopher and the practical man of wisdom, Robert Frost is like Emerson, of whom he reminds one in some ways only because they are so different. Frost's philosophy always derived from personal experience and his poems in detail are personal and objective. They are, as has been indicated, human, conversational, humorous, quietly dramatic (sometimes in an almost commonplace way)—and very local. Yet he is the most American poet and he universalizes everything that he touches. Truth is often hidden in a paradox. So with Frost. He seems interested only in the particular but the particular is for him the universal. He finds the center of the universe in every grain of sand that blows by his Vermont farm gate: the center of the universe is the focus from which the poet, who is also the philosopher, looks out in all directions upon the universe. Vermont, New Hampshire:—does a poet need to draw a map of the world to prove that a man in South Shaftsbury is the same man he would be in Moscow?

Because I wrote my novels in New Hampshire
Is no proof I aimed them at New Hampshire.

Robert Frost is both as a thinker and an artist subtle and elusive. It is his art most of all that proves him a great poet. It would be difficult to analyze the form of his poetry because it isn't a thing apart from the content. The form of one of Frost's poems fits the matter as if it had grown out of it and with it. Perhaps he has given the secret in "The Aim Was Song." Frost himself whimsically says that a poem ought to have a squirm of thought running through it. And perhaps if the form of the poem is properly twisted to the squirm of thought there results "the wind the wind had meant to be."

Before man came to blow it right
The wind once blew itself untaught,
And did its loudest day and night
In any rough place where it caught.

Man came to tell it what was wrong:
It hadn't found the place to blow;
It blew too hard—the aim was song.
And listen—how it ought to go!

He took a little in his mouth,
And held it long enough for north
To be converted into south,
And then by measure blew it forth.

By measure. It was word and note,

The wind the wind had meant to be—
A little through the lips and throat.
The aim was song—the wind could see.

To my judgment no richer volume of poetry has been produced in America since Poe's volume of 1845: a volume, this of Frost's, of one hundred and sixty-two poems no one of which might have been omitted to the poet's advantage. Robert Frost has been strangely made. Born in California of a Massachusetts father and Scottish mother, he was named for the Southern leader, Robert Lee. He was reared in New England, published his first poems in England, and living first in New Hampshire, then Vermont, has grown into the most typically American of all living poets. That phrase is of course a challenge. No foreigner would so quickly find Frost typically American as he would Sandburg or Lindsay, or Sinclair Lewis or Sherwood Anderson. But Frost is typical of the whole of America and of the traditions of America. He is typical as his own figures in his poems are typical, in that he is individual in a universal sense. The others are typical of something *in* America, some phase *of* America. But Frost has grown out of America like one of its forest trees. That great America of the mountain sides and the open fields, the small towns and the quiet homes in the cities; men and women, quiet, unmoved, and sound in heart and head; who never get on the front pages of the paper or run to the pier to meet the European celebrity: that is the America of which Frost is typical. He keeps his head in the midst of confusion: like the tree by his window every passing wind plays upon him

but the roots of his being are unshaken.

> The more a sensibilitist I am
> The more I seem to want my
>   mountains wild.

Geoffrey Grigson.
"Still Waters."
Saturday Review, 151
[London]
(April 4, 1931),
505.

The same experiences come to no two
poets, and all poets, therefore, who
deserve the name are original; their
relative greatness consists not in their
originality, but in the nature and variation of their experiences. Judged by
that rule Robert Frost can hardly be
called a great poet (how many can,
after all?). His experiences will strike
the critical reader as having been
valuable enough and felt to the
depths of his being, but their variation
is not wide or their nature anything
but quiet and level. If Frost be compared, for instance, with Wordsworth,
it becomes evident that he hears
something of the still, sad music of
humanity and feels a kinship with
nature, but does not experience in it
that

>   . . . . . sense sublime
> Of something far more deeply
>   interfused
> Whose dwelling is the light of
>   setting suns.

and so on to the end of a famous
passage. His manner of observation

and the use to which he puts it is
exemplified, to take a short and quotable poem, in 'Dust of Snow':

> The way a crow
> Shook down on me
> The dust of snow
> From a hemlock tree.
>
> Has given my heart
> A change of mood
> And saved some part
> Of a day I had rued.

In things or situations of beauty he is
constantly seeing analogies with
human problems or behaviour. The
way he does this is intellectual but
uncrabbed, as in the poem quoted, or,
better still, in those good but longer
poems 'For Once, Then, Something,'
'The Birches' and 'On a Tree Fallen
Across the Road.' Men and women
and the still sadness and half-sad
comforts of their existence are seldom,
if ever, absent from his work. They
fill many of his long blank-verse
poems in most of which he shows
himself a subtle observer of men and
women who are not typical but individual in every dimension. The environment of his verse—the New England of the old dwindling American
stock, the stiff soil and lonely or deserted farmsteads—has decided, or at
least enforced its tone, though one can
feel here and there a deep regret
which is perhaps wrung from him, in
spite of its fruits, by this localization
of place and mood. Consider, for instance, 'The Road Not Taken':

> Two roads diverged in a yellow
>   wood,
> And sorry I could not travel both
> And be one traveller, long I stood

And looked down one as far as I
    could
To where it bent in the undergrowth;

Then took the other as just as fair,
And having perhaps the better
    claim,
Because it was grassy and wanted
    wear;
Though as for that the passing there
Had worn them really about the
    same,

And both that morning equally lay
In leaves no step had trodden black.
Oh, I kept the first for another day!
Yet knowing how way leads on to
    way,
I doubted if I should ever come back.

I shall be telling this with a sigh
Somewhere ages and ages hence;
Two roads diverged in a wood, and
    I—
I took the one less travelled by,
And that has made all the difference.

Behind the charm of this and behind
poem after poem there is an emotional depth which does not always
give itself to a first or second reading.
The simplicity of his verse and his
quiet, gentle irony, or humour rather,
for it has not always the blade of
irony, are apt to keep it concealed.

In technique—and this again might
escape the casual tourist—few of his
contemporaries are more expert. In
some ways, but only on the surface,
he may seem like Crabbe (who had, of
course, none of his lyrical power). His
blank verse is even and slow and un-
excited, his manner conversational,
but he very seldom drops into the literal, matter-of-fact absurdity of bad
Crabbe or bad Wordsworth. In long or
short, in 'Dust of Snow' or 'The Death

of the Hired Man,' that masterpiece of
his peculiar genre, the same virtues
are evident of stern control and a
slow, steady progress from the first
idea to the ultimate version.

Taking this book all in all, I think
it the most important poet's collection
which has appeared for several years.
It is rare to find three hundred and
fifty pages of verse so consistently
good from cover to cover. It is rarer
still that a nature poet is so unliterary in the sense that he is free from
the stale influences of tradition. For
that reason alone I should put Robert
Frost far above his only rival on this
side of the Atlantic, who is, of course,
Mr. Edmund Blunden; and I am certain that his poetry deserves, and in
the fullness of time will earn, wide
and affectionate reading.

"Preferences." *Canadian Forum,* 11 (June 1931), 336-37.

Reading the *Collected Poems of Robert
Frost* which have come recently from
Longmans I have been struck with
the neat way this poet avoids all the
controversies. I don't mean that he
steers clear of the great world, its religious and political squabbles and
what not, though he does that too. A
cow and calf in a pasture, a chat with
a teamster, a shower of rain, a saw-
mill, a hired man, a woodpile, a
grindstone, a berry patch—any one of
these is enough to set him going. But
this is not what I was thinking of. I
was thinking of the way he writes. I
don't know any recent poet who so ad-
roitly sidesteps the great quarrel be-

tween the ancients and the moderns. Come to think of it, I don't know which to call him. As a practitioner in verse he is no more newfangled than oldfashioned. He writes or seems to write just as it comes to him; and, while he is not a Shakespeare, he has turned out a handful of things which no school of poets, I should think, would take pleasure in repudiating.

The secret of his quiet, but to my mind unassailable, success seems to be in this wise. On the one hand, he has recognized, as others have done, that the grand style is not for him, that there are sublime and austere regions of poetry which he cannot enter; and, on the other, he has perceived—more clearly and surely, I think, than anyone else—that there is an opposite sort of poetry which can meet all his needs. For want of a better word, I would call it 'the poetry of talking aloud.' Hardy and E. A. Robinson have drawn on it, but Frost uses nothing else. No compromise for him with the grand style or the poetic manner, no rhetoric, no stunts, no decorations. He just talks aloud all the time. He never writes a poem that lasts longer than a man might gossip—indeed I know many longer-winded gossips than he, if only they were poets—and he never lets his poetry rise above the accents of a man chatting with a friendly companion. I haven't found a poem—I have scarcely found a line—in all his goodsized volume which does not answer to this armchair test. Whatever he writes, you can hear him saying it over a log-fire, drawling a little with his Vermont accent—or is it New Hampshire?—and puffing, for all I know, at his cherrywood pipe. No matter what he touches, he does it nonchalantly, he doesn't let it disturb

him. The sight of our noblest Northern constellation rising over the hill-tops would make most poets put their jackets on, but Robert Frost takes the thing casually, cocking his eye at it as if it were a neighbour passing, yet missing nothing and setting it all down:—

You know Orion always comes up
   sideways,
Throwing a leg up over our fence of
   mountains

It is easy to see that the man who wrote that can manage quite well without the grand style. Like those pioneers who built their fences and log-cabins with never so much as a nail or a saw, making the homely axe do the work of all the other sophisticated tools put together, our New England poet swings his casual accents to and fro and says all he has to say. Nothing would I rather see than a good axeman at work; no poet that I know of offers a better substitute for the sight than Robert Frost with his easy, unpretentious, rough-trimmed voice, every word so sure, so spare:—

Something there is that doesn't love
   a wall,
That sends the frozen-ground-swell
   under it,
And spills the upper boulders in the
   sun

Now if Frost were some village-poet drooling his platitudes there would be no need to make much ado about it. But in what I have quoted—the two lines on Orion vaulting the hilly horizon and the three lines on the old wall and the stealthy winter freeze-up there is a largeness that you don't expect from his sort of poet. You may not notice it at first, it comes so quietly, but let the words lie around for a while in your mind and you will find that they can be quoted in good company. And there are moments in his poetry when he feels his way towards something better still. You will discover a hint of what I mean in the opening lines of 'After Apple-picking':—

My long two-pointed ladder's
   sticking through a tree
Towards heaven still,
And there's a barrel that I didn't fill
Beside it, and there may be two or
   three
Apples I didn't pick upon some
   bough.
But I am done with apple-picking
   now.

The hint is plain, for while he says nothing that a man mightn't say after a certain day in the orchard, it all has a sort of general significance, an applicability to a career lived and mused on, a sense that all life is or might be thus. If it were not that Frost seems to be shuffling the cards a little obviously for once—pointing his ladder somewhat too determinedly towards heaven, making quite sure that we get his meaning—I would say that these lines are a model of what philosophical poetry ought to be. There is so much philosophical poetry of the wrong sort and so little of the right. So much of the 'flower in the crannied wall' and 'God's in his heaven' and 'the child is father to the man' sort of poetry which is just philosophy, or the approach to philosophy, versified; and so little of the better sort in which the poet sticks to his business of rendering experience and letting the philosophy

come of itself. I don't mean that Robert Frost is as important a poet as these others I have quoted. He isn't. Yet he has something to teach them all the same.

But there are far better examples. To name three, there is first the poem on 'The Road not taken' which extracts its poetry from a mere cross-roads choice in the woods. There are two tracks, one beaten, one grass-grown; he chooses the latter, saying:—

I shall be telling this with a sigh
Somewhere ages and ages hence:
Two roads diverged in a wood, and
   I—
I took the road less travelled by,
And that has made all the
   difference.

He doesn't quite formulate the thought—the thought that all choice is a mystery and a fate, and the thought, too, of the nomad who goes aside—he lets it emerge unspoken from the simple account of what happened. Then there is 'The door in the dark,' playing on the same notion of chance and choice. As he gropes forward feeling for the door, it slips its edge through his guard and cracks him on the head. Again you can take what you like from it, but there is more there than a grin or a bump on the brow. The best of the three is 'The Armful':—

For every parcel I stoop down to
   seize,
I lose some other off my arms and
   knees,
And the whole pile is slipping,
   bottles, buns,
Extremes too hard to comprehend at
   once,

Yet nothing I should care to leave
    behind.
With all I have to hold with, hand
    and mind
And heart, if need be, I will do my
    best
To keep their building balanced at
    my breast.
I crouch down to prevent them as
    they fall;
Then sit down in the middle of them
    all.
I had to drop the armful in the road
And try to stack them in a better
    load.

I am not sure that these are Frost's
best poems. You might prefer some of
his short narratives, tragic or comic;
you might prefer that perfect little
thing called 'Stopping by woods on a
snowy evening.' But if you wanted to
get the better of Wordsworth or
Browning in an argument as to the
true way for poetry to philosophize
you couldn't do better than throw
Robert Frost's 'armful' at them and
ask them to stack it for you.

Frederick I. Carpenter. *"The Collected Poems of Robert Frost." New England Quarterly, 5 (January 1932), 159-60.*

The collection of the poems of Robert
Frost and their publication in a single
volume can only be welcomed by all
readers. Mr. Frost's reputation as one
of the leaders of contemporary poetry
has long been secure, and this collection of his poems will add to it. But

also, it must challenge the critic to
reconsider and re-define the reputation which Mr. Frost does enjoy, as
one of the clearest voices of "Our
Singing Strength." What are the qualities characteristic of this book?

To begin with, the volume of Mr.
Frost's poetry is comparatively small.
These complete and collected poems
occupy about 350 pages—printed not
very closely. And of this poetry, much
is narrative in form. Mr. Frost has
not been a prolific writer. This may
be due to a severely critical discrimi-
nation, or to a lack of fertility, or to
both. For, compared to other poets,
Mr. Frost does lack fertility.

To say this is perhaps pharisaical.
When was ever a poet judged on the
basis of quantity? Not quantity, but
quality is important. Well, then, what
of Mr. Frost's quality? By the common
consent of poets and critics, it is high.
His verse is perfectly modulated. It
expresses subtly all the shades of feeling which he wills. It bears delicately
the impress of his personality. It uses
new and unique rhythms. It is creative, in the best sense. His technique
is perfect; his feeling for words exquisite. But there is something, even
of quality, which he lacks.

Mr. Frost is a poet's poet. Critics
like Mr. Untermeyer, Mr. Aiken, Amy
Lowell, Professor Hillyer praise him
very highly. Many of them would put
him first among their contemporaries.
They appreciate the difficulty of his
task, and the perfection of his accomplishment. Their praise has authority.
But they are considering him as a
poet, only.

The fault of Mr. Frost lies merely in
this—that he is a poet, only. His criticism of life is merely poetic. He has
not the cosmic imagination which
creates its own world, as Walt Whit-

man had. He has not the tragic imagination which creates visions, as Mr. Robinson Jeffers has. He has not the epic imagination of Mr. S. V. Benet, nor the dramatic imagination of Mr. E. A. Robinson. His virtue, of course, consists in that he does not pretend to these. Rather, he is completely and perfectly himself.

So seldom does a man achieve this inner perfection that Mr. Frost's reputation is (and will remain) secure. But he has achieved this perfection by renouncing the possibility of becoming something greater. For the assurance of happiness, he has renounced the possibility of absolute greatness. This is not to criticise, but to define. Nevertheless, America, as a nation, has renounced happiness for the possibility of greatness. And so, in choosing a quiet happiness in preference to a turbulent greatness, Mr. Frost has merely cut himself off from the central American tradition. As Emerson once wrote: "You shall have joy, or you shall have power, said God; you shall not have both."

To illustrate by two of Mr. Frost's recent poems: "Once by the Pacific," and "Our Singing Strength." Once, gazing at the Pacific, Mr. Frost spent his boyhood. Then he returned to New England, and wrote of it. In his poetry he returned only once to the Pacific. Then he saw, vaguely, a portent:

It looked as if a night of dark intent
Was coming, and not only a night,
    an age.
Someone had better be prepared for
    rage.

Some one else had better prepare the tragic vision, not Mr. Frost. He, rather, has taken the course which he indicates in "Our Singing Strength." Instead of flying onward "with the driven flock," and striving to outdistance it, he has settled happily "back behind pursuit." He has chosen one way, but it is not the American way. Emerson and Whitman did not settle quietly "back behind pursuit," but left the driven flock behind them.

Although Mr. Frost disclaims the title of merely "the poet of New England," he is not, and can never become, "the poet of America." He lacks power.

Checklist of Additional Reviews

Mary Katherine Reely, ed. "A Selected List of Current Books." *Wisconsin Library Bulletin,* 26 (December, 1930), 347.

Louise Townsend Nicholl. "From the New Poetry." *Outlook and Independent,* 156 (December 10, 1930), 590.

"Robert Frost." *Booklist,* 27 (January, 1931), 197.

Louis Untermeyer. "One Singing Faith." *Saturday Review of Literature,* 7 (January 17, 1931), 529-30.

Elva L. Bascom, ed. *Among Our Books,* 36 (February 1931), 13.

C. Henry Warren. "An American Poet." *Fortnightly Review,* 129 (February 2, 1931), 282.

BOOK SIX

A
FURTHER
RANGE
BY
ROBERT
FROST

HENRY HOLT AND COMPANY
NEW YORK

A Further Range

John Holmes.
"In 'A Further Range'
Robert Frost Advances."
*Boston Evening
Transcript,*
May 29, 1936,
Book Review Section, p. 3

The first twenty years of Robert Frost's life were spent in coming of age, the second twenty in being an unrecognized poet, and the third twenty in being increasingly famous, until with his sixth book he stands undisputed as the first poet of his country. While he was waiting for poetic fame to get accustomed to him, he learned patience. Thus the intervals between his books have been long. "A Boy's Will" was published in England in 1913, when he was nearly forty. In 1914 "North of Boston" was also published there, and then both books appeared in the United States. Book Three, as he designates the volume when it was still in manuscript, was "Mountain Interval" when he decided on a title, and it came out in 1916. Then, having published three books in fairly rapid succession after waiting twenty years to do it, he let seven years pass before publishing "New Hampshire" in 1923. This brought him the Pulitzer prize, but

did not hurry him. Another five years went by, and in 1928 came "West-Running Brook." That was eight years ago, and now we have Book Six, called "A Further Range."

The title explains much that Mr. Frost's thousands of readers will have asked themselves about the book. He goes out beyond the New England farms and people for his subjects. Further to make this meaning plain, the volume is dedicated "To E. F. for what it may mean to her that beyond the White Mountains were the Green; beyond both were the Rockies, the Sierras, and, in thought, the Andes and the Himalayas—range beyond range even into the realm of government and religion." He goes still further to state his meaning by arranging the first group of poems in the book under the heading "Taken Doubly." Each one of these has a sub-title to point its other meaning, or one of its other meanings. Thus: "A Blue Ribbon at Amesbury, or Small Plans Gratefully Heard of." The accent is on "small," and that is about the extent of the comment on the world beyond the White Mountains. A farmer muses about breeding a greatly superior race of hens from his blue-ribbon winner; a small plan, a good plan, a plan to improve the quality of life at the source.

Then comes a section called "Taken Singly," and here are to be found most of the sort of poems that will have been expected from Robert Frost.

113

There are no sub-titles here. Then comes a group of "Ten Mills," to make a cent's worth of epigrams: this is followed by three poems, "The Outlands." There is a long poem near the end of the book, "Build Soil," delivered at Columbia in 1932, and two more short pieces, the last one called "Afterthought." His "Preface of Contents," as he calls it, lists fifty-one poems, the fifty-first being an intentional extra. Owners of his other books will be interested in the physical details of this one: there are no woodcuts in it at all: it is bound in a rather dark red, with large stamping in gold up the back. The type is excellent in appearance, bold and strong, and each page satisfying to the eye for that reason.

So much for the material data. The double-titling of the first poems is almost superfluous, except where a certain dry humor flavors them, because all of Mr. Frost's poems have always had an implied extra title, or several. During his Harvard lectures, he spoke of people asking him about the poem, "Mending Wall." "Doesn't it mean international boundaries, and that we must preserve them?" he was asked. "It goes much deeper than that," he answered. It does: that poem means that man will never build a wall or anything that will stand against weather and nature's destructiveness, but he will never cease trying, never cease repairing. He has always said things in this way; it is nothing new that he seems in "A Further Range" to be talking about Government and religion and certain mountains beyond those called White. It is simply that he points out specifically what he is doing. He is less hidden, more now the poet in the function of teacher or adviser or prophet. But there is no-

thing topical here; it is still universal at the same time that it is as regional as any poetry he has ever published.

Readers who seem to want their poets never to change, once they get used to them, will find their greatest satisfaction in the section called "Taken Singly." These are shorter, more lyrically intense, more personal in implication. Probably the most widely satisfying poems will at first be "Desert Places," "Leaves Compared With Flowers," "The Strong Are Saying Nothing," and "Neither Out Far Nor In Deep." At first, because they are like what is expected of Robert Frost. But the book grows steadily upon the reader, and like widening circles on a still pond, the understanding will reach the limits of all that is in the book. It needs no very great adjustment of the mind to accept the poet as shrewd commentator and preceptor. These elements have always been in Frost's poems and how he uses them.

His lines are surer than ever before if one can speak of degrees in the matter. For instance, in "Two Tramps in Mudtime," line after line speaks itself in the mouth with the turn and tone unmistakably intended; the poem reads itself. Not only that, but the poem, like many of the others, is a succession of small triumphs of perception and rapture. This poem is one of the best in the book, rewarding for the two reasons given. Favorites of this reviewer are the longest and the shortest pieces, the more than three hundred lines of "Build Soil" and the two lines of "The Span of Life." In the former, which is also called a Political Pastoral, Meliboeus the farmer and Tityrus the poet discuss the times, and how far out of joint they may be; both their last names are Frost. It is the poet who advises the farmer to build soil, and forget for a while about taking the produce to market, and he will do the same in kind.

In the new poem, "Neither Out Far Nor In Deep," which some hearers have mistakenly thought pessimistic, we get another statement of Robert Frost's attitude and belief that man will never conquer nature but that he will never cease trying. The first statement appeared in "Reluctance," in his first book:

Ah, when to the heart of man
　　Was it ever less than a treason
To go with the drift of things,
　　To yield with a grace to reason.
And bow and accept the end
　　Of a love or a season?

It has already been pointed out that the theme appears in "Mending Wall," man's ceaseless struggle against long odds. Again it comes in "Riders," in "West-Running Brook," where man buries his small fist in the mane of earth and will never be shaken off. Mr. Frost is too skeptical ever to be a romantic; to him nature is not at all the harmonious, beneficent, and purposeful force that the nineteenth century worshiped and created. He knows it objectively, no one better, but he does not pray to it. It is in the poem "Stopping By Woods on a Snowy Evening" that we see his philosophical position very clearly; he is called, he is tempted, but he "has promises to keep," and those promises are to mankind, and mankind is pitted against the dark woods forever. This is the modern attitude: Mr. Frost has always had it, and still has it.

He has continued to say the same sort of thing for twenty years, in six books, and found new ways, new tones

of voice. What we have in "A Further Range," then, is this attitude toward life re-stated, with a good deal more salt and bite than before, an even greater skill in sentencing, rhyming, and accenting, and a wider reach for his imagery and matter. The reader of Frost's earlier poetry will need time and effort to become used to parts of this book, but will find in it a perfectly satisfying number of poems of the sort he wants and expects, and will class them with the best the poet has ever written. Robert Frost has always been a man of wide knowledge, wide reading: he has never really confined himself to the one range of hills, but until now he has never so obviously pointed out the fact. That is really the only difference between this and any of his other five books.

"A Further Range" has been chosen as the June Book-of-the-Month, the second book of poetry so to be chosen, the first having been Edwin Arlington Robinson's "Tristram"; thus this is the first choice of a book of separate short poems.

Herschel Brickell. "Robert Frost's Book of Poems, 'A Further Range,' Filled With Expected Wisdom and Beauty." *New York Post,* May 29, 1936, p. 7.

... The familiar voice of Mr. Frost speaks in these poems, speaks with its accustomed deep wisdom and subtle humor, with its rugged strength, with a peculiar and individual beauty that is to be found nowhere else in the whole range of English poetry.

From the beginning Mr. Frost's complete originality has seemed to me to place him head and shoulders above any other American poet of his time, not because I set too much store by originality but because his kind is so much the distillate of a rare personality and has nothing to do with a deliberate flouting of tradition.

Those who know his work will find, then, what they expect to find in this book, and those who do not know it will discover a sufficient quantity of his best and most mature work to make them wish to read more.

There are fifty-one poems in "A Further Range," including the very short ones grouped under the subhead of "Ten Mills" and the longest is "Build Soil—a Political Pastoral," also one of the best, in which Tityrus, who is Mr. Frost, holds a dialogue with Meliboeus, "the potato man." . . .

Although there is more here [in "The Lone Striker"] than mere praise of solitude or meditation there is also the poet's own deep-rooted love of the country, which has nothing to do with a romantic or sentimental passion for "nature" and the back-to-the land cry of the neo-agrarians. . . .

My space runs short and I have said very few of the things I wanted to say. The truth is, that reviewing poetry, no matter how deeply it may move me, is not easy because of a lack of practice, but there is another truth in this case, which is that I know Robert Frost and consider him one of the few great and wise men I have ever met, greater and wiser even than his magnificent poetry, if it is possible to separate personality and work. Of course, it isn't really.

There is little reason to feel humble in the presence of most writers, but plenty here, and much in this new volume of verse to add to the feeling.

William Rose Benét. "Wise Old Woodchuck." *Saturday Review of Literature,* 14 (May 30, 1936), 6.

Two American poets of my time have possessed an integrity they wore so easily that no one could imagine them being otherwise. One is dead, Edwin Arlington Robinson, and one—we thank the gods—is still alive and writing with the same felicity and shrewd wisdom as of old. Of what does such integrity consist? One would say the chief element is being oneself. But then one really has to *be* someone in the first place. We soon find out what a man can do and how well he does it. But in the case of a major writer, the whole life becomes involved in the work. No matter how reticent he may be, or how objectively he may write, the whole man comes before us. A certain voice is speaking that is like no other. And that is not because he decides to adopt certain characteristics of style. His style grows out of his way of thinking and speaking. The commonplace, the specious, never achieve style. And no form of writing more betrays a man than the practice of what we call poetry.

Frost, I think, is a major poet, because he is, for one thing, a significant human being. He is definitely one certain kind of human being and has his own limitations; but he early decided to be his own man, and by so being he has developed his own special gift to the full. Probably there has only been one poet in the whole history of the world who could be all things to all men, and that was Shakespeare. Compared with that extraordinary phenomenon all other poets are minor, though all those we call major had their special gifts. But there is no use putting people into a pantheon too early, and it is of no particular importance, save to say that here is an American of whom we can rightly be proud as we are proud of Emerson, and that to me is saying a great deal.

But Frost is no transcendentalist. He is a close observer of the earth and the ways of man on the earth. When he first came into his own and wrote the line about "the highway where the slow wheel pours the sand" he demonstrated that he had the god-given faculty of reporting as a poet—of all beings at his best the most accurate—precisely what he saw. We have got used to that now, got used to his constantly opening our eyes to the things we overlook that he clothes with significance. He came before us quietly, with no blatancy, no fanfare, and at first we may have thought—we who were so romantic and so dramatic then—that it was commonplace. But how well he wears! No fuss and feathers. Just a man we like to listen to, because wisdom out of deep experience wells through his words.

So what?—says the young poet— you would have me become an admirable character first and all things poetic shall be added unto me? Unfortunately not. I am not forgetting the man of a craft. I suppose a thorough rascal might yet be a good stone-mason. That is a craft. So is verse. Frost is a craftsman of verse. But when verse somehow becomes poetry it certainly implies that you are not a rascal; at least, not a thorough one. Frost is a bit of a rascal at that. I think he is a bit of a rascal for being so intensely individual. But it is only that kind of rascality that gives tang to a man's work.

> Only where love and need are one,
> And the work is play for mortal
>   stakes,
> Is the deed ever really done
> For Heaven and the future's sakes.

And what does he say in the brevities of "Ten Mills"?

> Let chaos storm!
> Let cloud shapes swarm!
> I wait for form.

At a time of the most extravagant experimentation in verse, that is the craftsman speaking. No, young poet, you must learn the trade and how to use the tools! But brilliant as your performance then may be, behind it must be your own stature. Make no mistake about that! Nor, it has been doubted, is a cubit added merely by taking thought. But don't involve me in metaphysics!

> They cannot look out far,
> They cannot look in deep.
> But when was that ever a bar
> To any watch they keep?

When we find a man who can look out far and look in deep, and at the same time express himself clearly, to say that we should be grateful is understatement.

Frost's way of writing sometimes

looks so easy; it is only when you examine it closely and note the careful use of every word, and the way he has of stating anything with inimitable idiosyncrasy, that despair sets in. There have been some pretty good imitators, but they have not got far.

Why should I tell you what is in this new book? Read it! It is a small book, as books go; it is actually only the sixth book we have had from a man now with so large a reputation. And it is better worth reading than nine-tenths of the books that will come your way this year. In a time when all kinds of insanity are assailing the nations it is good to listen to this quiet humor, even about a hen, a hornet, or Square Matthew. Frost, as woodchuck, has been "instinctively thorough" about his burrow. Perhaps that is all it was from the first. Yet he has not only burrowed deep but sat often at the burrow-mouth to watch the great drift of the constellations. Wise old woodchuck! And if he has not got the whole "United States stated," he has got a good deal of life stated in original analogy and phrase. And if anybody should ask me why I still believe in my land, I have only to put this book in his hand and answer, "Well—here is a man of my country."

"Frost: He is Sometimes a Poet and Sometimes a Stump-Speaker." *News-Week*, 7 (May 30, 1936), 40.

Robert Frost doesn't subsist solely on potatoes any more. The old lean years are gone for good. Amherst College pays him a full professor's salary to have him around the campus a few months out of the twelve for informal readings and discussions. And other colleges and universities compete for his occasional lectures.

So he usually summers at his Vermont farm, turns to Amherst in the Fall, and moves to Florida in Winter, stopping at various ivy-clad auditoriums on the way back. There's plenty of time to write poetry, too. And magazines which rejected his stuff for two decades now print whatever fragments they can get.

But perhaps security and learned admiration have become a little too pleasant. Frost was not making the rounds of the colleges when he wrote such lines as these:

> Home is the place where, when you
>   have to go there,
> They have to take you in. . . .

His new book is disappointing. The 51 poems, quatrains, triplets and couplets—some of which have appeared in magazines—seldom attain the early heights. Frost's further range carries him beyond the Green and White Mountains into the realm of religion and government. But it is a downhill journey. "To a Thinker," admittedly directed at President Roosevelt, may well cause readers to wonder whether the author is a poet or a Republican.... "A Further Range" is worth its price. But readers who remember "North of Boston" and "Mountain Interval" must not expect too much.

Eda Lou Walton. "New Poems by Robert Frost." *New York Times Book Review,* May 31, 1936, pp. 1, 14.

In his introduction to "King Jasper," Robinson's last book of poetry, Robert Frost says: "But for me I don't like grievances. I find I gently let them alone whenever published. What I like is griefs—." This remark, made as preface to a statement about Robinson's own work, is a key to Frost's latest poems. These poems are, on the whole, more obviously humorous than is most of his earlier work. But under their humor runs a deep seriousness. In these new poems Frost takes account of this world of conflicting values. One must remember, of course, that he is in constant contact with young college poets, that he serves youth as a highly respected critic and confidant. As he himself says:

A youngster comes to me with half a
  quatrain
To ask me if I think it worth the
  pains
Of working out the rest, the other
  half.

I am brought guaranteed young
  prattle poems
Made publicly in school, above
  suspicion
Of plagiarism and help of cheating
  parents.

And youth, obviously, has been arguing with Robert Frost about poetry and propaganda, about the evil ways of the world, about socialism. Frost has been willing to listen, but, thinking all arguments over and reflecting on human nature in general, he comes to his own conclusions.

Essentially Frost concludes that the ways of the sturdy individualist are not altogether evil. He would have the farmer who loves the soil serve it, live on his farm and learn from it many values, not only economic but emotional. He does not like to see New England reaching out, by way of its pathetic hot-dog stands, for "city money." But he realizes the poverty of the stand owners. He does not believe poetry should be written "to move to action"—or that it will move to immediate action. But he is, on the other hand, certain that "the times seem revolutionary bad."

The question is whether they've
  reached a depth
Of desperation that would warrant
  poetry's
Leaving love's alternations, joy and
  grief,
The weather's alternations, Summer
  and Winter,
Our age-long theme, for the
  uncertainty
Of judging who is a contemporary
  liar
Who in particular, when all alike
Get called as much in clashes of
  ambition.

Frost notes from history the ways of mankind and concludes that these ways never run straight. As he puts it:

The last step taken found your heft
Decidedly upon the left.
One more would throw you on the
*   right.*
Another still–you see your plight.
You call this thinking, but it's
*   walking;*
Not even that, it's only rocking.

Throughout these poems, whether he is writing on modern conditions or on themes nearer to his heart, Frost draws together, by analogy, seeming contradictions and then laconically reconciles them as all pretty much a part of life and of man's ways of living it.

So much for the peculiar flavor of these last poems. Frost has left his "humanist" position, if he ever had it—which may be questioned—and become again pretty thoroughly himself. That he was ever named a "humanist poet" was due only to the fact that in his poems the moral is almost always implied. In his best poems, however, nothing didactic is forced. There was a brief period in Frost's writing when, probably because the poet had been made self-conscious by the critics, he inclined to moralize far too flatly. Actually, from the beginning, his work has shown two dangers, that of growing prosaic and that of growing didactic. But a fine, intuitive, poetic sensibility has, for the most part, kept him and his poetry safe.

Not, I think, a self-conscious, critical artist, Frost nevertheless knows instinctively what poetry is and what it is not. His poems, written in the

low key of reserved New England Yankee talk, simmer for a while over such pictures or events as his awareness singles out, then come to boil in such lines of poetic penetration and resolution as arise naturally from his subject. Again and again in Frost's better lyrics one hears the poet reflecting upon the humblest and the most touching aspects of daily living, then out of quiet speech the poet lifts his lines suddenly to ring with overtones of universal significance.

For I have promises to keep
And miles to go before I sleep
And miles to go before I sleep.

This poet knows his own power and gives his own type of advice:

At least don't use your mind too
*   hard,*
But trust my instinct–I'm a bard.

The poet, Frost is certain, must work from within. Today the world is forcing the poet to work too much outside himself:

We're so much out that the odds are
*   against*
Our ever getting inside in again.
But inside in is where we've got to
*   get.*

And "inside in" Frost touches most closely his own material. The best poems in this volume are not the arguments. Frost's genius is best expressed in his lyrics and in his dramatic monologues. "The Leaf Treader," a beautiful poem on age and possible death; "The Strong Are Saying Nothing," on much the same theme; "They Were Welcome to Their Belief," a poem on the hair turning white, are all new and splendid lyric poems. These poems enlarge Frost's unique place in our literature, a place that is, I believe, his for all time. Even the more amusing and lighter poems, "The Gold Hesperidee," on a New England farmer's solitary bacchanal, and "A Blue Ribbon at Amesbury," a poem on a prize pullet, are excellent. Close always to the center of his own feelings, able always to choose the correct detail to express himself, Frost holds his place as few poets of his generation do.

"The Lone Striker" tells us all we need to know of Frost's awareness of his world. First we have a picture of a workingman locked out because he was late. His machine, he reflects, will be idle. Then, philosophically enough, this worker begins to recall all that has been neglected in his factory life—friendship, fishing, solitude. And so he strikes:

The factory was very fine;
He wished it all the modern speed.
Yet after all, t'was not a church.
He never would assume that he'd
Be an institution's need.
But he said then and still would say
If there should ever come a day
When industry seemed like to die
Because he left it in the lurch
Or even merely seemed to pine
For want of his approval, why
Come get him—they knew where to
*   search.*

Such is Frost's position. He does not hate the mechanistic world as did Robinson. But he will not believe it rules all of a man's life. He recognizes necessity, yes, but that is all. "My right might be love, but theirs was need," he writes of two tramps begging a job of him when he was enjoy-

ing his own woodchopping. And this very quotation could, of course, be used against Frost by the young poets with whom he discusses the subject-matter of verse.

Frost's own life, one must remember, is his reason for his beliefs. Economically perilous it has been. But the poet did finally unite his avocation and his vocation. He farmed and he wrote of the farm and of farm people. He gave us poetry of the backwaters of a dying Puritanism, he preserved for us the speech and the thinking habits of a people who have not flourished in the modern age. Nevertheless, he would probably be the first to acknowledge that we have today poets unable to follow his advice, poets bred of cities and of collective living. Frost is aware of the new problems youth proposes and not scornful of them. He would, however, give to youth the truth as he has seen it.

These poems, like etchings in black and in white, are old New England to the core. And they are Frost, too. Who else could write a poem about two shoes, one wet in the Atlantic Ocean, one in the Pacific, because "two entirely different grandchildren got me into my double adventure" and conclude with such charm:

And I ask all to try to forgive me
For being as over-elated
As if I had measured the country
And got the United States stated.

The spirit of the man comes through this book as it has through all of Frost's volumes. Its meaning, given even in the dedication, "To E. F. for what it may mean to her that beyond the White Mountains were the Green; beyond both were the Rockies, the

Sierras, and, in thought, the Andes and the Himalayas—range beyond range even into the realm of government and religion," indicates that Frost has not stopped thinking. He is and has always been more a natural philosopher than a man given to theoretical or abstract thought. But today, even as in his youth, Frost is still taking in the world, making it a part of himself in so far as he is able. No one could ask more of a poet.

L. W. Payne, Jr.
"Robert Frost's New Book Has Characteristic Tone."
Dallas Morning News, May 31, 1936, Section 3, p. 10.

. . . Robert Frost has never belonged to any of these cliques or schools. He had long been interested in the making of poems—since his fifteenth year in fact—but he seemed satisfied to work alone and apart, absorbed, as it were in his own moods and thoughts, trying to learn how to "come into his own," trying to find which of the "two roads diverging in a yellow wood" to take. He finally decided on the path "less traveled by, and that has made all the difference." He seemed determined to find his own natural voice, to speak as an independent individual, to capture alive the speech-tones of the country folk, the natural rhythms of their every-day talk. In a conversation with me two years ago he declared that he remembered distinctly the moment when he found his own mode of expression, when he

ceased to be an imitative poet and became suddenly conscious of his own authentic and distinct voice, if still an unknown or unrecognized voice, in the poetic choir.

This was long before he went to England. For twenty years or more he had been working in the New England mills or on the New Hampshire farm which his grandfather gave him, or teaching in Pinkerton Academy, or bending steadily over his shoe (or poetry) last, when suddenly he quixotically sold his farm, gave up his several jobs, and went with his family to England to take a vacation, live leisurely and write poetry. In 1913 and 1914, respectively, he published in London two thin volumes, "A Boy's Will" and "North of Boston," and presently he found himself recognized as a new poet with an authentic voice, approved in England and also in America, where the two volumes were soon reprinted. From the date of his return to America Frost has been recognized as one of our major poets, and it now seems that he is at the very top of the list. . . .

"A Further Range" is Frost's sixth book, the other five having already in 1930 been gathered into "Collected Poems." It seems that it takes this poet just about half a dozen years to polish off enough of his authentic Frostian verse to make a small-sized volume. He keeps his pieces by him, mulls over them, coaxes them, tries them out on audiences, and finally, after so long a time, calls them finished poems. The fact that he revises incessantly, that he habitually keeps his poems by him and tinkers with them till they sing or speak in the authentic Frostian manner, has been amply proved in an article by R. S. Newdick which appeared in *Ameri-*

can Literature in the spring quarter, 1935. I could myself adduce similar evidence of numerous artistic improvements which Mr. Frost has made in the evolution of several of the poems in the volume now under consideration. For instance, I have before me early manuscript versions of the quaint little poem "Unharvested" and the playfully humorous and yet thoughtful one called "A Record Stride," the titles of which have been changed from the original ones of "Ungathered Apples" and "Past-Active Shoes," respectively; several verbal improvements and sometimes entirely new lines have been made for the final versions as they now appear in the printed form.

This new book, then, is altogether made up of authentic Frostian verse, but naturally not all of it is of equal value as poetry. I should say that the poet puts his best foot forward, giving his strongest and most significant poems in "Taken Doubly," the first division of the book; groups his most moving and singable lyrics in the second division, "Taken Singly;" follows with a less important group of eleven short philosophic aphorisms and humorous quips called "Ten Mills;" and finally fills up the balance of the volume with second-best material such as "The Outlands" and "Build Soil," this last being a long politico-humorous, pseudo-pastoral, riotously humorous poem. The book closes with "Missive Missile," a reverie on a prehistoric relic as an "Afterthought." ...

Newton Arvin. "A Minor Strain." *Partisan Review,* 3 (June 1936), 27-28.

One of the commonplaces about Robert Frost's work as a poet is that it renders so precisely and so fully the true essence of the New England spirit. Maybe it does, but surely that depends on what you mean by the phrase. Like all commonplaces, this one is compounded of truth and falsity in confusingly unequal proportions. There certainly is and, at least subterraneously, always has been a New England of which Frost's books are an authentic expression, and in the last two or three generations that New England has been peculiarly evident to the literary mind. It is the New England of nasalized negations, monosyllabic uncertainties, and non-committal rejoinders; the New England of abandoned farms and disappointed expectations, of walls that need mending and minds that need invigoration, of skepticism and resignation and retreat. How well one knows it!—that New England of so many unpainted farm-houses and so many frost-bitten villages and so many arid sitting-rooms. Yes, there is no denying that it exists.

It exists, and Robert Frost is its laureate. He has, at his best, the easiest and the truest touch a poet could have, and more than once he has found the perfect metaphor and the perfect cadence for that Yankee renunciation which, whatever else it is, is certainly what the Buddhists would call his own *dharma.* Everyone remembers the poem about the oven bird:

> The question that he frames in all
> but words
> Is what to make of a diminished
> thing.

Everyone remembers the poem about the bird at nightfall:

> At most he thinks or twitters softly,
> "Safe!
> Now let the night be dark for all of
> me.
> Let the night be too dark for me to
> see
> Into the future. Let what will be, be."

And—since no one expects that, even in a day when this philosophy seems as profitless as a dried-up well, Robert Frost will change his tune—everyone will be prepared to find the sentiment recurring, as it does more and more quaveringly, in this sixth volume of his. One of the metaphors now is that of clouds breaking, on a stormy night, in a not very starry patch of the heavens:

> Seeing myself well lost once more, I
> sighed,
> "Where, where in Heaven am I? But
> don't tell me!"
> I warned the clouds, "by opening on
> me wide.
> Let's let my heavenly lostness
> overwhelm me."

No doubt that is the way many people in New England, both plain men and intellectuals, have often felt, though certainly not, for the most part, very articulately. But it is not the way the Vermont marble workers seem to feel; it is not the way Roger

Baldwin acts as if he felt; and it is very far from being, in any absolute sense, the true essence of the New England spirit. On the contrary, it is expressive much more of the minor than of the major strain in Yankee life and culture; or of a strain that perhaps seemed almost the major one in a late, transitory, and already superseded period. Phillips and John Brown and Emerson and Ripley were quite as true New Englanders as Hawthorne and Emily Dickinson and Henry Adams: militancy, positiveness, conviction, struggle—such things have had a long and characteristic history in New England; they very evidently have as much life in them now as they ever had, and they are what Robert Frost has never succeeded—has, indeed, never wished to succeed—in expressing.

That, of course, was not his call as a poet, and though to say this does qualify, it does not minimize his admirable achievement. But it perhaps accounts for the disappointment one feels in reading these later poems collected in *A Further Range*. A writer naturally pays a price for committing himself to a point of view, and the price Frost has paid for cultivating a fruitless and rather complacent skepticism is apparently signalized by the gradual loss of the warmth and freshness of his early books and the relative dryness, emptiness, caprice, and even banality of some of the present poems. The best of them—a dozen, perhaps—are such as no other American poet could write. Most of them are pinched and poor in feeling and intellectually commonplace. Not much is added to the general fund of wisdom by the poem about the monkeys and the burning-glass, which ends with the line: "It's knowing what to do with things that counts." And surely a thousand minor poets could have told us what Frost tells us in the last stanza of "Two Tramps in Mud Time":

Only where love and need are one,
And the work is play for mortal
*   stakes,*
Is the deed every really done
For Heaven and the future's sakes.

Of such oracularities the worst one can say is that they will do no active harm: elsewhere in this volume one catches glimpses of the potential destructiveness in a way of thinking that might seem merely sterile. As Tityrus—in "Build Soil—A Political Pastoral"—Frost represents himself as explaining to his interlocutor, Meliboeus, the potato man, that bad as the times may be, they are by no means bad enough to justify a poet in taking sides in political or social conflicts:

Life [he says] may be tragically bad,
*   and I*
Make bold to sing it so, but do I dare
Name names and tell you who by
*   name is wicked?*

The answer is that Frost, with the splendid inconsistency of a systematic irrationalist, does dare to name names, and that like all professed non-partisans, he betrays his real animus when he names them. The potato man has asked him whether he thinks socialism is the thing needed, and Tityrus-Frost has answered that there is no such thing as "socialism pure":

There's only democratic socialism,
Monarchic socialism—oligarchic,

The last being what they seem to
*   have in Russia*

In these lines an old—and I should say a rather violent—bias reasserts itself. Remember the title poem of *New Hampshire:*

If well it is with Russia, then feel free
To say so or be stood against the wall
And shot. It's Pollyanna now or
*   death.*

From the poet whose ostensible refusal to take sides has resulted in complete silence on the savageries of Fascism in Italy, Germany, and elsewhere, I submit that these expressions come with something less than the best grace in the world.

On the jacket of this volume the publishers quote Mr. Mark Van Doren as saying that Frost's place "is and always has been singularly central." A less happy way of defining his distinction, it seems to me, could hardly be hit upon. His place has always been and still is on the sandy and melancholy fringes of our actual life, and his poetry derives its special, its estimable cachet, as well as its limitations, from that very fact.

James McBride Dabbs. "The Uses of Ambiguity." *Yale Review,* 25 (June 1936), 826-27.

I missed Robert Frost's recent talk on "The Uses of Ambiguity," but then I have his last volume of poetry. So far as that goes, he has always thought of life as an affair of hide-and-seek. Only he hides better now. Indeed, if he weren't so interesting when found—if found—his readers might stop looking. He plays the game with humor, and with courage. He's his own "Drumlin Woodchuck," sub-title "Be Sure to Locate"; but he doesn't tell us whether he means "Be sure to find," or the colloquial "Be sure to settle." Either makes sense; the first makes fun. He has a section, of brief poems, called "Ten Mills"—all I can think of is "Ten mills make a cent"—which contains *eleven* poems, one of them called "The Hardship of Accounting." There's method in this madness, but what is the clue? Nobody will ask him now; not after his warning, "If I had wanted you to know, I should have told you in the poem." So I shall never learn how near my guesses come unless I should catch him reading this review and surprise the proper twinkle in his eye.

The play goes on throughout the book. "A Further Range": beyond the White Mountains and the Green, "the Rockies, the Sierras, and, in thought, the Andes and the Himalayas—range beyond range even into the realm of government and religion"—where does the last range lie? Passing beyond the Andes, "The Vindictives," where one may perish "Of unsatisfied love of the high," he comes to the Himalayas, where the bearer of evil tidings turned aside from his useless journey, having found sufficient reason in a girl he met in a precipice valley in Pamir. Beyond the Himalayas, he comes to the Malverns ("but these are only hills," he says, trying to throw us off the track) where he finds

. . . The miracle

That never yet to other two befell,

the moon-made prismatic bow that

. . . Lifted from its dewy pediment
Its two mote-swimming
    many-colored ends,
And gathered them together in a
    ring.

Having come to the hills, the lowland-mountains (he still wants everything: earth and heaven—remember "Birches"?—dark woods and friends) he tells us how to stay at home there, in the hidden fields of a man's self, and build soil. *"This,* then is all." "But no, not yet." Beyond all two's, "he will sing us one-o." There is an "Afterthought," thought-of first, like a woman's postscript; a tragic, humorous afterthought, the story of the missive missile, the marked pebble thrown in vain across a million years. "Two souls may be too widely met."

Here, and in moods like this, where the play becomes deepest the poetry becomes best. And the beauty of it is that whoever wishes may penetrate immediately to this level, as in the lyrics of the section "Taken Singly." Here is the essential Frost: man taken singly: "Where, where in Heaven am I?" and the proof—and the bush for his hide-and-seek, if he wishes—is the music. Yet still he hides behind his smiles. Scientifically comparing leaves with flowers, he risks at last the singing lines:

Leaves and bark, leaves and bark,
To lean against and hear in the
    dark.

He teases even grief and care, how colloquially, and in what music!

"Yankee Poet."
Time, 27
(June 8, 1936),
83.

Robert Frost should be *persona grata* to two opposing parties: Yankees who never touch poetry and poetry-bibbers who shy at Yankees. For Robert Frost has a foot in both camps. New Englanders who pride themselves on their conservative shrewdness and rock-bound individualism think they recognize him as one of themselves; and poets know he is a poet. His prosiest lines are often lifted into verse by some piece of sly wit or canny wisdom, and at its best his poetry is as strong and simple as his Vermont landscape. . . .

Big-headed, heavy-lidded, unruly-haired Robert Lee Frost was 61 last March. That he was born in San Francisco is an unimportant accident: from his father back, his ancestors were New Englanders, and New England has been his home since he was 10. Something there was in Poet Frost that did not like a college, in his youth. He left Dartmouth after a few months, Harvard after two years. He worked as a mill-hand, a shoemaker, a newshawk, tried farming, then teaching. At 37 he sold his farm, took his wife and four children to old England. There he published his first two books of poetry *(A Boy's Will, North of Boston)*, made friends with such fellow-poets as Edward Thomas, T. E. Hulme, Wilfred Wilson Gibson, Ezra Pound. Thence he returned three years later to find himself a minor U.S. laureate. He turned to teaching again, for several years was "poet in residence" at the University of Michigan, now holds a similar position at Amherst. He has twice (1924, 1931) won the Pulitzer Prize for Poetry.

Admirers describe Poet Frost as looking like "Puck in a sack-suit," his voice as "the barking of an eagle." Others think he looks like a Yankee hired man, talks like one. . . .

Robert S. Newdick.
"Frost's Latest Poems."
Columbus Sunday Dispatch
June 14, 1936,
p. 6.

No one can say that Robert Frost floods the market with his books. This one, his sixth only, comes after a silence of eight years. But the thirty-eight poems in its hundred-odd pages example the forceful yet quiet perfection of feeling and thought and craftsmanship which Frost has always sought and attained.

The title of the book, "A Further Range," and the implications of a phrase in the dedication ("range beyond range even into the realm of politics and religion") may lead some to expect something strikingly new and different from the poet. There are, indeed, new emphases to be perceived, particularly in "Departmental," a fable told in terms of ants, in "To a Thinker," a piece with old origins but particularly applicable to the present, and in the brilliant "Build Soil," an avowedly political pastoral. Even these, however, are unmistakably Frostian, and most of the pieces in the volume are completely characteristic.

One's delight begins on first opening the book, for though there is neither a preface nor a table of contents there is a more than whimsical "Preface of Contents." The poems in the first of the six groups or divisions, headed "Taken Doubly," have secondary titles ("A Drumlin Woodchuck; or Be Sure to Locate"), ostensibly pointing out the underlying meanings, but really provided for the special delectation of the penetrating and understanding. Frost is sometimes a Puckish poet; not too often does one have him more than "loosely, as he would be held;" and that, to use the word with rich meaningfulness as he uses it, is part of the fun.

In the second group, "Taken Singly," the generally prevailing mood is different. After reading "Desert Places" or "Design," for instance, the reader will pause, not at all to smile, no matter how knowingly, but, much moved, to think. The variety of Frost is the variety of the full, rich life of one who has long felt deeply and thought profoundly.

Always, too, he is the poet, speaking the old with the freshness and vitality of an April shower. . . . Lovers of Frost's rendering of the out-of-doors in various places and seasons and moods will cherish especially his vivid "Iris by Night," the record of a stirring experience in the English Malverns, doubtless in company with his late friend, Edward Thomas. . . .

J. R.
"Mr. Frost Ranges Further."
Christian Science Monitor,
June 17, 1936, p. 14.

With the publication in 1913 of "A Boy's Will," Robert Frost was recognized as one of the few authentic voices in America. Since that time his place in modern poetry has been particularly individual. He has had nothing to do with extreme fashions. His compass has been wide enough to embrace any form, but he has never quite allied himself with any movement. He has maintained a certain dignity, a quietude of thought, which have held him to the center of his road.

Thus, in his new offering, "A Further Range," we find him still maintaining the "strong are saying nothing until they see." For him there are no "isms"; there is only man and his relation to nature and to his creator. And yet, strangely enough, the poet who has said, "most propaganda poetry is merely Marxian philosophy, thinly overlaid with verse," reveals himself, at this point in his career, as a propagandist. But with this difference: the Marxian poet is concerned with the philosophy of Marx, translated often into bad verse; Frost translates the philosophy of Frost into poetry.

"A Further Range" may seem, at first reading, a light book, a book of neat epigrams and homely wit. But a careful study is rewarding, for it contains much more than its surface may at times indicate. There are some poems here that the Frost of "North of Boston" might have written. But even these are a little more deeply penetrating, a shade more acute, perhaps, than even that excellent volume. In this section, for instance, we have a poem subtly comparing leaves with flowers. Again, the more familiar Frost shows himself in such poems as "Desert Places," "They Are Welcome to Their Belief," and particularly, "Iris by Night," which must stand as one of the most beautiful of the Frostian performances.

The indication that the poet had a double meaning in mind when he chose the title of his present volume is heightened and explained by his dedication, in which he says, ". . . beyond the White Mountains were the Green; beyond both were the Rockies, the Sierras and, in thought, the Andes and the Himalayas—range beyond range even into the realm of government and religion." Here indeed is a further range, not only of mountain but of thought, and yet the essential scene is unchanged, merely higher and more rarefied. Fundamentals have a way of remaining fundamentals. And one is able to go back to the first poem in Frost's first book and sum the whole matter up:

> They would not find me changed
> from him they knew—
> Only more sure of all I thought was
> true.

Elspeth Bragdon. "Robert Frost Again Sings New England." *Springfield Sunday Republican,* June 21, 1936, p. 7E.

The "constant reader" will find little to surprise him in the latest book by Robert Frost. "A Further Range" does step briefly into the field of political and economic conjecture, but in a manner so characteristic of its author that the venture is easily acceptable. For when Robert Frost writes of politics, he speaks as a man does who meets his neighbor in a country store or at a cross roads. "What's the world coming to?" the neighbor asks. With that certain knowledge possessed only by the dwellers in solitary places, Robert Frost answers. And good horse sense it is, too.

To say there is little of surprise is not to deny the familiar delight remembered in "A Boy's Will," "North of Boston," and "Mountain Interval." The easy swing of line and rhyme, the turn of speech that is as tangy as a McIntosh apple, the quick recognition of beauty down a dirt road—they are all to be found in this volume. Robert Frost can never forget his first love. The sun on New Hampshire hills will always quicken his pulse, the feel of an axe in his hand be kind and friendly. To him it is always new, and this feeling of discovery he shares with his reader.

For years critics went about proclaiming Robert Frost to be the spokesman of the American people.

That, of course, is extravagant. He is—and "A Further Range" is additional proof of the statement—primarily the spokesman of New England, of the corner of the states where granite fights an endless battle with crops, where the harvest is wrested from a grudging soil, and where the lush richness of valley and hillside mocks the average yield of the farmer's acreage. The very seasons are at war with each other in the country of which the poet writes, and man must of necessity, fight to win little or to lose greatly. He acquires an attitude of remoteness, this New Englander whom Robert Frost knows so well. What he must, he accepts, and with his own brand of philosophy. To know how stubborn a man can be, read "In Time of Cloudburst":—

"Let the downpour roll and toll!
The worst it can do to me
is carry some garden soil
A little nearer the sea.

"Then all I need do is run
To the other end of the slope.
And on tracts laid new to the sun,
Begin all over to hope.

The poem "At Woodward's Garden" is another parable of New England. Why bother to understand? "It's knowing what to do with things that counts." The countryman who sees the summer visitor whirl past in a motor car has learned the use and meaning of speed, and is not impressed. "The Master Speed" is the answer to those who are caught up in the rush of cities and who can still resent it—

"And you were given this swiftness,
not for haste.

But in the rush of everything to
waste,
That you may have the power of
standing still."

The old lyrical beauty which we have learned to associate with the poetry of Robert Frost is here in plenty. But, most precious of all, we find again the humor that is his peculiar gift. If, as in "Ten Mills" and "A Record Stride" the laughter is a little labored, remember that the farmer must fight for laughter as he does for everything he treasures. But it is right, this lumbering wit, shrewd and solid, echoed from the village post office when the mail is late. It is Robert Frost himself who tells us that "the way of understanding is partly mirth."

To his familiars, and, if there are any, to new acquaintances, "A Further Range" will prove a satisfying and heart-warming delight.

R. P. Blackmur. "The Instincts of a Bard." *The Nation,* 142 (June 24, 1936), 817-19.

It is a hard thing to say of a man grown old and honored in his trade, that he has not learned it. Yet that is what Mr. Frost's new volume, with its further range into matters of politics and the social dilemma, principally demonstrates. The new subjects, as they show themselves poetic failures, reflect back and mark out an identical weakness in poems on the old subjects. It is a weakness of craft, and it arises from a weakness, or an inadequacy, in the attitude of the poet toward the use and substance of poetry as an objective creation—as something others may use on approximately the same level as the poet did. Mr. Frost is proud of his weakness and expresses it in the form of an apothegm at the close of the poem called To a Thinker.

> At least don't use your mind too
> hard,
> But trust my instinct—I'm a bard.

If we may distinguish, and for more than the purposes of this review, a bard is at heart an easygoing versifier of all that comes to hand, and hence never lacks either a subject or the sense of its mastery; and a poet is in the end, whatever he may be at heart, a maker in words, a true imager, of whatever reality there was in his experience, and every resource of the mind must be brought to bear, not only to express his subject, to transform what Mr. Frost means by instinct into poetry, but also to find his subject, to know it when he sees it among the false host of pseudo-subjects. These are the labors of craft—in relation to which the bard's labors are often no more than those of a pharmacist compounding a prescription by formula. In the old bards we look mostly for history, in the modern for escape. Swinburne is the type of modern bard, Yeats of the modern poet. It may be that by accident a bard is also a poet—as Swinburne was; but a poet who writes with only the discipline of a bard writes unfinished poetry of uncertain level and of unequal value. That is the situation of Mr. Frost; and when, as now, he attempts to make poems of his social reactions without first having

submitted them to the full travail of the poetic imagination, the situation becomes very clear.

More precisely, taking the longest and most "serious" poem in the book, Build Soil—A Political Pastoral, which is a blank-verse dialogue between Tityrus the poet and Meliboeus the subsistence farmer, we find not poetry but an indifferent argument for a "one-man revolution" turned into dull verse. As bad religious poetry versifies the duty of an attitude toward God, bad social poetry versifies the need of an attitude toward society. Both the duty and the need may be genuine and deeply felt—it is our stock predicament and the great source of fanaticism and deluded action—but before either attitude can become poetry it must be profoundly experienced not only in intention but in the actuality of words. It is the object of craft, and only craft can secure the performance, to complete and objectify the act of experience. Craft in poetry is not limited to meter and rhyme, cadence and phrasing, gesture and posture, to any of the matters that come under the head of incantation, though it must have all these; for great poetry, craft is the whole act of the rational imagination. It must combine the relish and hysteria of words so as to reveal or illuminate the underlying actuality—I do not say logic—of experience.

Mr. Frost does not resort to the complete act of craft. His instincts as a bard do not drive him to the right labor, the complete labor, except by accident and fragmentarily, in a line here and a passage there. In a sense, his most complete and successful poems, the short landscape images where versification seems almost the only weapon of craft needed, are unfinished fragments. The good lines emphasize the bad, the careless, and the irrelevant, and make them intolerable; which is most often the case in activities which depend at critical points upon instinct. Instinct is only dependable in familiar circumstances, and poetry seldom reveals the familiar. A consideration of Desert Places, which is as good as any poem in the book, will show what I mean.

Snow falling and night falling fast
    oh fast
In a field I looked into going past,
And the ground almost covered
    smooth in snow,
But a few weeds and stubble
    showing last.

The woods around it have it—it is
    theirs.
All animals are smothered in their
    lairs.
I am too absent-spirited to count;
The loneliness includes me
    unawares.

And lonely as it is that loneliness
Will be more lonely ere it will be
    less—
A blanker whiteness of benighted
    snow
With no expression, nothing to
    express.

They cannot scare me with their
    empty spaces
Between stars on stars where no
    human race is.
I have it in me so much nearer home
To scare myself with my own desert
    places.

The same profound instinct that produced the first two stanzas of observation becoming insight allowed Mr. Frost to end his poem with two stanzas of insight that fails to reach the viable point of becoming observation. It may, practically, be a matter of bad rhyming in the fourth stanza, of metrical shapelessness in the third; but at the bottom, in so ambitious a poet as Mr. Frost, it must have been instinct that made the second pair of stanzas evade the experience forced into them by the first pair.

Horace Gregory. "Robert Frost's New Poems." *The New Republic,* 87 (June 24, 1936), 214.

For the past five or six years, Mr. Frost's critics have done him a curious disservice. They have insisted, both by implication and emphatic reassertion, that his poetry is the work of a major poet; they have assured us that Mr. Frost must take an embarrassed stand as the inheritor of a New England tradition which at its best includes the names of Emerson, Whittier and the recently rediscovered metaphysical poet, Jones Very. I doubt if Mr. Frost pretends to any such eminence, for to do so would place his work at singular disadvantage. If he were to step at any point crossing the paths of Emerson and Whittier he would be forced to carry an unwelcome load of social responsibility—and even, God save him!—give up forever "My own strategic retreat" and an obscure desire for a "one-man revolution."

No, Mr. Frost is not the kind of

poet, major or otherwise, that his critics have imagined him to be. I prefer to think of him in another set of associations where his virtues are more positive and his gains more genuine. I think of him as the last survivor of the "Georgian movement" which ran its course in England from 1911 to 1921. Of the poetry published during the first years of that period "A Boy's Will" was easily the best; it was Robert Frost, the American, who was to compress into one short line the philosophy of the entire movement: "Turn the poet out of door." His great advantage over his English contemporaries (such poets as Edward Thomas, Wilfred Gibson and W. H. Davies) was a quick ear for the use of the common words in everyday speech that are the property of uncommon poetry; and he has never lost his skill in using them, retaining even in his present book the familiar tang of Yankee vernacular.

Perhaps the title of his new book, "A Further Range," is half ironic; if not, I believe that he has heard too clearly the siren call of his unwise critics. It has always been Mr. Frost's particular virtue to make molehills out of mountains, to dig sharply, clearly and not too deeply into New England soil; so far as he has done this well, his integrity remains unquestioned. Beyond this range, however, he becomes self-defensive and ill informed; I refer to "Build Soil—A Political Pastoral," "To a Thinker," "A Lone Striker" and those thinly disguised platitudes in "Ten Mills"—all included in the present volume. If Mr. Frost sincerely wishes to identify himself with "A Drumlin Woodchuck" (one of the better poems in the book), to be "more secure and snug," why does he trouble his head about further

ranges into politics, where his wisdom may be compared to that of Calvin Coolidge?

There are two poems in this collection of fifty-one that are memorable examples of Mr. Frost's happiest insights and abilities: they are "The Master Speed" and "Provide Provide."

Leonard Feeney, S. J. "Coolidge with a Lyre." *America*, 55 (July 4, 1936), 309.

Robert Frost is said to possess an integrity all his own, one which has not yielded to the variations of present-day movements in poetry. This is true. It comes of his having a metaphysic of sorts. He believes, for instance, in an intrinsic difference between the intelligence of a man and an animal, doubting if a monkey will ever come "within a million years of an idea." He also is not exactly set against the idea of an after life. On this point he avers: "There may be little or much beyond the grave, but the strong are saying nothing until they see." Such a remark passes, as it were, for humility.

Frost also possesses a meager but very definite set of moral standards. He believes in work, thrift, in doing one's duty, in keeping one's peace, in minding one's business. "I can't help owning the great relief it would be to put these people out of their pain," he says of the city tourists who gather around the country roadside stands and infect the simple rural folk with their nervous ways of living. But he adds promptly: "I wonder how I should like you to come to me and offer to put me gently out of my pain." Such a remark passes, as it were, for charity.

Nevertheless, in the cramped world of those few certitudes which his mind allows him Robert Frost works with an unquestionable talent. His economy of expression and his ability to handle an intensely dramatic situation with a swift, apposite, home-spun phrase arouses one's admiration and exacts one's praise.

Frost is native neither to the White nor the Green Mountains, coming originally from California. But he passes for a Yankee and seems to take pleasure in being identified with the laconic, iron-shrewd characters he interprets. It is hard to believe that he chops nearly as much wood as he pretends to, or that cows, hens, and barnyards are his chief loves. He has been known to enjoy the tea life of social England and is at present a professor of poetry in a college. But this does not in the least detract from his quality as an artist. His poems are authentic because the people he treats of, while inarticulate themselves and unconscious to a great degree of their own dramatic value, are skilfully interpreted by this stranger and friend in their midst.

There is evidence in *A Further Range* that Robert Frost is in danger of mistaking his own powers. His *Build Soil—A Political Pastoral* is exceptionally bad. He is an artist, and only that, capable of reproducing in authentic accent the voice of a Vermonter in such a poem as *Voice Ways.*

His is not a wit, and his ten epigrams inserted in this collection are not successful. Neither is he capable of enunciating successfully an economic philosophy.

Rolfe Humphries. "A Further Shrinking." *New Masses,* 20 (August 11, 1936), 41-42.

There is an aspect of Robert Frost which criticism can dismiss with objugation; when you call him a reactionary————, or a counter-revolutionary————, you have, in essence, said it all. (Nor would Frost, who plays for it, care if you said so; he might be more het up if you were to denounce his poses and posturings in the presence of the young, for Frost, who professes to think Eliot a charlatan, has, for a long time, been getting away with a good deal in this regard.) Still, underneath the obduracy and all the affectation of homeliness, we were content to recognize something real, something racy and local, a tang and a twist, a combination of old Adam and New England (with more of old England than met the eye), a shrewd observation (though considerably less rustic than it liked to make out) of the foibles of beasts and men. And this (we thought at the time) was quite valuable.

Unhappily, the art of being sedentary is difficult to cultivate. You can't set [sic] indefinitely without running the risk of seeming paralytic, yet heightened reputation does not necessarily attend the act of getting up and going places. The man who, seated on his kallipyge, looks like Olympian Zeus, turns out, when he stands, to be of much less impressive stature, and when he strides the hustings, to be ridiculous and unimportant of gait.

So here. The further range to which

Frost has invited himself is an excursion into the field of the political didactic, and his address is unbecoming. The old Adam can still be recognized, but he wears his rue with a difference. His writing has always been more or less didactic, familiarly so, a product of ease rather than strain; if he fell short as poet, it was because his quarrel with himself was not sufficiently sharp. He falls short now because his quarrel with others is too much so; the new didacticism lacks authentic organic originality; it seems applied to the verse instead of pervading it, defective in the tone, color, and atmosphere that used to come from within and create a poetry harmonious, however low-pitched. Now Frost can be caught in the act of being what he most aims not to be—fuddled, garrulous, deaf, and ordinary. He does not bring to his art the discipline that he alleges for his wood-chopping. . . .

Critics of left critics are wont to allege that the latter do not find fault with, do not even notice, poor technique where the political ideology is acceptable. Often lamentably true; in our turn, we shall wait with pleasure for these others to point out, in Frost's present book, the tendency to prolong argument after the demands of art are satisfied, the failure of imagination, the uncritical inability to reject the bad material that weakens the good while making it look better, the clumsy prosodic accent, the homilies that sound like Guest instead of Frost. But we had better not hold our breath while we wait; maybe our adversaries will do these things, and maybe, as Ring Lardner had it, maybe San Francisco Bay is full of grape juice.

In so far as these are not wholly native deficiencies, the predestined consequences of original sin, they have been aggravated, in Frost's case, by the character of the audience he has attracted. The progress of any poet who professes himself a poet of individuality is bound to become involved in dilemma. What is the right number of hearers? Either he degrades himself with too many or isolates himself with none at all. Frost has found his most immediate audience on the college campus and its literary environs, a very select and upper-class type of village, to be sure, but hiatus of mind, countenance, and conscience can be found even here. What Marx describes as village idiocy is not limited to the steppes, and it is from his address to an admiring yokelry that Frost has undergone corruption, losing the precise effect in the general approbation, and substituting the poetic reputation for the poetic act. There is enough artist in Frost to resist these tendencies, but not enough to resist them entirely. We cannot be quite sure whether he has the saving grace to satirize his hick's apathy, or whether he is downright boasting when he remarks of his experience in Dives' Dive:

It is late at night and still I am
   losing,
But still I am steady and
   unaccusing.

As long as the Declaration guards
My rights to be equal in number of
   cards,

It is nothing to me who owns the
   Dive.
Let's have a look at another five.

Writing in *Partisan Review,* Newton Arvin has shown how Frost expresses "much more of the minor than of the major strain in Yankee life and culture"; and R. P. Blackmur, in the *Nation,* classifies him as a bard, rather than a poet, a bard being one who is "at. heart, an easy-going versifier of all that comes to hand, and hence never lacks either a subject or the sense of its mastery." In the old bards, Blackmur observes, we look mostly for history; in the new ones for escape.

These are valuable points from which co-ordinates of Frost's poetic position can be established. He has himself suggested another method of taking his measure—"How about being a good Greek, for instance?" If we look up his predecessors in the field of bucolic poetry, we have to conclude that alongside Theocritus, for instance, Frost looks like a pretty thin man. The Greek poet is much more joyous and zestful, his curiosity as a writer and observer more actively engaged, his variety of interest richer, his command of technique more sure. Nor is it the case that he was too simple-minded to know any better, too innocent to accept limitation; he possessed a highly sophisticated and civilized intelligence and lived in an age enough like our own to afford a fair comparison. Sicily and the island of Cos were to Alexandria not too different from what Frost's ideal New England is to New York. Material conditions would give Theocritus a little the better of it, and since material conditions not only help determine the boundaries within which the individual temperament works, but also operate on the individual temperament itself, perhaps we can blame on the state of New England the crabbed element in Robert Frost. Or should we leave it to our comrades

of the Freudian dispensation to account for the whys and wherefores of his insistence on narrowness?

A Further Range? A further shrinking.

Dudley Fitts. *"A Further Range."* New England Quarterly, 9 (September 1936), 519-20.

It is difficult to approach this book quite fairly. If only it were a first book, or if Frost's earlier work were less consistent in mood and technic, appraisal would be easier. As it is, one is distracted by a pre-established Frost manner: one expects certain idiosyncrasies of phrasing and diction, the texture apparently loose yet actually cunningly woven, the careful and felicitous colloquialism of tone, and consequently one is in danger of judging these poems not for themselves alone, but in the light of a preconceived notion of what they should be and what they should do. Accordingly, a good poem may seem invalid only because there is nothing in the manner to account for it; and a weak poem may achieve an apparent success because it evokes the glamour of a remembered excellence.

To be specific: one is perfectly at home with the short lyrics, such poems as "After-flakes," "Lost in Heaven," the fine "A Blue Ribbon at Amesbury," or "Desert Places." Here is Frost at his purest and best: no one else writes in this way, no one else has ever written precisely in this way. The quality is vibrant, eager, and curiously young; it is pure incantation, the more moving because it is managed by the simplest and homeliest means. In the same tradition are many of the longer, more dramatic pieces: "The Gold Hesperidee," for instance, and "The Old Barn at the Bottom of the Fogs." If these poems are generally less distinguished than the lyrics, it is because they are discursive, and because they more easily admit two elements which have marred much of Frost's work for at least one of his readers: an obvious didacticism, and a ponderous kind of playfulness.

It is in the long poems at the end of the book, however, that we encounter something unexpected. It is an extended statement of an attitude that has been only implicit before: a social attitude, satirically and most ambitiously exploited in "Build Soil—A Political Pastoral." And it is precisely here, where one would naturally have looked for the strongest writing, that the manner seems to break down completely. The voice is still the voice of Frost, it is true, and all the tricks are here; but the diction is faded, the expression imprecise, and the tone extraordinarily tired and uneasy. It is a strange thing that Robert Frost, pondering the problem of a sick society, should suddenly become ineffectual, should seem unable to deal abstractly with matters that he has powerfully suggested in many of his best lyrics. It is almost as though he had taken one of those incomparable lyrics—say "A Blue Ribbon at Amesbury," where much is implied—and drawn its essence out into an extended "message" poem, a diluted form of

Thanks, thanks to thee, my worthy friend,
For the lesson thou hast taught.

It is not that his social attitude suggests nothing new: is something new demanded? The trouble is that it suggests nothing at all so much as a man who wishes he had never brought up the subject in the first place. Whatever the reason, the "Political Pastoral," and three or four pieces like it, elaborate a quality hitherto not to be found in Frost: a sterility.

It is as a lyrist in a special field that Frost is supreme, and *A Further Range* is a book of the greatest distinction in so far as it is a reaffirmation of a standard already established. . . .

Louis Untermeyer. "Robert Frost: Revisionist." *American Mercury*, 39 (September 1936), 123-25.

With each new book, Robert Frost continues to establish himself as the most rewarding and likewise the most richly integrated poet of his generation. He has no contemporary rival in America, and only William Butler Yeats can challenge his pre-eminence as the most distinguished poet writing in English today. *A Further Range,* the sixth of his interrelated and yet varied volumes, solidifies his position.

By what name that position will finally be known will be determined by historians more detached than the present appraisers. Erudite and sometimes persuasive theses have been written proving Mr. Frost to be (a) a classicist, (b) a symbolist, (c) a humanist, (d) a synecdochist (Mr. Frost's own half-serious classification), and

(e) a glorified Neighbor. Lately, since the creation of political parties in literature, it has become the fashion to refer to him as a "centrist". All of the designations are plausible, all have some justification, and none is a satisfactory measure of the man. Actually, he is far more radical than the extremists. But his is an old radicalism not dependent on new slogans, or eccentricities of expression, or verbal vociferousness. It is a highly personal and intensely American radicalism, not unlike the individual insurgence of Thoreau and the quiet but thoroughgoing rebellion of Emerson. In the mellow and quizzical "Build Soil," which is subtitled "A Political Pastoral," and which is an undisguised Socratic dialogue, 1936 model, Mr. Frost reveals his freedom from cant and mob-thinking:

I bid you to a one-man revolution—
The only revolution that is coming.
We're too unseparate out among
     each other—
With goods to sell and notions to
     impart. . . .
Don't join too many gangs. Join few
     if any.
Join the United States and join the
     family. . . .
It is a bargain, Shepherd Meliboeus?

To which the other pastoral poet, Mr. Frost's alter ego, replies:

     . . . . I agree with you;
We're too unseparate. And going
     home
From company means coming to our
     senses.

But, though there is little politics in most of his poetry, the verse is not without broader challenge. From the early "Mending Wall" to the just-published "The White-Tailed Hornet," Mr. Frost has questioned routines of thought. He has disguised his intransigence in understatements, in offstage whispers, in whimsical circumlocutions, but his penetrations have been none the less thorough. He challenges the pat conclusions of the formalist in art and education; he scorns a stereotype in expression no more (and no less) than an emotional cliché. In "The White-Tailed Hornet" he cannily—and completely—upsets the favorite theory that instinct in the lower animals is a sort of higher intelligence. "Desert Places" exposes the platitude of the external dark and frightening space by quietly suggesting the vaster deserts within. So with most of his poems old and new, the longer ones to be "taken doubly", and the lyrics to be "taken singly", many of which are among Mr. Frost's deepest. If I were called upon to add to the categories, I would drop the classicist, the bucolic realist, and the localist. I would call him a revisionist. It is the power not only to restate but to revise too easily accepted statements which is one of his great qualities, and it has been overlooked to a surprising degree.

If it were not for the columnist and vaudeville connections which belittle the term, I would be tempted to add "humorist" to the categories. Not that Mr. Frost would resent the appellation, debased although it has become. Introducing E. A. Robinson's posthumous *King Jasper* a few months ago, Mr. Frost slyly satirized novelty for its own sake and insisted that the style was not only the man, but that "style" was the way the man takes himself. "If," he continued, "it is with outer seriousness, it must be with inner humor. If it is with outer humor, it must be with inner seriousness." The sentences were, primarily, a tribute to Mr. Robinson; essentially they are an almost perfect description of Mr. Frost. His style, so characteristic, so seemingly simple and yet so inimitable, so colloquial and so "elevated", has a way of uniting opposites. It combines fact and fantasy with a baffling, even a matter-of-fact, tone of voice. Or, rather, it is not so much a combination as an alternation, an intellectual prestidigitation, in which fact becomes fantasy and the fancy is more convincing than the fact. The inner seriousness and the outer humor continually shift their centers of gravity—and levity—and it must be plain to all but the pedants that Mr. Frost's banter is as full of serious implications as his somber speculations, that his playfulness is even more profound than his profundity.

In *A Further Range,* in which even the title is a deprecating and yet sentimental pun, the playfulness is extended further than in any of his five preceding volumes. Sometimes it takes the form of straightforward jocularity (as in "Departmental, or My Ant Jerry," and a few of the epigrammatic "Ten Mills"), by no means a new note for the author of "The Cow in Apple Time" and "Brown's Descent, or The Willy-Nilly Slide," to say nothing of the privately printed one-act one-page "play" entitled "The Cow's in the Corn." Sometimes the humor is subtler, as in "The Gold Hesperidee" and "At Woodward's Gardens"; sometimes it is sagely critical, as in "To a Thinker" and "The Vindictives." And, to balance the side-spring and the satire, the new collection contains some of Mr. Frost's quietest and richest

speculations. "The Lone Striker" and "Two Tramps in Mud Time" must be set down among the poet's finest soliloquies; "Lost in Heaven," "Desert Places," "A Leaf Treader," and "The Strong are Saying Nothing"—three of these originally published in THE AMERICAN MERCURY—will take their place among his most memorable and moving lyrics.

The reader is grateful to Mr. Frost not because he has learned something, but because he has experienced something. He has been fortified by the poet's serenity, strengthened by his strength. He has been intellectually revised and spiritually revived.

LeGarde S. Doughty. "More Good Poems." *Commonweal,* 24 (September 1936), 450-51.

One has learned to expect of Frost just what this new work gives: elegant simplicity, and a degree of inspiration that precludes any tack toward such legerdemain as takes in some critics completely and makes others wonder if, after all, the hand is quicker than the eye. When Frost fails it is not through subterfuge. Except when toying with consciously trivial verses, he is resolved to be the poet at every onset; and his failures are intermittent sinkings into anemia, when his eyes see and his tongue speaks, poetically, but his blood becomes thin. Singularly, some of Frost's greatest poetry occurs near the border line of this lassitude; then he is master of emotion, and will not go to the other extreme by losing his balance in any eruption of sublimated mob spirit.

A past winner of the Pulitzer prize, Frost, in his narrative pieces, has a kinship with the current winner. Both have a propensity for New England genre; and Coffin's trochee opposed to Frost's iambus is more the distinguishing mark than any essential. . . .

A chart of the present book would show a horizontal line of moderate elevation running from the first to the central pages; there it would rise perpendicularly to the position of Frost at his uppermost; it would culminate in "Iris by Night"; near the close it would drop to its first level and run thus to the end, except for a sharp rally at the longish "Build Soil—a Political Pastoral," a grand achievement in poetical logic. . . .

Edgar C. Knowlton. "Poems by Robert Frost." *South Atlantic Quarterly*, 35 (October 1936), 460-62.

It is a pleasure to have another characteristic volume of poetry from Robert Frost so soon after his remarkable introduction to *King Jasper,* the last poem of his friend, E. A. Robinson.

The manner of Robert Frost has never been pontifical. From the days of the invitation of "I shan't be gone long. You come too," he has shown a winsome humility. With that grace are independence and respect—a respect for others and for oneself. It is a

grave mistake to believe that this duality lacks social vista and ignores the fundamental perspectives of society at large. For example, many of us today either want work or know of others who are out of a job. "Two Tramps in Mud Time" submits a report on several related aspects of the present (yet recurrent) difficulties of living. A doctrine now in vogue opposes a man's splitting wood for the love of doing so; rather he should leave the job to a professional, an expert, on the ground of the latter's need. And an amazing parallel dictum avers that no man should love the work in which he is engaged. Mr. Frost retorts:

My object in living is to unite
My avocation and my vocation
As my two eyes make one in sight.
Only where love and need are one,
And the work is play for mortal
    stakes,
Is the deed ever really done
For Heaven and the future's sakes.

One Marxian critic, granting that Mr. Frost is truly a poet, has found in him an absence of views on industrialism, of disruption from scientific hypotheses, and of Freudianism, and fears that the lack, despite advantages, will prove in the long run deplorable. But is the deficiency genuine and fundamental? The poem quoted is surely an example of ideas applicable to industrialism. In typical half-humorous verses on the white-tailed hornet, a competent hawker "for flies about the kitchen door," Mr. Frost examines the age-old doctrine of a basic distinction existing between man and animal, or in this instance, between a man and an insect. Man makes mistakes because he has reasoning power, and can choose, because he has consciousness; no wasp-creature of instinct should aim at a real fly and miss it, even if it errs with nail heads in the floor or pretends that a huckleberry is a fly. But put theory to the test of observation, and no longer is it true that

To err is human, not to, animal.

Mr. Frost therefore asks, "Won't almost any theory bear revision?" And he concludes modestly,

Nothing but fallibility was left us
    [men],
And this day's work made even that
    seem doubtful.

Such a remark can scarcely be anything but an allusion to the latest science and psychology as well as to ancient dogma.

Repeatedly the poet performs a service by his isolation of the traits and qualities of man, and by pondering on them in connection with the homely phenomena of grasshoppers, hens, woodchucks, bluebirds, the bark, leaves, and blossoms of trees. By so doing, he suggests, we may "take upon's the mystery of things, as if we were God's spies," and in our own generation strive toward re-ascertaining the fundamental principles of life. Thus perhaps Freudianism becomes but a phase of a more all-embracing difficulty: how shall we deal sensibly and effectively with any misdirected regulation of the natural, of human nature?

Nobody was ever meant
To remember or invent
What he did with every cent.

In "Build Soil—A Political Pas-toral" occur copious hints—some playful, some earnest—about naming names, about socialism and forms of government, about free-this-and-that, and the like. He rejects extensive cultivation as any sound farmer, responsible to the future, in all the history of agriculture has done. "Build Soil" means intensive cultivation. Common sense understands that there should be only born farmers for this work.

It is a genial experience to perceive unexpected beauties in our surroundings, and to exchange understatements and unexpressed meanings with this representative of New Hampshire, to stand quietly with him on a secure height, seeing range rise beyond range toward the horizon.

E. Merrill Root. "Here Is Victory!" *Christian Century,* 53 (October 7, 1936), 1329-30.

Today is not the time for a definitive estimate of Frost. This, his finest book, indicates no end, but magnificent growth toward a final word that he may take two books to reach. But to appraise this book, I must retrace the foot-hills and mountains he has already climbed before, on this further range, he salutes the sun.

Frost began with the grace of "A Boy's Will"—like a day in March, with chime of melting snow, old-porcelain skies, straight black trees against snow-pale hills. It was no mountain, but a birch-embroidered hill. Then upon a world surprised into acclaim of poetry far too good for it, came "North of Boston"—tanged, earth-based, shrewd—with its smiling tenderness for the little calf that totters, the singing bounce of "The Code," the lilac grace of "Blueberries," the moon that hit the little cloud and made a dim row (and beauty never surpassed in American poetry). It was a mountain on whose shoulders people dwelt; whose summit was dark with pines and white with clouds. "Mountain Interval" was a savoring of this world of a Yankee Virgil—the white exquisite dream of "Birches," the grace notes of one who wandered out of beaten ways, half searching for the orchid Calypso, a high peak of backward vision. "New Hampshire" was an even finer book—of etched fire and ice, of a man stopping immortally by snowy woods, of azure water-lizards running from under the bearskin-rug of snow, of the ghost's lightning-scribble of bones, of the spring piper's silver canticle that winter death never kills. It was a book of color rich yet cool; of lilac grapes against snowy birches; of stars moving in white fire over even higher mountains. "West Running Brook" was a bolder venture from the world north of Boston into the inner weather of Robert Frost. He dipped the moon in water, and watched the colors run and wonder follow; or, in "Acquainted with the Night," "West Running Brook," "Bereft," wrote perfect artistry of black-and-silver. It was a mountain of transfiguration, where he saw east, and west, and "the something sending up the sun."

But what *is* the essential Frost? The usual nonsense of the usual nit-wits is often the inversion of his truth. He is called "realist," "objective," a "New England" poet. But a realist is one who subordinates the infinite center to the finite circumfer-

ence; Frost uses the finite circumference only to give form to the infinite center which forever troubles him with beauty. An objective artist flees his own heart; Frost puts out a bold hand amid the harp-like morning-glory strings of beauty, and plays the unseen tenderness that moves about us. A "New England" poet splashes local color; Frost catches the timeless essential American. Moreover, New England to him is only the stage of a four-dimensional life extending beyond the *sigmas* and *taus* of the constellations, or the homesickness of Ruth amid the alien corn. He slyly entitles "North of Boston" what is really *Center of Robert Frost;* and "New Hampshire" what is really his *Song of Myself.* Finally, instead of being hard, cold, objective, his poetry sings and shines; builds rhododendron-colors of splendid imagery; glows with magic like witches' oils.

Also he is one of those forever *growing* poets (like Shakespeare) who strangely develop *not* in "worldly wisdom" but rather, by contact with the world, find ever more deeply and express ever more perfectly their own difference from the world. Only the greatest poets grow, like Frost, ever more surely into themselves.

Finally, Frost seeks always to hint infinitely in the finite, making each symbol a focal glass that gathers the diffused sun into white fire. If we see only the thing that he says, we shall forever miss what he says; like the greatest artists everywhere, his music lies on the other side of sound. His birches are only a flying trapeze to heaven; his Drumlin woodchuck only the eternal Thoreau of the human heart.

Thus we reach "A Further Range." It is, indeed, a further range—rugged and eternal, whence a "lone striker" with his "one-man revolution" gives his shrewd rugged individualism of the heart—the eternal anarchic and yet communal individualism that transcends all revolutions. It is in the great American mood, and tradition, yet as modern as a roadside stand, as much Frost as his own flesh. His art was never more potent, his speech never more tanged, his symbols never more perfect. Here is quintessential Frost. The book ranges from sheer rhododendron beauty of color (see "Two Tramps in Mudtime"), through the wistful tenderness and sly understanding humor of "A Roadside Stand," into the transcendent smashing wisdom of "To a Thinker" and the cosmic victory of "In Time of Cloudburst"—most triumphant word yet spoken in contemporary America. And how much this omits! There is singing wisdom in "Build Soil" comparable to Lao-tse; criticism of totalitarian states in "Departmental" like the edge of a surgeon's laughing knife. "A Leaf Treader" is perhaps the most beautiful, strange, profound lyric ever written in America, a dark wind from beyond the world, fanning the enduring soul to whiter flame, in words and music of beauty so terrible the heart almost breaks with joy.

Here is victory! Here is a man who has come through; who has grown quietly, steadily, toward perfected art and a self to express; who savors and evaluates and sees and says. It is augury and portent, triumph that is heartening in time of cloudburst. Where else in modern American literature do we discover a man who has humor, and earth-based tang, and fearless vigor, who is also a mystic in touch with the fourth dimension, seeing eternity transcending time and

life laughing at death? Serene amid collapse and catastrophe, above the plangence of the wars and revolutions of time, yet earth-vivid, flesh-accepting, here is the artist of victory!

To try to review "A Further Range," is like picking blueberries in a New England pasture: always the fruit of sky upon these turquoise orchards lures and teases you with a richer and newer beauty just beyond, till there is no end. It will take America two hundred years to garner and savor all this fruit of sky, and then we shall only have begun: for here is eternity.

Morton D. Zabel. "Poets of Five Decades." *Southern Review*, 2 (1936-1937), 171-73.

Neither Robert Frost nor Marianne Moore has encountered these extreme needs and distresses of "growth." They possessed their characteristic manners from the beginning of their public careers, and maintain them inimitably down to the present moment. They have met no necessity of adapting or changing their styles in order to sustain public interest, since one of them discovered a permanent hold on popular approval from the start, and the other has found none whatever. Both have published sparely: Frost's new volume, *A Further Range,* is his first in eight years, and Miss Moore's luxurious book adds only five new poems to the eleven additions she made last year in her *Selected Poems.* At every point their talents diverge except in their consistency of purpose.

Frost practices his readable art of homely phrase and tough Yankee shrewdness; Miss Moore exercises again the severely calculated technique of an uncompromising originality.

Frost's new poetry does not differ essentially from his earliest in *A Boy's Will.* If it has advanced beyond the delicate sensibility of that charming volume, it does so by the sharper accent of its eccentricity, and by an exchange of younger impressions for the cannier skepticisms of maturity. His work from the beginning has described the provincial hinterland of the American conscience; it has worked out its salvation far removed from literary fashions and the discords of intellectual society. It has profited by the same kind of stoic detachment that Robinson employed in holding to his viewpoint. Frost's foreword to Robinson's posthumous volume of last fall, *King Jasper,* was an interesting indication of how these two men formed their judgments of the modern world without ever mixing in its perils. Frost praised Robinson for having a sense not of life's grievances but of its grief. This meant an estrangement from the rebel generation now around him, and stated his belief that individual tragedy is more essential to a poet's purposes than the ephemeral passions of mass protest. Thus he still concentrates upon the humblest figments and minutiae of human wit or misery, writing largely within his own rumination, and employing the *sotto voce* of conversations with himself. When he says in "Ten Mills" that

I never dared be radical when young
For fear it would make me
    conservative when old

he shows himself temperamentally a noncombatant, a tolerant pacifist. This is both a sound and a cynical view of the destiny of human causes; it is a view capable of shrewd wisdom but rather dry poetry. And in *A Further Range* his fortitude unfortunately takes on in many poems the rather complacent mock-innocence already hinted at in *West Running Brook.*

The time particularly needs genuine disinterestedness in its poets, and Frost stands beyond all suspicion of the risks or histrionics of political activity, but the question rises whether he describes the human conscience in a form sufficiently robust to bring his insight to mean much beyond a personal satisfaction in honesty, or even a discreet contempt of more reckless forms of honor. There is here no discernible advance in his powers. He includes poems of trivial oddity like "A Record Stride," and gnomic bits of philosophy like "The White-Tailed Hornet" and "At Woodward's Gardens." There is comparatively little to rival his finest work, but a good deal to make one fear that a certain vanity has bred stiffness in his sympathies and vision. The poet, in other words, has sunk beyond a safe degree into that unconscious animal patience which characterizes his New England farmers. He shares their obliviousness of keener struggles instead of treating it, in the manner of Hardy, as a symptom of heroic trust. Frost's best work resists such reproof fully; it made classic use of the spiritual temperament of the American peasant. Here there are signs that this moment of classic realization has passed. Uncritical indulgence has allowed pieces of dull writing and petulant wisdom to enter this volume. There are, however, some poems of great beauty, notably the sonnet "Master Speed." . . .

Basil De Selincourt. "Poets and Pessimism: Idealism in the Storm." *The Observer* [London], April 4, 1937, p. 5.

Well, here is Robert Frost, his voice not, I candidly admit, the voice of a people, though one would be right to call him a typical New Englander: a typical New England individualist, the upholder of a great cultural tradition, a man of courageous hope and constructive counsel, an unrepentant idealist, and as sound an artificer in words as any living. I suggest that the kind of poetry he writes, with the kind of message appropriate to it, the message he delights to deliver in subtle and sly hints, as a special aptitude to the critical conditions of our day, and that it is peculiarly worth our while to enjoy it and ponder it and make it our example. . . .

Build soil, he says; and in another connection he might have said, take ballast. The scheme is, not to loose the idea, but to get somewhere with it. The scheme is to work it and know how it works, and to give it out only as it overloads you with its success and solidity. And that, I may say, is just as much a poetical as a practical scheme: Milton, of course, propounded it and did it dazzlingly and gigantically; but it holds proportionately at all levels.

There is probably such a thing in poetry as survival value; and it may

be because his lot has been cast in an age of soaring ideals and annihilating disasters, that Robert Frost, offering us the virtue of his poetry as an almost imperceptible leaven, administering his nectar to our malady in homeopathic doses, has maintained equilibrium and serenity, where so many others have foundered or capsized. His work is possibly a suggestion to us that the times have their new demand for poetry too. No doubt in a Fascist or Communist state poetry can continue to be written out of a mass emotion which must of necessity rest on illusion in the main. But if, in a free society, we more and more recognise that truth lives only as the individual sees and realises it, then surely individual vision, individual embodiment, with its nicety, its personal distinctiveness, its poised and piercing articulation, becomes, in a sense, a presupposition of our poetry. Our poetry must be in a new sense individual before it can be shared; it must not presume on universality but attain, if it should attain, to it by slow degrees.

Frost is a poet of delicatest degrees, but universal in this sense that he sees in these degrees the very secret of truth. And, one more point, the poet, in his eyes, is the man who, whatever he has to do, does it completely:—

Let me be the one
To do what is done

is a favourite motto of his; even if what is to be done is nothing better than splitting beech logs, he likes to go ahead in the spirit of poetry—for necessity itself is poetry if you can learn to take it so. I think I would give my prize in his new volume to the piece, "Two Tramps in Mud Time," where not so much as a syllable strays in nine packed stanzas, at end of which he resigns to the out-of-works the chopping he would so much have liked to do himself; meditating for consolation thus:—

But yield who will to their
   separation.
My object in living is to unite
My avocation and my vocation
As my two eyes make one in sight.
Only where love and need are one,
And the work is play for mortal
   stakes,
Is the deed ever really done
For Heaven and the future's sakes.

"Ever" and "really" are the vital words; to do it some time, somehow, we can all manage—with hopes, of course, of scrambling into Heaven.

Robert A. Newdick. "Robert Frost Speaks Out." *Sewanee Review,* 45 (April-June 1937), 239-41.

Those simple readers who expect a poet early to set his course and always thereafter to steer that course unswervingly will be somewhat disappointed in Robert Frost's latest book, for with firm if unuttered insistence, symbolically made clear in the dedication, in *A Further Range* he lifts up his eyes to other than the customary hills and in characteristic metaphor speaks out even on such

hitherto unwonted subjects as government and religion.

No sluggard, and in crisp couplets of iambic trimeter as effective as a rapid succession of left hooks, in "Departmental" he goes to the ants for his funereal parable on regimentation, restraining himself in sharp conclusion to the tellingly litotic exclamation:

It couldn't be called ungentle.
But how thoroughly departmental.

(Some admirers will regret that the sophisticated connotations of "frightfully", the adverb first employed, gave way in revision for book-publication to the more suave "thoroughly".) In "To a Thinker", a title originally extended on editorial supplication by the phrase "in Office", he says his say—lightening it with an abundance of sub-malicious humor—on glib-tongued political opportunists.

Obviously the most notable of the pieces in which Frost provocatively projects his philosophy with regard to the problem of the individual and society is "Build Soil", a "political pastoral" spoken at Columbia University, May 31, 1932, that is, before the national party conventions of that year. Much like the title-poem in *New Hampshire,* "Build Soil" is essentially conversational, Frost talking as only Frost can talk, searchingly, socratically, consecutively, though here, in the character of Tityrus, with Meliboeus for a foil, and, throughout, with more marked compactness and point. The old-new emphasis is, of course, on the greater strength of individualism:

I bid you to a one-man revolution—
The only revolution that is coming.

We're too unseparate out among
each other—
With goods to sell and notions to
impart.

. . . .

We congregate embracing from
distrust
As much as love, and too close in to
strike
And be so vert striking. Steal away
The song says. Steal away and stay
away.
Don't join too many gangs. Join few
if any.
Join the United States and join the
family
But not much in between unless a
college.

Other pieces which might well be
spoken of in connection with Frost's
views on government and problems in
which government has lately taken a
hand are "The Old Barn at the Bottom of the Fogs", "A Roadside Stand",
and several of the illuminating
flashes labelled "Ten Mills" (of which,
in quiet fun, there are eleven), particularly "Precaution". As with Archibald MacLeish's recent *Public
Speech,* neither communists nor fas-
cists will find their kinds of prop-
agandistic utterance in *A Further
Range,* but with regard to Frost the
volume ought to lay once and for all
the absurd strawman representations
of such straining thesis-critics as
Granville Hicks and Michael Gold.

Beliefs and convictions, religious
and quasi-religious, in terms of personal philosophy, lend ample expression through all of Frost's books. In
the present book, for those who care,
the focus is sharpened suggestively in
such moving poems as "Desert
Places," "Lost in Heaven," "Neither

Out Far Nor In Deep", and, perhaps
least mistakable, in "The Strong Are
Saying Nothing":

There may be much or little beyond
the grave,
But the strong are saying nothing
until they see.

Which incidentally may be read as in
part an answer to such former waste-
landers as are now scurrying to
shelter under the doubtfully almighty
wing of authority.

As Frost grows older his emphases
naturally shift perceptibly from the
lyric left to the more meditative right,
yet the familiar Frost remains to
cheer and delight the pattern-
squirrels, humorously and wisely in
"The Gold Hesperidee", whimsically
and thoughtfully in "Two Tramps in
Mud Time", and in "Moon Compasses"
with an intimate and perfect lyric the
peer if not the superior of the already
classic "Fire and Ice" and "Nothing
Gold Can Stay".

Merrill Moore.
"Poetic Agrarianism:
Old Style."
Sewanee Review, 45
(October-December
1937),
507–509.

Robert Frost is still the New England
philosopher-poet in this, his sixth
book. And that is to say that he still
retains the distinctive flavor and outlook which have made him, for the
past twenty or more years, poetically
unique.

Cognizant of the times and the discussion being evoked by them, he retains an unruffled core and is only mildly disturbed while other poets are seeing red. While admitting that "the times seem revolutionary bad", a teasing, semi-humorous Yankee outlook enables him to take the world not too seriously while still being aware of it. The present volume is the most cheerful book he has published. He can measure the present with the past—which quality is always conducive to philosophic calm, in his case not the calm of a Plato but that of the New Englander close to the soil.

The last step taken found your heft
Decidedly upon the left.
One more would throw you on the
  right,
Another still—you see your plight.
You call this thinking, but it's
  walking—
Not even that, it's only rocking—
. . . .

Just now you're off democracy
(With a polite regret to be),
And leaning on dictatorship;
But if you will accept the tip,
In less than no time, tongue and
  pen,
You'll be a democrat again.

So speaks Robert Frost. But his tone is not entirely flippant. He is enough of the staunch New Englander to hold a belief in the individual which he feels to be worthy of defending. Chary of collectivist schemes of living, he clings to the older faith, and bids you "to a one-man revolution—the only revolution that is coming", to "steal away and stay away", and not to "join too many gangs." This is his political philosophy as voiced in the long, rambling "Build Soil" which critics

might claim comes far from being poetry, but which at least gives the author space for airing his views.

The modern mechanistic world is, likewise, not harshly repugnant to him. He still retains his middle-of-the-road position, although he does revolt at the sight of rural New England reaching out with its pathetic hot-dog stands for city money.

Sometimes I feel myself I can hardly
  bear
The thought of so much childish
  longing in vain
The sadness that lurks near the open
  window there
That waits all day in almost open
  prayer
For the squeal of brakes, the sound
  of a stopping car—

Frost is possibly so completely a part of his New England scene that he is not as aware as some others of the grimness of the forces which encircle it. There is at times a faint, almost pathetic, tinge to his lines suggestive of an order of life which is passing away. To some readers his refusal to become ruffled may smack of complacency, especially when he tells his rather idyllic tale of the lone striker who decides to leave the factory and retreat to the tall trees.

The factory was very fine;
He wished it all the modern speed,
Yet, after all, 'twas not divine,
That is to say, 'twas not a church . . .

There may be some sufficiently realistic to wonder how many factory hands are in a position to retreat. Some may go even further and question whether the factory may not have destroyed the vision and the very yearning for "tall trees".

But Robert Frost has never been a harsh realist. Nor is he a propagandist. In this book, as always, he is at his best in his lyrics in which he writes of humble things. Outstanding is "A Blue Ribbon at Amesbury" which describes with a distinctly Chaucerian flavor a noble prize-winning fowl. There is an abundance of lines full of that quality which has so long delighted Frost enthusiasts.

You know how it is with an April day
When the sun is out and wind is still,
You're one month on in the middle of May.
But if you so much as dare to speak,
A cloud comes over the sunlit arch,
A wind comes off a frozen peak,
And you're two months back in the middle of March.

Although this new volume contains nothing to surpass those poems which have endeared themselves to all and have become American classics, *A Further Range* is a sheaf of poems which is worthy of standing alongside of those others which have come before. It shows Frost still secure in the position he has won, and which he seems likely to retain for all time.

Checklist of Additional Reviews

Christopher Morley. *"A Further Range,* by Robert Frost." *Book-of-the-Month Club News,* May 1936, pp. 2, 3.

Lewis Gannett. "Books and Things." *New York Herald Tribune,* May 30, 1936, p. 9.

Arthur H. Nethercot. "Professor Nethercot, Reviewing Robert Frost's New Book, Finds That the Poet Still is a Non-Intellectual." *Evanston Daily News-Index,* June 4, 1936, p. 5.

Marion Strobel. "Robert Frost Charms Again With Volume of Singing Poems." *Chicago Daily Tribune,* June 6, 1936, p. 10.

Wilbert Snow. "Cheerful New England Poems." *New York Herald Tribune Books,* June 7, 1936, p. 4.

Philip Brooks. "Notes on Rare Books." *New York Times Book Review,* June 14, 1936, p. 20.

"A Further Range." Booklist, p. 32 (July 1936), 315.

Herschel Brickell. "The Literary Landscape." *Review of Reviews,* 44 (July 1936), 12.

"Literary Horizon." *Current History,* 44 (July 1936), 6-7.

Reely, Mary Katherine, ed. "A Selected List of Current Books." *Wisconsin Library Bulletin,* 32 (July 1936), 84.

John Holmes. "Up the Sleeve." *Boston Evening Transcript,* July 11, 1936, Book Section, pp. 6, 8.

Hariett F. Whicher. "The Book Table." *Amherst Graduates' Quarterly,* 25 (August 1936), 407-408.

James Norman Hall. *"A Further Range* by Robert Frost." *Atlantic Monthly,* 158 (September 1936), n.p.

T. M. *Catholic World,* 143 (September 1936), 756.

E. R. "Best Selling Books." *Delineator,* 129 (September 1936), 55.

Dorothy Emerson. "Poetry Corner." *Scholastic,* 29 (September 19, 1936), 6-7.

James Stephens. "Mr. Frost's New Poems." *London Sunday Times,* April 4, 1937, p. 9.

Ralph Thompson. "Books of the Times." *New York Times,* May 5, 1937, p. 23.

COLLECTED
POEMS OF
ROBERT FROST
1 9 3 9

NEW YORK
HENRY HOLT AND COMPANY

Collected Poems of Robert Frost

Louise Bogan.
"Verse."
The New Yorker, 15
(March 4, 1939),
68-70.

Robert Frost's "Collected Poems: 1939" brings together six books, beginning with "A Boy's Will," first published in England in 1913, and ending with "A Further Range" (1936). A preface called "The Figure a Poem Makes" describes Frost's poetry process, illustrated with a poem's beginning and development ("There is a glad recognition of the long lost and the rest follows"). "A Boy's Will" should bring back to some readers the freshness its delayed American appearance let into literary parlors: a fragrance wholesome as the smell of new hay, which, more than twenty years ago, showed up the sad, unaired condition of American poetry. The lambrequins and antimacassars then disturbed have been put aside and all sorts of new and foreign breezes have since flowed in and out. Frost's first book was close to English prewar Georgian verse (also bucolic), but was saved from that school's sentimentality by the sensitive accuracy (akin to Thoreau's) reapplied to the long-neglected New England landscape.

"North of Boston," which also had to be imported, as it were, from England, did something more: it put New England speech into literature. Reading these poems again, one is struck by their solidity in comparison to even the best of a thousand poetic narratives derived from them. Frost never stretched his narratives to any great length. His good sense has kept him from running any of his tendencies into the ground. That same good sense, on the other hand, has kept him from developing, in any broad way, beyond his first work.

Frost has for a long time been one of the most popular poets of our day. Some of this popularity can be put down to the fact that he has always expressed, with imaginative sincerity, American nostalgia for a lately abandoned rural background. His love for the soil, his intimate knowledge of "country things," and his rejection of an industrial civilization's special values appeal strongly to readers who have been compelled to accept these values. If Frost had allowed his philosophy to remain completely implicit in his poetry, he would have escaped the occasional querulous tone apparent in his later books. It is not the province of the pastoral poet directly to preach. If one has chosen na-

151

ture and eschewed cities, the choice must be absolute and unrationalized. If the pastoral poet sees fit to defend his chosen mode of life, he immediately lays it open to criticism in turn—is it not a backward and recessive development of the civilization he has thought to escape? Frost has broken out every so often in diatribe against the city and its machines, although since his recognition by the public—late enough he admits—the results of his successful dealings with the printing press have enabled him to live as he pleases.

The best of Frost's lyrics are impermeable to criticism. They appear in his latest book as purely as in his first. But one reads "Collected Poems: 1939" waiting for a crack of upheaval, with some roughness of unforeseen growth thereafter. The tone is curiously static throughout. The emotion in the best lyrics, and particularly in Frost's greatest lyric, "To Earthward," does not "Broaden down" from youth to maturity; it sounds intermittently. And the reader who holds these lyrics in deep respect somehow feels that Frost's later carping and conservatism should never appear in his work at all.

"More than once I should have lost my soul to radicalism if it had been the originality it was mistaken for by its young converts," Frost says in his introduction. For the poet, the point is to lose his soul, to whatever wisdom or folly, and then to regain it. "The best way out," he once said, "is always through." The ordinary man may be able to conceal his evasions; in the poet, the evasion shows. In the later Frost, the mold, unbroken, has stiffened a little.

Alfred Barrett. "Collected Poems of Robert Frost." America, 61 (April 29, 1939), 70.

Three Pulitzer Prizes awarded to him have confirmed the position Robert Frost holds among the arbiters of contemporary literature. But his books also command a large popular sale or his publisher would not dare to be so lavish in the format of the present volume, which includes the contents of all six of his best-known books and a new preface, "The Shape a Poem Makes."

Frost, the philosopher, and especially the political philosopher, is too flavorous of Emerson to be taken very seriously. He does not need the nod of the second Roosevelt, any more than his friend, the late Edwin Arlington Robinson, was the better poet for receiving the smile of the first. With the exception of *Death of a Hired Man,* the longer pieces of Frost do not, for me, possess the validity of such lyrics as *After Apple-Picking* and *Stopping by Woods on A Snowy Evening.* Having written the American *Shropshire Lad* in his shorter poems, Frost is entitled to follow Housman's *The Name and Nature of Poetry* with a theoretical disquisition of his own, which may explain and does not distract from the magic of the poems following it.

"Bookwright."
"Reprints, First Editions."
New York Herald Tribune Books, May 14, 1939, p. 17.

The new prose preface, called The Figure a Poem Makes, to Robert Frost's COLLECTED POEMS (Holt, $5) has as much form and precision, as much intensity and clarity as any poem in the volume. "The object in writing poetry," he says, "is to make all poems sound as different as possible from each other, and the resources for that of vowels, consonants, punctuation, syntax, words, sentences, meter are not enough. We need the help of context—meaning—subject matter. That is the greatest help towards variety. All that can be done with words is soon told. So also with meters—particularly in our language where there are virtually but two, strict iambic and loose iambic . . . The possibilities for tune from the dramatic tones of meaning struck across the rigidity of a limited meter are endless. And we are back to poetry as merely one more art of having something to say, sound or unsound."

Of course there must be wildness too. "If it is a wild tune, it is a poem." But poets trying "to be wild with nothing to be wild about" find themselves kicking "in all directions as of a hot afternoon in the life of a grasshopper. Theme alone can steady us down. Just as the first mystery was how a poem could have a tune in such straightness as meter, so the second mystery is how a poem can have wildness and at the same time a subject that can be fulfilled." To put it another way, a poem "begins in delight and ends in wisdom. . . . It has an outcome that though unforeseen was predestined from the first image of the original mood—and indeed from the very mood. . . . It finds its own name as it goes and discovers the best waiting for it in some final phrase at once wise and sad."

The Necessity of Surprise

"No surprise for the writer," Mr. Frost goes on to say, "no surprise for the reader. For me the initial delight is in the surprise of remembering something I didn't know I knew. . . . There is a glad recognition of the long lost and the rest follows. Step by step the wonder of unexpected supply keeps growing. The impressions most useful to my purpose seem always those I was unaware of and so made no note of at the time when taken, and the conclusion to come to is that like giants we are always hurling experience ahead of us to pave the future with against the day when we may want to strike a line of purpose across it somewhere." The poet cannot advance merely by logic, because "logic is backward, in retrospect, after the act." He must feel rather than see before him, as in prophecy. His poems must be "a revelation, or a series of revelations, as much for the poet as for the reader. . . .

"Scholars and artists thrown together are often annoyed at the puzzle of where they differ. Both work from knowledge; but I suspect they differ most importantly in the way their knowledge is come by. Scholars get theirs with conscientious thoroughness along projected lines of logic; poets, theirs cavalierly and as it happens in and out of books. They stick to nothing deliberately, but let what will stick to them like burrs when they walk in the fields.... A schoolboy may be defined as one who can tell you what he knows in the order in which he learned it. The artist must value himself as he snatches a thing from some previous order in time and space into a new order with not so much as a ligature clinging to it of the old place where it was organic....

"Originality and initiative are what I ask for my country. For myself the originality need be no more than the freshness of a poem run in the way I have described: from delight to wisdom. The figure is the same as for love. Like a piece of ice on a hot stove the poem must ride on its own melting. A poem may be worked over once it is in being, but may not be worried into being. Its most precious quality will remain its having run itself and carried away the poet with it.... It can never lose its sense of a meaning that once unfolded by surprise as it went."

Besides all the poems of the collected edition of 1930 the new volume contains those of "A Further Range" (1936).

"The Muse; Collected Poems of Robert Frost." *Time,* 33 (May 15, 1939), 83-85, 87.

From Homer on, hardly a serious poet has been without a guardian conscience which he called his Muse. To the Greek poets, the Muses were goddesses who led a life apart from the bullheaded and goatish gods but were, like them, bland absentees. After paganism, when Christianity started trying to hatch out a more personal and better world, the Muse turned from goddess to angel—like Dante's Beatrice, who spoke to him from heaven. But with the Renaissance, poets found their angels nearer home and less angelic: in Elizabethan times, on the streets and in the Court; in the 18th Century, in the boudoir or the salon; among the Romantics, anywhere outdoors. But whether divine, semi-divine or human, the Muse was always a woman.

The Muse of **Robert Frost,** No. 1 of living U. S. poets, has been his wife. Since her death, a year ago, he has gathered practically all his published poetry (about a third of what he has written) in his *Collected Poems.* In the book's characteristically half-evasive, half-outspoken foreword, *The Figure a Poem Makes,* Frost says: "It [a poem] begins in delight and ends in wisdom. The figure is the same as for love." Frost's book begins in knowledge and ends in perplexity; but the figure it makes is Frost himself.

Robert Lee Frost, a ninth-generation New Englander (whose Yankee father expressed his Southern sympathies by naming his son after General Robert E. Lee), was born in San Francisco, where his father had become embroiled in politics, in 1875. After his father's death, his school-teacher mother moved the family back to New England. Frost went to high school in Lawrence, Mass. At school, a passage in Virgil's *Georgics* suddenly made him understand what it was to be poet. He began to write; but meanwhile, after Dartmouth proved too academic for him, he set out to make his living in a Lawrence mill.

When he was 20 he married Elinor Miriam White and two years later entered Harvard for a final wrestle with culture. Two years were enough; he quit and began to teach. He also made shoes, edited a weekly paper (the Lawrence, Mass. *Sentinel*), finally became a farmer.

For eleven years he and his wife lived in Derry, N.H. in almost complete isolation. Four children were born and he wrote constantly, but except for a few poems printed in the (now defunct) *Independent,* a religious weekly, none of his poetry was published. He scraped a barer and barer living from his farm. But meanwhile he was writing his intensest poetry. This intensity was the natural consequence of living face to face, side by side with a living Muse:

I left you in the morning,
And in the morning glow,
You walked a way beside me
To make me sad to go.
Do you know me in the gloaming,
Gaunt and dusty grey with roaming?
Are you dumb because you know me
*   not,*
Or dumb because you know?

Almost all of Frost's earlier poems

were attempts to make himself more completely known to this womanly presence who was his chosen judge. But never once did his wife give his poems a word of praise, though she knew them like the palm of her hand. Frost's early poems read like invocations of a conscience which, if it left him, would leave him lost—yet whose presence made every day, however perfect, a judgment day. But even these early poems show Frost almost as willing to play hide-&-seek with judgment as to face it.

We make ourselves a place apart
Behind light words that tease and
*   flout,*
But oh, the agitated heart
Till someone find us really out.

At the end of this period—when his farm finally sank under him, Frost took to schoolteaching again—the Frosts thought of moving into even deeper isolation, considered going to Vancouver. At this juncture Mrs. Frost made the only romantic remark her husband ever heard her make: "Let's go to England and live under thatch." Frost sold his farm and the family sailed for England in September 1912. There, in a thatched cottage in Beaconsfield, he began to associate with literary professionals (Lascelles Abercrombie, Rupert Brooke, Wilfrid Gibson, Edward Thomas). In England he published his first book of poems, *A Boy's Will* (1913).

A Boy's Will, containing several of the best lyrics in U.S. literature, attracted some attention. A year later he published *North of Boston*, a "book of people" so full of New England scenery and New England tones of voice that even foreigners could get the lay of the landscape and the hangs of its inhabitants. His U.S. reputation thus established by his English success, when Frost returned to the U.S. in 1915 he found himself regarded as a famed American poet. In the next 22 years he received honorary degrees from 13 colleges, was thrice awarded the Pulitzer Prize for poetry.

‑ He became Poet in Residence successively at Amherst, University of Michigan and Harvard. Crowds turned out, as they still do, to hear his lectures and readings of his own poetry. In a creaking, cranky voice as of one grinding his own poetic ax, and with the mannerisms of a Yankee hired man who knows more than he lets on and somewhat despises his boss for knowing less, he dropped hints that poetry was the most important thing in the world. Then he would read from his own poems, as evidence.

The theme of Robert Lee Frost's life is a conflict between staying and going. Staying, for him, has meant standing by a poetic conscience such as has been given to few American poets—in complete disregard of any lesser audience. Going has meant playing the artist more than the man—and winning a public success which he never intended and partly distrusts. Frost did most of his staying in his first three books *(A Boy's Will, North of Boston, Mountain Interval)*—and his later books contain many poems that testify to his ability to stay. But he has written many poems about going, too—poems that unsay the unspoken contract between him and his Muse:

Ah, when to the heart of man
Was it ever less than a treason

To go with the drift of things,
To yield with a grace to reason,
And bow and accept the end
Of a love or a season?

As they wear onward, Frost's *Collected Poems* show an increasing self-complacence of poetic purpose: from the initial effort to write true things acceptable to his Muse to writing good things acceptable to himself—no small achievement, since Frost is a hard man to please. As the craftiest artist among American poets, he has attracted an audience who like his poems' sound and sense—without quite knowing which is which. Sometimes Frost seems to strike a perfect balance, as in his famous *Stopping by Woods on a Snowy Evening. . . .*

Harvest time in Frost's career as an artist was *New Hampshire*—his fattest book and one that contains almost all his characteristic art-forms: a long conversation piece, aphoristic verses, autobiographical riddles, lyrics, blank-verse "novels"—all written in words of archaic clarity and rasping directness. Frost's later books *(West-running Brook, A Further Range)* are aftermath. In them the poet goes over & over his familiar field, gleaning it with unhurried but anxious care. . . .

His Yankee humor is as self-contained as ever, but as a social or political commentator he tends to carp and crack like General Smedley D. Butler, whom he fleetingly resembles. Otherwise Frost, at 64, resembles nobody but himself: a grey, wonderfully good and faintly rascally poet whose Muse is dead, a man with no particular place to go, no particular place to stay, and one always occupied with the complicated task of simply being sincere.

James Southall Wilson. "The Figure a Poet Makes." *Virginia Quarterly Review*, 15 (Spring 1939), 303-305.

Sir Henry Irving said that a good actor makes the mold for his own form in the company with which he acts. He cannot fit himself into the mold left by another actor. The figure pleases me at the moment for it suggests Robert Frost's phrase in the preface to the beautiful new volume of "The Collected Poems of Robert Frost": "The figure a poem makes. It begins in delight and ends in wisdom. The figure is the same for love." The first line commits the poet and he moves on, surprised himself at the poem that forms. The figure is the same, too, for a poet. He begins in delight and ends in wisdom, and between the beginning and the ending is formed the pattern of the life that a poet lives.

Frost has been called a realist and also an idealist. It is one of the several paradoxes of his nature that he is both and neither. His comment—though I think he has never put it in print—has often been quoted as to the kind of realist he is. He does not hand you the potato with all the dirt on it. He scrubs the potato to form. He has said in a talk that he is not an idealist but an "idea-ist." He has not seen a vision of a perfect world

through parting clouds in the sky. He believes in working, with what implements and methods there are, toward the realization of the best ideas you have been able to think through in your own mind. He is an individualist, not an institutionalist. A man needs the courage that grows out of his loneliness, he needs the strength he develops by standing alone. I think all the virtues, for Frost, begin with one, and grow from one to two, and two by two. He invites you as a poet not in groups but singly. "You come, too," he says in "The Pasture," a poem that is the foreword poem in each of his collected volumes. The moral in his early poem, "The Tuft of Flowers," is that no man works alone; but the message of the uncut blossoms that the reaper left comes to the other worker by himself. Frost is not a collectivist. I believe that is true of his religion, his sociology, his politics, his economics, his aesthetics; in short, of his whole philosophy. His conception of the adequate man is as self-centered, self-contained, self-directed, but not self-sufficient. Not every man by himself, to himself, for himself; but every man in himself, through himself and from himself. I do not think of Robert Frost as talking about "duty." "It begins in delight and ends in wisdom." The figure is the same for love. That is the secret of a good poem or a good axe helm. It is also the secret of a good poet and a good life. Lovers are by twos and twos and the revolution in America that will count is a one-man revolution. With no arithmetic but twice one is two he gets in all, because somehow every two is one and all the ones make together the sum of the whole. That is a paradox, also, that the institutionalist cannot re-

solve. Emerson said in effect somewhere that a general's philosophy is
more important than the number of
his troops. A man is what he believes,
he meant. I think Frost would judge a
man by what he loves. What counts is
what begins in delight and ends in
wisdom. The obligations, the require-
ments, the other person's standards
are not what really matter. The test
of this view is in his poems almost
anywhere. Home is not "the place
where, when you have to go there,
they have to take you in," it is "something you somehow haven't to deserve." It's yours by force of love or
something like it, for loyalty is a degree of love.

Perhaps an understanding of Robert
Frost's philosophy of every man's
right to his own life and his own way
of life is the best explanation of his
position in the United States today.
Foremost living American poet and,
since Yeats' death, first of living poets
of the English tongue, he stands
neither as a great national figure nor
even as a great symbol as Yeats did.
He stands as a great and individual
figure of a man and a poet. He seems
even a lonely figure. Yet, he has
friends everywhere. He belongs to no
group, he has established no cult. We
shall not say "After Frost," as they
say "After Pound" or "After Eliot."
But his "tuft of flowers" gladdens and
will gladden the hearts separately of
thousands who never heard the sound
of his scythe. An understanding of
him begins in delight and ends in
wisdom. The figure is the same for
love. That is the figure, too, that a
poet makes.

Muriel Rukeyser. "In a Speaking Voice." *Poetry,* 54 (July 1939), 218-24.

Soon after he started to publish, in
1912, it was evident that Frost was to
have a curative effect on the speech of
poetry. A special effect. From the beginning, he said nothing that did not
placate and soothe and reconcile. All
the disturbances were natural, nothing was said that could not be
stated without raising the voice. Patience and resistance and the pains of
responsibility temper his lines, in
lyric, short dramatic piece, or narrative, with his neighborhood stamped
on all his work. Frost stands now, in
this latest collection of his poems, as a
mean in the measure, with no effort
to rake up to consciousness, or to im-
pose a unity of meaning from above;
he stands at the level of articulation
into conversation. Average, if you
like, in tone; reliable in the solid garden way, plus its articulation, so that
the constant and delightful play of a
combining charm is on the surface.
He makes a place his own; coming
from California to New England, he
took over as unmistakably as Jeffers,
traveling opposite, took over the
Coast; but without the great expanded
images, the stridings, the toppled
forests and families and the vic-
timized love. Here is photography of
the effects of snow and heat, sorrow,
exuberance *to a point,* sun in the
pines, on the bushes, lives turning
slowly as leaves under warmth,
householders living day-to-day; a realism of the senses, Frost gives us,

blueprints of that countryside. New England, which he came to young, and claimed; the wild, neat states of exaggerated seasons.

There is not much development in over four hundred pages. There is re-working and turning over, and one looks naturally to farm comparisons. The first book has the voice already, and much of the later craft, in *Storm Fear, October, A Tuft of Flowers, Mowing*. But the language is stilted; one questions how it could ever have appeared honest: "and lo," "fay or elf," "abide," "aloof," "zephyr," "limns," "The languor of it and the dreaming fond." What saves the book and marks it is its flatness, inflection of casual speech, scapes laid on stroke by stroke:

The crows above the forest call;
Tomorrow they may form and go.

and

When the wind works against us in
　the dark,
And pelts with snow
The lower chamber window on the
　east. . . .

The next book, the successful *North of Boston*, which had its English furore and set Frost's standard, contains sixteen of the most sufficient, local, and convincing poems he has done. The list begins: *Mending Wall, The Death of the Hired Man, The Mountain, A Hundred Collars, Home Burial*. . . . If you open the book and read straight through, it is during these poems that you get taken up, catch the rules of conversation and attitude, and see the limitations the man has set himself. He comes through now, as a mild man set to orient himself by the most per-

manent facts he can find: seasonal force, constants in life and work and death to see him through his responsibilities. All of these poems, with three exceptions, are narrative, and dramatic, and conversation-pieces; the three are *After Apple-picking*, one of the most beautiful poems Frost has ever written; *The Wood-pile,* and the final lyric. The stories are lifelike, typical, moving, against static backgrounds; the two startled people confronted by a face at the dark house; the descendants of Starks, met at a rainy reunion; the house with a room-size cage for the insane uncle; the clenched father who had dug his child's grave and come into the kitchen for weather-gossip; the collector drinking in a shared hotel room—exposing their lives in the calm monologue that Frost makes the world speak.

The third book, *Mountain Interval,* has the short uneven poems whose top level is struck in *The Hill Wife, Birches,* and *The Bonfire.* England was put behind, and Frost was living in New Hampshire, famous, after the foreign success. Twenty years of obscurity and inability to get published were over. It seems now, from the outside and much later, that here was a place for choice. There was no turn; *Mountain Interval* was a variation on the one established theme; and *New Hampshire,* published seven years later, summed up all the previous work, taking the three books along together, repeating the early words with more affection, greater intimacy, a finer intimacy, a finer precision of the senses. From the title-poem, through *Fire and Ice,* and *Good-Bye and Keep Cold,* and *Gathering Leaves,* the level comes up in sureness of handling. *West-running*

Brook, published in 1928, and *A Further Range,* which appeared in 1936, take Frost back into the compact lyric, becoming more and more didactic, sorrowful, affectionate and cross.

Frost has his theme. He was recognizable from the beginning, and he never chose again. He stokes and banks, and gauges the fires; there is little work of enduring intensity. Fancy and imagination are very close in all his work; when the description is clean, striking the senses immediately, a lasting impression is made; but there is a double exposure, and behind the picture is a quiet and in many ways a desperate man, keeping his grip on his poems, but forcing them to be distal to his own much more intense problems and choices. The poems are end-products, and Frost has contempt for

> . . . poets
> Who fall over each other to bring
>   soil
> And even subsoil and hardpan to
>   market.

Markets are what he hates, but he has his product, and is at his counter; and when he chooses to be a plain New Hampshire farmer, in answer to the literary choice,

> Choose you which will you be—a
>   prude, or puke,
> Mewling and puking in the public
>   arms,

he still does not choose to farm. His obligation as poet has kept him at his self-controls, until one wonders whether he has not turned himself out a self-controlled prude, a self-controlled puke, by not choosing either of them, but choosing self-control. He falls into fears he says he has escaped. He writes

> I never dared be radical when young
> For fear it would make me
>   conservative when old.

And is conservative. Look, here is the mild man, quick to see, quick to love glints and delicacies, and sturdiness and thrift. He has no dependence on a shabby personal legend, none of the city shabbiness. He walks around an object, delimiting it, catching the surface well, doing this at the normal speed of walking and talking; not at the speed of the imagination, not seizing hold nor letting go fast. This is not poetry that strikes immediately at invention and the spirit; it is delimiting, and at the end one knows the object in area and in impact on the senses; but whatever insight there is comes as recognition.

Frost took a country that he came to very young, and received it fresh on himself. It was lucky that he was not born in New England; he chose his home. He chose his work; caring enough for college to leave Dartmouth and return to Harvard, caring enough for academic standards and the classic, as Untermeyer points out in *Modern American Poetry's* useful introduction to Frost, to get his best marks in Greek, and leaving it all behind in his work—except, perhaps for the true bucolic flavor, which becomes New England flavor of apple and blueberry, snow and granite face—traveling, having his family, teaching, he cuts all of this out of his life in poetry, gripping hard for faith to New England simples. With this passage of time, we see that he has the colors and sharp tastes of his countryside, and remember startled how he used to be accused of being colorless. But the strain and violence and sharp contrasts have been controlled out of his poems. They are in his country, and one sees them in his rejections; he has stayed away from them. He has his responsibility, he is firm in his craft, with a steady checking influence on the language of American poetry, in the line of recorded speech that includes Frost, Robinson, Masters. Of the three, Frost evades most. He comes to the edge: read *The Bonfire,* and *A Servant to Servants,* and *Two Witches*—he almost goes over the edge. One need not require a line of development from Frost, any more than from Fearing—these are people working and always working with one implement. But Frost has developed through certain apprehensions, with a certain nervousness. One thinks of Yeats, his generous full developing mind. Frost stays close, and guards. He is a village-spirit, deep in village-life. I started to re-read many of these poems (and they should be dated, and they should have an index) believing that I admired them and that they were not enough what I needed to hear to let me like them. But as I read, I knew they were near, I did like them too; I was occupied by their warmth and mocking and turning, by the neat perception of physical detail, strict enough to let one smell these trees and animals, I saw that glare on snow. I wanted more, by then. Frost has articulated much that was not spoken for. Early in life, he drew his circle around himself, and plainly said, "I will deal with this." The attitude does not come through as self-control, but as a rigid preconception of life. He wants his poem to have "the wonder of unexpected supply;" he says "it begins in delight and ends in wisdom" in his note to this book, *The Figure a Poem Makes*. He cultivates his own garden, grouping with art so that everything there may be discussed in the same tone of voice. Meet him on these his own terms, and there is fine work, rewarding place-love, folk-love, solemn or gay recognitions. They are the recognitions of a man desperately determined that this is really all there is, and that this will be enough. It is not all, and it is not enough.

John Ritchey. "The Figure a Poet Makes." *Christian Science Monitor Weekly Magazine Section,* July 22, 1939, p. 10.

These collected editions of the poems of Robert Frost take the reader through "A Further Range." Of course they are not the complete collected poems, happily. They do, however, between them provide two valuable additions to the 1930 edition. First, there is in the Holt edition a preface entitled, "The Figure a Poem Makes." It may be worth the difference in price to most readers. Certainly it is a Frostian key to the poems. . . .

The second valuable addition to these new collected editions is that both contain the complete text of "A Further Range." You can read through the bucolic first volumes and, at last, find yourself in a suave, faintly urban setting. The subtitle might read: "From Rags to Riches." It is not that wholly, of course, but the implication is inescapable. The early poems mark the struggle of the Frost of the furrow, a man who got himself a country to come from and they bear the scars of difficult years. By the strange alchemy of poetry the scars of this life came out, not scars, but something between hurt and joy. In these early pages are poems that are poems in the final sense that poetry is always a little beyond the reader and behind the poet. They are experiences in space and time.

What happens, then, when the struggle, at least the conscious struggle for material necessities, is over and the battle won? Let's look at the record. You see, nothing happens at once. The reason? Refer to the passage quoted from the preface. You go on writing as long as the experiences hurled before you last. After that you write "A Further Range."

The man who once lived on the little rocky farm is the man who goes by in a swift motor and notes that the little farm has a roadside stand now. That is because its occupants are poorer than the poet was. Life is even crueler now, the prices are lower; they offer what they grow to the motor traffic. He hears of a plan to move these folk away from the farm to the city. That is worse than hunger, he concludes. It wasn't for him; he reaps what the land sowed in him. But one Frost a century is nature's economy.

Again the Frost of the air-conditioned Pullman car looks out at twilight and sees a lone cabin and a figure in the doorway:

He stood unshaken, and if grim and
gaunt,
It was not necessarily from want.
He had the oaks for heating and for
light.

He had a hen, he had a pig in sight.
He had a well, he had the rain to
catch.
He had a 10-by-20 garden patch. . . .

Who is the sad man now, who is the lost, the figure in the doorway or the poet? Is looking deep in as happy an occasion as looking deep out? That is the reversal in "A Further Range." Such poems are a long way from "The Times Table" and "To Earthward." About as far as the distance between the lone figure and the man in the Pullman.

* * *

But is that to stand as blame? One critic, at least, has said so. On what basis could such a conclusion be reached? The implication is that success turns one from a liberal to a conservative. But he claims to be neither. He dislikes such labels, thinks them as useless as they are silly. Poetry is out of experience, it cares little for the double talk of politics, per se. Its politics consists in having no politics except the experience of here and now so built as to carry over into the future. That I suspect, is what Frost intends to do. When most successful this method produces poems of great social significance. I think the following lines are among the most significant social observations of our time. Speaking of mankind, the poet asks:

Why is his nature forever so
hard to teach
That though there is no fixed
line between wrong and right,
There are, roughly, zones whose
laws must be obeyed. . .?

What basis there may be for finding

something unsatisfactory in the poem of the Pullman is largely in the manner. The old edict of being witty is carried like a chip on the shoulder. Who says I am not funny? I'm the funny man of serious poetry. A great poet should be easy. This is how it is done. The hand is quicker than the eye.

What law is it, though, that allows no latitude for the great poet. There are a half-dozen poems in the volume of the Pullman poet to place against all the rest of the collected poems. That's more than a fair average—even for a Frost. And there is "Provide, Provide," doing what the poet preaches, marrying wit to wisdom:

Some have relied on what they
    knew;
Others on being simply true.
What worked for them might
    work for you. . . .

What Frost is surest of and what the reader is surest to get is the theme of freshness, a fresh way of looking at an old world so as to make it seem new. A poem, he says, should run from delight to wisdom. Most of his poems do more than that: they run both ways. He remains a poet to measure against poets.

Vrest Orton. *"Collected Poems of Robert Frost,* 1939." *New England Quarterly,* 12 (September 1939), 563-67.

Here, in one volume, at last, are all Robert Frost's books, the first collected edition in nine years. It begins with *A Boy's Will,* written by an unknown young man who had fled from an America always tardy to recognize genius in any of the fine arts, and issued by an obscure British publisher twenty-six years ago. It ends with *A Further Range,* published in New York in 1936 as the product of America's best-known living poet. We have gone through two different worlds since that first slender brown volume appeared without pretension in 1913—and now hardly anything seems permanent except the very thing that Robert Frost has been doing. That is why we may safely reserve a place for him beside Hawthorne, Thoreau, Emerson, and Whitman.

This reviewer is not going to try to chart the course of modern poetry over the last quarter century—that, he believes, should be left as an easy task for some erudite young English doctrinaire. He proposes to tell how he feels about Frost simply because he is sick and tired of reading heavy-laden, academic comments on poetry, or the hoity-toity, heliotrope words of poetasters who write for little "arty" magazines. Strange that the combination has not driven people away from verse forever! Poetry has got to be pretty good to find its way through this literary labyrinth to reach, at last, the minds and the hearts of the people it is meant for—and pretty strong, too.

Frost's poetry is both good and strong. Nothing anyone says about it can ever hurt it. Yearning spinsters who lay claim to poetic genius review Frost's work with an envy not easy to conceal. Hard-boiled Marxians scold the author for not composing banners to be carried in parades. Smart, slick writers for the smart slicks drive by Frost as if he were a tramp too rough to stop for. And modern abstractionists who, having nothing to say, choose to say it in an obscure and knowing fashion, try to patronize Frost because he uses language so plain that thought opens without a key. All these people do not care for Frost. They fail to hurt him. Their words pelt against him and run off, like rain against a granite cliff.

Again, a lot of people like Frost. One day I went over the mountain from my home to his. We sat and talked all the forenoon, a serene day in early autumn. Absorbed, I was not aware that the room had become a little chilly. Frost suggested that we go out back, get some wood, and build a fire. There was a run or two of good maple there. Frost hauled down a couple of sticks and started, like a veteran, to swing his axe. He wouldn't let me do anything. As I stood there, I saw a young man lolling beneath an apple tree, on the side hill, not far from the barn. He was reading a book. He looked like a long, strong young fellow, and I said so. Frost stopped, sunk his axe into the chopping-block, and looked up.

"Yes, he's staying with us."

"Why don't you have *him* chop the wood?" I asked.

Frost smiled and turned back to his work.

"He doesn't chop wood," he said, without the slightest emphasis on any word; "he's a poet."

While many of our neat and stylish American poets are reading away all their quiet afternoons under well-sheltered trees on sunny hillsides, seeking inspiration, Frost, the rugged, gnarled American workman, has been busy chopping wood. In the course of this plain, honest work of more than twenty-five years he has achieved enough, certainly, to know that he has earned his niche in perpetuity.

He is the most independent of men—independent even to the exasperation of his best friends.

> . . . Steal away
> The song says. Steal away and stay
>   away.
> Don't join too many gangs. Join few
>   if any.
> Join the United States and join the
>   family—
> But not much in between unless a
>   college.

Frost has refused to compromise, to muddle, or to beat around the bush. "The best way out," he has said, "is straight through." This is the way he has always gone.

No one else has quite his craftsman's way with words. He uses them as a good blacksmith uses iron. They have no special shape until he begins on them. He bends, twists, and pounds them out with sure, sharp blows. They come out in all kinds of shapes, sometimes rough—like a sensible sled-runner—and at other times fine and delicate, like a wrought-iron gate, or a lovely candelabrum. The point is, though, that they are all made of sound iron—no adulterations, no wood painted black, no papier-mâché—and they come out as Frost desires. And like the blacksmith who must heat every piece in the forge before he shapes it, Frost first heats words in his brain and his heart.

A poem, he says, should begin in delight and end in wisdom. Try the lovely "To Earthward" as evidence. This happens only because Frost is what he is. He has set down great truths, in common speech, about common things. Like Benjamin Franklin, he is as great a man and a philosopher as he is a writer. Franklin transcends his work. So does Frost.

New England gave up making men like Frost a century ago: that is why he is something special. He thinks and feels things out. He is not afraid to put his mind against yours. Moving from complexity to simplicity, as all real artists must, Frost has gained an audience for poetry while other writers have been losing it. Their retreat into the dark caves of cryptic symbolism has only moved Frost more up-to-date than ever—to the point where he agrees with young Lewis and Spender, who believe poetry should be the "private language of personal friends." Poetry, Frost says all the time in his poems, is something warm and personal and felt—never in intellectual exercise or a stunt. He has made the simple things his, but given to them a fresh meaning so that we can better make them ours, too. He is a man of earth, and every permanent thing of earth—mountains, trees, rocks, meadows, grass (and men who deal with these)—he knows intimately. To ordinary things Frost has given new magic and new beauty—and that is precisely what a poet is for. We have enough star-gazers: what we need most is a man who can see the world in a grain of sand, and then show us how to see it with him.

Of course our contemporary socio-economic critics will protest. We are all "modern"; some of us believe in, some of us will fight for, a grave new world of social justice, free from slavery to money. We hate chains; some of us detest Hitler and Mussolini and their mobocracy; others think the whole world is going to hell. But this has nothing to do with one's attitude toward Robert Frost. He is outside and above all this. There are some who are sorry he has even attempted to touch upon it—as in a recent poem or two. Regardless of how we feel about the future or what view we take of society, we shall always (it is to be hoped) wish to know and love trees, mountains, and grass. We can find plenty of people to deal with the changing, fast-moving world, but not many so capable as Frost of dealing with the permanent.

             . . . to me
The times seem revolutionary bad.
The question is whether they've
     reached a depth
Of Desperation that would warrant
     poetry's
Leaving love's alternations, joy and
     grief.
The weather's alternations, summer
     and winter,
Our age-long theme, for the
     uncertainty
Of judging who is a contemporary
     liar—

Who in particular, when all alike
Get called as much in clashes of
    ambition.

Frost, they say, is an old nine-
teenth-century rebel. His work is
mere nostalgia for the outmoded individualism that we have now left behind for a twentieth-century collec-
tivism. He clings to the agrarian
philosophy of Jefferson, and he represents the escape-motives of Thoreau
and Emerson. They say. . . .

Like Whitman, we are told, Frost is
the last flowering of an age now done
for—always brightest just before the
doom. Some great poet, artist,
philosopher, these people say, always
seems to rise to put his period into a
time-capsule just an hour or two before oblivion. One gathers that they
disparage the fellow for having come
late. If all this be the truth, and produced Whitman and Frost, so be it!

In this unsafe time when we are
likely to lose faith in a world which
seems to be headed for barbarism and
bestiality, it is good to have a man
like Frost to hang to. He restores, he
even strengthens our faith in mankind. He confirms beauty in common
things, the only things that last. We
who are going to be lost in the twentieth century, cast up on a desert island while the revolution rages, will
have Frost and his poetry—good,
nourishing bread, better than anything fancy. Our brave friends of the
Marxian persuasion will scoff at all
this, and shout: "You can't have your
cake and eat it, too. You can't keep
one foot in one world and the other in
another." Possibly not, but no one is
going to shoot us for *desiring* to do
so—yet.

"Harvest of Poetry: Studies in To-day's Contrasts." *Times Literary Supplement,* November 18, 1939, p. vi.

. . . Mr. Frost's qualities as a poet are
now fully recognized. The essential
fact, however, that his poetry springs
direct from the soil, that it has matured slowly like a forest on a hillside
and is fertile to its roots, has,
perhaps, been unduly stressed at the
expense of the animating spirit informing it, a mind as exquisitely re-
sponsive to the humour and pathos of
simple people as to the life of small
natural things, and as tenderly fanciful as it is incorruptibly honest in its
regard of fact. In a short preface to
his "Collected Poems," entitled "The
Figure a Poem Makes," he emphasizes
the importance of subject-matter. In
his own words—"Theme alone can
steady us down." Yet this basis of a
chosen theme, as he makes clear, is
but a condition of true creative surprise, as the theme unfolds and is fulfilled in the poet's hands in wholly
unexpected ways.

This glimpse which Mr. Frost gives
us of the way in which his own poetry
takes shape is valuable in itself and
helps to explain how the figures of
speech, of which he is so sparing,
grow inevitably out of the organism of
his poems. These may be drab at
times, but it is never the drabness of
mere realism. Each of them makes a
figure which, in his own words, like

love "begins in delight and ends in wisdom."

Checklist of Additional Reviews

Henry G. Leach. "Poetry of Permanence." *Forum and Century,* 101 (April 1939), 240.

Edward L. Tinker. "New Editions, Fine and Otherwise." *New York Times Book Review,* April 2, 1939, p. 24.

Cyril Clemens. "The Quarterly Recommends." *Mark Twain Quarterly,* 3 (Spring 1940), 19-20.

A

WITNESS

TREE

BY

ROBERT

FROST

HENRY HOLT AND COMPANY

NEW YORK

A Witness Tree

Stephen Vincent Benét.
"Frost at Sixty-Seven."
*Saturday Review of
Literature,* 25
(April 25, 1942),
7.

This is a beautiful book, serene, observing, and passionate. It has the characteristic music made out of common speech which is one of Mr. Frost's great gifts—no matter where you met a poem like "Come In" you would know it was by Mr. Frost—it has the Yankee taste for philosophic laconics which makes him one of our most indigenous products—but, most of all, it has a lyric force and intensity that shows how a mind may know age without losing youth. Mr. Frost has never written any better poems than some of those in this book. Nor are any of these merely repetitions and rephrasings—as sometimes happens to the later work of a man who has done a good deal of work. There are poems, to be sure, that could fit in earlier books—"To a Young Wretch," for instance, with its very Frostian, "It is your Christmases against my woods"—"Wilful Homing," with its characteristic first line, "It is getting dark and time he drew to a house." But the brief run of notes called "Carpe Diem"—well, there it is,

quite perfect in technique, quite different in technique from any of the others, and quite entirely his. Nor will you write a poem like "The Subverted Flower" by being young, old, middle-aged, modern, classical, American, English, or what have you—but when the lightning strikes.

Reviewing such a book is no easy task. What are you going to say of a man who, at sixty-seven, produces work that is both firmer in texture and fresher in impact than that of so many of his juniors? You can recognize the tart individual flavor in such lines as the closing lines of "A Considerable Speck":

I have a mind myself and recognize
Mind when I meet with it in any
  guise.
No one can know how glad I am to
  find
On any sheet the least display of
  mind.

and wonder, uneasily, if there is a certain advice there for reviewers as well as animalculae. You can read such lines as those which conclude a poem named "The Most of It" and note the precise description, the rising music, so strongly and effortlessly handled till the inevitable close.

* * *

And that is in the great manner of

English verse—that is all. It is going to last, it is going to resist breakage. It has Mr. Frost's particular signature on it—note the tenth line. But it goes beyond particular signatures.

There are other such poems in the book—such poems as "The Wind and the Rain" in one vein, as "Of the Stones of the Place" and "Trespass" in another. There is a narrative poem which isn't a narrative poem but a philosophic one, doesn't succeed entirely, and yet has half-a-dozen lines which might have come out of "Kilmeny." There is "The Literate Farmer and the Planet Venus" which I can't admire as much as some people do and at least one quatrain "On Our Sympathy with the Under Dog" which I can't admire at all. In other words, out of forty-two poems not all are successful. But the ones that are, by themselves, would make a reputation, though Mr. Frost had written no others.

I hold your doctrine of Memento
    Mori
And were an epitaph to be my story
I'd have a short one ready for my
    own.
I would have written of me on my
    stone:
I had a lover's quarrel with the
    world.

So Mr. Frost at the end of "The Lesson for Today." The statement is very like him and we are all the richer for the quarrel. For here is a book to read, a book to remember, and a book that will be part of our inheritance.

Mary M. Colum. "The New Books of Poetry." *New York Times Book Review,* May 3, 1942, p. 5.

In his sixties a poet's lyrical days are supposed to be over; that is, his verse is no longer the thing on wings that lyric poetry is. But here in "The Witness Tree" by Robert Frost is the lyric in all its intensity, indeed, with a greater intensity than the lyrics the poet wrote when he was young. It is, to be sure, the philosophic lyric, that which Yeats also wrote in later life, and on which the reader has to set his mind working if he is to get the full significance of it. These lyrics of Frost's have that wisdom, that power of revelation that is time's last gift to the mature and powerful mind. In them we have a summing up of life and experience and the poet's certainty that from the destructiveness of time which has destroyed the Seven Gates of Thebes and the gilded monuments of princes, he has rescued something. What has the poet rescued? "What I myself have held"— that is, time has only taken from him what time can destroy:

I would give all to Time except
    except
What I myself have held . . .
And what I would not part with
    I have kept.

In the Winter of 1914 at the Poetry Society of America many people, including the present reviewer, then a young person, heard Robert Frost's poetry for the first time; it was read by the then president of the society with accompanying encomiums from the pen of the English critic Edward Thomas. It was an unexpected sort of poetry for many present: it was the said thing rather than the sung thing, and not only were the rhythms different from those of the English poetry we had been used to, but the psychic content, the psychic direction, the landscape, were different. This made it all the more remarkable that an English critic was the one to appraise this poetry at its worth, and, even more remarkable, an English publisher the one to bring it out. . . .

These new rhythms, this new content, was non-English, non-European; even single lines gave an insight into shapes of life that were distinct from Europe's. In a single line like "Something there is that does not love a wall," Frost was opening out something characteristic of America. Walls in old countries somehow kept together and lasted; walls of all kinds, indeed were one of the central facts in old countries. In America a wall was temporary and was meant to crumble away after a while. This work of his came to stand in his readers' minds for a part of the history of the country, because Robert Frost had that uncommon power, the power of integrating his work with the country and that really only a few of the poets in any literature have had. . . .

There are many different moods in "The Witness Tree": we have poems like that earlier one, "Fire and Ice," where the sharp, the bitter wit bites the lines into the memory so that after a reading or two one never forgets them; there is the mood of

subtle humor and Horatian sophistication as in "The Lesson for Today" where he tells us what he would do

If this uncertain age in which
*   we dwell*
Were really as dark as I hear
*   sages tell,*
And I convinced that they were
*   really sages.*

He would get up his medieval Latin and go back to the writers of the world's undebatably dark ages and find out what they had done. They weren't overcome by the darkness:

They slowly led old Latin verse
*   to rhyme*
And to forget the ancient
*   lengths of time,*
And so began the modern
*   world for us.*

What discoveries in language, what a mastery of technique is in this mixture of humor and reflection become poetry! The sense of rhythm here never breaks; indeed, a rhythm that never breaks is the characteristic of all the poems in "The Witness Tree." That Frost deliberately did not send his line swinging upward in incantation, that he chose to *say* rather than *sing*, made it even more than usually necessary a power of using the inevitable, the unique word; it meant that he had to keep his poems even more than ordinarily self-contained and never go a line beyond the boundary. Robert Frost has always been a master at getting an end to his poems: in most of them the last lines are a real climax, not merely a dramatic climax but a kind of spiritual climax. He has always been good, too, at the story in verse form: "The Subverted Flower"

in this volume is a short story in lyrical form and in a very modern shape.
Here, again, we see the psychic shape
peculiar to this continent, a shape
that is in the work of Henry James.
Henry James, however, would have
taken a good many pages to say what
is in these three pages.

There are many poems in his earlier volumes that are as fine as the
poems in "A Witness Tree," but few of
them bear so strong an impress of the
poet. Through the work of a lifetime
Robert Frost has been molding himself into what is himself, with all the
accidents chiseled away. If we make a
free translation of Malarmé's great
line in the sonnet on Edgar Allan
Poe, *Tel qu'en Lui-mome enfin l'eter-
nité le change,* "molding himself to
what is eternally himself"—this is
what Robert Frost has done with himself, that is what he really means
when he says

I would give all to Time
   except–except
What I myself have held.

* * *

Wilbert Snow.
"Robert Frost, Dean of American Poetry."
New York Herald Tribune Books,
May 10, 1942,
p. 5.

Robert Frost has made such a distinctive contribution to American poetry
that almost any reviewer is inclined

in advance to say gracious things
about his worth when called upon to
appraise an additional volume. In the
back of the reviewer's mind such
poems as "Stopping by Woods on a
Snowy Evening," "Birches," "The
Road Not Taken" and a dozen more
induce him toward partiality. When,
therefore, upon opening the new volume, he discovers a number of poems
he can whole-heartedly praise as
worthy of these old favorites, he feels
himself the recipient of a rich legacy,
and wants to impart the good tidings
to others.

"A Witness Tree," Frost's latest
volume, contains a half dozen poems
which have a right to stand with the
best things he has written. Of these
half dozen, "Come In" is probably destined to be the general favorite.
Without departing from the conversational tone which is Frost's especial
hall mark, this lyric has color, music,
and a triumphant sense of life bubbl-
ing through it. "The Silken Tent," a
love sonnet, carries through an unusual figure with a sureness of touch
which only a master could achieve.
"Carpe Diem" is a wise criticism of
those who tell us to snatch the present hour. "I Could Give All to Time"
is a variation of the same theme,
"Time," the last stanza of which
reads:

I could give all to Time except—
   except
What I myself have held. But why
   declare
The things forbidden that while
   the Customs slept
   I have crossed to Safety with?
For I am There,
And what I would not part with I
   have kept.

"To a Young Wretch" describes the poet's feelings as he ponders what he should do to a youngster who, without asking, has cut a spruce out of his pasture for a Christmas tree. I will venture to call it the finest Christmas poem in American literature. It concludes:

> And though in tinsel chain and
>   popcorn rope,
>   My tree a captive in your window
>   bay
> Has lost its footing on my
>   mountain slope
> And lost the stars of heaven,
>   may, oh, may,
> The symbol star it lifts against
>   your ceiling
> Help me accept its fate with
>   Christmas feeling.

"The Gift Outright" is a poem which we need to contemplate in our present disturbing crisis. In sixteen blank-verse lines, crowded with overtones, the poem summarizes the story of American culture—our too-long dependence on the Old World and the fatal weakness such dependence brought us. . . .

My arbitrary half-dozen mark is already reached and I find I have omitted an unusual poem which originally appeared in one of our magazines under the title "The Geode," and is now called "All Revelation"—a poem which locates everything in heaven and earth in the human mind:

> Eyes seeking the response of eyes
>   Bring out the stars, bring out
>   the flowers,
> Thus concentrating earth and skies
> So none need be afraid of size.
>   All revelation has been ours.

I find I have omitted also "Happiness Makes Up in Height for What It Lacks in Length," a singing lyric which attributes the lasting sense of warmth and light to the memory of one cloudless day. Nor have I included "The Most of It," with its matchless picture of a buck swimming across a river: "Pushing the crumpled water up ahead." And what could be more Frostian than "A Considerable Speck," a poem in which the author ponders over the presence of a tiny insect on a sheet of white paper, rejoicing to find there what many teachers of English composition have so often failed to discover on sheets of paper, manifestations of life?

> No one can know how glad I am
>   to find
> On any sheet the least display of
>   mind.

The keynote of Frost is fierce New England individualism; this it is that gives his work an integrated unity. In the new collection he includes a poem written in 1900 "To a Moth Seen in Winter," and its strong individualistic assertion enables it to seem at home here, and yet every book of Frost's seven has some one quality which sets it off from the others. In this volume he has left the "lovely, dark and deep" woods of northern New England and turned into the darker and deeper forests of the human mind. Two of the first six poems I have mentioned deal with the concept of time. The fascinating Harvard Phi Beta Kappa poem, "The Lesson for Today," contrasts the dark ages of the past with the encircling gloom of our present-day civilization, and a portion of the poem deals with the effect of the concept of space on human thinking. One whole section of the book is made up of brief gnomic sayings in verse which shows that Frost has been brooding over the wisdom of the East. In other words Frost is turning more and more toward philosophy, although, of course, he has always been more or less of a philosopher in the school of Thoreau and Emerson. Some of the poems here are little more than rhymed fancies; others lack the bullet-like unity of structure to be found in those I have singled out for special praise. The narrative in the book is not equal to the great dramatic narratives to be found in "North of Boston." But he has given us enough first-rate poems here to satisfy the most exacting critic, keep us all in his debt, and leave him secure in his enviable place as the dean of American poetry.

"Poetry."
Time, 39
(May 18, 1942),
91-92.

Like an ancient Vermont maple putting forth its leaf in due season, 67-year-old New England Poet Robert Frost this April brought out his seventh book of poems, his first new book in six years. During those years he lost his son (his youngest daughter died in 1935, his wife in 1938); yet the only lines in his book that refer to personal loss read as follows:

I could give all to Time except–except
What I myself have held. But why
* declare*
The things forbidden that while the
* Customs slept*
I have crossed to Safety with? For I
* am There.*

And what I would not part with I
* have kept.*

A *Witness Tree* is a testimony and a revelation of what Frost has managed to keep, through the happy and tragic years of his life. On the plus side is his passion for the passion that makes flowers bloom, trees scrape stars, and some people love each other. In his latest book, as in his first, Frost still goes for this heavenward earth-love as a horse goes for oats—see parts of his *Come In,* for instance. When he goes limpingly, as he does on many pages of his book, it is less because of his age than because he has come more & more to favor his worst poetical fault—his rascally independence, based on preternatural self-esteem. When full of this—and he is only occasionally entirely free of it—Frost writes like a wise man ensconced in a pickle jar.

But the plus outweighs the minus in *A Witness Tree,* and Frost remains in this book a first-rate poet and a natural American. . . .

Whatever America becomes, she will bear, to her lasting beautification, the pioneer trace of Robert Frost.

Adam Margoshes.
"Robert Frost,
Semi-Poet."
Current History, 2
(June 1942),
302-303.

When André Gide was asked whom he considered the greatest French poet, he replied "Victor Hugo, alas!" In the same spirit it must be admitted that Robert Frost is one of the leading contemporary American poets. In his latest book, the first in seven years, he has produced some of his best verse. His writing is clearer, more pointed, simpler, and richer than it ever has been. "Come In" is probably the best thing he has done; there is a note of poignancy and true lyricism here that he has not captured before:

The last of the light of the sun
That has died in the west
Still lived for one song more
In a thrush's breast.

Far in the pillared dark
Thrush music went—
Almost like a call to come in
To the dark and lament.

But if Frost has gained by advanced age rather than lost, as most lyric poets have, it is perhaps because he is not essentially a poet at all. In his homespun optimism, his somewhat self-conscious love of the more barren aspects of New England, his intellectual's anti-intellectualism there is something pedestrian and prosy. For example, in a poem about an insect that has crawled across a page he was writing on, he says:

I have a mind myself and recognize
Mind when I meet with it in any
guise.
No one can know how glad I am to
find
On any sheet the least display of
mind.

Or again, we have this complete poem:

We dance around in a ring and
suppose

But the secret sits in the middle and
knows.

An attempt is made to disguise the dry character of such thought by forcing it into rhyme, but the effect is often that of doggerel:

Oh, stormy, stormy world,
The days you were not swirled
Around with mist and cloud,
Or wrapped as in a shroud, etc., etc.

Sometimes, and quite unintentionally, a few lines reach the level of Ogden Nash's nonsense:

The slave will never thank his
manumitter;
Which often makes the manumitter
bitter.

There is no excuse for such poetic poverty, especially since it offers no compensation in thought or feeling. Perhaps the entire message and significance as well as the tone of this little book can be summed up in the presumably proud line:

I advocate a semi-revolution.

Frost himself is certainly nothing better than a semi-good poet—or a semi-poet. If he is among the best we have in America today then what American poetry needs is a complete revolution.

W. T. Scott.
"Frost's Seventh Book."
Poetry, 60
(June 1942),
146-49.

We live in a time when a writer's "attitude"—specifically his political or social attitude—is of intense concern to critics and to other writers. No doubt this is less true than it was two or three years ago, now that the war has hurled us all into one big pot; and where, as often in the 1930s, this concern itself reacted in terms of literary politics it could be, and often was, either ridiculous or vicious, or both. Yet insofar as a writer's attitude defines his work—shows, as Mr. Frost's symbol of the marked or witness tree intends, where and how he is "not unbounded"—others' concern with it is not only legitimate but necessary.

It is not, in the case of Robert Frost, of primary importance, but those who want further clues to his conception of society and of his relation to it will find them in this latest collection of his verse and will decide, I think, that Frost is a philosophical anarchist. Frost is not only a believer in the imperfectness of man but also in the imperfectability of man or (the same thing) of man's society. He remarks that there are no blessed isles and that he doubts the achievement of a golden age. If, Frostian like, he finds a wistful sadness in this he treats it, as usual, with a barely wistful humor and, in the best didactic poem in the book, *The Lesson for Today,* he even guys liberalism:

I'm liberal. You, you aristocrat

Won't know exactly what I mean by
    that.
I mean so altruistically moral
I never take my own side in a
    quarrel.

But he concludes:

I would have written of me on my
    stone:
I had a lover's quarrel with the
    world.

It is the live-and-let-live attitude, a genuine part of Frost's tradition and salted by plenty of opinions of its own. It is distinguished in our time—whether you like it or not—by its refusal to convert. It has given Frost the objectivity of his character and story poems, and it has given him the wit that sparkles in his work. It is at its barest and best in the poem just mentioned, where Frost, with particular literary intention, scoffs at those who find the times especially dark. The point is that all times are pretty dark, and there is the humor of it.

The Lesson for Today as an exception, most of the plainly moralistic verse of *A Witness Tree,* especially in the very brief poems, is flat and even smug. But these and a few other poems that somehow lack the sharpest point of Frost's best innuendo and wisdom make perhaps a third of the collection; the rest is an often astonishingly able continuance of Frost's most characteristic triumphs, and several of the lyrics should stand with his best. Here, it seems to me, is the matter of primary importance.

All the lyrics in the first part of the book would appear to refer to personal loss and grief, and in one of them, the very beautiful *The Wind and the Rain,* Frost says "And there is always more than should be said." The line, standing alone, almost demands to be snatched out for use as literary comment, and I only hope it will not be used exclusively as one more prop to the New England platform on which (to suggest a change of metaphor) Frost has been all but nailed. Perhaps it has some regional relevance, yes; but we had better note that the line states a principle of poetry wherever and whenever written. Frost, wherever he has lived, has been one of the poets of our time to know its truth and to honor it.

The other magnificent example in his practice, and it is here in this book as in all his books, lies in his use of the contemporary speech as the basis, even as the substance, of poetic speech.

Far in the pillared dark
Thrush music went—
Almost like a call to come in
To the dark and lament.

But no, I was out for stars:
I would not come in.
I meant not even if asked,
And I hadn't been.

There, as throughout a flawless lyric called *Come In,* is the Frost genius for raising perfectly common, seemingly simple, speech to a moving and memorable experience. This seems to me characteristic of all his best work. It shapes even the talky *North of Boston* type of poem; but its real triumph—Frost's real best, after all—comes in the surprising number of lyrics in which that weight of implication and that ease of words combine to indisputable and lasting poetry.

This is what matters most, and I can give a small, typical example of its power. As I write this view on a bright April afternoon I can see near the windows some maples coming into flower, some forsythia, some new grass; but I cannot see them without thinking—on such afternoons as this, year after year—"Nature's first green is gold." So, because of *Come In,* I expect I shall hereafter have exactly the right words for a country road near a woods in the early night:

Now if it was dusk outside,
Inside it was dark.

The very simplicity is the rightness. It is that "old way of being new" in poetry that Frost preaches. And in this new book in his sixty-seventh year, Mr. Frost adds several occasions to those many on which he has said what we already knew in such way the words become our own as though we had known them, too, all the time.

George F. Whicher.
"Frost's Seventh."
Yale Review, 31
(June 1942),
808-10.

Robert Frost's seventh book of poems has its roots in the previous six. There is no great departure here from what he has done supremely well before. But thinking back to "A Boy's Will" and "North of Boston" after reading this book is like following back a river to where trees can stretch across it. The new poems are the Frost we have always known, yet with a plenitude never before realized.

An unsuspected breadth of his poetry opens before us in the striking narrative called "The Discovery of the Madeiras," based on a page in Hakluyt which tells how a stolen lady and her lover reached these unknown isles and how the lady there "died of thought." This phrase might well fascinate one who delights to recognize "the least display of mind," and the poet has supplied for the lady's brooding an incident similar to that in Swinburne's "Les Noyades" (though probably not derived from it), which neatly cleaves asunder the masculine and the feminine attitudes towards giving all for love. What in the original was merely romantic, under Frost's handling becomes profound.

"The Literate Farmer and the Planet Venus," another of the longer pieces in this volume, is like the dialogues of Frost with his neighbors or with himself (it doesn't matter which) in "North of Boston" and subsequent books, and nothing he has ever done in this kind is gayer or more surprising as a texture of reflection. With it I should group some ten or a dozen shorter poems under the general head of country experiences—a species as characteristic of Frost as the dramatic lyric is of Browning. In the homely-lovely category "Come In" and "The Most of It" add unforgettable memories of thrush and buck deer to the long series of animal, bird, insect, and flower poems that runs a close second to the human interest, if it can be separated from it, in Frost's total work.

Cosmic experiences, or adventures while ranging the Zodiac, another favorite type with this confirmed stargazer, are represented by four poems as fine as anything he has ever

conceived in this sort. About an equal number, of which "I Could Give All to Time" is representative, might be called poems of philosophical reflection, while another cluster of four or five continues the vein of political comment which was first notably opened in "A Further Range." Of these last "The Lost Follower" seems to me incomparably most significant, but that may be because I have known it longest. Frost's poems have a way of growing on you.

Two magnificent compliments to women, though not unparalleled by previous poems, attain an effect of novelty by sheer perfection. "The Silken Tent" is as full-bodied as an epic simile from Virgil, and one would call it ultimate if it were not so beautifully exceeded—as the commendation of Martha by that of Mary—by the tender unspoken implications of "Never Again Would Birds' Song Be the Same."

A whole section of sparkling and unexpected epigrams carries on the playful note of "Ten Mills" in the book before this. A strange, and to me puzzling, bit of melodrama, "The Subverted Flower," might be bracketed with "The Lovely Shall Be Choosers" to the confusion of those who overlook the deeps in Frost's nature. Finally, such pieces of pure humor as "Wilful Homing," "To a Young Wretch," and "A Considerable Speck" bring to the surface the hidden current of fun that underlies much else in this and Frost's other books. Offhand I cannot think of any kind of thing that he has previously done that is not equalled or surpassed in the present volume, and all the kinds are here.

I have kept till the last what seems to me one of the greatest poems that Frost has ever written, "The Lesson for Today," a poem that may be grouped with "New Hampshire" and "Build Soil" as one of the sort that he calls "cartoons," though this is a very highly finished specimen. Here Frost imagines a somewhat one-sided dialogue between himself and Charlemagne's Master of the Palace School as to which is living in the darkest of dark ages. After pointing out in lines of exquisite badinage that moderns are dwarfed by their conception of space as much as mediaevals were belittled by their idea of God's majesty, he concludes:

One age is like another for the soul,

and with resolution (rather than resignation) to accept his share of incompleteness, the universal fate, offers as his epitaph:

I had a lover's quarrel with the
world.

It may be so, but one would say after immersion in the sunny, silvery wisdom of this book, that the quarrel had been well made up. At least our world, which foolishly sets such store on poems distilled from other poems, cannot long afford to remain at odds with the most original and inimitable poet now alive.

"Life and Nature." *Times Literary Supplement,* July 3, 1943, p. 322.

The qualities of honesty and plain-speaking, and of closeness to the labour of plain people, which have always characterized Mr. Frost's poems, are to be found in this new collection. But there is more in it of mental discovery than of rural incident. As he writes in "A Considerable Speck," a musing on a minute insect which invaded the sheet of paper he was writing on,

I have a mind myself and recognize
Mind when I meet with it in any
   guise.
No one can know how glad I am to
   find
On any sheet the least display of
   mind.

Typically the display of mind he welcomes is embodied in the humblest of living creatures, and in several of these poems he sagely reproves the poets who in "this uncertain age" have been decoyed from the object, however small, which pulsates with life and mind into abstract wildernesses, writing, for example, in "The Lesson For To-day":—

They've tried to grasp with too much
   social fact
Too large a situation. You and I
Would be afraid if we should
   comprehend
And get outside of too much bad
   statistics

Our muscles never could again
   contract:
We never could recover human
   shape,
But must live lives out mentally
   agape,
Or die of philosophical distension,
That's how we feel—and we're no
   special mystics.

Mr. Frost's own deep respect for fact
and his Puritan fear of the fluent
word or the merely sensuous image
can leave him stranded in prosaic
flats, as in the concluding lines of
"Our Hold on the Planet." But generally his reflective impulse is enriched
by a tender and individual fancy as
well as by an intimacy with nature.
"Never Again Would Birds' Song Be
the Same" is a good example of this:—

He would declare and could himself
   believe
That the birds there in all the
   garden round
From having heard the daylong
   voice of Eve
Had added to their own an
   oversound,
Her tone of meaning but without the
   words.
Admittedly an eloquence so soft
Could only have had an influence on
   birds
When call or laughter carried it
   aloft.
Be that as may be, she was in their
   song.
Moreover her voice upon their voices
   crossed
Had now persisted in the woods so
   long
That probably it never would be lost.
Never again would birds' song be the
   same.
And to do that to birds was why she
   came.

The reflective mood weighs rather
heavily upon the lyrical in some of
these verses, but when the two blend
most happily in some of his shorter
lyrics, the kind of sunny sanity which
gathers up into it the shadows of experience has in it something of a
proverbial wisdom, though the angle
of vision and the turn of expression
are so distinctively his own. Who but
he, for example, would have suddenly
seen a mountain he was climbing as a
slanting book held up before his eyes
or have written of the "obstinately
gentle air" that it

      may be clamoured at by cause
         and sect
   But it will have its moment to
      reflect.

That "obstinately gentle air" breathes
through his verses, even in the narrative poem "The Discovery of the
Madeiras," the tale of which is taken
from Hakluyt and which has a roughness, even an uncouthness, in parts,
which the theme demands. It is a fine
example of his gift for dramatic and
colloquial condensation. His irony is
less successful when it is explicit in
the rather laboured discourse of "The
Literate Farmer and the Planet
Venus" than when embedded in his
sensitive but unsentimental view of
life.

K[atherine] B[régy]. *"A Witness Tree."* *Catholic World,* 155 (August 1942), 626.

There is a different sort of whimsey and wistfulness whispering through the branches and up from the roots of A Witness Tree; and while Robert Frost has conscious kinship with the stars, his music might be fancifully compared to the level rays of the setting sun. Today he stands as the greatest of our contemporary American poets—the one with the richest creative harvest behind him and the creative spirit still alive and intact. Here is the man who back in 1914 helped to inaugurate our "New" Poetry Movement by his *North of Boston*—and had to go to England to see it published. A quarter of a century has done the work it should with him. It has undone nothing, for as he prophesied in his first book,

> "They would not find me changed
>   from him they knew—
>   Only more sure of all I thought
>   was true."

Here again are honestly beautiful nature poems, true to nature and to himself, with the kind of originality that is part of personal integrity. With fine irony and finer wisdom he gazes across the centuries, facing the good and the ill of passion, the heedlessness and loveliness of the daily pageant, the "waste of nations warring" and of much human activity. He is not free from disenchantment (who can be?) but has the playful profundity of the philosopher who would be written down in his final epitaph as one who "had a lover's quarrel with the world."

I, for one, did not suspect that he who was past master of free verse and the couplet could write so delicately inevitable a sonnet as Frost's "Silken Tent." Altogether the volume is one of which American literature may be proud. And many of us, in these days of flux, will like to have the poet and seer to remind us—

> "We dance round in a ring and
>   suppose,
> But the Secret sits in the middle and
>   knows."

William A. Donaghy. *"Three Contemporary Poets."* *America,* 67 (September 4, 1942), 607-608.

Robert Frost's high place in contemporary letters is secure and we confidently expect posterity to ratify our judgment of him. This latest book of new poems, his seventh, we can hand on as important testimony. It is Frost at his best.

Gone is the raucousness which not infrequently broke through in his previous work; though even yet, in *The Discovery of the Madeiras* and *The Subverted Flower,* there is some rugged realism. But those poems which fall naturally into the unique genre which Frost has perfected, are warm with a fine mellowness and tenderness: *Wilful Homing,* for example, *The Gift Outright, Of the Stones of the Place, Trespass* and *A Serious Step Lightly Taken.* Here is the language of the people, colloquial, homespun and touched to glory by superb technique and a "moral earnestness" which, as Untermeyer noted, cannot be denied to Frost.

A definite Horatian thread runs through the book and somehow I feel that Mr. Frost would have done better to stay in New England. Maybe it is just that I like Falernian neat; or, at least, not mixed with cider. Again, the poet's historical sense is not uniformly sound, as appears from *The Lesson for Today*.

My main regret, though, is that such a great artist should have his vision obscured by a kind of agnostic irony. "We're either nothing or a God's regret" is not Mr. Frost's own personal sentiment; but one feels that he would not repudiate it. Still, even when he is mystified or angry, his sympathetic humor softens any harshness. This book truly is the work of a great and sincere poet who sums up by saying, "I had a lover's quarrel with the world."

Checklist of Additional Reviews

"Briefly Noted." *New Yorker,* 18 (May 9, 1942), 79-80.

Booklist, 38 (May 15, 1942), 344.

Robert Hillyer. "Atlantic Bookshelf." *Atlantic Monthly,* 169 (June 1942), n.p.

Mary Katherine Reely, ed. "A Selected List of Current Books." *Wisconsin Library Bulletin,* 38 (June 1942), 95.

Open Shelf, May-June 1942, p. 12.

Louis Mertins. "Silver-Fish," *Southern Literary Messenger,* 4 (July 1942), 327.

Bookmark, 3 (May-August 1942), 9.

Kenneth Porter. *"A Witness Tree." New England Quarterly,* 15 (September 1942), 547-49.

Pratt Institute Library Quarterly Booklist, Series 6, No. 10, December, 1942, p. 16.

Notes

A MASQUE OF REASON

BY

ROBERT FROST

HENRY HOLT AND COMPANY

NEW YORK

A MASQUE OF REASON

Frances Alter Boyle.
"The Masque of Reason."
Library Journal, 70
(March 1, 1945),
219.

The poet whose "North of Boston" and "West Running Brook" have become American classics, here attempts a seventeenth-century masque in verse, without the elaborate trimmings characteristic of the form. The cast includes Job and his wife and later, God, with one speech by Satan. Job, respectfully, and his wife not too awestruck, attempt to find the reason for God's proving Job's sanctity. Doesn't come off for this reader who reread "The Book of Job" with increased delight. . . .

Leonard Bacon.
"Robert Frost and the Man of Uz."
Saturday Review of Literature, 28
(March 24, 1945),
24.

This is a very strange poem, which can be read in half an hour, though it will take most of us much longer than that to understand it. This is not unnatural, for the work is a continuation of another poem, which many have found difficult of interpretation for the last three thousand years. The final line of "A Masque of Reason" is as follows:

"Here endeth chapter forty-three of Job." There is at least as much mystery in this chapter as in any of the preceding forty-two.

Mr. Frost's hand is as skilful and sure as ever. And there is something aromatic in the work, Sabaean odors from the shore of an Araby along which he has not always chosen to cruise. Nor is there any falling off in his power of making what we take for granted glow with unfamiliar fluorescence. This has always been a mark of fine poets. In spite of the studied colloquial style, or perhaps because of it, the poem is bound to take hold of anyone who will pay appropriate attention. Now for the particulars.

Job and his wife Thyatira, whose works are greater than her patience (see Revelations, 2., 19.), lie at their ease in one of the oases of the Desert of Eternity. Presently they see God caught in his burning bush (or is it a Christmas tree, or the tree of Alexius Comnenus?), from which he quickly frees himself. God seizes the opportunity to apologize in form for any inconvenience Job may have suffered in the past and excuses Himself on the ground that together Job and He demonstrated the truth that reason cannot make a connection between what men do and what they endure. Job, by his competent assistance, has relieved God of the theoretical necessity of rewarding good and evil in kind, a great convenience for any deity, the world being what it is. But this proves to be merely the statement of the official point of view. Job and Thyatira (the latter much exercised because this is an androcentric universe) demolish the position, Job because he wants a reasoned and well-ordered system ("The artist in me cries out for design"), and Thyatira because she feels that Job has been put upon to no reasonable purpose. Although Thyatira sleeps a good deal during the debate, gradually Job and she extract from their Creator the reluctant admission that He gave Satan power over the just merely to show off the superiority of his supporters. This reminds Job of the Adversary, who by invitation joins the party, appearing "like a sapphire wasp that flickers mica wings." The guest appears on the whole greatly to interest Thyatira, who twits him unmercifully but helps God and Job save him from a tendency which is running

away with him. At the end of the poem Thyatira poses the three protagonists for a group photograph, at the same time telling them that it will be better to look pleasant, whatever they may have settled, if anything. This sounds farcical in the paraphrase, but somehow it is not in the poem.

If the reviewer understands the parable, which is open to question, Mr. Frost's meaning is much like the late Arthur Ryder's, as set down in his brief, grim, diverting, and powerful "Job": "Evil is not a problem but a fact." In spite of the dialectic sport the metaphysicians have had in and around the subject, it would appear that all the contradictions might be liquidated, if the philosophers actually took pains about definitions. The clash between fate and free will, we are informed, ceases to trouble when the controversialists realize that they don't know enough to define either except provisionally. Mr. Frost has some pertinent remarks:

. . . Science goes self-superseding on.
Look how far we've left the current
    science
Of Genesis behind. The wisdom
    there though,
Is just as good as when I uttered it.

It is too. And it may be observed that those generalizations which remain valid are seldom connected with the dogmas of sects. Rather, for the most part, they are statements about inescapable experience and concern the sweat of the brow and the eating of bread. What has been called the embroidery of the theologians is produced later in monasteries and universities by comfortably situated persons, who enhance the dignity of their order by introducing intellectual refinements of the subtlest kind and of no importance whatever. It is not denied that such occupations stimulate the mind. The Neoplatonists and the Scholastics are not wholly lost motion, but their activities look pretty nebulous beside the less ambitious but more exact operations of the mathematician and the physicist, which are not asymptotic to the wisdom alluded to by Mr. Frost.

For all its brevity and beauty this is a difficult book. And, as hinted above, the reviewer is by no means convinced that he has read it aright or interpreted it properly. He is, however, of the opinion that men of many kinds will be charmed and excited by the wit and the grace of mind which play over the pathetic spectacle of finite logic at her Psyche task, forever trying to force the Infinite into nice, reasonable, satisfactory, digestible categories. The reviewer has had occasion before this to remark that Mr. Frost is not only a very wonderful poet but a very wise man. Nothing in this little book has suggested to him any reason for receding from the position.

Leo Kennedy. "Now Robert Frost Essays the Full-Length Biblical Poem." *Chicago Sun Book Week,* March 25, 1945, p. 3.

Sooner or later, but usually before he reaches the unread eminence of a padded poet, every major poet has a whirl at a full-dress piece on an Old Testament theme. Like measles in childhood, it is traditional and inevitable; by the same token, it is rarely fatal.

Such side-trips into our pre-Christian cultural past are likely to irritate critics who have the poet's career clocked and charted; they annoy the biographers who will have to explain away their darling's fall from grace. And they rarely sell.

Well, Robert Frost has written his sabbatical book, and traveled in it as far from "North of Boston" or "A Further Range" as any poet could conceivably go. Slyly, he calls it "Chapter Forty-Three of Job," and into it has written a diverting though reverent commentary on chapters one through forty-two.

"A Masque of Reason" isn't much of a masque in the Elizabethan sense of that word, though equipped with trick props and mechanical devices. It opens with Job and his wife, a thousand years after the former's trials, reclining in a heavenly oasis in a heavenly desert. Close to them the "intense-bearing tree" breaks into flame to become the Burning Bush or the Christmas Tree, as you will.

> Job: Smell the rosin burning?
>   The ornaments the Greek
>   artificers
>   Made for the Emperor Alexius,
>   The Star of Bethlehem, the
>   pomegranates,
>   The birds, seem all on fire with
>   Paradise.
> And hark, the gold enameled
>   nightingales
>   Are singing. Yes, and look, the
>   Tree is troubled.
>   Someone's caught in the
>   branches.

It is God. "I'd know Him," Job's wife says, "by Blake's picture anywhere." God leaves the Tree and pitches his throne, a plywood flat, a prefabricated job that he puts lightly upright on its hinges. Job, deciding this is Judgment Day, comments:

Here's where I lay aside
My varying opinions of myself
And come to rest in an official
*   verdict.*

God recognizes Job and greets him:

I've had you on my mind a
*   thousand years*
To thank you someday for the
*   way you helped me*
Establish once for all the principle
There's no connection man can
*   reason out*
Between his just desserts and
*   what he gets.*

He is grateful to Job for having assisted Him shake free of the role imposed by the Deuteronomist:

You changed all that. You set me
*   free to reign.*
You are the Emancipator of your
*   God.*
And as such I promote you to a
*   Saint.*

Job's wife, Thyatira, is rather hot for women's rights, and especially for witches' rights. (The Jewish community of the Lydian city of Thyatira was given over to superstitious and magical practices, my Bible dictionary points out.) She is reasonable, logical and a scold. Every husband will find her vaguely familliar. Of Job she says:

I told him not to scratch: it made
*   it worse.*
If I said once I said a thousand
*   times*
Don't scratch!

Thyatira presently goes to sleep and Job broaches what has long been on his mind. God's recorded explanation to Job for that good man's trials never has contented him:

I need some help about this
*   reason problem.*
I waived the reason for my
*   ordeal—but—*
Why did you hurt me so?

He expresses a rather general uncertainty:

We don't know where we are, or
*   who we are.*
We don't know one another; don't
*   know You;*
Don't know what time it is. We
*   don't know, do we?*
I'm sick of the whole artificial
*   puzzle.*

God answers Job's long monologue on this theme:

I was just showing off to the
*   Devil, Job,*
As is set forth in chapters One
*   and Two.*

As indeed it is. Job is jolted by the revelation.

Job: God, please, enough for now.
*   I'm in no mood*
For more excuses.

God: What I mean to say:
Your comforters were wrong.

Job: Oh, that committee!

The poem is full of jinks and jollity. Satan is invoked but speaks only two lines: He makes a literary joke. Job's wife is thrilled:

Oh, he speaks, he can speak!
That strain again! Give me excess
of it!

which is pretty good gagging, too.

The masque ends with God, Job and the Devil posing for a photograph which Thyatira takes. Reasonably, she gets in the last word:

There, that's just the right
arrangement.
Now if you three have settled
anything
You'd as well smile as frown on
the occasion.

Of course they have settled nothing. Thyatira has shrewdly observed that. Robert Frost has settled nothing; he did not even settle the poem which breaks off suddenly like a snapped stick. But he has written a delightful trifle which is full of tolerance and sly humor. Then, it will send many readers back over the ground Frost covered to write it: the Book of Job. That is a very good thing too.

Lawrance Thompson. "Robert Frost Rediscovers Job." *New York Times Book Review,* March 25, 1945, p. 3.

"I have written a wicked book," Melville said of "Moby Dick," "and feel spotless as the lamb."

Apparently Robert Frost did not feel quite so spotless after he had completed "A Masque of Reason," an unholy one-act play in which the major characters are God and Job, with Job's wife and the Devil taking lesser parts. Frost caught pneumonia, and as he lay on his Job-like bed of pain he wondered if he were going to die; wondered if perhaps God had thus smitten him for his own wickedness in twisting the tale of Job. Fearing the worst, he stoically made no repentance promises—merely waited for the verdict. He lived—he will be 70 tomorrow—and boldly published his wickedness.

If Robert Frost is one who believes it is unnecessary to experience death before discovering the excruciations of Hell, he may be braced for what's coming. Although the ideas expressed in "A Masque of Reason" are but satirical variations on themes already hidden away in his poems, it is inevitable that he *will* catch hell from his more orthodox admirers because he has dared to make light of sacred themes.

In defense, he may point out that his version of Job's questions and of God's answers represents a studied commentary on the inscrutable problem of Evil; that Melville had more reason to feel wicked because "Moby Dick" contains an allegorical theme of negation, while "A Masque of Reason"—slight as it may be by comparison—merely lampoons false affirmations. A further glance will permit the reader to draw his own conclusions.

When the curtain goes up on the "Masque" it is obvious that the time is the present. The setting of the action is Heaven—by no means the traditional Heaven, but rather a skeptic's definition of what Heaven (and life therein) may be like: "A fair oasis in the purest desert. A man sits leaning back against a palm. His wife lies by him looking at the sky." Quite naturally, the traditional characters have accumulated a welter of information which gives anachronistic flavoring to their conversation when they refer to such diverse items as Blake's likeness of God and of Einstein's theory of relativity. The blank verse give-and-take between the major characters begins when God happens along to pass the time of day and asks how Job is feeling.

Aside from "a reminiscent twinge of rheumatism," Job admits he's fine and that "the let-up's heavenly." Enlightened· by his own words, Job asks if he has stumbled on a definition of Heaven: "Escape from so great pains of life on earth that it gives a sense of let-up calculated to last a fellow to Eternity." God isn't telling secrets— even to the dead. Instead, he changes the subject by thanking Job for his contribution to human understanding as to the divine scheme of Good and Evil. Job helped prove, God says, that

There's no connection man can
  reason out
Between his just deserts and
  what he gets.
Virtue may fail and wickedness
  succeed.
But it was of the essence of the
  trial
You shouldn't understand it at
  the time.
It had to seem unmeaning to
  have meaning.
My thanks are to you for
  releasing me
From moral bondage to the
  human race.
You are the Emancipator of
  your God.

Job is not satisfied with such an unexpected answer to the age-old problem of Fate and Necessity. Is it possible that his own classic suffering helped prove that reasoning man may as well put away his God-given reason when it comes to understanding the purpose of God? Why is God being so secretive, after all these years? God tries to explain that Job misunderstands his own importance in the divine scheme:

We groped it out together.
Any originality it showed
I give you credit for. My forte
  is truth,
Or metaphysics, long the world's
  reproach
For standing still in one place
  true forever,
While science goes self-superseding
  on.

To Job's perplexed questions as to whether it matters as to who first thinks an idea through to meaning. God reassures him that He has always done His best thinking through human beings—and through the Devil, who has been a constant inspiration. Together, God says, He and Job

Found out the discipline man
*   needed most*
Was to learn his submission to
*   unreason;*
And that for man's own sake
*   as well as mine,*
So he won't find it hard to take
*   his orders*
From his inferiors in intelligence
In peace and war—especially
*   in war.*

Like medicine, Job perceives: "So he won't find it hard to take his war."

Continuing to wrestle with his collaborating Adversary, Job persists that God must have had some ulterior purpose in permitting the Devil to torment him so dreadfully. Pressed long enough, God merely falls back on chapters one and two of "The Book of Job" and points out that of course he was also showing off to the Devil.

These are but a few of the high points in the little play—and for those who are not squeamish about the mischief in the poet, "A Masque of Reason" will prove both entertaining and stimulating. Robert Frost's familiar cunning and slyness flash constantly through varied twists of words and phrases. His wickedness may seem virtuousness to those who believe that the divine scheme requires man's growth through searching. Those ideas expressed here frequently remind the reader of earlier poems. "All revelation has been ours," he said, in one of them.

Consistently, he has thrown his skeptical criticism in the face of care-less affirmations, because he rebels against shallow answers to profound questions. Like Emerson, he makes a principle out of nonconformity and declares there is nothing more sacred than the integrity of his own heart and mind. For him, no final questions are resolved either by the dogmas of religious dualism or of philosophic monism.

Nevertheless, the searcher will find in Frost's poems sufficient affirmations close-knit enough to offer valid design for human conduct. Long ago he gave prose expression to one of the most penetrating bits of wisdom in this new poem. He began that prose passage by making fun of those who wanted to claim credit for having suffered in the worst of all possible worlds. All ages of the world had been bad, Frost pointed out—a great deal worse, anyway, than Heaven. If they hadn't been, then the world might just as well be Heaven immediately and get it over with.

"One can safely say," he continued, "after from six to thirty thousand years of experience, that the evident design here is a situation in which it will always be about equally hard to save your soul. Whatever 'progress' may be taken to mean, it can't mean making the world any easier a place in which to save your soul—or if you dislike having your soul mentioned in open meeting, say your decency, your integrity." Obviously, Frost is a New England moralist.

Curiously, however, the play-on-ideas in "A Masque of Reason" has a disarming twist in the present context. These unholy liberties taken by Frost permit him to speak through these holy characters until he has defined his own quality of rebellion against some of those same Puritanical concepts which tortured Melville. There is no connection, Frost says, between man's just deserts and what he gets. But does he really believe what he says? Is he completely free from his New England heritage on this point? If so, how shall we explain the cause-and-effect thought which crossed his mind during his pneumonia crisis?

Mark Van Doren. "Why Robert Frost Is Ageless at Seventy." *New York Herald Tribune Weekly Book Review,* March 25, 1945, pp. 1-2.

Robert Frost at seventy is not much different, I imagine, from what he was at forty or even thirty. I first knew him when he was fifty, and he was no different then. I am speaking of the poet, not the man. The man grows older, but the poet was always old. The poet called Robert Frost has from the beginning been in on a very important secret. It is the secret of humor, the greatest and rarest secret poetry knows. A man who is in on it has no particular age. You could say as well that he is always young. But that has the wrong sound, and suggests ignorance, attractive or otherwise. It is better to say old, and mean well-aged, which in its turn suggests ageless. This has more to do with the Frost we read, with the Frost whose poems we cannot remember not knowing, though when we read them

now they are as fresh as they would be if they had to make their way all over again, as love does, and fear, and loneliness, and snow.

Plenty of poets have wit—think well, and write well—but few poets at any time have humor. Frost is the only one alive who has it all over and through the body of his work. That is probably why he is not only the best living poet but the most popular. People never fail to honor this gift, for it is what makes the poet able to know what they know, it is what makes him interesting. There may be a dozen poets today as "good" as Frost, but none of them is so interesting. And they will never know why. I shall not pretend that I do, but I am willing to guess that it is humor.

Not wit, though wit is nothing to despise, and in the English poets of the seventeenth century it was the name of the thing they took for poetry itself. But of their wit I should say that it was, like Frost's wit now (for Frost is full of it), wrapped and soaked in humor. Or buried and embedded in it. Humor is, of course, the larger, the deeper thing. It is what makes any man good to know, it is what most easily moves us to call a person real—because he is like ourselves, but also because he is unmistakable. It is what makes us trust him, too, when he is serious. For he can be serious, and indeed, in a fashion which we scarcely understand, he is always serious. The humor I mean does not consist of jokes, or of saying what you don't believe. It consists of saying exactly what you do believe, in language which though common would not have been used by any other man. It consists of using words in such a way that nothing leaks out of them, none of the original juice that was in them or you. It consists of always remembering who you are and what the whole world has seemed to you to be like.

The humor of Robert Frost is so serious that it regularly takes the form of reminding us how hard the world is.

> I may as well confess myself the
>   author
> Of several books against the world
>   in general.
> And were an epitaph to be my story
> I'd have a short one ready for my
>   own.
> I would have written for me on my
>   stone:
> I had a lover's quarrel with the
>   world.

By which Frost means, I think, not merely that he has found the world a hard place, as all of us do, but that he has found us ridiculously unaware that we do. His quarrel is half with us for not remembering original sin. Original sin is easy for him to remember because of the whole view he keeps, and keeps by the way so well that the entire range of his subject matter is present in any poem he writes; all of his poems are about the world, yet each is characteristic of him.

The world he writes about is one whose difficulty must not be falsified. It was, is, and will be tough going for the soul. "All ages shine with equal darkness."

> There's always something to be sorry
>   for,
> A sordid peace or an outrageous war.
> Yes, yes, of course. We have the
>   same convention.

> The groundwork of all faith is
>   human woe.
> It was well worth preliminary
>   mention.
> There's nothing but injustice to be
>   had.
> No choice is left a poet, you might
>   add,
> But how to take the curse, tragic or
>   comic.

The golden age never was and never will be Now. Gold is something to think about, not to have—if gold, he means, is metaphorical metal, as it usually is in poetry and morals. To have it would be to lose it after all where it could do most good. To have heaven, for instance, would be to sacrifice our richest prospect.

> Earth's a hard place in which to save
>   the soul,
> And could it be brought under state
>   control.
> So automatically we all were saved.
> Its separateness from Heaven could
>   be waived;
> It might as well at once be
>   kingdom-come.
> (Perhaps it will be next millennium.)

This theme recurs with special force in Mr. Frost's new poem, "A Masque of Reason," which claims to be the forty-third chapter of the "Book of Job." It is a witty poem, but it is also a humorous poem—that is to say, it manages not to miss the most important things. The speakers are Job, Job's wife, and God; also, for a few seconds at the end, Satan. The key speech is by Job's wife:

> Job says there's no such thing as
>   Earth's becoming

An easier place for man to save his
  soul in.
Except as a hard place to save his
  soul in,
A trial ground where he can try
  himself
And find out whether he is any good,
It would be meaningless. It might as
  well
Be Heaven at once and have it over
  with.

This is what I mean by humor in
Mr. Frost. It is the thing in him
which reminds us, if we are willing to
be reminded, of a certain immemorial
wisdom concerning the one way for
men to feel good. "The Fall is the only
cheerful view of human life," some
one once said to G. K. Chesterton.
The only way for men to feel good is
to admit that the world was not designed for them to do so, and to understand that no miracle will ever
improve the design.

To Mr. Frost it is funny that men
forget this, and go on asking for
machinery which will outmode
morals. Contraptions always break
down, for the simple reason that the
soul can be a part of no machine. Mr.
Frost is old-fashioned enough to be
exclusively concerned with the soul.
But it is a fashion that comes in
again. Knowing which is still another
thing that makes him humorous.

His principle is right and clear, but
recently he has fallen a little in love
with the pleasure of merely stating it.
If he has lost anything with the
approach of age it is the power to
apply it. He has not escaped the
danger there is for a poet in having a
voice. The advantages of a voice are
famous—no poet can hope to succeed
without one. But there is also the
danger that a man who *has* a voice

will decline a man who *is* one. Then
he becomes a sage. To be a Voice is
not to be enviable, for it means taking
whatever you say as valuable merely
because you hear yourself saying it.
Mr. Frost has been charged with such
a decline, and too harshly. But there
is this much in it. It has become a bit
too easy for him to apply his principle
of cussedness in the world. He takes
short cuts and applies it in wrong
places, defeating thus the principle itself. I should say, for example, that he
is missing the point these days about
war, which he refuses to wish away
because he identifies it with his principle. But war as we shall henceforth
know it is probably the worst enemy
of that principle. Mr. Frost wants
difference and strife. But what is war
doing if it isn't making us all alike—
helmets on everybody, sirens in every
ear, and the same news every day?
World laws to prevent this would
bring back the differences Frost loves,
and the little wars he really, I think,
prefers. He needn't fear that law
would give us too much justice. It is
merely the thing that lets us live with
our enemies without having to love
them. The war we now know may not
let us live at all. I can't believe he
would like that, though in effect he is
for it. It is thus, and only thus, that
age has shortened his sight, permitting him to confuse principle with
case.

However all that may be, the poems
he has written have the best chance
of any I know these days to live. The
author of such lines as these has little
to fear from time:

The fact is the sweetest dream
  that labor knows.

Something there is that doesn't
  love a wall.

Home is the place where, when
    you have to go there,
They have to take you in. I
    should have called it
Something you somehow haven't
    to deserve.
With the slow smokeless burning
    of decay.
Or highway where the slow
    wheel pours the sand.
All out of doors looked darkly in
    at him.
Loud, a mid-summer and a
    mid-wood bird.
And miles to go before I sleep.
Great waves looked over others
    coming in.
I bid you to a one-man revolution.

And many more are bound to be remembered. But it is a pity to take even these lines out of the poems where they belong. Robert Frost's unit is the poem, not the line. The Oven Bird, or Once by the Pacific, is as perfect as any poem can afford to be. I mention two at random, which is not a bad way to proceed. The others will stay where they are, waiting good-naturedly to be recalled.

Anne Fremantle.
"A Masque of Reason."
Commonweal, 41
(March 30, 1945),
592-93.

This slim septuagenarian volume of verse—it lacks the essential element of surprise that would lift it to poetry—will add nothing to the reputation of the author of the fine, grim, tombstone-granite verses in "North of

Boston." It does not seem that Mr. Frost's *forte* is thought, or the use of reason. His explanation of evil is that God "was just showing off to the devil"; that "the tempter comes to Me and I am tempted, I've had about enough of his derision, of what I valued most in human nature, He thinks he's smart." And in an attempt to make the Deity use the language of Goethe and Peer Gynt—blank verse salted with colloquialisms—he succeeds in reading like a Buchmanist's rendering of the works of the late Mr. Humbert Wolfe. "How is that for a mix-up, Thyatira?" "Two pitching on like this tend to confuse me," "I'm a great stickler for the author's name" and "My kingdom, what an outbreak" are hardly sentences one would wish put into the mouth of a prophet who wrote some of the greatest sentences in any language, and of his Creator, about Whom one of the things we definitely know is that He is the Word. The dust cover is delightful.

Mark Shorer.
"A Masque of Reason."
Atlantic Monthly, 175
(March 1945),
133.

The dramatic element has always been strong in Mr. Frost's lyrics, and it is not surprising that he should now produce a kind of ballet in verse, for that is in a sense an extension of his lyrical method. The surprise consists rather in the tone of *A Masque of Reason* and in its sources—in, that is, Frost's choosing to write a sequel to or a satire on (as you wish to view it) the Book of Job, and to divorce himself from speculations and sentiments which hitherto have been attached quite explicit to a locality and to the somewhat dogged pieties which comprise its picture of itself.

A Masque of Reason is presented as the forty-third chapter of Job. The ancient sufferer, still unsatisfied by God's answer of His inscrutability, demands to know the reason why. So does Job's wife, a theological feminist. God replies:—

> . . . Job and I together
> Found out the discipline man needed
>   most
> Was to learn his submission to
>   unreason.

This, still, does not satisfy Job, and at last God confesses, with considerable anxiety:—

> I was just showing off to the Devil,
>   Job,
> As is set forth in chapters One and
>   Two.

Job replies:—

> 'Twas human of You. I expected
>   more
> Than I could understand and what I
>   get
> Is almost less than I can understand.

And in so far as *A Masque of Reason* is to be read for metaphysical intentions, this seems to be its essence.

It is clear, however, from the tone of bantering irreverence and from the accidents of situation and of language (puns, for example, and constant contemporary allusions) with which Mr. Frost supplements Biblical considerations, that he is at least as intent on writing an entertaining poem as he is on writing a philosophical one. That they need not be distinct, *A Masque of Reason* amply demonstrates, and no more clearly than at its end.

God calls in the Devil, finally,

> More to give his reality its due
> Than anything;

for he has lost stature of late (or apparent stature) through "Church neglect and figurative use." The Devil does not wish to speak, and does not, in fact, wish to remain. (Denis de Rougement points out in a new book that the Devil's first trick is the escape into anonymity.) He steps on a "tendency."

> . . . like the Gulf Stream,
> Only of sand not water,

and, without himself moving, begins to move away; but Job's wife, who is determined to take a picture of the three of them, pulls him off it and makes him stay. No humor could be more metaphysical.

Yet what is most memorable about *A Masque of Reason* is not so much its humor or its metaphysics as the tone of voice in which these characters speak at all times except the few occasions when topicality drowns them ðut: the tone of ancient wisdom, which carries with it the full weight and weariness of that skepticism to which intelligence is doomed.

Kenton Kilmer. *"A Masque of Reason." Best Sellers, 5 (April 1, 1945), 3.*

The position of the child in the Anderson tale "The Emperor's New Clothes" is one that every now and then confronts a reviewer, as the position he must adopt if he is, like the child, to be honest. This is such an occasion for me. Here is Robert Frost, venerable, certainly one of our finest poets, a man known for homely wisdom, writing a playful philosophical conversation in which join God, the devil, Job, and Job's wife. I find myself more afraid to belittle Frost than Frost seems to be to belittle God! Trembling, I read the words of the blurb: "With each rereading the total import deepens and widens, for this extraordinary poem constitutes a still further range of the power, the imagination, and the technique of Robert Frost." Can I be wrong? For me the total import is deep enough and wide enough, in all conscience—it is a blank abyss of nothingness.

The matter which Job and his wife discuss with God is the problem of suffering; specifically, the question of why Job had to suffer so much. God answers several questions, some sensibly and some frivolously, and neatly evades others. Job's wife contributes some of the most illuminating remarks on the subject. But the upshot of the discussion is the flat failure of all three, as well as of a most diaphanous and shy devil, to answer the basic question. Perhaps the closest God comes to a valid answer is this:

The discipline man needed most
Was to learn his submission to
*   unreason:*
And that for man's own sake, as well
*   as mine,*
So he won't find it hard to take his
*   orders*
From his inferiors in intelligence
In peace and war—especially in war.

The final scene is of Job's wife arranging God, Job, and the devil in a pose for a snapshot.

The whole is artificial, amusing, frivolous, done with skill and urbanity. Line after line, strangely, would serve aptly as criticism of the whole affair; such as:

This is polite society you're in
Where good and bad are mingled
*   everywhichway,*
And ears are lent to any sophistry
Just as if nothing mattered but our
*   manners.*

or:

We will be talking anyway
And may as well throw in a little
*   sense.*

or, finally:

The chances are when there's so
*   much pretense*
Of metaphysical profundity
The obscurity's a fraud to cover
*   nothing.*
I've come to think no so-called hidden
*   value's*
Worth going after. Get down into
*   things*
It will be found there's no more given
*   there*
Than on the surface.

It appears to me that in this masque celebrating his own seventieth birthday Frost has given himself the birthday present of representing God as unable to answer a question Frost himself can't answer. There seems little harm in that if it is not taken seriously, and I don't believe Frost himself takes it seriously. There seems no reason, however, to recommend the book except to those who wish to have as rounded a knowledge as possible of Robert Frost.

J. Donald Adams.
"Speaking of Books."
New York Times Book Review,
April 8, 1945,
p. 2.

Publication of the poem which marked the arrival of Robert Frost's seventieth birthday has set the reviewers to scratching their heads. A short play in blank verse, which Mr. Frost, with tongue in cheek, offers as chapter forty-three of the Book of Job, it has called forth differing reactions and interpretations. Some think it represents the poet at his best, others that it adds nothing to his stature. And nearly all give the appearance of straining hard to extract the poem's meaning.

"A Masque of Reason" is, in truth, a modern postscript to what I sometimes think is the greatest book in all the Old Testament. What would be mere imprudence and effrontery in a lesser writer, what would be woundingly irreverent in one less obviously seeking truth, may here be accepted as justified in its intention and in-

offensive in its humor. I think that no truly religious person need take umbrage at Mr. Frost's off-handed manner with the Deity. His humor is puckish, not arrogant, and I would think better of a Supreme Being who could accept it with a smile.

The play consists of a conversation between Job, his wife, and God, and, for the space of a moment, the Devil, whom God brings in "more to give his reality its due than anything." The time of the conversation is now; it contains contemporary references. Its theme is as old as man: the presence of evil in the world, and the fact that it is inescapably a part of man's lot on earth. The talk revolves about the question which Job, after all these years, puts to God: "Why did You hurt me so?"

When he speaks of this play Mr. Frost protests that he did not undertake to resolve anything, and that he hopes his critics will not search too far for its meaning. He thinks it salutary now and then to approach the gravest themes in a playful spirit, and I for one wholeheartedly agree. But even though "A Masque of Reason" shows us Robert Frost at his humorous ease (and he is one of those rare poets whose entire work is underscored and shot through with humor) it is humor with depth, such as the truest kind must have, and the play is also, it seems to me, Frost at his wisest. He would be among the last, I think, to call the wisdom in this case his own; the recognition and acceptance of it are his, but the wisdom itself, for the most part, is the wisdom of the poet of the Old Testament. Nevertheless, some of the poem's lines drop a plummet as deep as any Frost has written.

One word of warning may be in place: the poem can be enjoyed with only the average memory of Job's story, but to extract its full savor a rereading of the forty-two preceding chapters is not amiss. One needs to keep in mind God's negotiations with the Devil before Job, "with safeguards," as Frost reminds us, was delivered into his hands. One needs, too, a clear recollection of the words of Job's comforters, and their rebuke.

Mr. Frost leaves the central problem pretty much as it was left for us in the Bible story, but his asides provide some of the most delightful and some of the most suggestive lines we have had from him. All we know is that it is necessary for man to learn to take his orders, "to learn his submission to unreason." And so, Frost interjects, "he won't find it hard to take his war."

There is a line that pays high tribute to the intelligence of women. He has Job's wife say: "There isn't any universal reason; and no one but a man would think there was," to which she adds, "You don't catch women trying to be Plato." And there is Frost's own profundity in God's answer to Job's question why the demonstration afforded by his trials had to be at his expense. "It had to be at somebody's expense," says God.

Society can never think things
    out:
  It has to see them acted out by
    actors,
  Devoted actors at a sacrifice—
  The ablest actors I can lay my
    hands on.

Or when Job's wife observes of the Devil: "Look how he takes no steps! He isn't really going, yet he's leav-ing." And were the sea-changes suffered by science ever as well phrased as in the line, "while science goes self-superseding on"?

Once again, it seems to me, Robert Frost has given us what he once declared to be the final function of a poem—"a momentary stay against confusion." It is that "momentary stay against confusion" that he has contributed in larger measure than any other American writer of our time. And once again, one is struck by the continuity in Frost's work, by its sustained development and power.

I venture the guess that he is the only one of our living poets to whose collected work readers will turn generations hence with the same delight as we now do; others will live on in the anthologies, but in Frost's work the stones are laid end to end; even as each poem of his is an indivisible unit, so are they all inseparably joined. It is true of him, as it has been of so few writers in our time, that his work is corporate. It rises and holds fast together like an arch in stone. He seems to me to be the first of our poets since Whitman who will, beyond any question, belong to the world! There is in him, I think, even more of universal quality than there was in Whitman. His New England is a microcosm, and his wisdom is such wisdom as men have found anywhere, at any time.

Conrad Aiken. "Whole Meaning or Doodle." *New Republic,* 112 (April 16, 1945) 514.

Robert Frost's new long poem, *A Masque of Reason,* is another example of "whole-meaning" method. Here too the poet has begun with his end, has known in advance every move on the board; but although Mr. Frost starts us off with one of his very happiest openings, and takes us with dexterity to one of his most amusingly inconclusive conclusions, one cannot help feeling that through a good deal of the poem the "whole meaning" goes, unfortunately, a little bare. Dare one whisper, of a poet to whom one so gratefully owes so much, that a little more affectionate and affective care with his blank verse might have prevented its becoming *quite* so—and frequently—unrewardingly blank? It's all great fun, of course, and not too dangerously unorthodox; but there are times when the cracker-barrel wisecrack grates a little, and when the texture and text alike become too thin. Mr. Frost himself once reminded us that good fences make good neighbors—but he himself doesn't much like a wall. Far indeed from the art that conceals art, is this (if we may say it without impertinence) the artlessness that conceals artlessness? But Mr. Frost is no doubt laughing up his sleeve at us, and this remains a most engaging little *jeu d'esprit,* and is not intended, like Hardy's "God's Funeral," to give us a real pause.

F. W. Dupee. "Frost and Tate." *The Nation,* 160 (April 21, 1945), 464, 466.

Fortunate in the fine adequacy of his rural symbolism and native style, Robert Frost has always seemed the most self-sufficient of living poets. But now on his seventieth birthday he has published a poem, "A Masque of Reason" (Holt, $2), which is not only unique among his writings, but is also in obvious debt to other poets. In this dialogue in heaven between Job, Job's wife, and God on the subject of divine justice, the heaven is an artificial paradise reminiscent of Yeats's Byzantium. More oddly still, God has a "prefabricated" throne, liable to sudden and embarrassing collapses as in some modernistic fantasy of Auden's.

But Yeats and Auden here fuse—if they fuse at all—into a whimsicality typical of no one but Frost himself. The trouble with such humor in Frost is that it is too often not a laugh but a smirk—the reflex of an incorrigible complacency. Least apparent in those beautiful poems in which he is the observer, at once realistic and visionary, of New England objects and occupations, it is apt to become overwhelming at those times when he is explicitly the philosopher. And "A Masque of Reason," with its unearthly setting and despite all its rustic banter and horseplay, is pure speculation. . . .

"Book Window." *Christian Science Monitor Weekly Magazine,* April 21, 1945, p. 12.

Out of the fullness of experience, confident of his position in the world of letters, Mr. Frost has amused himself with writing a *jeu d'esprit*. A conversation between God, Job and his wife, and Satan—such is the imaginary form which it takes. It is, of course, smooth and expert work; moreover, it is primed with humor which is none too usual a circumstance in free verse. But as to precisely what Mr. Frost means to convey, perhaps none of his readers will be quite sure. One thing is certain: Mr. Frost is hiding inside Job and asking God all the questions he would like to have answered. He naturally does not receive the answers, and so the poem becomes merely an entertaining trifle. Mr. Frost has added little to the great discussion of the problem of good and evil, with which the world has been concerned for so long.

"New England Questions." *Time,* 45 (May 7, 1945), 99-100.

Shortly after completing this 23-page verse-play, 70-year-old Robert Frost came down with penumonia, lay wondering if God were punishing him for having written it. Happily—and justly—he recovered. A poet whose work has often been explicit drama, Frost is outright dramatist in *A Masque of Reason*—and still the New England philosopher asking questions about the nature of things.

They are embarrassing questions, and one of the dramatic values is the embarrassment of God, of whom the questions are asked. Job, the afflicted, who asks the questions, is embarrassed, too. Only his wife is not: she is too impatient with the two male colloquists. (And too bored: once, she falls asleep.)

The play's setting is "a fair oasis in the purest desert" of the afterworld. Job, his wife, God and the Devil are the actors, and the theme is the place of reason (or lack of it) in man's lot under God's hands. Says God (who, like his servant, is pure New Englander in sense and idiom):

I've had you on my mind a thousand
*   years*
To thank you some day for the way
*   you helped me*
Establish once for all the principle
There's no connection man can
*   reason out*
Between his just deserts and what he
*   gets. . . .*

God finally confesses to Job that, in making him suffer, He was really just "showing off to the Devil"—for which He is somewhat apologetic, now.

When God agrees to call in the Devil (in response to Job's suggestion of "a good old get-together"), Job's wife perks up, runs for her camera.

"Now if you three have settled
*   anything*

*You'd as well smile as frown on the
    occasion."*

Which is about what the reader
does—seeing that nothing is settled,
but a good deal of wit and sly wisdom
have been released. The 23 pages are
good latter-day Frost: the ruminative
philosophic wit whose pentameters
are salted with gentle satire and unobtrusive learning.

Louis Untermeyer. "Submission To Unreason." *Virginia Quarterly Review,* 21 (Spring 1945), 286-89.

On the eve of his seventieth birthday,
the most respected of our living poets
and the (seemingly) most recognizably
traditional of New England voices has
published his most questioning and
controversial poem. It is like nothing
hitherto composed by the author of
"North of Boston" or, for that matter,
by any other poet. It is called a masque;
but those readers who might be
led to expect a pretty piece of semi-
Shakespearian dumb-show will be
vividly shocked, although the lines—
even to the stage directions—are in
decorous blank verse. "A Masque of
Reason," apparently a one-act play,
opens in "a fair oasis in the purest desert." Underneath a palm—time and
place not stated—a man and a woman
sit staring at the sky. A tree (which is
part Burning Bush, part Christmas
Tree) is on fire, and something caught
in its branches struggles to get out.

What emerges (prefabricated plywood
throne and all) is God, and the man
and woman are not, as the reader is
inclined to guess, Adam and Eve, but
a more argumentative and far more
interesting couple, Job and Job's wife.
It transpires that the occasion is the
Day of Judgment, and it is God who
has come to be judged.

But God, an old and skillful dialec-
tician, is not to be tricked into solving
the humanly insoluble. . . .

It develops that it was the very essence of Job's (or any man's) trial that
its agony could not be understood by
suffering humanity. God insists that
he tried to appease man by following
man's arbitrary choice of good and
evil "with forfeits and rewards he understood," that Job changed all that
and thus became the Emancipator of
God; as such, Job is promoted to
sainthood. But Job's wife (who recognized God at once by Blake's picture)
is not comforted. She pursues God
with protests; she demands reasons,
asks why injustice still prevails, cau-
stically inquires who invented earth.
Perversely enough, or because of the
natural confraternity of males, Job
defends God:

. . . God must await events
As well as words . . .
God needs time just as much as you
    or I
To get things done. Reformers fail to
    see that.

And God agrees that he and Job
worked out a great demonstration:
that the discipline man needed most
was "to learn submission to unreason." And when Job not unnatu-
rally inquires why it had to be at his
expense, God logically replies:

It had to be at somebody's expense.
Society can never think things out.

Nevertheless the man in Job is not satisfied with God's ex-post-facto excuses and the artist in him "cries out for design."

I fail to see what fun, what
    satisfaction
A God can find in laughing at how
    badly
Men fumble at the possibilities
When left to guess forever for
    themselves.
The chances are when there's so
    much pretense
Of metaphysical profundity
The obscurity's a fraud to cover
    nothing . . .

It is here, when Job's demands grow most godlike, that God is most human. The suffering of Job was an answer to Satan—"a showing off to the Devil," a temptation God could not resist. It was God's trial as well as Job's, made easier for the Deity since God knew he could count on Job, and since (as Job's wife puts it) the Devil is God's greatest inspiration. Satan, precipitated from the desert air, appears and is twitted by Job's wife, who brings the poem to a close on a teasing domestic note. The rest is a cryptic silence.

The reader's first reaction will be one of surprise. Both the material and the manner seem to be worlds apart from the homely scene and accent of "Mending Wall," "The Death of the Hired Man," and "Birches," as well as "Come In" and the other lyrics. Yet the Frostian touch is there; it is even bolder in its mingling of profundity and playfulness, more daring than ever in its philosophical banter and

metaphysical fancy. The whole poem is a play in paradox. It is a continual alternation of purpose and cross-purpose, of meaning and mockery.

Most paradoxical of all, it is a young man's poem: a half questing, half querulous search for ultimates. The years have sharpened the wit of America's most probing and most representative poet. They have emphasized the character of the man who transcended his own rustic material and who, in poem after poem, lifted the regional into the universal. "A Masque of Reason" is his latest triumph—a curious but logical complement to the early monologues which startled us thirty years ago in "North of Boston." It is a richly speculative piece of exegesis that is no less wise for being so tantalizingly whimsical.

George F. Whicher. "Chapter Forty-Three of Job." *Yale Review,* 34 (Spring 1945), 549-51.

Spring is the mischief in Robert Frost as much in this metaphysical fantasia, published in honor of his seventieth birthday, as in "Mending Wall," printed before he was forty. The thirty years and more of his public career as a poet have seen a broadening out of his range of reference, but no blunting of his wit and wisdom. Never has he written with more assured control of philosophical implication and verbal intonation than in the imaginary colloquy in blank verse that he has now constructed on the basis of the Book of Job.

In "A Masque of Reason" (called a masque, he has said, because it isn't one) Frost has travelled a long way from the region north of Boston where his imagination once seemed to have settled for life. His scene is now "A fair oasis in the purest desert" where time has become a space dimension with room to turn around in, with the result that his characters, though projected from the Old Testament, move upon a plane of mental abstraction where all historical periods are scrambled together. A figure of God modelled on the drawings of William Blake emerges from a prevailingly Byzantine burning bush and proceeds to "pitch" a collapsible, plywood throne. The Devil manifests himself as a sapphire wasp with mica wings, since "church neglect and figurative use" have attenuated him to a shadow of disrespect. Job, Job's wife, God, and the Devil quote Shakespeare, Milton, Herrick, Lovelace, Emerson, and Browning at each other with weird effect.

It might be expected that persons in a play conceived without the support of the homely rusticity that Frost has so often reproduced in his country idyls would melt into thin air as readily as the actors in Prospero's masque, but the reverse is true. All the speakers have an authenticity of voice that makes itself felt from the first words they utter. God, who begins by proclaiming a grandiose theological reason for his treatment of Job but at last confesses that what really moved him was the desire to show off before the Devil, is molded more nearly in man's image than perhaps becomes an Ancient of Days with flowery beard, yet he at least is no lay figure. Job is

deferential, but nobody's fool, not even God's. The Devil in his brief appearance is an incarnate smirk. The great triumph of the piece is the characterization of Job's wife, here named Thyatira. She turns out to be an advocate of "witch-women's rights," who nurses a grievance because prophets are nearly always men and wants to know what God would do with "a prayer that started off Lord God of Hostesses." Though she dozes through most of the high discourse between God and Job, she wakes up again with the instinctive perception that all that the talk amounts to is "the Devil being God's best inspiration." None of the many country women in Frost's dramatic lyrics is more convincingly portrayed than this epitome of feminine downrightness, a character not planted by intention but come upon unexpectedly like a wild flower of the mind.

Underlying the playfulness that is a constant feature of Frost's poetic thought is a bedrock of serious meditation. The theme of the little play is the function of reason in a mortal existence which has come to seem less like a boat descending a stream under some control of oar and rudder and more like the irresistible lapse of the stream itself. As compared with man's will, whether used as motor or as brakes, reason may be thought of as a steering-gear. But in view of the unaccountable flux of things in general, reason is powerless. When even God must wait for events, the chief lesson that man needs to learn is that of "submission to unreason." Yet, as Job notes, man cannot help being concerned with reason even while disparaging it. As he states it:

. . . We're plainly made to go.

We're going anyway and may as well
Have some say as to where we're
    headed for;
Just as we will be talking anyway
And may as well throw in a little
    sense.

Such a rationalization may satisfy Job, but Thyatira is not willing to accept God's sovereign unaccountability. She does not expect from Him any single solution of the mystery of things, but she puts it up to God that there must be

. . . lots of unsystematic
Stray scraps of palliative reason
It wouldn't hurt you to vouchsafe the
    faithful.

Convinced in the end, however, that "you won't get any answers out of God," she frankly doubts if his kingdom on earth has any valid meaning and loses interest. But as for the Devil, "He's very real to me and always will be." She snatches him off a "tendency" that like a strip of moving carpet was carrying him away—

. . . I hate
A tendency. The minute you get on
    one
It seems to start right off
    accelerating.—

And at the close of the play she is engaged in posing God, Job, and the Devil for a candid camera shot of their "good old get-together celebration."

One need not argue about Frost's distinction. The proof of a poet lies in what he can do. Where else can we find work that both rewards a casual reading by its whimsical wit and still holds substance for long pondering? It may be said of other poems that

. . . when there's so much pretense
Of metaphysical profundity
The obscurity's a fraud to cover
    nothing.

But in "A Masque of Reason" there is no pretense. It is the ripe product of a writer who is both philosopher and poet.

Checklist of Additional Reviews

Springfield Sunday Union and Republican, March 25, 1945, p. 4D.
Orville Prescott. "Books of the Times." *New York Times,* March 26, 1945, Sec. 1, p. 17.
"We Recommend." *Boston Daily Globe,* March 28, 1945, p. 17 [evening edition].
Booklist, 41 (April 1, 1945), 221.
"Jehovah, Satan, and the Jobs." *Newsweek,* 25 (April 2, 1945), 100-102.
Louise Bogan. *New Yorker,* 21 (April 7, 1945), 83-85.
Mary Katherine Reely, ed. "A Selected List of Current Books." *Wisconsin Library Bulletin,* 41 (May 1945), 53.
Open Shelf, May-June, 1945, p. 11.
E. S. Forgotson. "A Shift of Scenery and a Change of Cast." *Poetry,* 66 (June 1945), 156-59.
U. S. Quarterly Book List, 1 (June 1945), 7.
Thomas F. Opie. *Churchman,* 159 (July 1945), p. 19.
Katherine Brégy. *Catholic World,* 161 (September 1945), 522.
Theatre Arts, 29 (October 1945), 607.

STEEPLE BUSH

BY

ROBERT FROST

NEW YORK

HENRY HOLT AND COMPANY

Steeple Bush

Leonard Bacon.
"Robert Frost's 'Intricate Simplicity.' "
Saturday Review of Literature, 30 (May 31, 1947), 15.

The hill pastures of "the one state of ours that is a shire" are in season apt to be full of spiraea tomentosa, alias hardhack, alias steeple bush. Outsiders hardly notice the close-packed Gothic panicles, but the native and the enlightened summer visitor recognize a strict and upright beauty in the vertical spikes, to which more spectacular flowers can lay no claim. Nor could any flower be a better symbol for what someone has called Mr. Frost's "intricate simplicity."

There are forty-three poems in this little volume, most of them brief and all of them interesting for one reason or another. There is no falling off. There has been no resting on oars or on laurels. And we can still thank God for the "barbed image," the penetrating wisdom, the inconspicuous grace that half conceals its own elegance, and the lancinating wit.

And we can thank God for something else. It was said of some Frenchman that while his rivals thought about writing, he wrote about thinking. This hits off Mr. Frost quite well. He is the most careful of workmen, but he always has something worth his while to work on. Any one of his poems is the incarnation or symbol of something completed in the mind. It may involve philosophies. It will force you to draw conclusions. You must decide yes or no. It isn't strange that Lucretius appears several times in these pages. Lucretius shared that passion for the explicit and the clear. He too hoped that he would not be misunderstood in what he meant. And he apparently meant to mean. Certainly Mr. Frost does. And yet for all the sober almost mathematical approach, where in all our American scene is there such a burning?

The reviewer might easily have written a formal notice of "Steeple Bush." He could have dwelt with pleasure on the bewildering beauty and the extraordinary evocation of mystery from the familiar which characterizes "Directive," a poem impossible to forget once it is read. The sharp imagery of "An Unstamped Letter," the savage satire of "Etherealization," all such matters a respectable critic should deal with justly, not forgetting to supply the poet with a ready-made system of esthetics and some good advice as to his future artistic conduct. This the present writer will not do. Mr. Frost is too great a poet.

Why not say so and be done with it?

Randall Jarrell.
" 'Tenderness and Passive Sadness.' "
New York Times Book Review,
June 1, 1947,
p. 4.

Reading through Frost's new book one stops for a long time at "Directive."

Back out of all this now
   too much for us,
Back in a time made simple
   by the loss
Of detail, burned, dissolved,
   and broken off
Like graveyard marble sculpture
   in the weather,
There is a house that is
   no more a house,
Upon a farm that is no more a farm
And in a town that is
   no more a town . . .

One climbs there along a road quarry-like with glacier-chiseled boulders, not minding the "serial ordeal" of the eye-pairs that watch from forty cellar-holes, not minding "the woods' excitement over you/That sends light rustle rushes to their leaves. . . ."

Where were they all not
   twenty years ago?
They think too much of having
   shaded out
A few old pecker-fretted apple trees.

Finally, on"the height/Of country where two village cultures faded/Into each other. Both of them are lost,"

you too are lost, "pull in your ladder road behind you," and make yourself at home with the only field left, "no bigger than a harness gall," with the shattered "playthings in the playhouse of the children." ("Weep for what little things could make them glad.") Then, passing the "house in earnest" that has become "only a be-lilacked cellar hole," you go to your destination, "a brook that was the water of the house,/Cold as a spring as yet so near its source,/Too lofty and original to rage," and at last you find

. . . hidden in the instep arch
Of an old cedar at the waterside
A broken drinking goblet
   like the Grail
Under a spell so the wrong ones
   can't find it,
So can't get saved, as Saint Mark
   says they mustn't.
(I stole the goblet from
   the children's playhouse.)
Here are your waters and
   your watering place.
Drink and be whole again
   beyond confusion.

There are weak places in the poem, but these are nothing beside so much longing, tenderness, and passive sadness. Frost's understanding that each life is tragic because it wears away into the death that it at last half-welcomes—that even its salvation, far back at the cold root of things, is make-believe, drunk from a child's broken and stolen goblet hidden among the ruins of the lost cultures. Much of the strangeness of the poem is far under the surface, or else so much on the surface, in the subtlest of details (how many readers will connect the "serial ordeal" of the eye-pairs with the poem's Grail-parody?), that one slides under it unnoticing. There are no notes in the back about this Grail.

There is nothing else in "Steeple Bush" like "Directive"; probably the nearest thing is the dry mercilessness of "The Ingenuities of Debt." But most of the poems merely remind you, by their persistence in the mannerisms of what was genius, that they are productions of somebody who once, and somewhere else, was a great poet. The man who said that he learned from Marlowe to say his prayers: "Why, this is Hell, nor am I out of it"; who could be annoyed at a hornet for not recognizing him as "the exception I like to think I am in everything"; who in poems like "A Servant to Servants," "The Witch of Coös," or "Home Burial," had a final identifying knowledge of the deprived and dispossessed, the insulted and injured, that one matches in modern poetry only in Hardy—this poet is now, most of the time, an elder statesman like Baruch or Smuts, full of complacent wisdom and cast-iron whimsy. (Of course there was always something of this in the official role that Frost created for himself; one imagines Yeats saying about Frost, as Sarah Bernhardt said about Nijinsky: "I fear, I greatly fear, that I have just seen the greatest actor in the world.")

"Steeple Bush" is no book to convert intellectuals to Frost. Yet the ordinary "highbrow" reader is making a far greater mistake when he neglects Frost as commonplace, than the academic reader makes when he apotheosizes him, often on the basis of his most complacent or sentimental poems.

Frost is one of the subtlest and saddest of poets; and no other living poet has written so well about the actions of ordinary men. But anyone should know this after reading "Home Burial," "Two Witches," "A Servant to Servants," "Neither Out Far Nor In Deep," "Design," "Acquainted with the Night," "Provide, Provide," "Desert Places," "Directive," "The Gift Outright," "An Old Man's Winter Night"; or guess at it after reading

But now he brushed the shavings
from his knee
And stood the axe there on
its horse's hoof,
Erect, but not without its waves,
as when
The snake stood up for evil
in the Garden. . . .

Esther Willard Bates. "For Humbly Proud Thinkers." *Christian Science Monitor,* June 16, 1947, p. 16.

Beautifully named is STEEPLE BUSH, by Robert Frost, the latest volume of poetry to come from America's Dean of Poets. Steeple bush is the rich, stiff spires of rose pink, which some of us call hardhack, and which we see dotting the August hillsides, planting its flag amid dark green junipers and outcrop of pudding stone. In midwinter, when the drifting snow has buried grass and fern, it holds high above the icy land its panicled tips, brown, perhaps, but undaunted.

The verse in this volume is also uncompromising and enduring, but rich and unforgettable. As happens with older poets, the music and a certain loveliness go, but the wisdom increases. So is it here. This is poetry such as Hardy might have written, had Hardy possessed Frost's hope and courage.

The titles of the poems tell the reader what to expect. "Something for Hope" advises us to retain our patience and look away ahead. Frost sounds again and again the note of timelessness, the sense of space, both of which keep before our vision a certain unearthly beauty.

He writes of a long-departed Ancient, who left his unmistakable traces in the delta of a brook, of crumbling cellar holes of houses long since vanished. In other and earlier volumes, Frost had us pausing with him in a snowy wood to hear the swish of snowflakes and see the little horse shaking his head. Now, when we pause with him outdoors, we are spending "all night with universal space." Something has driven him into the uttermost fields of the sky where one may search out wisdom with Job.

But there he has found what he sought, a word to hear to take firm hold on. The sun is in the sky; the sap runs; spring breaks from its cold prison and man again plants his pitchfork in the tough and fibrous clay.

Frost's correlatives are plain and dry, but the elements of fire, air, earth, and water are in them, too. His rhythms are broken. There is a rough metrical going but it suits the rocky road that man must travel on.

And yet, no one should imagine that Robert Frost has lost his love for the human occupants of this earth in his imperative preoccupation with the remote destinies of men. One of his loveliest, "An Unstamped Letter in Our Rural Letter Box," is in this late volume, only waiting to be snatched at by anthology makers. There is a brief and shattering poem to an enemy. There is a satire on a Mrs. Someone who's been to Asia, etched in caustic, and a lovely and haunting "Roger's Group." Still and all, this is no book for a dreamer. It is for thinkers who are humbly proud.

George F. Whicher. "Ripeness of a Poet's Wisdom." *New York Herald Tribune Weekly Book Review,* July 6, 1947, p. 2.

Notwithstanding bonds of continuity that makes Frost always Frost, there is never any guaranty that he will be found twice in the same place. His eight principal volumes distributed over thirty-four years represent a considerable segment of the life-cycle possible to a poet, and each volume holds a distinctive position. He does not write in his seventies imitations of what he was writing in his forties. Where there is likeness there is increase of skill. The present gathering of poems mainly written during the last three years is more topical, more sharply intellectual, and more given to teasing than any of its predecessors. Frost, as he long ago predicted he might, has grown more sure of all he thought was true.

A dozen poems massed at the end of

the book under the heading of "Editorials" are devoted to a playful mauling of current attitudes for which Frost has little use. Like Tolstoi, his deep sense of the rhythms of nature make him distrustful of interferences by government. Many of his antipathies are roused by variations on the assumption that our earth was intended to be or can be made a place where human beings can live at ease. He is not impressed by the schemes of Utopian planners, nor is it true that

With him the love of country means
Blowing it all to smithereens
And having it all made over new.

Still less is he impressed by prophets of disaster. He likes a world stormy enough to make survival rank as an achievement. The contortions of statesmen, the cocksureness of scientists provide him with all the amusement he needs. And if anyone is incautious enough to suppose that the evils of an industrial era are peculiar to America, Frost will remind him that human nature is perennially and everywhere the same, a contention maintained in one of the most striking final couplets in recent poetry:

Teach those Asians mass production?
Teach your grandmother egg suction.

Abstract verse comes in for a fling in a sonnet called "Etherializing," one of a number of highly individualized treatments of the traditional form that appear in this collection. Scattered through the book are a few outbreaks of pure delightful whimsy, such as "In the Long Night" and "Two Leading Lights," and a few bits of sheer cleverness like "Iota Subscript," a masterpiece of ingenuity, and "Lu-

cretius vs. the Lake Poets." Readers who cannot bear to think that high poetry can ever be sportive may avert their earnest eyes.

They will be better pleased with a considerable group of meditative poems, philosophical and even religious, which attest the ripeness of the poet's wisdom. Over the years poems of this type have been growing more frequent in his work. His interest in the range of human knowledge is wide, extending from archaeological inferences about primitive man to the latest speculations of astronomers about the cosmos.

There is only a little work in this volume that recalls the intense lyricism of "Mountain Interval" and parts of "New Hampshire," but the few lyrics are of the finest quality. Indeed the poem called "One Step Backward Taken" seems to me certain to be recognized among the greatest lyrics of the twentieth century. Beginning as an innocent description of a mountain freshet it suddenly changes into an image of our tormented epoch so powerfully reverberant that it takes the mind by storm as only the handiwork of a master can.

But there are also three utterly charming poems at the beginning of the volume, "A Young Birch," "Something for Hope," and "Directive," which picture country things as only Frost can picture them. Here again we encounter the poet of stone walls and birch trees, of overgrown pastures and "belilaced" cellar holes, and the poignancy of affection that he so well knows how to evoke. No doubt to many readers the best part of the book will be this assurance that the poet has not altogether changed from him they knew.

George Snell.
San Francisco Chronicle,
July 13, 1947,
p. 20.

Robert Frost's quality as a poet has long since been confirmed; his new volume, "Steeple Bush," shows no diminution of poetic power. The peculiarly Frostian flavor is in these poems, with the New England bite and the American tang. The lyric ease and the flow of thought and its complete communication, are continued delights. Such beautifully fashioned poems as "To an Ancient" or "Were I in Trouble" seem enough to cause one to say, here is America's best living poet. It is indeed a pleasure to contemplate the constant, if not increasing, mastery of Robert Frost.

Louis Untermeyer.
"Still Further Range."
Yale Review, 37
(September 1947),
138-39.

This may not be Robert Frost's heaviest or happiest book, but it is one of his shrewdest. It is salted with wit and peppered with satire. Although it is a small book—only sixty-two deeply margined pages—the range is wide: songs, soliloquies, whimsical lyrics, somber speculations, bitter conclusions. The section titles give the key to its variety: "Steeplebush," "Five Nocturnes," "A Spire and Belfry," "Out and Away," "Editorials."

The skeptic note is immediately apparent. Frost is a dogged examiner; he appraises the world without being deceived by its cherished illusions; he doubts both its pretenses and its desperations. Rarely has the poet written so grimly as in "The Broken Drought," "Bursting Rapture," "Why Wait for Science," "No Holy Wars for Them," and particularly "The Ingenuities of Debt," with its pitiless beginning and end:

These I assume were words so deeply
     meant
They cut themselves in stone for
     permanent
Like trouble in the brow above the
     eyes:
"Take Care to Sell Your Horse
     before He Dies;
The Art of Life Is Passing Losses
     on." . . .
Sand has been thrusting in the
     square of door
Across the tessellation of the floor,
And only rests, a serpent on its chin,
Content with contemplating, taking
     in,
Till it can muster breath inside a
     hall
To rear against the inscription on
     the wall.

This is a far and lonely cry from the personal bucolics of "North of Boston," the little lyrics of "A Boy's Will," the appealing pastorals and monologues of "Mountain Interval," "West-Running Brook," and "A Further Range." But the new book is not without some of the old tenderness and the rough half-concealed grace. "A Young Birch" and "Something for Hope" (and especially, "Directive") recall the genius for understatement which is essentially Frost's. Such poems supply added emphasis to that simplicity which is so deceptive and so subtle. Rarely has the sadness of age and the hopelessness of inevitable ruin reached out so tragically as in "Directive." Yet there is no breast-beating, no loud anguish. On the contrary, the tone is detached and seemingly impersonal, lightly if falsely casual:

> Back out of all this now too much for
> us,
> Back in a time made simple by the
> loss
> Of detail, burned, dissolved, and
> broken off
> Like graveyard marble sculpture in
> the weather,
> There is a house that is no more a
> house
> Upon a farm that is no more a farm
> And in a town that is no more a
> town.
> The road there, if you'll let a guide
> direct you
> Who only has at heart your getting
> lost,
> May seem as if it should have been a
> quarry—
> Great monolithic knees the former
> town
> Long since gave up pretence of
> keeping covered. . . .
> Make yourself up a cheering song of
> how
> Someone's road home from work this
> once was,
> Who may be just ahead of you on
> foot
> Or creaking with a buggy load of
> grain. . . .

I have implied that this is neither Frost's most commanding nor his most co-ordinated volume. But it is highly characteristic of the man at seventy-three and the poet at any age. It cannot be by-passed. It must be read as part of the still-growing work of America's most considerable contemporary poet.

Donald A. Stauffer. "The New Lyrics of Robert Frost." *Atlantic Monthly*, 180 (October 1947), 115-16.

In New England, steeple bush is a weed that has evidently as poignant and specific associations as loco in the West or aspidistra in London. Steeple bush crowds out the edible grass and is in turn crowded out when the maple, birch, and spruce take over. It is, then, halfway between cultivation and something dark and deep and primitive. That is Robert Frost's position in his latest volume, *Steeple Bush*.

The cultivation is still there: in his "post Franconian, recent Riptonian" period, Frost can make of a drinking cup and a brook near an abandoned house a poem as clear and refreshing as any that have celebrated Falernian wine or the Bandusian fountain. But there is more Lucretius now than Horace, more granite than herbs. Though Frost may be ironically aware of his own limits in "The Middleness of the Road," such poems are no contented celebrations of the Golden Mean, but realizations of stars, sky, space, and time, of

> the absolute flight and rest
> The universal blue
> And local green suggest.

Even in such a perfect reflection as "A Young Birch," tenderness and beauty become elegiac in the contrived succession of the Order of Contents.

These poems, then, are not so much simple as they are elemental. Precipices and dark chasms open beyond the walls of the world, and the vistas through time make a century like the tick of a pendulum. Frost is uncompromisingly aware of an agonizing universe, and creates apocalyptic twentieth-century visions no less grim than Hardy, Yeats, Eliot, and Auden. Frost collects "Five Nocturnes" in this book; there are not an equal number of *aubades.* "I put no faith in the seeming facts of light."

The underpainting for *Steeple Bush* is an unforgiving cosmos. But in poetry, subject matter—or even emotional situation—is trivial in comparison with what the poet *does* with his material. Beauty may be born out of its own despair. This little volume of forty-three poems is inspiriting. Frost is one of the very small company of living poets whom it is an immediate pleasure to read. No harm can come from revealing his open secret, for although it may be described, it cannot easily be imitated. His mastery depends upon absolute control of technique and of thought.

While other writers talk about the problem of including the multiplex modern world in a poem, Frost goes ahead and does it. Wordsworth wrote of poetry as "the smile upon the face of science." If this means anything at all, what better example could we find than these lines from Frost's "Skeptic," addressed characteristically to a far star?

I don't believe what makes you red
   in the face

Is after explosion going away so fast.

To put into two lines a whole astronomical theory of the present state of the universe, including the supporting data dependent upon the wave lengths of light, and then to add psychology and philosophy to science by denying the theory, is perhaps as much metaphysical complexity as is good for half of any quatrain. Yet Frost is accused of simplicity!

What he achieves, of course, is the reduction to common speech, almost as Dante does, of difficult ideas, yet without destroying overtones. He seems simple only because of his language, and because he has done in advance the work of resolution and thought which other poets, more lazy or careless, are content to leave to their readers. Where Yeats threw aside the old embroideries of language to discover that "there's more enterprise in walking naked," Frost from the beginning has more consistently taken what he calls "my barefoot stand." His capacity to generalize in ordinary terms makes him quotable and memorable on every page. Take two noble single-line meditations on restraint:—

He has the greatness to refrain.
Too lofty and original to rage.

Opposed to those many moderns who strive for the unusual and clashing adjective or the puzzling turn of thought, Frost seems to work for a kind of harmonious inevitability which triumphs most when its easiness passes unnoticed. Calculation is made to appear instinct, and the writer's labor becomes the reader's pleasure. Frost's serious puns are no accidents:—

While the trees put on their
   wooden *rings*
And with long-sleeved branches hold
   their *sway.*

Or:—

Something was going *right* outside
   the hall.

Or (for an Eskimo speaker protected
from the long Arctic night):—

As one *rankly* warm insider.

His structures are no less pleasurable. "Were I in Trouble" is a lesson to poets in patterning minute sound effects. One of his most successful forms is the triple wave of a Shakespearean sonnet followed by a turn or conclusion, though not necessarily in the proportions of 4-4-4-2. "The Planners," for example, comes out in fourteen lines, but the divisions are three triplets in parallel thought and a five-line conclusion. And "The Middleness of the Road" is cunning craftsmanship: its sixteen lines are divided by structure into four quatrains, and by sense into 3, 4, 4, and 5, so that the quatrains run on, coalesce, and slip together into a single firedrop of lyric. If this were the place, a whole review might be spent on the singing qualities that Frost builds from interjecting three-syllable feet in basic two-syllable patterns, or from rhyming monosyllables with two- or three-syllable words.

The imagery is no less his own. It grows out of respect for little things and for one's native land and language. A "belilaced cellar hole" of a deserted house slowly closes in "like a dent in dough." The myth of the lock of hair turned into a constellation, which Pope modulates at the end of *The Rape of the Lock* and which Yeats intensifies in

And after, nailed upon the night
   Berenice's burning hair

becomes, in Frost's wry speech:—

It may not give me hope
That when I am translated
My scalp will in the cope
   Be constellated.

What George Herbert did for the church at Bemerton, Frost does for the country around Ripton, Vermont, using "A Steeple on the House" as Herbert used "The Pulley" or "The Collar" or "The Altar."

The bells are in full chime in Frost's belfry—imagery, structural harmony, language, singing rhythms. And the steeple stretches toward the sky.

The central drive of the volume cannot suggest its variety—its wistfulness toward the "Young and unassuming," its ancestral ruminations in "A Cliff Dwelling" and "To an Ancient," the humorously magnificent compliment of "Iota Subscript" (the love poem of Browning's grammarian), the metaphysics of near and far, of a thinking reed in an icy universe. The satiric note is strong. Frost includes the most devastating and funny quatrain of hate since the days of Doctor Fell, and in the course of the volume draws blood (it may be a mere pinking, it may be a decapitation) from the planners, the wagers of holy wars, the believers in clichés and mass opinion, the worshipers of size and of abstraction, the officious, the fearful, the philological deans, the fashionably intellectual, and the scientific materialists. The satire proceeds to the final page of owlishly uninformative "Notes" which would not be so effectively ridiculous if Eliot's *Waste Land* and Auden's *New Year Letter* had not preceded them.

The gayety, and at times the extravagant abandon, of the style is a necessary balance to the dark philosophy which makes many of Frost's contemporaries look like his callow fanatic whose "Mind is hardly out of his teens." Frost's mind grows clearer and sharper, less sentimental, with the years. Although he may deliberately protect the independence of "all those who try to go it sole alone," although he may assume the value of skepticism and the need for reticence, *Steeple Bush* contains its trinity of intimations on hope, courage, and love. He still knows that the withered leaves of a young beech in March may be, in some strange world of truth, "the Paradise-in-bloom."

Yeats took for his symbol as an artist the singing metal bird. Here Frost has chosen steeple bush, intervening for a century as an interval of rest is the cycles of the cultivators of the soil. Its spire points toward heaven, and in its rocky pastures it allows us to develop hope and patience, "to make up for a lack of meditation" in case we are too serious, too hurried, and too cultivated in our economics, our pacifism, our etherealizing, our learning, and our scientific "complacent ministry of fear." There is partial irony in calling steeple bush "a lovely blooming but wasteful weed."

Malcolm Ross. *"Steeple Bush." Canadian Forum* November 1947, p. 191.

There is little in this volume to please the admirer of Frost's best and characteristic work. Where once metaphysical suggestion stole secretly from simple Yankee birches, one encounters a self-conscious strain, a striving for "modernity," and only rare moments of lyrical lift. The jacket tells us "that Frost's shrewd comment on national and world affairs seems sharper and more provocative than ever before." But unfortunately, the topical poems read like mediocre newspaper editorials set to rhyme. The volume is technically uneven, often lapsing into amateurish doggerel. We are sadly aware that this is Frost's old age and that it is no Homer who nods here.

Gladys Campbell. " 'A World Torn Loose Went By Me.' " *Poetry,* 71 (December 1947), 145-49.

Robert Frost has been recognized as an important poet by most important critics for almost thirty years. During these years he has published a dozen books, and new poems have constantly appeared in magazines. Through text-books and anthologies some of his poems are so well-known to school-boys that they are amazed to find that Frost is a living poet. He belongs with Tennyson, Wordsworth, Longfellow—all those who are to be read before examinations. The works written about him are extensive, and by thoughtful people. And now comes a thin volume called *Steeple Bush,* dedicated to six grandchildren. One hesitates to say more than "Here is another book of lyrics by Robert Frost." The time is long past for casual contemporary evaluation. But since any book by Frost is likely to have a unity as structurally sound and clear as the form of his lyrics, to look for this unity may be an exploration worth our time.

The title *Steeple Bush* comes not from the first poem but from the second of the seven which comprise the introductory group called "Steeple Bush." The other groups are: "Five Nocturnes"; "A Spire and a Belfry"; "Out and Away"; "Editorials." Each of these parts has a complex of ideas which relate to those of the others: the relationships progress as a series. Since, in spite of simple diction and homely instance, Frost's poetry is highly symbolic and metaphorical, a simple prose statement of this progression would violate its meaning. The book presents nothing so simple as a problem and a solution. Yet certainly its major concern is contemplation of the journey of life in the world of 1947. It suggests possible bad roads, possible good roads, sympathetic insight into fears; and it reports flashes of hope lighting the way, even though they come in fiery fusion of stars or lightning of storm.

Perhaps a few selections will not falsify the structure too much if they are used merely to indicate a characteristic color. In the first group, the first poem has special importance since it precedes the title poem. It is about *A Young Birch* that was "once in cutting brush along the wall . . . spared from the number of the slain." When it matured, anyone could see

It was a thing of beauty and was
    sent
To live its life out as an ornament.

The second poem, *Something for Hope,* introduces the steeple bush which gives title to the volume. It is a "lovely blooming" but wasteful, not good to eat, and it crowds out the edible grass. No plow can change the situation, but give nature time and the cycle of weeds, forest, and grass will move around in about a hundred years.

Thus foresight does it and laissez
    faire,
A virtue in which we all may share
Unless a government interferes.

. . . .

Patience and looking away ahead
And leaving some things to take
    their course.

The group ends with *To an Ancient,* which points out that immortality was achieved for a prehistoric man by one eolith and his own bone. It ends:

You made the eolith, you grew the
    bone,
The second more peculiarly your
    own,
And likely to have been enough
    alone.
You make me ask if I would go to
    time

Would I gain anything by using
  rhyme?
Or aren't the bones enough to live in
  lime?

The second short group seems in a lighter mood, but the implications are not light. The subjects are: fear of the dark; distant lights that give false comfort; ever imminent danger; a satiric watcher of the void, checking off the stars to see if anything happens. The last poem of the group, with its scene laid in the Arctic regions, is a kind of inverse pastoral. Two friends in an igloo, instead of on the hills of Arcadia, pour oil on their fire, recite to each other, crawl out to look at the Northern Lights, share their fish and oil with visitors. The poem and the group end:

We can rest assured on eider
There will come another day.

The third group, "The Spire and the Belfry," might, less freshly, have been called "The Flesh and the Spirit."

A spire and a belfry coming on the
  roof
Means that a soul is coming on the
  flesh . . .

We find the courageous groping of men after war.

They renew talk of the fabled
Federation of Mankind.

. . . .

They will tell you more as soon as
You tell them what to do
With their ever breaking newness
And their courage to be new.

One aspect of a solution seems to be suggested in the whimsical *Iota Subscript,* which is nothing in itself but merely a subscript to "you."

The poems in the fourth group on first reading may seem somewhat unrelated, but after rereading we appreciate the ambitious attempt to cast a shadow of ourselves on the cosmic screen. The first directs our attention to consideration of the near and far, the universal and local, the absolute.

The mineral drops that explode
To drive my ton of car
Are limited to the road.
They deal with near and far.

But have almost nothing to do
With the absolute flight and rest
The universal blue
And local green suggest.

In the context of "The whole Goddam machinery," one little four-line poem carries a good deal:

The play seems out for an almost
  infinite run.
Don't mind a little thing like the
  actors fighting.
The only thing I worry about is the
  sun.
We'll be all right if nothing goes
  wrong with the lighting.

The last group is frankly called "Editorials." These poems are more explicit, perhaps, and seem sometimes limited and specific, as in *U. S. King's X,* but there is always far-reaching suggestion, if not universal comment. A serpent of sand still rears its head to obliterate the mottoes of the city that took pride in its art of *Passing Losses On.* The book ends with a poem *To the Right Person,* telling of a splendidly situated district school planned for coeducation.

> But there's a tight shut look to
>   either door
> And to the windows of its
>   fenestration,
> As if to say mere learning was the
>   devil
> And this school wasn't keeping any
>   more
> Unless for penitents who took their
>   seat
> Upon its doorstep as at mercy's feet
> To make up for a lack of meditation.

Now it would be foolhardy to take these passages and translate them into a thesis—and it would also misrepresent the book. But perhaps they do indicate that the poetry, after the fashion of poetry, is saying a good deal about the confusion of our world, its illness and its hope, though it talks of stars, rivers, ancient bones, cliff dwellings, igloos, and steeple bush. A few of the poems may seem to go too far toward exposition in their direct literal statements, but the book should be read as a whole. A fundamental sequence in a richly varied pattern begins in the beautiful thing, the ornament of the land, and moves through the good heart, ignorance and fears, natural purification, exaltation of the spirit, to hope in humility and learning if the two are kept together. It has its by-paths that seem insignificant, its plateaus that stretch too far, but the mountains rise, and the total landscape is worthy of its author.

Checklist of Additional Reviews

Gerald McDonald. *Library Journal,* 72 (June 1, 1947), 889.

"Briefly Noted." *New Yorker,* 23 (June 7, 1947), 112.

Booklist, 43 (June 15, 1947), 328.

"Hardy Perennial." *Time,* 49 (June 16, 1947), 102-104.

United States Quarterly Book List, 3 (September 1947), 242.

Katherine Brégy. *Catholic World,* 166 (December 1947), 279.

A

MASQUE OF

MERCY

BY

ROBERT

FROST

HENRY HOLT AND COMPANY

NEW YORK

A Masque of Mercy

Sidney Cox.
"Mr. Frost's Blank
Verse Dialogue."
*New York Times Book
Review,*
November 9, 1947,
p. 6.

Robert Frost's mind being a true source he can let wisdom and counter-wisdom play as in a play and himself enjoy and be relaxed. Most of "A Masque of Mercy" is light, despite the depths from which the dramatis personae of ideas have through long years risen. And for him there is no fixed boundary between the truths that "are God's white light retracted into colors," and banter about a woman changing her analyst because she didn't love the doctor she had before. He teases fellow writers, comments on recent politics, offers a new and convincing explanation of how scientific method led, through the discovery of fire insurance, to the concept of compulsory "mass mercy," all in the same blank verse dialogue which illuminates the profoundest mysteries. And the composition, none the less though not quite obviously, is a unit.

The carriers of the ideas, themselves representing persons of our times as well as reincarnations, are four. Jonas Dove, alias Jonah, is a fugitive from God, having lost his "faith in God to carry out the threats he makes," because God always lets him down on the doom he orders him to prophesy on "the city evil." My Brother's Keeper cannot make a living at his bookstore and is a kind of revolutionist, and Jesse Bel (Jezebel), his wife, is sick of everything and her "cure will lie in getting her idea of the word love corrected." Paul, the analyst, is Jesse Bel's doctor. Late in the play Jonah calls him the apostle. His mind is, however, subtler, mellower and freer than the sermonizer and theologian in the New Testament.

The humor of the masque is proportional to its seriousness. Reading it is difficult delight. It is worth many readings. And it would be exciting to watch great actors perform it on a stage.

William Carlos Williams.
"The Steeple's Eye."
Poetry, 72
(April 1948),
38-41.

Now Jesse was the father of David and David was a great king; but Jezebel was a streel who would see the righteous persecuted and in the end the dogs licked up her blood in the streets. You can't get very far that way in trying to decipher the origin of the name *Jesse Bel* which Mr. Frost uses for one of the characters in his *A Masque of Mercy.* There are three other characters, all men, *My Brother's Keeper,* husband of *Jesse Bel,* and joint proprietor with her of a bookstore where, on closing for the night, one customer, *Paul, a doctor*—presumably with literary leanings—has been locked in. The fourth character, *Jonas Dove,* comes banging at the door after it has been closed, a fugitive from God.

Jonas and *Dove* are synonymous in the Hebrew—or so the Mask seems to say. The Dove then is the victim and the argument of the play centers about him and his fate. For he refuses to prophesy as God seems to want him to do, but instead, has fled from the very stage of a New York lecture platform (as Vachel Lindsay fled in mid-lecture from a Princeton platform many years ago) rather than compromise himself. Justice is what he seeks, not mercy, for with justice mercy would not be necessary. The three in the bookstore give him sanctuary, then proceed, in forthright Vermont fashion, themselves to judge him, each according to his own lights. It is a good situation for Mr. Frost to develop and he goes to it with a will.

But whatever Bible history has said and Mr. Frost intended by his thinly disguised characters, (I myself particularly like *My Brother's Keeper,* the Unitarian) there is one thing I will not do in reviewing this book, that is to try to separate the characters from their "meaning" in order to make that clear for the general reader. The meaning, if I judge rightly, was never meant by Mr. Frost to be made clear

in that way, rather it was densely integrated with the characters and as far as I am concerned must remain so.

We have, at the beginning, an opposition of country to city though I don't think this theme is sufficiently developed as the story goes on—the bookstore being in the country to which from the city Jonas has fled. The country is, I presume, Vermont. Looks like it. Someone has fled the whorish city—the New York that is riding a geologic fault, a fault in the rock under it, a shelf from which, given a God-sent earthquake, it may very well, one of these days, be sloughed off into the sea—with no tears shed by Mr. Frost, though they would be copious, I am sure, from the eyes of many a bookstore proprietor.

After this, the play proceeds, to end finally upon the eternal dilemma of the individual conscience (the Bible being put ahead of the more popular *Moby Dick* in this case—the Bible, God's only book), man's conscience facing the cellar-hole of finality without relief. In the Masque this cellar-hole is simply the bookstore cellar where the others will hide *Jonas Dove* against his Pursuer, and where, according to *My Brother's Keeper, Dove* will find a crucifix painted on one of the walls by a Mexican artist—suggestive of the Dartmouth Library.

Thus, in this décor, a moral fugitive has come to judgment crying out for justice. Frost has appointed the judges; who wins the case each reader will have to decide for himself—for in Vermont that is how it is done. It calls to my mind the argument between the Devil and Dan'l Webster with many of the overtones there revealed but lifted here to a somewhat more elevated plane and without loss of humor.

The style represents a wedding between the abstract and the colloquial to good effect, as in the best of Frost, crotchety and tough-minded. It is in a very plainly figured blank verse, often with two anapests to a line. The lack of rhyme is pleasant though I can't say the many inversions of phrase such as "but in a butt of malmsy I was drowned," while inoffensive, give me any feelings of pleasure. I frankly don't like it, but find that just there the invention which modern verse needs to revivify it has lost another opportunity.

The beauty of the verse, for it is primarily in the verse of Mr. Frost's writing that I am interested, lies in certain of the longer speeches which amount sometimes to well sustained philosophical lyrics full of spicy rhetoric. You feel that under the almost casual speech of four lay figures, as in the *autos da fè* of Lope de Vega perhaps (this is not Milton), a profitable form is being exploited for us: we may still use the Bible heritage of our environment for pithy statement if we pursue it diligently enough under the right circumstances.

My own taste would call, however, for a richer verse than Mr. Frost prefers, richer in verbal resources and metric than I find in this Masque. But if the plainness of the speech is once accepted the effectiveness and beauty of the lines rise, at times, as spires above the countryside, with references far removed from their immediate limitations. Like *Jonas Dove* in his predicament they call for mercy, for without mercy who of us would in the end find justice? Upon this theme *My Brother's Keeper, Jesse Bel* and *Paul, the doctor,* as well as *Jonas Dove* himself, have their say.

Lawrence McMillin. "A Modern Allegory." *Hudson Review,* 1 (Spring 1948), 105-107.

In *A Masque of Reason*, published two years ago, and in the recent *A Masque of Mercy*, Robert Frost has fostered the revival of an old and bastard poetic form. He has recognized the possibility of combining some of the best elements of the Platonic dialogue, the Puritan allegory, and the closet drama in a modern philosophical and religious form of masque. What makes these masques remarkable does not, however, make them successful poetry.

A Masque of Reason is a twentieth century revision of Job. This twenty-three page dialogue, more clever than weighty, gingerly moves about the vast problem of reconciling the tribulation visited upon the just and unjust alike with the notion of a reasonably benevolent God. The characters are God, Job, the devil, and Thyatira, Job's apocalyptic wife. God is such a vain and incompetent old buffoon that Mr. Frost may be making fun of the fundamentalists and twitting his own skepticism as well. Job appears as a wealthy retired nomad. The devil looks like "a sapphire wasp that flickers mica wings," and God agrees with Job that the devil has lost his vitality. To Job's contention that "We can't leave him out," God replies:

> No. No we don't need to.
> We're too well off.

Later God elaborates:

> church neglect

And figurative use have pretty well
Reduced him to a shadow of himself.

The fundamental impropriety of the
poem is in its philosophical burlesque
and anthropomorphic horseplay. God's
excuse for allowing Job to suffer ("I
was just showing off to the devil,
Job") is neither amusing nor original.
Thyatira's remark:

That's God. I'd know Blake's picture
anywhere.

is clever, but inappropriate. Such
theological banter is revolting to the
orthodox, bewildering to the faithful,
and unconvincing to the secular mind.
Milton, the master of English prophetic poetry, and his masters, the Hebrew psalmists and prophets, knew
that the poet, to clothe the letter with
the life of myth and prophecy, must
resist the temptation to let wit get the
better of judgment.

Perhaps Mr. Frost has been over-
conscious of contemporary taste.
Perhaps he is appointing us to forsake
the cult of intellectualized sensation
by reintroducing the theme of man's
concern with the Unknown. Nevertheless, what is substantially lacking is
that sense of tragedy without which
the theme of human tribulation becomes a cosmic joke.

A connecting link between the first
and second masques is the name Mr.
Frost gives Job's wife. Thyatira is one
of the seven churches in the Book of
the Apocalypse. The church of Thyatira is reprimanded for tolerating a
false prophetess named Jezebel who
was (or will be) mixing prophecy with
fornication. In *A Masque of Reason*
Job's wife querulously asks God why
prophetesses should be persecuted
more frequently than their male col-

leagues. In *A Masque of Mercy* the
prophetess Jezebel turns up as Jesse
Bel, an archetype of the modern
woman of the nineteen-twenties. Both
Thyatira and Jesse Bel are petulant
feminists; Mr. Frost, like Mr. Shaw,
has gleaned rather than borrowed
from the wealth of Christian love, but
less successfully. Comedy is not
equally at home everywhere and com-
plexes of wit can be wasteful effort.

In the more successful *Masque of*
Mercy, Mr. Frost is manipulating per-
sonalities with which he is somewhat
more familiar. The Keeper of a pro-
letarian bookstore opens his door to
Jonas, an agrarian Jonah who is escaping from a storm and trying to escape the commission of his God. Besides Jesse Bel, Keeper, and Jonas,
there is Paul, a modern off-shoot of
the first Christian missionary and
theologian. These characters work
and act out a tentative solution to the
problem of mercy and justice in the
Christian God's relation with man:

Nothing can make injustice just but
mercy.

The kind of piety which results
from this conclusion is an heroic metaphysical vitalism. The uncertainty
whether even our sacrifice, the best
we have to offer, may be found acceptable in heaven's sight causes a
profound metaphysical fear within us
which seems to be a near relation of
what the Existentialists call anxiety.
We must take courage, the necessary
complement to our basic skepticism,
in order that we may persevere to
great accomplishment. The characters
reach the conclusion that St. Paul's
New Testament mercy, not Keeper's
Marxist or Jonas' Old Testament justice, can save us from the perils of

uncertainty. The clamor for justice becomes a futile arrogance, making uncertainty unbearable.

A Masque of Mercy has greater density, solidity, and relevance to its theme than the earlier masque. The poem in spite of itself departs from the desperate flippancy and impertinent ingenuity which have been the curse of much recent reflective poetry. Nevertheless, it suffers more than the first masque from technical defects which stem from a similar failure to suit emotion to the theme. It is hard to believe, for instance, that Keeper should think that Rockwell Kent is the author of *Moby Dick*. Jesse Bel's erratic intellect is unconvincing. Sometimes she talks in the manner of a simpleton; sometimes in the manner of a female Socrates. At times, the characters' behavior is abstrusely mechanical; the emotional response of Keeper, Jesse Bel, and Paul to Jonas' death is particularly inadequate. Mr. Frost has unsuccessfully tried to turn the Miltonic trick of transforming his characters into particularized universals. He has packed much traditional material into this second masque without seeking the formal unity characteristic of Miltonic drama and epic. Such witty irrelevancies as a quip about *The New Yorker* magazine do but flounder in the mass of traditional philosophy and religion both symbolically and directly expressed. Mr. Frost has not created myth.

Turning to the question of style, I question whether the trim, deft line and the simple syntax of which Mr. Frost is master, are fitting or adequate for the purposes of prophetic poetry. Milton could never have succeeded by employing the styles and forms of his contemporary, Robert Herrick. But Mr. Frost is in general to be commended for his courageous if ill-executed attempts to redirect poetry in these days of existential anxiety and psychosomatic medicine. If he succeeds, the soul may gain a poetic currency which it has not enjoyed since the commencement of the Cartesian era.

Checklist of Additional Reviews

Lawrence Olson. *Furioso*, 3 (Spring 1948), 50-51.

Walter Wood Adams. "Drama and Ballad." *Voices,* 132 (Winter 1948), 49-52.

COMPLETE

POEMS

OF

ROBERT

FROST

HOLT, RINEHART AND WINSTON

NEW YORK

Complete Poems of Robert Frost

Leo Kennedy.
"He looks like a poet—
he is a poet."
Chicago Sun-Times,
June 20, 1949
p. 44.

This book bulges with richness. It contains all the poems that Robert Frost wishes to keep. It retains several that his most earnest admirers could wish he would throw away.

From the deceptively simple first poems of "A Boy's Will" to the wry metaphysics of "A Masque of Mercy," everything that's Frost is here: the feeling for nature and the sense of oneness with it, the later, high Tory attitudes, the nursery rhyme simplicity of language, the craggy individuality of the New England man.

How Frost feels about the poems that he and others make in a churned, hysterical time is put down tightly and sometimes ambiguously in a four page preface called "The Figure a Poem Makes." It is the best possible kind of preface to the body of Frost's lifework because it is a kind of credo.

This preface is a synthesis of Frost's convictions as an artist and his reflections as an aging man. It does more to clarify Frost's creative philosophy than the whole body of Frost criticism that has piled up, volume by volume, over the years. It's worth scrutiny here.

Of his elusive, double-talking contemporaries, Frost says: "Abstraction is an old story with the philosophers, but it has been like a new toy in the hands of the artists of our day. We bring up as aberrationists, giving way to undirected associations and kicking ourselves from one chance suggestion to another in all directions. . . . Theme alone can steady us down."

From general to particular is a short step, and of his own work Frost writes: "[A poem] begins in delight and ends in wisdom. The figure is the same as for love. It begins in delight, it inclines to the impulse, it assumes defection when the first line is laid down, it runs a course of lucky events, and ends in a clarification of life.

"It has denouement. It has an outcome that though unforeseen, was predestined from the first image of the original mood. It is but a trick poem and no poem at all if the best of it was thought of first and saved for the last. It finds its own name as it goes and discovers the best waiting for it in some final phase at once wise and sad."

In the front of the book there's a recent and perfect photograph of the aged Frost. In it he looks like a gnarled and knobby old apple tree with a thatch of whiteish blossom on its top. Any poet would hope to look like that some day and any poet worth his active verbs would hope to have a lifework like this to look back upon.

"The Intolerable Touch." *Time,* 53 (June 27, 1949), 94, 96, 98, 100.

Since Robert Frost is only 74 and sound as a hickory ax handle, this book is not likely to be his last. It does, however, contain his lifework up to the present, including several poems not printed in book form. And though this is not the sense intended, the title is correct about the poems: almost every one of them is complete as a work of art. Moreover, Frost is a complete poet, one of the few who ever stuck it out as such in a tough country for poets. Frost's reputation has been secure for 35 years; he is America's most popular living poet of the first rank; but only lately, and to the keenest readers, has he begun to seem as subtle, as haunting and hurting a poet as in truth he is.

The New England in which this slow man got his seasoning was the land of what Henry James called "the classic abandoned farm of the rude forefather who had lost patience with his fate." In 1906, Frost had been farming for six years outside Derry, N.H., and had begun to teach school. He showed his verse to his wife, who liked it but never praised it. Frost kept this up until 1912, when he was 37; only then did he have enough

money to buy passage to England for his family. As a poet he had no name whatever.

Robert Frost was 38 before he ever sat down with another poet to talk about poetry. That was in London; the poet was Ezra Pound; the poetry was Edwin Arlington Robinson's "Miniver Cheevy." "I remember," Frost said many years later, "the pleasure with which Pound and I laughed over the fourth 'thought' in

Miniver thought, and thought, and thought,
And thought about it.

Three 'thoughts' would have been 'adequate,' as the critical praise word then was. There would have been nothing to complain of if it had been left at three. The fourth made the intolerable touch of poetry. With the fourth, the fun began." Few others but Frost would have seen and described the quality of true poetry as "intolerable" and "fun" at the same time.

For the Ages. Frost's first two books, *A Boy's Will* and *North of Boston,* came out in England first; published soon after in the U.S., they had made him famous before his return in 1915. They were masterly first books; the poet's own obscurity had delayed them until he was almost 40, his early experience digested, his resolutions tempered, his vanity under control, his craft long practiced and well in hand. He had wrought and sweated to make himself intelligible, and had done it well enough by that time to know that the results would last.

I shall be telling this with a sigh
Somewhere ages and ages hence;

Two roads diverged in a wood, and
I—
I took the one less traveled by,
And that has made all the difference.

In dramatic monologues and dialogues Frost never improved on these early works. One of them, "The Generations of Men," is as sad and lovely an American romance as anything of Hawthorne's; two others, "A Servant to Servants" and "Home Burial," are as torturing records of the life of men with women as New England could provide. Frost went back to farming near Franconia, N.H., and in 1924 won his first Pulitzer Prize with *New Hampshire.* After that the sturdy, deliberate man with the tousled head and bright blue eyes became a public figure.

The cause of Poet Frost is the cause of Emerson, Thoreau, and all the spiritual freeholders who fought for life against the slamming and banging, the smoke and slums and sham, the fragmentation of experience in an urbanized and industrialized republic. The essence of what all his work affirms ·and pleads for is the value of wholeness—the union of lives in marriage, the union of form and substance in art; beauty in ordinary things, spirit in matter, the past in the present; the dead remembered, nature cherished. All this got across to the hearts of the harried people who read Frost and loved him as a sensitive fighter for what any heart desires:

But yield who will to their
separation,
My object in living is to unite
My avocation and my vocation
As my two eyes make one in sight;
Only where love and need are one,

And the work is play for mortal
stakes,
Is the deed ever really done
For Heaven and the future's sakes.

Vain & Smug? New England, Frost's home country and his chosen scene, was a lens through which he brought the world to focus in his best work. During the '30s, the tremendous pull of social distress and reforming talk loosened his roots a little. The immediate result was a number of didactic poems in which dislike for New Dealing glibness of his own, likened, by the unkind, to that of Calvin Coolidge. Even sympathetic critics suspected that Frost's work was done. Some people found him vain and smug. Wrote critic Louise Bogan of his *Collected Poems* (1939):

"His good sense has kept him from running any of his tendencies into the ground. That same good sense, on the other hand, has kept him from developing, in any broad way, beyond his first work ... One reads ... waiting for a crack of upheaval, with some roughness of unforeseen growth thereafter." The fact was that an upheaval had by that time taken place.

Myth & Maple Sirup. The poems in *A Witness Tree,* in 1942, were the work of a more profound and at times a triumphant Frost. He had lost his wife in 1938; love, grief and faith have never sung more perfectly, or more discreetly, together than in "I Could Give All to Time," "The Wind and the Rain," and other poems affected by that loss. He had worked his way out of whatever limits of time & space New England had imposed on him, and could write with austere and touching grandeur about the American experience from a vantage point beyond it:

The land was ours before we were the land's.
She was our land more than a hundred years
Before we were her people. She was ours
In Massachusetts, in Virginia,
But we were England's, still colonials,
Possessing what we still were unpossessed by,
Possessed by what we now no more possessed.
Something we were withholding made us weak
Until we found out that it was ourselves
We were withholding from our land of living,
And forthwith found salvation in surrender.
Such as we were we gave ourselves outright
(The deed of gift was many deeds of war)
To the land vaguely realizing westward,
But still unstoried, artless, unenhanced,
Such as she was, such as she would become.

Frost was, at last, going back in time to the richly and fearfully storied past; he had taken the way that only the greatest modern men of letters—Joyce, Mann, Eliot—have been able to take without being engulfed, into the mystery of the long ago that becomes myth. Though he took his humor and toughness with him, his Grail-poem, "Directive" (1947), has a sorrowful magic like nothing he had written before. If this was the old man's intolerable touch of poetry, *A Masque of Reason* (1945) and *A Masque of Mercy* (1947) carried on his vein of fun.

Last week Robert Frost was on his farm near Ripton, Vt., where this spring, with his partner, Stafford Dragon, he manufactured 60 gallons of fine maple sirup. He had also, in the course of the school year, visited and lectured at 20 colleges; but his Homer Noble farm (named for a former owner) is where he spends the longest stretch of the year. He passes his time there, reading history and biography, sometimes working around the rugged mountain farm. When he gets to the Homer Noble farm the arrival is, in a geographical way, something like the one he wrote about not long ago in another sense:

I could give all to Time except—except
What I myself have held. But why declare
The things forbidden that while the Customs slept
I have crossed to Safety with? For I am There,
And what I would not part with I have kept.

John Holmes. "Designs of Self-Discovery." *Saturday Review of Literature,* 32 (July 16, 1949), 9-10.

It was 1913, in England, that Robert Frost's "A Boy's Will" was published, a small book, fifty pages, by an unknown poet forty years old. Now we have a volume of eight books in one, with two masques, three new poems, and a preface. The fame he hoped for so long ago he has long had. Robert Frost is our established first living poet, well read, much taught. This new book has the look and the lift of durability: 640 pages of devotion, a life. Its publication is literary history, its contents literature.

It would seem complete, but, knowing Robert Frost, one suspects his kind of reservation in the date, 1949; complete for now, but the climax will be capped. It is in the nature of his master design that it will be. In "The Figure a Poem Makes," a compact prose preface to this book, he speaks of a poem's sources, mystery, and wildness; subject and pattern imposed. He says, "Step by step the wonder of unexpected supply keeps growing." Robert Frost's source of supply is so deep, and has been shaped from the ore so skilfully, that his poems will be unspent for a long time.

Frost has always composed his books with care. The sequence, the divisions, the variety, become an additional poem, one more piece of design than listed. When he sat on a floor in an English farmhouse some thirty years ago and spread out the poetry he had written, he "composed" "A Boy's Will" by giving the poems subtitles in the table of contents. "North of Boston" was composed by selection of long meditative pieces only. Certainly he had written in other lengths and shapes, but he saved these for other books. He has been known to save a poem ten or twenty years for the right book. This is composition on a still large scale, not of one poem, not of one book, not even of this "complete" works, but of his working-ever-present, and his long future fame.

His design can be seen more obviously in the later books: six sections in "A Further Range," to account for his growing wish to write epigrams, satires, prophecies; but always the lyrics. "A Witness Tree" has five parts. The increasing variety of his subject matter calls for categories of the personal, the shared-with, the outside-himself, the regional, and so on. In "Steeple-Bush" he frankly calls one whole section editorials, and so maps a growing area of his poetry. He likes to advise his country how to grow, and does.

A hardy wisdom, a skill like that with tools, and a wise individualism go to make Robert Frost's poetry, spoken in a timeless international Yankee language, the best idiom heightened and tightened. He is conservative in the same way an independent thinker has always been conservative: with that wildness, that reckless mystery he speaks of in the new preface.

The making of Robert Frost's books has been a happy publishing achievement, and a handsome one. As books in the hand, all have been a delight, and, as the collector knows, there are ten times as many variants as the ten volumes. All have appeared in trade and limited editions. The limited edition of this new "Complete Poems" is a beautiful piece of book design. Other titles have appeared in British reprints, low-price reprints, and so on. Of these, the "Pocket Book of Robert Frost's Poems," which is an enlarged version of Louis Untermeyer's "Come In," is surely the best buy in poetry today at the price. A number of Frost's books, and Christmas leaflets, have been illustrated by J. J. Lankes, most appropriately. His publisher's designer has always done finer things for each new book, each variant edition, each leaflet.

Design is what we can learn from Robert Frost, who has such shrewd and sensitive knowledge of it. He taught himself. Few helped him, in the early years, and many have praised him in the later years. He always had his own way, and still has; that is his triumph. He is a major part of American literary history. He is more read, studied, loved than any living poet. He composes well, as he himself might say, and as this new volume testifies.

There remains the wildness. "A poem may be worked over once it is in being, but may not be worried into being. Its most precious quality will remain its having run itself and carried away the poet with it." Robert Frost has never worried a poem into being. He has always waited for his own kind of wildness to complete a poem, to bring the singing line, like "The woods are lovely dark and deep" or "Snow falling and night falling, fast, oh, fast" or "Winds blow the open grassy places bleak." Such lines were never planned when the poem started.

He says in the new preface, "It must be a revelation, or a series of revelations, as much for the poet as for the reader." "No surprise for the writer, no surprise for the reader." This latest gathering of Robert Frost's poetry is from a lifetime of self-discovery; for readers there will be revelations for a long time to come.

Rolfe Humphries. "Verse Chronicle." *The Nation,* 169 (July 23, 1949), 92-93.

So here are the "Complete Poems," to date, at least, of Robert Frost. With the volume in hand, knowing the poems, knowing also what one knows, or thinks one knows, or has heard about the poet aside from the poems, one hesitates to open the pages, indulging, first, in a little utterly idle speculation. What would have happened had Frost gone off on some road not taken? Suppose, for instance, he had spent his years of growth, or his artistic maturity, not in New England, nor old England, either, but Ireland or France, Paris or Dublin. Suppose he had had his native simile jarred, suppose he had knocked around in, and been knocked around by, the company of his peers, with a ribald Gogarty or a wild old wicked Yeats, a Verlaine, a Rimbaud, a Baudelaire, looking over his shoulder or arguing far into the night. Up to a point, I think, no one would want Frost different: it is when his paths diverge, and he chooses, not one of two ways, but two at once, that one regrets the split, the waste of energy, the element of denial.

Creatively, there are at least three Frosts—the actual artist, the legendary public character, posed and professed, and the latent, potential poet that might have been. The fellow in the middle, it must be said to his credit, has interfered very little with the first; he has, however, I think considerably stunted the growth of the last. Everybody knows, and too many admire, this character, the local wiseacre, rural sage, town whittler, Will Rogers and Cal Coolidge combined, village idiot (in the Greek sense of the noun). To a sophisticated, Alexandrian, professional, academic, middle-class, urban audience, this version of pastoral has great appeal; we do not see too clearly how much it is of the bourgeois, by the bourgeois, for the bourgeois. This is the side of Frost that speaks for the first time, and for the first time with smugness, in the title poem of the collection called "New Hampshire," his fourth book and one which contains some of his finest work; it is occasionally heard thereafter, intermittently, the slightest soupçon, in "West-Running Brook," becomes a good deal more insistent in "A Further Range," culminating in the ugly editorials in "Steeple Bush," and the arch gerontic garrulities and mock sapience of the two masques. On this side of Frost it is not very pleasant to dwell.

As actual artist Frost has won double triumph, in fields which would seem to lie far enough apart so that a conqueror seldom invades both with success. There is the fine and beautiful lyric poetry—Reluctance in "A Boy's Will"; The Road Not Taken, The Sound of the Trees, in "Mountain Interval"; Fire and Ice, In a Disused Graveyard, Stopping by Woods on a Snowy Evening, in "New Hampshire"; Bereft, Acquainted with the Night, in "West-Running Brook"; Come In, in "A Further Range"; A Nature Note, in "A Witness Tree"—these are not all, only the most conspicuous that can be cited.

What is not so often found in the lyric poet is the ability to turn outward, to manage the modes of speech as well as those of song, to be dramatic as well as personal, to get out of the self and into insight into the selves of others. No single adjective, like lyric, can be found to apply to this side of Frost's excellence—what shall we say, dramatic monologue, bucolic idyl, epyllion, to describe those somewhat longer poems of Frost's, so many of which are so good? The Death of the Hired Man, almost all the poems in "North of Boston" (one or two are flops, to be sure, for example A Hundred Collars, but there are interesting elements even in the unsuccessful items); Out, Out, and Snow, in "Mountain Interval," the first missing melodrama, perhaps, only by its terrible brevity and economy; The Witch of Coös in "New Hampshire"—what can be said about poems like these is that they stand with Chaucer's and Browning's, a little less in good cheer and gusto, and a little more in sensitive and reserved compassion. And the ear for speech as superlative as Lardner's.

To have succeeded in two areas as diverse as these would seem to be almost enough for one man to have accomplished, and I was going to rest my case there, but I find, as I run through the pages, another kind of poem that I cannot resist delighting in and praising. That would be the kind of poem that uses, mainly, the cadence and line of the ones mentioned in the paragraph above, and devotes itself to observation, of nature, or occupation, with a little commentary, humorous, it may be, or semi-rueful: After Apple-Picking is a case in point, An Old Man's Winter Night, that wonderful accuracy of The Grindstone, A Hillside Thaw, The Runaway, the middle stanza of The White-Tailed Hornet. Some of the dogmatism in Two Tramps in Mud Time gets my back up, but who could resist:

Good blocks of oak it was I split,
As large around as the
    chopping-block;
And every piece I squarely hit
Fell splinterless as a cloven rock. . . .

The sun was warm but the wind was
    chill.
You know how it is with an April
    day
When the sun is out and the wind is
    still,
You're one month on in the middle
    of May.
But if you so much as dare to speak,
A cloud comes over the sunlit arch
A wind comes off a frozen peak
And you're two months back in the
    middle of March

Well: and after all this, Frost being this good, how dare anyone be disappointed in him, or wish him to have been better? A fair question, however difficult, and deserving a serious answer. In a way the dissatisfaction is the compliment; Frost himself all through his work, more or less, offers clues as to the kind of thing he might have done, the line of a frightful and fascinating interest that he almost dared to follow. The road not taken.

"Here error is all in the not done/all in the diffidence that faltered"—Frost states the case, for (and against) himself:

The bearer of evil tidings
When he was halfway there,
Remembered that evil tidings
Were a dangerous thing to bear

Frost has been halfway there, or farther, much more than once: as early as The Fear, in "North of Boston"; as late as The Subverted Flower, in "A Witness Tree"—and there are other poems which show where he has turned off the woodland trail, briefly, toward the heart of some deeper forest, jungle, sinister tarn—Fire and Ice, The Bonfire, The Lockless Door, Bereft, The Lovely Shall Be Choosers, with its cadences broken, out of dreams, and here and there very frightening, Desert Places, The Rabbit Hunter, The Night Light, Design. Reading such poems as these, one cannot escape the impression that they are much more truly the essence of the poet than the plain New Hampshire farmer is, or Meliboeus the potato man, or whoever; one wishes he had been a little less fearful of evil tidings, less scared of his own desert places. One wishes he had wasted less time being sane and wholesome, and gone really all out, farther than he did beyond the boundaries of New England's quaintness into its areas of violence, madness, murder, rape, and incest (for *New England's* read *humanity's*). "Any eye is an evil eye/that looks in on to a mood apart"; the heart of man is desperately wicked; I (read Everyman) am a villain. It is this night side of life and nature that Frost's art has, I think, scamped reporting, and not because he did not know it; no American poet in our time, no American poet, nor Poe in his stories, has come closer to Baudelaire.

Robert Fitzgerald.
"Patter, Distraction, and Poetry."
New Republic, 121 (August 8, 1949), 18-19.

As for the new books by Americans, none but Robert Frost's *Complete Poems* requires attention. Frost is a master within his range, and a reading of his lifework makes it clear that his range is wider than people often suppose. The controlled development of his talent, and the finality and grace of statement in his best poems, are of moral no less than artistic value, exemplary for all who practise this art. Where he has not been an influence in American poetry he has been a presence, of which curious marks are to be seen, for example, in the early work of Eliot. His vein of romantic triviality and perversity is not hard to distinguish, and it may be indulged.

That stern critic, Yvor Winters, considers Frost an Emersonian and therefore untrustworthy sage; but he would probably concede that on occasion Frost has had a harder edge and eye than Emerson, more humor, and more of the fear of God. It would be going too far to think of him as a religious poet, but his work tends toward wholeness, and thus toward a catholicism of the heart. The economy and caution that have kept his mind

provincial, and prevented him from essaying the great assimilative effort of Pound and Eliot, is very much in the tempo of the older America that persists in the new; and that is not so bad, either. If he has not been a "culture hero," neither has he been a culture ruin. Some of the most gifted of the young American poets have acknowledged a debt to Frost: Randall Jarrell, Robert Lowell, Karl Shapiro; but to demonstrate it I shall quote, not from their work, but from a still younger man who is less well known. Here is the first stanza of a poem called "The Death of a Toad," by Richard Wilbur (from *Poetry*),

> A toad the power mower caught,
> Chewed and clipped of a leg, with a
>   hobbling hop has got
> To the garden verge, and
>   sanctuaried him
> Under the cineraria leaves, in the
>   shade
> Of the ashen heartshaped leaves,
>   in a dim,
>   Low, and a final glade . . .

Wilbur's immaculate verbal choice, his freshening of the sense of life within a rigid metrical frame, and not only within it but by means of it, recall Frost's writing at its best.

Peter Viereck.
"Parnassus Divided."
Atlantic Monthly, 184 (October 1949), 67-68.

An unusual variety of new books of poetry has appeared in recent months. In a comparative reading several superlatives suggest themselves. The most important book of 1949 is the *Complete Poems of Robert Frost* (Holt). It is—to make a point-blank value-judgment—the year's "best" by any American poet. . . .

Robert Frost's name is rarely heard among the exquisities of *avant-garde.* His poems are like those plants that flourish in the earth of the broad plains and valleys but will not strike root in more rarefied atmospheres. The fact remains that he is one of the world's greatest living poets. Frost, W. H. Auden, Wallace Stevens, and William Carlos Williams are the contemporary poets in America whose styles are most intensely original, most unmistakably their own. Of the four, Frost is the only one to be widely read in terms of general circulation and the only one who has never been adequately subjected to the Higher Criticism of the *doctores subtitles* of the Little Magazines.

On first reading, Frost seems easier than he really is. This helps account both for the enormous number of his readers, some of whom like him for wrong or irrelevant reasons, and for the indifference of the coteries, who become almost resentful when they can find no double-crostics to solve. Frost's cheerfulness is often mistaken as smug, folksy, Rotarian. This fact, plus his reputation for a solid New England conservatism, frightens away rebel youth and "advanced" professors.

In truth, his cheerfulness is the direct opposite of Mr. Babbitt's or even of Mr. Pickwick's. It is a Greek cheerfulness. And the apparent blandness of the Greeks was, as Nietzsche showed in his *Birth of Tragedy,* the result of their having looked so deeply into life's tragic meaning that they

had to protect themselves by cultivating a deliberately superficial jolliness in order to bear the unbearable. Frost's benign calm, the comic mask of a whittling rustic, is designed for gazing—without dizziness—into a tragic abyss of desperation. This is the same eternal abyss that gaped not only for the Hellenes but for such moderns as Pascal, Kierkegaard, Nietzsche, Baudelaire, Kafka. "Pascal," wrote Baudelaire, "had his abyss that followed him." In the case of this great New England tragic poet, the desperation is no less real for being a quiet one, as befits a master of overwhelming understatements. His almost too smooth quietness is a booby trap to spring the ruthless doubt of the following typical Frostian quatrain:—

It was the drought of deserts. Earth
    would soon
Be uninhabitable as the moon.
What for that matter had it ever
    been?
Who advised man to come and live
    therein?

Or ponder upon the following four lines, where again the meaning sneaks up on you imperceptibly and leaves a sense of ephemeral human smallness in the eons it takes for the sun to burn out:—

The play seems out for an almost
    infinite run.
Don't mind a little thing like the
    actors fighting.
The only thing I worry about is the
    sun.
We'll be all right if nothing goes
    wrong with the lighting.

Or this:—

A voice said, Look me in the stars
And tell me truly, men of earth,
If all the soul-and-body scars
Were not too much to pay for birth.

Let those who consider Frost obvious or superficial brood a bit upon the last line of "Never Again Would Birds' Song Be the Same." Consisting only of simple monosyllables yet subtly musical and full of "the shock of recognition," that concluding sentence is perhaps the most beautiful single line in American literature, a needed touchstone for all poets writing today:—

He would declare and could himself
    believe
That the birds there in all the
    garden round
From having heard the daylong
    voice of Eve
Had added to their own an
    oversound,
Her tone of meaning but without the
    words.

. . . .

Moreover her voice upon their voices
    crossed
Had now persisted in the woods so
    long
That probably it never would be lost.
Never again would birds' song be the
    same.
And to do that to birds was why she
    came.

Many writers have described nature's brutal threat to mankind, but rarely with so strong a metaphor as Frost's description of the hills of earth in "Sand Dunes":—

Sea waves are green and wet,

But up from where they die,
Rise others vaster yet,
And those are brown and dry.

They are the sea made land
To come at the fisher town,
And bury in solid sand
The men she could not drown.

But the poem ends with hope, for man remains free to think. This hope is based not on the pollyanna of easy optimism but on the tragic wisdom of those who through the ages have not only stared into the abyss but have outstared it. This is probably the final message of Frost's *Complete Poems.*

A word about his metrics and his diction. Frost is one of the few poets today who dare use contractions like "as 'twere" and "e'er." I don't care for this sort of thing, especially in a poet who makes a point of catching the idiom of everyday speech. But I don't let this annoying anachronism spoil my enjoyment of him. Equally old-fashioned, but this time in a better sense of the word, is the fact that his meters scan with a beat-by-beat regularity, usually in the form of rhymed iambic pentameters. In this connection, do not overlook his thoughtful preface on poetic techniques and meters.

Frost's stubborn conventionality of form makes many young poets and readers think his is also a conventionality of meaning. On the contrary, he is one of the most original writers of our time. It is the self-conscious *avant-garde* rebels who follow the really rigid and tiresome conventions.

Checklist of Additional Reviews

David Daiches. "Enduring Wisdom From a Poet-Sage." *New York Times Book Review,* May 29, 1949, p. 1.

Mark Van Doren. "Our Great Poet, Whom We Read and Love." *New York Herald Tribune Weekly Book Review,* May 29, 1949, pp. 1, 11.

Charles Poore. *New York Times,* June 2, 1949, Sec. 1, p. 25.

J. H. Johnston. *Commonweal,* 50 (July 8, 1949), 324-25.

Booklist, 45 (July 15, 1949), 396.

Open Shelf, July-August-September, 1949, p. 15.

Gerald McDonald. *Library Journal,* 74 (September 15, 1949), 1327.

"Briefly Noted." *New Yorker,* 25 (October 15, 1949), 127.

Bookmark, 9 (October 1949), 4.

Notes

IN THE CLEARING

BY

ROBERT FROST

HOLT, RINEHART AND WINSTON

NEW YORK

In the Clearing

John Ciardi.
"Robert Frost: American Bard."
Saturday Review of Literature, 45
(March 24, 1962),
15-17, 52-54.

On March 26 Robert Frost will be eighty-eight years old. His birthday will be doubly marked this year. It will be publication day for his first new book in fifteen years, "In the Clearing." And it will be the occasion for a banquet to be given in Washington, the invitations for which have been jointly issued by Secretary of the Interior and Mrs. Udall and by Mr. Frost's publishers, Holt, Rinehart and Winston. Unless he is prevented by affairs of state, President Kennedy is expected to lead the list of distinguished guests.

For many years now, Mr. Frost's birthdays have been almost national observances. But though each new birthday has brought fresh honors, it is probably the eighty-fifth that will remain most memorable to literary historians.

For that occasion, at a banquet given at the Waldorf by Mr. Frost's publishers, Lionel Trilling read a paper in homage to Mr. Frost and thereby set off a hot if meaningless controversy, while at the same time illustrating an attitude of our more sophisticated critics that, though it passed without comment, remains far more ponderable than the bone that was worried in print during the following weeks.

Trilling saluted Mr. Frost as "a poet of terror." All angry voices to the contrary, I could find nothing wrong with Trilling's choice of words. That he meant nothing but praise is obvious. In fact he compared Mr. Frost to Sophocles in this sense. What man could fail to feel honored at being so paired? On this point I find Trilling's assessment both just and central to the Frostian genius.

Let the School System make a whited saint of Mr. Frost if it must; and as, alas, it will. The man himself remains an *hombre*. If he is half radiance he is also half brimstone, and praise be. His best poems will endure precisely because they are terrible—and holy. All primal fire is terrible and holy. Mr. Frost could climb to heaven and hear the angels call him brother—*frater,* they would probably say—but he could as well climb Vesuvius and equally hear every rumble under his feet call out to him. The darkness in his poems is as profound as the light in them is long. They are terrible because they are from life at a depth into which we cannot look unshaken. What else is the power of such poems as—to name only a few—"To Earthward," "Reluctance," "Home Burial," "Death of the Hired Man," and "Fire and Ice"?

It was some such homage, I am sure, that Trilling meant to pay, and to worry the word "terror" as if it contained a slur is nonsense. What reader will not prefer the terror of Frost to the sweetness of many of his contemporaries?

What appalled me that night at the Waldorf was Trilling's confession that it had only been within the preceding few years that he had grown aware of the depth and power of Mr. Frost's poetry. And then, as if to toss the whole tribute into the abyss, Trilling added something to the effect that he had been unable to grasp the poems until he came to them through a reading of D. H. Lawrence!

What I think I heard Trilling describe was a failure sufficiently common to the New or Academic Critics to serve as a reproach to all of them. There stood Professor Trilling, one of our leading men of letters, a master of literary subtlety and complexity, paying homage to America's foremost poet by confessing years of professional neglect, and then capping the insult by suggesting that the key to Mr. Frost's poetry lay in D. H. Lawrence, a writer I am bound to believe Mr. Frost would incline to think of as half madman and half charlatan (a guess, let me add, that certainly does not bind Mr. Frost, and that is not at all my personal assessment of Lawrence).

What is there to conclude except that our best critics have suffered too long from a fear of simplicity, and that, misled by the surface simplicity of Mr. Frost's poems, they have dismissed them as being simple—all the way down? It is a rueful irony that brought together America's first truly national poet and a representative of America's first truly-formed school of literary criticism, only to show that it took the critic something like thirty years to recognize the real thing when it happened.

By now the New Criticism has pretty much adjusted to Mr. Frost, at least to the earlier Frost. As I mean to discuss in a minute, I find two main stages of the earlier Frost: the poet of passion and the poet of wit and whimsy. The adjustment of the New Critics, as nearly as I have been able to sense it, has been to praise the poet of passion and to dismiss the poet of wit. I wonder what the New Critical verdict will be on this new Frost. For it is a new Frost one finds in these poems; a Frost not unprecedented in his own past, but a new Frost all the same. What Mr. Frost called "editorials" in "Steeplebush" (published in 1947) were already long on the way toward his new way of writing—or perhaps one should say, rather, toward his new way of taking himself. And the fact that most of these new poems have long been familiar to close followers of Mr. Frost, through his readings and Christmas cards, does take the full burst of surprise from them. Yet put together as they are now in a new book, the poems make bold the announcement that this Frost is impressively different from the more familiar one of the public image.

Trying to parse anything as complex as Robert Frost into categories is a bit like trying to put spirit into a box, but granting the inadequacies of all such boxes, let one be called, as noted, passion, and the other, wit and whimsy. It was basically as a poet of impassioned light-and-dark that Mr. Frost made his appearance on the scene and many of his first reviewers were moved to speak of a background sense of terror that haunts his New England landscape. This Frost burns with the appetites of life. The essence of tragic characters is that they ask of life more than ordinary men are moved to ask. They are terrifying and exalting because they are seared by passion:

I craved strong sweets but those
Seemed strong when I was young;
The petal of the rose
It was that stung.

Now no joy but lacks salt
That is not dashed with pain
And weariness and fault;
I crave the stain

Of tears, the aftermark
Of almost too much love,
The sweet of bitter bark
And burning clove.

When stiff and sore and scarred
I take away my hand
From leaning on it hard
In grass and sand,

The hurt is not enough:
I long for weight and strength
To feel the earth as rough
To all my length.

Call it terror in the Sophoclean sense, or call it the impassioned life force, this is lyricism at a kindling point of the soul. This poet is not only the lover but the demon lover.

His passion, moreover, was always toward the privacy of the self, toward the rescue of the self from the world's demands. So in "Love and a Question," one of his earliest published poems, he dramatizes the world's intrusion upon the privacy of love, choosing for his symbol of the world's demand a needy wanderer who seeks shelter in the bridal house. At this point of his development, the poet frames the question without answering it. The poem ends:

The bridegroom thought it little to
    give
    A dole of bread, a purse,
A heartfelt prayer for the poor of
    God,
    Or for the rich a curse;
But whether or not a man was asked
    To mar the love of two
By harboring woe in the bridal
    house,
    The bridegroom wished he knew.

The same impassioned sense of two-against-the-world cries out in "Not to Keep." And the converse of that theme may be found in "Two Look at Two," a poem in which the lovers, in joy, recognize the exaltation of what is their most private ground.

That theme is everywhere in the early Frost. In "Two Tramps in Mud Time" the question is given a new and terrifying setting, this time to be firmly answered. The speaker of the poem, a farmer, fiercely in love with the muscle and sweat of his labor of chopping wood, feels the world's demand in the presence of two lumberjack tramps who want to take his work from him for pay, because they need the pay:

The time when most I loved my task

These two must make me love it
    more
By coming with what they had to
    ask.

And this time the demand is rejected:

Nothing on either side was said.
They knew they had but to stay
    their stay
And all their logic would fill my
    head:
As that I had no right to play
With what was another man's work
    for gain.
My right might be love but theirs
    was need.
And where the two exist in twain
Theirs was the better right—agreed.

But yield who will to their
    separation,
My object in living is to unite
My avocation and my vocation
As my two eyes make one in sight.
Only where love and need are one
And the work is play for mortal
    stakes,
Is the deed ever really done
For Heaven and the future's sakes.

By whatever force of the rational
mind this poet frames his reasons, the
life force in him cries out "Keep off
my acre!"

Perhaps with a touch of whimsy
but, if so, with the anger unabated,
that cry rings out again in "The Egg
and the Machine." There the poet
meets the intrusion of a locomotive
upon his private haunts by digging up
a clutch of turtle eggs. Armed with
them as his grenades, he issues his
challenge:

'You'd better not disturb me
    anymore,'

He told the distance, 'I am armed for
    war.
The next machine that has the
    power to pass
Will get this plasm in its goggle
    glass.'

That dark, impassioned, and reclu-
sive Frost has not entirely disappeared from these new poems.
Whether "A Draft Horse," for example, is entirely a new poem or one
newly brought out of older workbooks,
it moves as darkly and yet as resil-
iently as any of Frost's early ven-
tures into shadow. Here it is entire, a
poem of terror enough for any darkness:

With a lantern that wouldn't burn
In too frail a buggy we drove
Behind too heavy a horse
Through a pitch-dark limitless
    grove.

And a man came out of the trees
And took our horse by the head
And reaching back to his ribs
Deliberately stabbed him dead.

The ponderous beast went down
With a crack of a broken shaft.
And the night drew through the
    trees
In one long invidious draft.

The most unquestioning pair
That ever accepted fate
And the least disposed to ascribe
Any more than we had to to hate,

We assumed that the man himself
Or someone he had to obey
Wanted us to get down
And walk the rest of the way.

With "A Draft Horse" may be grouped

"Ends," "A Peril of Hope," and "Questioning Faces" (the last of which first appeared in *SR*) as poems more nearly in Mr. Frost's first voice, the voice of impassioned love, of dark and of radiance, and above all of a fierce commitment to the private acre of the individual the essential ground that must be protected from the world's intrusion.

If I am right in taking whimsy to be the second voice in Mr. Frost's developing range, I do not mean to imply that there were not touches of whimsy in the poems from the beginning. There is a happily whimsical touch in "The Pasture," the first poem in the first book ("A Boy's Will"). And more than a touch in as early and as deeply felt a poem as "Mending Wall." There the speaker, thinking to draw out his neighbor says:

Spring is the mischief in me and I
    wonder
If I could put a notion in his head.

and later:

    I could say 'Elves' to him
But it's not elves exactly, and I'd
    rather
He said it for himself.

The difference between Frost as the poet of passion and Frost as the poet of wit is one of degree and the mixture of the two tones in many of the poems may require a considerable adjustment of one's standard "poetic" expectations. As Mr. Frost himself notes in a typical touch of whimsy:

It takes all sorts of in and outdoor
    schooling
To get adjusted to my kind of
    fooling.

Nevertheless the difference is real. The poet of passion is a singing man and deeply committed. The poet of whimsy is a speaking man and coolly detached, concerned, yes, but evasive, his eye forever on the relation of the individual and society, but warily. . . .

Walter Harding. "At 88 His Poems Still Show the Master's Touch." *Chicago Sunday Tribune Magazine of Books,* March 25, 1962, p. 1.

Tomorrow, March 26, Robert Frost marks his 88th birthday by the publication of his first volume of new poems in 14 years. It is a collection of 40 poems, ranging in subject matter from butterflies on milkweed to the cow jumping over the moon in an age of rockets, from the Wright brothers at Kitty Hawk to a conversation between Mist and Smoke. In length they range from two-liners to a 400-line narrative. In form they vary from blank verse to sonnets, with an interesting new [for Frost, that is] preoccupation with a rollicking Skeltonic short-line verse. But enough for technical matters—I mention them only to indicate that age has not narrowed Robert Frost's range. If anything, it has enlarged it.

The joy of "In the Clearing" is that it contains so many poems that should rank among Frost's best. There is

"Pod of Milkweed" with that same exuberant love of nature that we find in the old familiar "Tuft of Flowers." There is "The Draft Horse" that has caught the humor of the New England farm folk as well as had "Brown's Descent." Or "A Cabin in the Clearing" that has caught their diction as had "The Hill Wife." I don't mean to imply that Frost is repeating himself, but rather that he is continuing to equal the achievement of his earlier years.

It is true at times he perhaps strains a bit for comic effect, as in:

"I wish I may I wish I might"
Give earth another satellite.

or, in speaking of Columbus and Queen Isabella:

Here he was
Without one trinket from Ormuz
To save the Queen from family censure
For her investment in his venture.

But he fairly warns us:

It takes all sorts of in and outdoor
    schooling
  To get adapted to my kind of
    fooling.

Beneath the surface comedy there is depth.

Speaking of the surprise overnight visit of a stray Dalmatian pup, he says:

A symbol was all he could hope to
    convey,
  An intimation, a shot of ray,
A meaning I was supposed to seek.

Such intimations can be found in most of the poems, and the search for them can be most rewarding.

It is understandable that now his thoughts should frequently turn to other-worldly ideas, as they do in this new volume. But so obvious is still his vital love for life . . . that I am not surprised to find him saying:

I am assured at any rate
Man's practically inexterminate.
  Someday I must go into that.
There's always been an Ararat
  Where someone someone else
    begat. . . .

In recent years Frost has received honors in a multitude accorded no other literary figure in our history and has won the admiration and devotion of reading audiences from the most unsophisticated to the most critical. In his typically modest fashion he thanks us with:

Breathes there a bard who isn't
    moved
  When he finds his verse is
    understood
    And not entirely disapproved
  By his country and his
    neighborhood?

We can rejoice in the publication of "In the Clearing" and hope that Frost will be with us at least another 88 years.

Richard Wilbur. "Poems That Soar and Sing and Charm." *New York Herald Tribune,* March 25, 1962, p. 3.

Tomorrow Robert Frost will be 88. This new collection of his poems will be published on his birthday.

"In the Clearing" has an epigraph borrowed from Frost's early poem. "The Pasture"—"and wait to watch the water clear, I may." This illuminates both the old poem and the new book, and it brgins to mind something which Frost once said: "All we do in life is a clarification after we stir things up." And then there is a charming poem in the book called "A Cabin in the Clearing." It is a dialogue between the chimney smoke and garden mist which hover about a house encircled by forest, eavesdropping on the earnest talk of the couple within. The "clearing" of this poem is a little area of human coherence, a bit of the universe become a colony of mind. Frost's title, then, has to do with mind-activity, with clarification, with the penetration of nature by human thought and effort.

This is a high-spirited, high-minded book. Despite its Frostian skepticisms and paradoxes, it is sweepingly assertive, and ought to satisfy the sort of critic who values poetry for the philosophy which may be shaken out of it—as some children eat the Cracker Jack for the sake of the prize. A verse "frontispiece," excerpted from the long poem "Kitty Hawk," argues that

"God's own descent
Into flesh was meant
As a demonstration
That the supreme merit
Lay in risking spirit
In substantiation."

Or as Emerson put it in prose, "There seems to be a necessity in spirit to manifest itself in material forms." If men are considerably less than divine in apprehension, if they cannot create "One least germ or coal," nevertheless Frost holds that we, the only creatures who have "thoughts to think," are under divine orders to penetrate matter as far as we can, claiming it for intellect and imagination. The fall from Eden he sees as the "instinctive venture" of a creature designed to enquire, and he makes Jehovah say to Jacob (retracting a few of His recorded injunctions):

"Have no hallowing fears
Anything's forbidden
Just because it's hidden.
Trespass and encroach
On successive spheres
Without self-reproach."

It may surprise some readers that Robert Frost should write a book full of the word "venture," a book whose longest poem celebrates unlimited reaching-out—soaring planes, soaring capsules, soaring thought. These attitudes seem hardly to suit with those of, say, that great focal poem "The Mountain," in which an earlier Frost advised a retreat from change, confusion, and "too much" generally into the coherence of local tradition. But after all there has been no fundamental change of mind: first and last, Frost's concern has been for wholeness of life and character, and he is now defending, by a new strategy and on a broader front, the Emersonian values he embraced. In late years, he has become more and more the conscience of his country, and taken upon himself the burden of its confusion: what certain of these poems are directed against is the fear that our society, cowed by its own dangerous powers and potentialities, will go back on those things in man which Frost sees as highest and most human.

"Ours is a Christian adventure into materialism." Frost said not long ago, and the political poems of "In the Clearing" all insist that Americans must see themselves not as ingenious materialists but as riskers of spirit in the realm of matter. "America Is Hard to See" reproaches Columbus with having, in his appetite for Cathayan gold, failed to recognize our continent as "The race's future trial place. A fresh start for the human race." "Our Doom to Bloom" and "The Bad Island—Easter" attack the cynicism of welfare-state thinking while in "How Hard It Is to Keep From Being King," King Darius is counselled to give his people "character and not just food." The lines "For John F. Kennedy His Inauguration" look to the new Administration not for an exacted benevolence but for courage, the pursuit of glory, the bold exercise of power, independence of the mob, and a spirit "answerable to high design." The effect of the whole book, as it bears upon the political poems, is to invest with idealistic vigor a number of ideas which, in earlier embodiments, may have seemed nostalgic, negative and ungenerous. It is a considerable clarification.

But what about the poems as poems? The percentage of "editorials," jokes, aphorisms, and humorous wisdom-verse is high, and of these the present writer prefers the long "Kitty Hawk," which seems to ramble but ends as quite a structure of notions, and two delightful light pieces, "In a Glass of Cider" and "The Objection to Being Stepped On." Still, my reactionary taste is for the lyric and dramatic Frost, who in this volume happily persists. "The Draft Horse" is a sinister yet amusing symbolic poem on Frost's old theme of acceptance, and "Questioning Faces"—a six-line glimpse of an owl just missing a window-pane—is as ponderable as the densest haiku. As for the first four poems in the book, they are rightly placed, and every one a beauty. "Pod of the Milkweed," like Frost's brilliant sonnet "Design," charges some insects and a flower with vast implications: in this case the implications of spirit in matter. Of "A Cabin in the Clearing" I have spoken already. "Closed for Good," a version of which appeared in "Complete Poems," is here revised and shortened for the better. And this poem, "Away!", is perhaps the best of all:

Now I out walking
The world desert,
And my shoe and my stocking
Do me no hurt.

I leave behind
Good friends in town.
Let them get well-wined
And go lie down.

Don't think I leave
For the outer dark
Like Adam and Eve
Pull out of the Park.

Forget the myth.
There is no one I
Am put out with
Or put out by.

Unless I'm wrong
I but obey
The urge of a song:
I'm—bound—away!

And I may return
If dissatisfied
With what I learn
From having died.

That is a poem so perfectly dexterous as to seem easy: a gay, venturesome poem to go away by. But stay with us, Mr. Frost. Earth's the right place for happy returns and may you have many more.

W. H.
"From the Sierra to Outer Space."
San Francisco Chronicle,
March 25, 1962
p. 30.

Breathes there a bard who isn't
    moved
When he finds his verse is
    understood
And not entirely disapproved
By his country and his
    neighborhood?
                    —Robert Frost

Tomorrow, on the eighty-eighth birthday of Robert Frost, Holt, Rinehart & Winston will publish "In the Clearing," a book of new poems by this beloved American. The final poem was written as recently as January 12 of this year. The book consists of some 40 entries by this four-time winner of the Pulitzer Prize for poetry, including "For John F. Kennedy: His Inauguration," written in dedication to the President. At the time of the inauguration, the poet also quoted the short piece, "The Gift Outright," which first appeared in "A Witness Tree" in 1942. This is the only poem in this book which has appeared in a former collection by Robert Frost, and is included here to retain the spirit of the occasion.

Mostly Mr. Frost writes about the woods, man, nature—from the Sierra to outer space. All of it is "understood," and certainly none of it could be "disapproved by his country and his neighborhood."

Although born in San Francisco in 1874, Frost has lived most of his life in New England, where generations of his family lived before him. Once he was reminded that his "Collected Poems," a volume of some 600 pages, represented 60 years of writing. "This means," he replied, "that I've been writing less than ten pages a year. It's discouraging."

The poet does not force himself to write. He prefers to wait until he can write at his best. "It takes me two days to unscrew and two to screw up again," he once said. He also noted: "A complete poem is one where an emotion has found its thought and the thought has found the words."

Mr. Frost still writes his poems completely in this sense.

John Holmes.
"All the Robert Frosts
Are In His New Book,
'In the Clearing.' "
*Christian Science
Monitor,*
March 29, 1962,
p. 11

The great poem in Robert Frost's new book is "Kitty Hawk," perhaps the profoundest statement he has ever simplified into his kind of language, an ultimate in a lifetime's vision. That he means it as the chief piece we know at once, because he uses eighteen lines of it as "Frontispiece," such a surge of hope and belief as his skeptical mind has never quite said aloud before.

His achievement in this poem is a curious and exciting study, because there have been preliminary published versions, and apparently the book has been delayed these five or six years till he could get it right. But it is right now, for him, and for our wider understanding of modern life. "Kitty Hawk" is a major poem, partly autobiographical, partly a far-fetched and successful identification with the Wright brothers' leap into air, mostly a grand gathering of the forces of American character.

There are all the other Frosts in this book, the rural Frost we fondly think is the only one; the topical Frost we are less accustomed to but find deep and shrewd; the later political Frost, still wise and earthy; the mischievous, epigrammatic Frost; and the magical, the fabulous Frost that invents timeless tales; the direct-descriptive Frost; the ironic-tragic; and the Frost of the classical and American perspective in a responsible world-view.

The title of the book comes from a poem called "A Cabin in the Clearing," sent out to friends in 1951 as Christmas greeting. It is a dialogue between Mist and Smoke, watching two human beings, and ends, "Than smoke and mist who better could appraise/ the kindred spirit of an inner haze." Frost's way of saying that the spirit persists has always been metaphored in effort, as in the earlier "Tree at My Window"; by his naming this book "In the Clearing," one feels the certainty of at least a clearing in the woods. Into this clearing we walk with him after a full life, as we did in "Into My Own," in his first book. Unless I am too much stretching it, this sort of connection is one of many sensed in the cunning articulation of the book. A charming jacket-photograph shows a white-haired Frost with a finger at his lips, "Hush! . . . Listen! . . . ."

Of course, the two Kennedy inaugural poems are included, not conspicuously. The longer one, which unfortunately and yet affectingly Frost could not read on the occasion, reads nobly and powerfully here, a call to glory, "a golden age of poetry and power." His intention, years in the making, is to bless government's recognition of the arts, including poetry, and his foresight was true: the Kennedys have done it. The 1942 poem, "The Gift Outright," is reprinted. With this famous pair go "America Is Hard to See," a longish one about Columbus, and shorter, lighter ones on the same theme. The strain of Frost the comprehensive, national elder counselor is in all these.

Among the apparently casual (but never underestimate this poet, especially when he is casual) couplets and bits at the back of the book is one called "From Iron." He has often told the story in public. A huge ball of almost pure iron ore was mined in Sweden, and sent by the King to the United Nations, with the hope that it might be set up as a one-world symbol. An Indian representative of the UN, Ahmed S. Bokhari, called on Mr. Frost to invite him to write some lines to be done in bronze about this symbol. It must have tempted the poet. But he could not so perpetuate his approval of this oneness. All his thinking and writing had worked out the opposite concept. And so what the Indian delegate got, and all we get in this book, is a couplet, but it comes from the heart and center of all the poet's belief:

Nature within her inmost self
    divides
To trouble men with having to take
    sides.

Frost's last book of new poems was "Steeple Bush," published in 1947; a long time since. His assembly and demonstration of himself from the years between—and earlier—is of masterly and instructive interest. Here is "Accidentally on Purpose," with its last quatrain,

And yet for all this help of head and
    brain
How happily instinctive we remain,
Our best guide upward further to the
    light,
Passionate preference such as love at
    sight.

Here are "One More Brevity," about the Dalmatian; and "Escapist— Never," concluding with "All is an interminable chain of longing"; and here, to my own delight, is the second longest poem in the book, "How Hard It Is to Keep from Being King When It's in You and in the Situation." It first appeared on one surprising Sunday in the New York Herald Tribune book section, and shortly thereafter in a hard-cover edition of 300 copies, in 1951.

This is Frost the parabalist. A King of old abdicates, but his son, to whom he offers the throne, declines the honor and leaves with his father. In another kingdom the ex-King becomes cook to a sovereign who first appreciates good food, then good advice, from his superior kitchen help. Excellence cannot hide itself; but the poem gives us the extra invention of the cook-King's son as poet. Here the didactic old arbiter Frost says what poetry is and isn't, should be and shouldn't be. Suddenly he is speaking of Carnegie grants, free verse, Whitman, Sandburg, and iambics, which he here defines:

Regular verse springs from the
    strain of rhythm
Upon a metre, strict or loose iambic.
From that strain comes the
    expression *strains of music.*
The tune is not that metre, not that
    rhythm,
But a resultant that arises from
    them.
Tell them Iamb, Jehovah said, and
    meant it.

This playfulness is a long passage for working poets, yet in the total structure of the book it is almost buried, one more of the gathered finalities. A first impression of the whole book might, in fact, be of miscellany. But the more one reads, and relates groupings of ideas, theme, and their cross-allusions, the more powerfully one is impressed that "In the Clearing" contains essences of most of the thoughts and convictions Frost ever had—with the great addition of "Kitty Hawk." Never underestimate Frost the book-planner.

And I must return to "Kitty Hawk" as a summation of the poet's thinking and as an almost documentary piece in our literary history. In 1894, Frost ran away from home in Massachusetts, wandered south aimlessly, found himself on the sands of Kitty Hawk and "Nag's Head"—of course, long before the Wrights—and returned to Lawrence, and marriage with his high school sweetheart, Elinor White. In all the later poems of temptation into the dark woods, he pulls back, but this once, and early, he ran recklessly and far.

Next, in tracing the poem's long evolution, we would have to point out epigrams, satires, and public talks in the 1930's, that were concerned with national and political party affairs; Frost the elder, the friend of Henry Wallace, the outraged critic of Franklin D. Roosevelt. But a little earlier, he had been invited by Herbert Hoover to the dedication of a memorial shaft at Kitty Hawk. This is the point when, by my guess, Frost began to want to identify himself with the Wrights, and the air age, and Washington, D. C.

He had never forgotten that he was on the scene, and he mightily strove, and he mightily succeeds, in identification. He did meet the surviving Wright, and told him he had been there first. Wasn't it as important that a poet could fly off that beach as

that a biplane could? This would be the poem's problem.

The first version was the 1956 Christmas pamphlet, 128 lines of three rapid, freely rhymed beats. In the 100th anniversary issue of the Atlantic Monthly, November, 1957, this became a 203-line Part I: the second half is mostly the same, the new part is first. The Atlantic version had a whole new Part II, of 219 lines.

In the final version, in this new book, Part I is subtitled, "Portents, Presentiments, and Premonitions." Part II, now lengthened to 289 lines, is sub-divided as "Talk Aloft," "The Holiness of Wholeness," and "The Mixture Mechanic." Throughout the several expansions of the poem, the single-word changes, the line-omissions, the shifts of verse-paragraphs, and the long caring over the whole poem are strikingly evident. It was in this prolongation of the poem that Frost reached a depth of deliberation and insight that enabled him to put his own interpretative blessing on what has always made the American materialist uneasy.

"Kitty Hawk" is a manifesto, a major statement on American character and American achievement in mechanics, issued by our greatest modern poet, who has at last made his peace with science, which he has so long thought the enemy of poetry. He has brought about a magnificent, hard-won triumph; my rather arithmetical demonstration is meant only to prove the triumph. In this long poem, as in the seemingly artless combinations of the other poems, he has forgotten nothing of all he ever knew, he has managed to show off all the aspects of a lifetime's speculation, and told us the best he knows about life.

Lest anything or anyone be omitted, "In the Clearing" was published on Frost's 88th birthday Monday, and the dedication mentions Louis Untermeyer, Sidney Cox, and John Bartlett. A reminding line beneath the book's title is, "And wait to watch the water clear, I may," from the first poem in his first book. The title poem is dedicated to his publisher, Alfred Edwards. Even in "Lines Written in Dejection on the Eve of Great Success," he prophesies Astronaut Glenn's orbit. He reaches far back to a California memory of being swooped at but not carried off by an eagle, in "Auspex." And he closes the book with a very simple poem about chopping down one maple tree, which will defeat neither nature nor himself. This small quiet image is summary: man active, nature ceaseless, neither one winning or losing, which is the core of Frost's belief.

Adlai E. Stevenson. "Robert Frost at Eighty-Eight." *New Republic,* 146 (April 9, 1962), 20-22.

The alliance of poetry and politics is very old. Poets from Vergil and Dante to Frost himself have paid tributes to statesmen in their own stock in trade: verse. But what is to be done when the roles are reversed? What can I, a dealer in international politics, do for our renowned poet? What is *my* stock in trade? Perhaps I can make him a present of a problem—such as the cold war; or disarmament; or the rule of law. And I have many more. . . .

But I can tell you, in part at least, what the public servant has to give to the poet—it is the defense of the society in which the man like Robert Frost will still have, in his own words: "the freedom of my material— the condition of body and mind now and then to summon aptly from the vast chaos of all I have lived through." That is all a poet needs from society; the rest, the power to reveal truth and clarify paradox, he has inside himself.

In Robert Frost, the American people have found their poet, their singer, their seer—in short, their bard. Fortunately, Mr. Frost concurs with at least part of our judgment. In a quatrain—clearly aimed at lawyers and politics such as I have been, he says:

So if you find you must repent
From side to side in argument,
At least don't use your mind too
     hard,
But trust my instinct—I'm a bard.

He once defined a poem as he would define love. "It begins," he says, "in delight and ends in wisdom." I am grateful to him for describing with such precision the reason why, for me, his poetry lives and speaks. You hardly need to read two pages before you encounter the first of these delights—the sudden brilliant image of mankind's "outer weather"—that natural environment of tree and bird and stone which his words make more vivid than even our senses can—"the whirr of sober birds," the "whelming east wind . . . like the sea's return"—we smell, we taste, our eyes are freshened and renewed, we see better because the poet has seen for us.

And he is the poet of our "inner

weather" too. No living poet describes more passionately and compassionately the sea changes of the human heart—or has more sly humor to debunk the pretensions and pomposities we mistake for living. Sometimes it is a casual aside:

A small bird flew before me . . .
He thought I was after him for a
   feather—
The white one in his tail; like one
   who takes
Everything said as personal to
   himself.

Sometimes the light tone and the punch line cover a sad and serious thought.

I turned to speak to God
About the world's despair.
But to make matters worse,
I found God wasn't there.

God turned to speak to me
(Don't anybody laugh)
God found I wasn't there—
At least not over half.

But humor—and beauty—do not alone make a bard. He begins in delight. He ends in wisdom. A lot of things, it seems, pass for wisdom these days— flag-waving, super-patriotism, frenetic business confidence of the don't-sell- the-country-short variety, conformity, anti-conformity, the power of positive thinking. We'll find nothing like that in Robert Frost. His wisdom does not shirk the risk of suffering and injustice and disaster. It measures it. Indeed, not many poets have expressed the anguish more directly:

A voice said, Look me in the stars
And tell me truly, men of earth,

If all the soul-and-body scars
Were not too much to pay for birth.

It is just because there is no naïve optimism, and the abyss is recognized for what it is—the possibility of ultimate despair—that Robert Frost's constant extolling of a quiet, unsensational, dogged courage is more than a conventional theme. It is an inspiration and a force.

I for one do not believe that these are days of halcyon weather for America or for the world. We need poets who help us to gird ourselves for endurance, and who walk with us on dark roads where the end is not in sight. And if you asked me to name one poem which enshrines for me the spirit in which as a nation we should confront our troubled future, I would quote you the last of these familiar lines:

The woods are lovely, dark and deep,
But I have promises to keep
And miles to go before I sleep,
And miles to go before I sleep.

M. L. Rosenthal.
"The Two Frosts."
Reporter, 26
(April 12, 1962),
50-52.

Everyone knows there are at least two Robert Frosts. Each of them does some talking in the new book. One of them is a natural, sometimes broodingly bitter or fearful lyric poet and storyteller. He has a fine ear for traditional English metric and combines it beautifully with the tones of native

American speech. This, most of us would say, is the "real" Frost. His home is in rural New England, his spirit shy and elusive. It may be true that he became eighty-eight just a week or two ago, but he has always had the delighted eye and voice of ageless youth. He was forty when he published "The Pasture," which begins:

> *I'm going out to clean the pasture*
> *   spring;*
> *I'll only stop to rake the leaves away*
> *(And wait to watch the water clear, I*
> *   may);*
> *I sha'n't be gone long.–You come too.*

He uses the third line of this stanza for his present epigraph, I think to suggest that he has now actually seen what he long ago set out to see, and that we readers have "come too" and seen it with him. How delicately accurate, and how absorbed in pure observation, he can still be we may discover from the opening poem of the new volume, "Pod of the Milkweed":

> *Its flowers' distilled honey is so sweet*
> *It makes the butterflies intemperate.*
> *There is no slumber in its juice for*
> *   them.*
> *One knocks another off from where*
> *   he clings.*
> *They knock the dyestuff off each*
> *   other's wings—*
> *With thirst on hunger to the point of*
> *   lust.*
> *They raise in their intemperance a*
> *   cloud*
> *Of mingled butterfly and flower dust*
> *That hangs perceptibly above the*
> *   scene.*

Often this first, truest Robert Frost has the gloom of a great Russian writer. One of his early poems expresses the desire to disappear into a dark forest, "fearless of ever finding open land." Another presents him convincingly as one "acquainted with the night." And altogether, we are constantly surprised by what sad, grim poems he has planted in his books among the happier visions of "these flowery waters and these watery flowers" of spring and the humorous pictures of provincial life. Leaf through the *Collected Poems* (1949) and you will find a long series of forever memorable close-ups of grief, of neurotic agony, of irremediable suffering. Among American poets not even Robinson has matched the horror-filled awareness of woman's vulnerability in poems like "Home Burial," "The Lovely Shall Be Choosers," and "A Servant to Servants," to name only a few. Faulkner himself has not managed to show such vistas of grossness and pain as that last poem provides without any eccentricity or waste motion. Doubtless Frost is talking about more than a plant when he writes, in "Pod of the Milkweed" again:

> *And yes, although it is a flower that*
> *   flows*
> *With milk and honey, it is bitter*
> *   milk,*
> *As anyone who ever broke its stem*
> *And dared to taste the wound a little*
> *   knows.*

Sometimes the feeling is not so much shock at the grotesque brutality that marks the common life as it is a deeply nostalgic and ambiguous melancholy. The extraordinary poem "Directive" in the 1947 volume *Steeple Bush* was of this order, a tracing back toward buried meanings in the traumatically destroyed and irrevocably eroded past. The little poem "Ends" in the new book, though very much slighter, is of this order in its impulse at least:

Loud talk in the overlighted house
That made us stumble past.
Oh, there had once been night the
*   first,*
But this was night the last.

Of all the things he might have said,
Sincere or insincere,
He never said she wasn't young,
And hadn't been his dear.

Oh, some as soon would throw it all
As throw a part away.
And some will say all sorts of things,
But some mean what they say.

This reminds me on the one hand of the deliberately sterile little marriage poems of the very contemporary Robert Creeley, not in form but in ultimate manner—the dry casting away of all sensational detail in a sort of minimal approach to catastrophe. And, in quite another way, it is like some late minor piece by Yeats, "Quarrel in Old Age," say, or one of his little but heartfelt political outbursts. It is poetry that doesn't give a damn about anything except to make an accurate, telling foray *toward* the truth. As ancient Hebraic lore hath it, "It is upon us to begin the work; it is not upon us to complete the work." Two other somewhat ambiguous poems, "The Draft Horse" and "Closed for Good" (reprinted from *Collected Poems* without its original opening and closing stanzas), add to the sadness of *In the Clearing* a note of dauntless acceptance of fatality. They are like the very touching, deliberately doggerel "Away!" in their val-

edictory tone, although "Away!" is altogether out in the open and ends with the cockiest of threats:

And I may return
If dissatisfied
With what I learn
From having died.

But there is of course a second Robert Frost, and we hardly know what to do about *him*. He is the handsomely craggy-faced sage and official bard who was chosen to compose a poem for the inauguration of President Kennedy and whose birthday this year was celebrated at a formal affair sponsored by the Secretary of the Interior. For two decades now he has frequently donned this sage's mask and costume, as of a Good Grey Walt Whitman without beard or other taint, and treated us to verse-sermons on sundry topics: science, religion, socialism, capitalism, his own brand of twinkling-eyed pragmatic idealism right out of the cracker barrel, and almost anything else. Except in stray patches, it is as if when he begins sermonizing he loses all his poetic strength and capacity for self-irony and becomes merely the "smiling public man" Yeats once, but how wryly, called himself. Take two of the poems in the new volume, "For John F. Kennedy His Inauguration" and the even longer "Kitty Hawk." Both blandly affirm the technological values of American society today. The inaugural poem suggests as well that we are at the beginning of a new "Augustan" era of splendor and progress under the aegis of the Kennedy administration. Now we cannot reasonably say these are bad poems because of their ideas. On the contrary, we must all hope they prove themselves valid—and besides it is thrilling to see the "mad" absorption of certain great artists, in their later years, in transcendent ideas that so often prove saner than mean common sense can ever understand. But that is just the trouble. It is not "madness" but the descent into literal ordinaries, into Panglossian optimism, and—more to the point—into a style to go with them that makes the second Frost so dismayingly unreal:

> Come fresh from an election like the
>   last,
> The greatest vote a people ever cast,
> So close yet sure to be abided by,
> It is no miracle our mood is high. . . .
> There is a call to life a little sterner,
> And braver for the earner, learner,
>   yearner.
> Less criticism of the field and court
> And more preoccupation with the
>   sport. . . .

Where are we, anyway? Thinking of these unhappy matters and rather baffled by them—there is still so much of the "true" Frost with us too—I cannot help remembering Kenneth Rexroth's somewhat melodramatic lament for the alienated American poets of Frost's generation:

> What happened to Robinson,
> Who used to stagger down Eighth
>   Street,
> Dizzy with solitary gin?
> Where is Masters, who crouched in
> His law office for ruinous decades?
> Where is Leonard who thought he
>   was
> A locomotive? And Lindsay,
> Wise as a dove, innocent
> As a serpent, where is he?
>   Timor mortis conturbat me.

I do not know what it is that has made the difference among the present members of that great generation. Of them all, at least those still resident in this country, perhaps only William Carlos Williams and E. E. Cummings stand with the perpetual opposition. (Marianne Moore and Carl Sandburg liked Ike.) Say what you will against him, Mr. Cummings will never be anybody's official anything; and though somewhat more amenable, Dr. Williams will have to wait until the ideal anarcho-Bohemian-socialist-fraternitarian society of the future to march to the rostrum with his honor guard of loving young poets around him. But they have had a certain salutary neglect by comparison with Frost. They have not had to respond to a public at once interested in hearing them speak prophetically and less concerned with the content than with the air of their wisdom.

But I was going to say that Frost's case is more hopeful, and more complex, than all this may imply. Actually, the "real" Frost is interested in "issues" of all kinds too, though always in small doses and at great intervals. When *he* speaks, he does not shrink so far within a sage-disguise that his own natural voice is lost. His voice is then irrepressible:

> Forgive, O Lord, my little jokes on
>   Thee
> And I'll forgive Thy great big one on
>   me.

That pops up in *In the Clearing*. It reminds me of a little poem in *Steeple Bush* that shows how capable our poet is of satire in the great tradition, the quick, spontaneous thought of a free-mind with the twin gifts of wit and discipline. The poem is "U.S.

1946 King's X." It has the kick of personality and the ability to jeer at oneself lacking in the Kennedy poem:

Having invented a new Holocaust,
And been the first with it to win a
war,
How they make haste to cry with
fingers crossed,
King's X—no fair to use it any
more!

In the Clearing, too, gives us the truly thoughtful little poem "Our Doom to Bloom," which stands out coolly against the more ponderous and characterless "wisdom" pieces. Asked for a right definition of Progress, the Cumaean Sibyl replies:

. . . if it's not a mere illusion
All there is to it is diffusion—
Of coats, oats, votes, to all mankind.
In the Surviving Book we find
That liberal, or conservative,
The state's one function is to give.
The bud must bloom till blowsy
blown
Its petal loosen and are strown;
And that's a fate it can't evade
Unless 'twould rather wilt than fade.

The sadness of this poem is like that of Jeffers's "Shine, Perishing Republic," from which in fact its epigraph is taken. It contains a quiet but sobering recognition that a country like ours must lose its uniqueness as it helps other peoples advance; and it makes its point without too much expansiveness and, finally, through a most appropriate figure. If we look back over Frost's work we shall find that his social and political comments are always best made in this way, for instance the thoughts on war in "Snow," "To E.T.," "The Bonfire," and

"Not to Keep," or the thoughts on organized society and its economics in "A Lone Striker." In the long run we shall not be terribly troubled by the second, or false, Frost and the almost innocent garrulity with which he too often beguiles himself and his trusting public. We shall mostly forget the work of that sort, and move among the frightening depths and bright or shadowed surfaces of his characterizations and impressions of places and of significant moments. What we shall remember most, very likely is his intense repossession of psychological states, whether the near-nightmare richness of "After Apple-Picking," the deep, drowsy acceptance of weakness and death's nearness in "An Old Man's Winter Night," the hilarious though grisly matter-of-factness of "The Witch of Coös," or the coarse and savage erotic strangeness of "The Pauper Witch of Grafton." And the music!—

Ah, when to the heart of man
Was it ever more than a treason
To go with the drift of things,
To yield with a grace to reason,
And bow and accept the end
Of a love or a season?

Burton A. Robie. "Poetry." *Library Journal*, 87 (April 15, 1962), 1616.

Robert Frost has published a new book of verse and it was the pleasure of this writer some months ago to hear him speak one of the pieces at a small gathering in one of the Yale

Colleges. Now upon reading the work in print ("One More Beauty" in which a transient canine becomes for one night the great star Sirius), it becomes blindingly clear how much the art is inseparable from the man. Frost, the poet and faithful lover of his world and country, needs no introduction or commendation from this reviewer. As ever, in these poems he is as much at home in the fields and forests as in the mysteries of the universe and demonstrates in a wise, humble, not unhumorous way that he has come to terms with life. All have much to learn from and share with him. If ever there should be a Poet Laureateship in this country (and why not) his would be the certain honor.

Peter Davison.
"Robert Frost, His Own Tradition."
Atlantic Monthly, 209 (May 1962), 100-101.

Robert Frost more than spans in his lifetime the distance between nineteenth- and twentieth-century poetry, and yet he is more a poet of his age than many younger poets writing today. Though he was born in 1874, his verse was not published in book form until 1915, and since then he has kept even with his times, if not frequently ahead of them. Frost, in a queer way, is a tradition unto himself. While his ideas owe much to the stoical doctrines of antiquity and to the writings of Emerson and others who expressed their aspirations for the American republic, his style and tone owe little to any other poet. Frost has created his own style in English verse—a style as distinct as T. S. Eliot's in the twentieth century or Milton's in the seventeenth.

While other poets, moreover, have found specific guidance and refreshment in re-establishing contact with the poetry of the past, Frost has not changed or looked back, but, in his own words, written more than fifty years ago, has grown "Only more sure of all I thought was true." He is surely the most independent of our poets and stands apart from obvious poetic tradition. Yet who would venture to say that he is untraditional? His work is rooted neither in poetic convention nor in colloquial speech, but in the movement of our language, in the rhythms of our talk, in the innate sound and structure of English, as well as in the verse forms that have taken shape in our language over the centuries.

It cannot help but be odd to think of Frost as a contemporary—not only in years but in preoccupations—of Grover Cleveland as well as of John F. Kennedy; and it seems strange that a poetic career which has continued after the death of Dylan Thomas should be the lifework of a man who was attending Dartmouth in the year that Tennyson and Whitman died. Yet these are accidents of the calendar. It is no accident that Frost continues to embody in his verse as subtle a spirit as that of anyone else writing. The times have a way of catching up with themselves. Frost's recent poems are often topical, but you would not be making a bad bet if you gambled on the timelessness of at least a few.

Things will have to settle down for

a while, of course, before the question of Robert Frost's place in the history of our poetry can become certain, partly because his long career has made him the contemporary of so many and such disparate poets, and partly because he is so much his own man. He differs, too, from his contemporaries of this generation not only because he stands above them but also because he stands, in a way, ahead of them, looking forward rather than back. His new collection, *In the Clearing,* is his first in fifteen years. It contains thirty-eight new poems, two of them quite long. No other poems being written today resemble them in tone or rhythm, and few have the power to stretch the reader's mind in just the way that these do.

The longest, most central poem is called "Kitty Hawk," and, more ambitious than his youthful contemporaries, Frost has here attempted what most poets would shy from—to understand and make lyrical the aspiration at the heart of science. In some five hundred lines he reflects, in shifting contexts, on the impulse that occasioned man's first vault from the earth in the Wrights' biplane on the sands of Kitty Hawk,

Off on the unbounded
Beaches where the whole
Of the Atlantic pounded.

and summons, in prophetic terms, the history and force of man's inspired wrestle with nature over the centuries past and in the years ahead:

We are not the kind
To stay too confined . . .
Don't discount our powers;
We have made a pass
At the infinite,

Made it, as it were,
Rationally ours . . . .

It is a most extraordinary poem, and, in my opinion, one of the major poems in Frost's work. The poem is a little forbidding in a way peculiar to Frost's habit of "fooling" about things—it sounds trivial on the surface.

He is a poet who has always tried (sometimes so successfully as to be misunderstood) to disguise the largeness of his own poetic statements. Though "Kitty Hawk" is perhaps the highest flying "skylark" he has ever written, he conceals his intention within an apparently rigid, rhymed structure of three-beat trochaic lines—a line so difficult to vary that, since the time of Skelton, it has seldom been used in English except for short, light lyrics. Frost seems to have felt that the broadest theme demanded the most constricted form, and therefore required himself to modulate his rhythm across the tight confines of this meter and yet keep plenty of sweep for such trumpet blasts as:

But God's own descent
Into flesh was meant
As a demonstration
That the supreme merit
Lay in risking spirit
In substantiation.

The secret of bringing off so ambitious, not to say so seemingly impossible, a trick as this lies in Frost's profound fascination with the behavior of rhythm and meter as much as in the determination to master the conflict between form and substance and make them one. In another long poem Frost digresses:

Regular verse springs from the
   strain of rhythm
Upon a metre, strict or loose iambic.
From that strain comes the
   expression *strains of music*

And throughout this collection the serious play with metrics is part of the poet's game. Some rhythms are spare and bald, others flow in the unmistakable accents of the poet who years ago invented his own brand of blank verse and left his stamp on it forever:

MIST: I don't believe the sleepers
        in this house
        Know where they are.

SMOKE: They've been here long
         enough
         To push the woods back
         from around the house
         And part them in the
         middle with a path . . .

Other poems take on the quizzical, deceptive, facetious manner that is more common in Frost's work of the last twenty years. Here are the opening lines from one of his best jokes:

At the end of the row
I stepped on the toe
Of an unemployed hoe . . . .

Some of the comic poems (which are, of course, never purely comic in Frost's work) take on a silliness, a reaching for the unconsidered laugh that you may find disappointing, but most of them contain a great deal more than meets the eye, like this rueful remark about the iron that goes into tools and into weapons:

Nature within her inmost self
   divides
To trouble men with having to take
   sides.

Robert Frost has taken the privilege of age in this volume; he has turned his back, for the most part, on the soft lyrical manner of many of his earlier poems and has set aside the details of nature in favor of nature in the large, in favor of political and philosophical speculation. One of the finest poems is an engaging blank-verse fable called "How Hard It Is to Keep from Being King When It's in You and in the Situation." Throughout them all, however, no matter how speculative they are, the reader hears rather than sees the truly independent personality of this poet, putting a good face on the rocky reality of the world, calling from himself the strength to summon a smile at our confusion, to cope with the terrible moments of inner darkness, to temper our ineluctable stubbornness, to celebrate the rewards that nature offers us for being ourselves. At the age of eighty-eight such a confrontation of reality shows at least no less courage than it would in a younger man; and if Frost's work as a whole reveals that it is easier for him to confront some orders of reality than others, yet his most recent collection shows him still courageous in the face of the same losing odds as ever. "Forgive, O Lord," he asks, apparently blithely,

Forgive, O Lord, my little jokes on
   Thee
And I'll forgive Thy great big one on
   me.

Rosemary F. Deen. "Frost's New Power." *Commonweal,* 76 (May 4, 1962), 155.

In the Clearing appears as Robert Frost's culminating book. The title suggests a breakthrough—at once escape *(in the clear)* and clarification. But Frost resists finality. As a verb, *clearing* suggests an action going forward; as a noun it means only the "overthrow" of a few trees and not the defeat of nature. These ironies of title make one thing clear—that the years turn Frost ever more surely into himself.

The bulk of the book consists of poems of "philosophic talk." Whether you like them or not depends mostly on whether you share the "philosophy." Another Frost specialty is the fable in which a commonplace object takes on life and (often malicious) purpose. Readers who remember the grindstone and the ax-helve will recognize the "malice prepense" of the "unemployed hoe" in "The Objection to Being Stepped On." But the best poems are the lyrics, which freshly continue Frost's old themes and symbols. The theme of "wanton waste" and the image of flowers and butterflies appear in "Pod of the Milkweed"; frailty and the image of whiteness compose "A Peril of Hope"; the idea of escape/exploration figured in the solitary walk produces "Away."

Possibly the best poem, "The Draft Horse" ranks with "Design" in that special category perfected by Emily Dickinson and Frost: the frightening poem. It is the tale of a poorly-equipped pair going a night journey through woods. The fear in it is conveyed as much by the form as by the events—for example in the curious emptiness of the connectives in this stanza:

And a man came out of the trees
And took our horse by the head
And reaching back to his ribs
Deliberately stabbed him dead.

In the last two stanzas the fright deepens in the irony beneath the unquestioning acceptance of the pair. For the complacency of their reaction is countered by the enormous effort of the one long, winding sentence in which it is expressed:

The most unquestioning pair
That ever accepted fate
And the least disposed to ascribe
Any more than we had to to hate,

We assumed that the man himself
Or someone he had to obey
Wanted us to get down
And walk the rest of the way.

This mountain of labor produces this mouse of good will. Stanza One reminds us, after all, that "the rest of the way" lies through "a pitch-dark limitless grove."

In a way the most remarkable thing about this book is its evidence that Frost's lyric gift remains perfectly fresh and alive. Sometimes it is exercised in evocatively simple diction and stripped-down phrases:

Now I out walking
The world desert
And my shoe and my stocking
Do me no hurt.

Here the commonplace *shoe* and *stock-ing* are given symbolic status by the grand, echoing quality of *world desert.* Another example is the transition between the dream-like opening of "In winter in the woods alone," (with its echo of Emily Dickinson's "In winter in my room") to its final expression of conflict between Nature and the self. It must be from this Antaean opposition that Frost draws new strength.

Richard Kell.
The Guardian,
October 19, 1962,
p. 6.

Robert Frost's *In the Clearing* though much wider in range and more companionable [than Robert Graves' *New Poems 1962*] is also less serious. It contains more skilful light versification than poetry:

When clever people ask me where
I get a poem, I despair.
I'm apt to tell them in New York
I think I get it via stork . . .

"A Never Naught Song"—in the section called "Cluster of Faith"—summarises huge concepts in tiny featherweight lines:

It was in a state
Of atomic One.
Matter was begun—
And in fact complete,
One and yet discrete
To conflict and pair.
Everything was there
Every single thing
Waiting was to bring,
Clear from hydrogen
All the way to men.

These two quotations are representative: chatty monologues of a veteran with a lively mind, a warm heart, and a twinkle in his eye. The tight-lipped will say "homespun wisdom" and toss the book aside; but to read it solemnly would be to drink ginger pop with a soup spoon. Frost could not have made his reputation on stuff like this, but at the tail-end of a distinguished career it is unexceptionable. A thing is more enjoyably said in good light verse than it would have been in good light prose, if only because verse is more ingenious. The freshness of the rhyming alone is enough to put "America Is Hard To See" 'way ahead of a prose equivalent.

D. J. Enright.
"The Muse's House."
New Statesman, 64
(October 19, 1962),
530.

The characteristic lilt of Robert Frost's poetry, the eruption of excitement from a meditative base, have given way in this new collection, the first for 15 years, to craftsmanship, the sort of sureness of touch which almost conceals the fact that nothing much is being touched, and an insistent humorousness or good-humouredness which sometimes falls flat. The longer pieces ramble amiably, and the light verse tends half-heartedly towards Ogden Nash. But what is saddest is the noisy way in which the blurb holds its breath over "the unprecedented honour" granted this distinguished old poet of reciting a poem at President Kennedy's Inauguration. Perhaps some of the honour was on the other foot.

In the Clearing does contain some enjoyable poems, including the Inaugural recitation itself and "America Is Hard to See," and originalities rub shoulders with trivialities on practically every page. No one else, it is true, could have written these poems. As Robert Graves says, they are "stamped all over with his own seal": we know it is Robert Frost's seal from seeing it stamped more clearly and deeply elsewhere.

William G. O'Donnell. "Robert Frost at Eighty-Eight." *Massachusetts Review,* 4 (Autumn 1962), 213-18.

With the passage of the years reviewing a new collection of poems by Robert Frost has become an increasingly difficult task. For a long time now, Frost's poetry has been hard to separate from Frost the talented reader of his own lines, the remarkably gifted public entertainer, and the striking personality and man of wisdom. After Mr. Frost appeared at the Inauguration of President Kennedy and was seen and heard by a television audience estimated at more than 60,000,000 Americans, the critics' difficulties began to multiply. More recently, Frost's journey to the Soviet Union, climaxed by a much-publicized talk with Premier Khrushchev, has added another dimension to the Frost legend and, by making the writing more famous than ever, has made it at the same time somewhat less accessible.

In the Clearing, Frost's eighth collection in a career that goes back to the early 1890's, was published on the poet's eighty-eighth birthday, March 26, 1962, and six months later was still maintaining a place on bestseller lists throughout the nation. Not for more than thirty years has a collection of poems enjoyed so wide a sale in America. The question raised by the popularity of the hundred-page, forty-poem volume are obvious enough.

How does *In the Clearing* compare with previous Frost volumes from *A Boy's Will* through *Steeple Bush?* What are its best poems? Does it contain any pages to be added to the list of poems that Frost has safely "lodged"—to use one of his own favorite metaphors—beside the finest achievements in American writing?

Understandably enough, *In the Clearing* was handled with great circumspection by the reviewers who helped introduce the book in the spring of 1962. Twenty-five years earlier, with the publication of *A Further Range,* Frost had been misinterpreted and underestimated by several of the nation's most penetrating critics, and this time everyone seemed determined not to say anything that would betray a hasty or insensitive reading of the poems. Some of the reviewers cautiously skirted the whole issue by writing essays on Frost's significance in general rather than his achievement or lack of it in the new volume. Not to be overlooked, furthermore, was the attitude on the part of certain reviewers that critical analysis is inappropriate when one is dealing with a symbol of America as enduring as the Flag or Robert Frost.

The volume's distinctive quality, which must be defined before any evaluation of individual poems can be attempted, is its bardic tone. Even the lyrics of *In the Clearing* are marked by this characterizing voice. The bardic role is nothing new for Frost, of course, since he began assuming it years ago. Until the present volume appeared, however, he had never played it with genuine ease and full conviction; in earlier decades the bardic stance was sometimes marred by a tendency to lapse into the narrowly conservative attitudes of "A Brook in the City" or "To a Thinker" or the prosiness of "Build Soil." The years since *A Further Range* have witnessed a liberalizing of Frost's opinions—he would naturally deny the reality of this shift—and a corresponding refinement and improving of the bardic poetry. With *In the Clearing* the culmination of this aspect of Frost's career is reached. America has had bards in the past, but, except for Walt Whitman, it has never had one who fully appreciated the poetic possibilities of the role.

The best poems of *In the Clearing* include—to mention several in the order of their occurrence within the volume—"A Cabin in the Clearing," "Closed for Good," "Escapist—Never," "Forgive, O Lord," "Auspex," "Questioning Faces," "The Objection to Being Stepped On," "In a Glass of Cider," and "In Winter in the Woods Alone"—more than enough for the core of an excellent collection. The two long poems, "How Hard It Is to Keep from Being King When It's in You and in the Situation" and "Kitty Hawk," are interesting as experiments that illuminate some of the lesser known facets of Frost's mind and personality; but the first is too relaxed and garrulous to rank with Frost's major achievements, and the

ambitious, seventeen-page "Kitty Hawk," although full of brilliant passages, does not entirely succeed, perhaps because the barrier in the use of a strange, five-syllabled, three-accented line is not finally surmountable. The dignified Inaugural effort, "For John F. Kennedy," the only "occasional" poem Frost has ever published, sums up the poet's admirable sentiments on the subject of America's revolutionary and anti-colonial origins; like "Kitty Hawk" and other things in the book, it exalts the virtue of courage and finds that a willingness to risk all in a bold venture of the spirit is one of the saving American qualities. Among other substantially constructed poems is "America Is Hard to See," where Frost, in spite of a comic tone, gives a bleaker picture of his native land and its prospects than he does in the patriotism of his tribute to the President's "beginning hour." Finally, the volume has two or three items that are not so much light or comic poems as poetic hoaxes, part of an old poet's bag of tricks, useful for public performances, perhaps, but awkward when printed side by side with perfectly fashioned lyrics.

"A Cabin in the Clearing" and "Escapist—Never" demonstrate once again Frost's continuing mastery of a highly original, constantly evolving blank verse. The rhythmical variety that Frost achieves here in the most traditional verse form in the language is one of the volume's successes. Frost's ability to control the deeper subtleties of blank verse, an ability he shares with the later Elizabethan and the Jacobean dramatists, is unequalled by any British or American writer in the twentieth century:

He is no fugitive—escaped, escaping.
No one has seen him stumble
    looking back.
His fear is not behind him but beside
    him
On either hand to make his course
    perhaps
A crooked straightness yet no less a
    straightness.

Yeats, Wallace Stevens, and Edwin Arlington Robinson struggled with the great form—stumbling block for many a poet since the seventeenth century—but rarely attained the marvellous flexibility of these lines from "Escapist—Never," with their assured freedom inside a strict convention and their curiously shifting accents and added syllables.

Frost's accomplishments in blank verse, in poems ranging from the narratives and dramatic monologues of *North of Boston* through "Two Look at Two" in the 1920's to "Escapist—Never" or "A Cabin in the Clearing" from the new collection have never been given their due. Not since Webster and Ford has there been a blank verse that so thoroughly and effectively exploits the rhythmical and idiomatic resources of the English language; yet the years of Frost's life have seen the growth and virtually universal acceptance of a belief that blank verse has outlived its usefulness. A generation ago Ezra Pound started convincing people that blank verse in the twentieth century was an impediment to making language move in the sequence of the spoken or the musical phrase; as Pound understood the problem, the form belonged to the past, to the theater in the days of Elizabeth and the Stuarts, and had no relevance in modern literature. After the erection of "the Chinese Wall of Milton," said T. S. Eliot in 1919, blank verse began to suffer "not only arrest but retrogression." The Pound-Eliot doctrine, which announced that good blank verse could no longer be written and should therefore not be attempted, confronts Frost's accomplishments in the form, not simply a few lines here and there, but more than a score of poems and hundreds of lines composed over a period of six decades.

In the new volume Frost continues his pursuit of the idomatic essence of his language, a pursuit that commenced in *North of Boston*. As much as anything else in his writing, it is this unending search for an appropriate colloquial form that gives Frost cogency as a modern rather than an old-fashioned or traditional writer. His love of the prepositional constructions that lie at the heart of idiom in English and are not translatable into any other language is as strong and characterizing a trait as it ever has been:

Forget the myth.
There is no one I
Am put out with
Or put out by.

The accent is unmistakable here. Frost understands how much the distinctiveness of his style depends upon idiom and how much idiom, in turn, depends upon the range of effects possible in the various prepositional and prepositional-adverbial usages. He has never tried to reveal the secret of his creativity, how a poem first begins in his mind, but one imagines that a sudden flash of idiom, forming an image-idea, must have marked the starting point of a great deal of the writing. He seems to go through life searching for these simple yet profoundly suggestive phrases to use as building-blocks. The total number of strikingly idiomatic lines may be relatively small in any of these poems since idiom, as a writer's distinguishing quality, is not so much a matter of frequency of occurrence as it is of emphatic or climactic position. Part of Frost's genius with idiom is a matter of correct timing, of knowing exactly when to introduce a colloquial, conversational phrase so as to counterbalance a passage composed in the less idomatic language of standard literary English.

A dominant feature of the collection is the brilliance of a number of the shorter poems. "Questioning Faces," complete in its six lines, will come to be accepted as one of Frost's best nature poems, an example of his unequalled ability to capture a simple natural event in all its beauty and immediacy and, even while doing so, to draw the characteristic line that always separates the well-loved, closely-observed outer world from the world of human beings in these poems:

The winter owl banked just in time
    to pass
And save herself from breaking
    window glass.
And her wings straining suddenly
    aspread
Caught color from the last of
    evening red
In a display of underdown and quill
To glassed-in children at the window
    sill.

"In a Glass of Cider" is a masterpiece of playful, comic poetry, a medium in which Frost's imagination often moves with a greater freedom in establishing remote but convincing associations than it does in the more "serious" verse. "In Winter in the Woods Alone," the most recent poem of all, concludes *In the Clearing* with a moment of characteristic optimism, Frost's feeling of being unwilling to quit until he is finished.

These short lyrics and bardic or gnomic utterances belong to a genre that becomes more and more common in the collections since *A Further Range*—that is, the poem in which every detail, no matter how minute, is an imaginative necessity. Perhaps poems of this type—brief, polished, and wise—can be written only by very old poets, men who have seen much of the world, have learned something from their long experience, and have become deeply skeptical of the value of the grand style and grand words. It would be incorrect, of course, to suggest that the genre has been limited to Frost's last years since a few examples may be found in the earlier period as well. The beautiful "Dust of Snow" appeared in the 1920's, and "In Neglect," which was quoted in the first review of Frost's work in 1913, is typical of one element in *A Boy's Will*. It is true, however, that in Frost, as in Yeats, the poem of the utmost brevity and compression is more characteristic of age than of youth, although in neither writer is this fact indicative of an inability to follow a long effort through to completion.

Frost has tried to escape the boredom that a good many people nowadays object to, no doubt wrongly, in certain parts of the long poems of the past. His aim, like Poe's, has been to create poems in which all lines and phrases are poetic. The American writing that Frost has most often admired—Emerson's poetry and the perfectly formed sentences of Emerson's essays—helped to confirm this aim. A writer who complained of the monotonies of epic novels, especially those in the Russian manner, and read the Greek Anthology and the Roman epigrammatists with intense pleasure was probably bound to find out what, if anything, could be done with the six-line, four-line, and two-line poem.

Like "An Answer" from *A Witness Tree,* "Forgive, O Lord" from the new collection will probably become a classic example of the genre and proof that such a thing is really a possibility:

Forgive, O Lord, my little jokes on
     Thee
And I'll forgive Thy great big one on
     me.

The meaning of this complicated witticism, which delights Frost's audiences, is something of a mystery. Frost places it in a group to which he gives the title "Cluster of Faith," and since its companion pieces are all expressions of the poet's passionately held belief in purpose and design and his rejection of an accidental evolution as a sufficient explanation of man's origin and destiny, "Forgive, O Lord" is undoubtedly intended as a positive assertion, not a denial. Frost, who is more religious than people think he is, knows that jokes about God can be reverent and devout as well as Voltairean. But there is at least a suggestion that the design revealed here is a negative one, "a design of darkness to appall," to use a phrase from a celebrated sonnet. In this sense the poem embodies, to some extent, a feeling that life is basically absurd and meaningless, a joke at

man's expense, but not, however, a joke that demonstrates man's spiritual greatness. Perhaps the poem's secret is that a positive meaning exists in the two lines and predominates in spite of the negative undertones of skepticism and doubt.

Several of the poems are more affirmative than anything Frost has previously written, and some of the lines imply, without any precision of statement, a whole vista of religious and theological suggestion in the background. The collection begins with a "Frontispiece" taken from a lyrical passage in "Kitty Hawk":

But God's own descent
Into flesh was meant
As a demonstration
That the supreme merit
Lay in risking spirit
In substantiation.

Exactly what Frost intends this to mean we are probably not going to discover, just as we are not supposed to press too insistently for meanings in any of the more poetic paragraphs of Emerson's essays. It is sufficiently clear, however, that the passage is a positive assertion. On the other hand, a few poems in *In the Clearing* capture a familiar mood of incertitude:

And still I doubt if they know where
     they are.
And I begin to fear they never will.
All they maintain the path for is the
     comfort
Of visiting with the equally
     bewildered.
Nearer in plight their neighbors are
     than distance.

Here, in the moving, blank verse rhythms of "A Cabin in the Clearing," the poet seems as hesitant about asserting too much as he is willing to assert all in parts of "Kitty Hawk." If there is a fault here—and there probably is one—it may lie in Frost's failure to place the divergent moods, the antagonistic tendencies, within the unified structure of a single poem and thus achieve a rich complexity of utterance rather than an impulsive shifting from one sentiment to another. Frost's greatest poems, "Directive" in particular, have a quality of doubleness in their manner of combining statement and counter-statement, affirmation and denial, assertion and an undercutting irony. At times the new volume takes the easier way out and follows Emerson in trying to be honest to the sentiment of the moment while hoping that in the long run the direction will be "A crooked straightness yet no less a straightness."

In the Clearing places value upon a sense of clarification as well as a sense of direction. The title is a phrase from the poem about the people who have subdued nature and made a human clearing in the wilderness; it is to be read, Frost indicates, in the light of a line from "The Pasture," "And wait to watch the water clear, I may." The search for insight, for understanding, for the moment of clarification after a preliminary stirring up of the spirit, is the main theme established through much of the collection. This time Frost seems to be hoping for insights that will be more than momentary stays against confusion, to use a phrase from "The Figure a Poem Makes," and at least part of his hope is realized. *In the Clearing* may have no supremely accomplished poems, like "Two Look at Two" or "Directive," but when it is added to the *Complete Poems,* it will take an honored place in the Frost canon beside the seven collections that preceded it.

Louise Bogan. "Briefly Noted." *New Yorker,* 38 (November 17, 1962), 242, 244.

"In the Clearing," a new collection by Robert Frost (Holt, Rinehart & Winston), published on its author's eighty-eighth birthday, with celebration and applause, is written in American, a language that still has a good deal of life and heart in it. Frost has always equated patriotism with responsibility. This resolute belief, with others, he now frames in admonitions rather than as straight demands for this or that kind of action. Rhetoric is conspicuously absent; the old lyric voice takes over from time to time. The atmosphere is clear and tonic, with the admonitory remarks often coming through in aphorisms that might belong to Poor Richard or, more likely, to his poetic successors, R. W. Emerson and Henry Thoreau. Very formal, very direct; very dry, very nice.

William Meredith.
"Robert Frost in Book
Reviews and Under the
Aspect of Eternity."
Poetry, 101
(December 1962),
200-203.

In the Clearing is the latest addition to the most successful work-in-progress of poetry in our language. To describe the book this way is only to insist that, in the constancy of its concerns and of its success, Robert Frost's work is a single work. It has grown like a tree of a new species: the layer of live wood is a perennial miracle of new life, but the tree itself is what is altogether astonishing—*a new tree*—even before it was the giant it stands today.

In the almost fifty years that Robert Frost has been publishing books of poetry, twelve reviews have appeared in this magazine, which had started the year before *A Boy's Will.* Perhaps the best were the second one by Ezra Pound (who had also written the first) and the latest one by William Carlos Williams. Most of them were written by poets and they represent articulately the judgments that were made of the work, volume by volume, as it grew—a work that has survived many parochialisms of time and looks as though it would survive them all.

    Things must expect to come in front
       of us
    A many times—I don't say just how
       many—
    That varies with the things—before
      we see them,

Brother Meserve tells us in *Snow,* and surely this is truer of works of art than of most things.

In 1929 Harriet Monroe, the remarkable woman who fashioned *Poetry,* noticed that the quality of Frost's work was beginning to fall off. This simple, relatively lovable error has been repeated with every book since then, though not often in these pages where it stands as just another of Miss Monroe's famous *firsts.* The volume she was reviewing contained *Spring Pools, Once by the Pacific, Tree at my Window, The Flood,* and *Acquainted with the Night,* and it was called *West-Running Brook.* "Well, these poems are Frost's all right," that wonderful woman wrote, "but none of them may be ranked among Frost's best. . . . The title poem is a slight affair . . ." etc. (The people who have believed that they invented Robert Frost, and like the telephone and the airplane he is widely claimed, have been particularly subject to this error about new works, which are bound to seem apocryphal if not indeed by a spurious hand.)

Another critical error (which was seen at its most intelligent and pigheaded in George W. Nitchie's book called *Robert Frost: A Study of a Poet's Convictions*) is to review the opinions or philosophy that can be attributed to a poet on the basis of a work or a fragment of a work. But a poet speaks through many characters. He has many visions of the things that deeply concern him. The subjects to which he returns, as Richard Wilbur has observed, are those which vex him. Poems talk to each other about the ambiguities of life. "And there is always more than should be said," Frost himself says in *The Wind and the Rain.*

At the end of a rather friendly review of *A Masque of Reason* in 1945 E. S. Forgotson took exception to the poet's view of the responsibility for human trouble. "It had to seem unmeaning to have meaning," Frost's God has said to Job about his suffering. Like the book of Job, Frost's book is sophisticated enough to lay most of the blame on God. Mr. Forgotson goes on to say that happily there is a "less stultifying" view of man's plight than this, and then he quotes (you hardly know where to put the *sic!* in a sentence like this) an article by Ruth Benedict from *Partisan Review* to the effect that "the chief evils of our time, such as war and fascism, economic depression and individual neurosis ... are consequences of man's having arranged his affairs to his own disadvantage." I have no quarrel with this as anthropology, but I can't feel that the *Masque* has been confronted, any more than Mr. Nitchie confronts the poems when he says they yield or gyres nor yew trees and therefore are less serious than Yeats or Eliot.

William Carlos Williams, writing of the second masque in 1948, shows how a poet takes meaning. "There is one thing I will not do in reviewing this book, that is to try to separate the characters from their 'meaning' in order to make that clear for the general reader. That meaning, if I judge rightly, was never meant by Mr. Frost to be made clear in that way, rather it was densely integrated with the character and as far as I am concerned must remain so." Since Frost is committed to the view that "everything is as good as it is dramatic", Dr. Williams's position is soundly applicable to the lyric as well as the overtly dramatic poems. Yet most of the people who have quarreled with Frost's stature have done so on the basis of this simple error: they take

certain dramatic utterances, few or many, and make a creed of them which they then find insufficient.

As the poems accumulate they give a rather complete account of the universe. It is a compendious rather than an edited account—"at least I will not have it *systematic*," as one of the independent-minded quatrains says.

The poems in the new book argue with the *Complete Poems* like old cronies. *Pod of the Milkweed* is one of a series of discussions of prodigality, including *November, Carpe Diem,* and *In Hardwood Groves. Away* takes up the theme of death in a tone like and yet unlike the tones of *Misgiving, In a Disused Graveyard, To Earthward,* and a dozen others. *A Cabin in the Clearing* reminds you, in its account of the limits of human knowledge, of *Neither Out Far Nor In Deep* and the *The Star-Splitter,* but in its affection for the householders it reminds you of the young people in poems like *Two Look at Two* and *A Rogers Group. The Draft Horse* is one of the most perfect poems in the new collection. It reaches back in our minds for all that has been said since *A Boy's Will* about the debate between good and evil.

The Draft Horse

With a lantern that wouldn't burn
In too frail a buggy we drove
Behind too heavy a horse
Through a pitch-dark limitless
    grove.

And a man came out of the trees
And took our horse by the head
And reaching back to his ribs
Deliberately stabbed him dead.

The ponderous beast went down
With a crack of a broken shaft.

And the night drew through the
    trees
In one long invidious draft.

The most unquestioning pair
That ever accepted fate
And the least disposed to ascribe
Any more than we had to to hate,

We assumed that the man himself
Or someone he had to obey
Wanted us to get down
And walk the rest of the way.

A reviewer who confines himself to
pointing to a poem like this, or to the
frontispiece poem abstracted from
Kitty Hawk, and saying, this is what I
mean by a poem firmly lodged—there
is a reviewer playing it safe with
posterity.

"The Old Masters."
Times Literary
Supplement,
December 21, 1962,
p. 987.

Both these volumes have a little worried reviewers. Mr. Frost is nearly
ninety and the poems in *In the Clearing* have the odd, chirpy, grasshopper
lightness, the strange lack of *gravitas,*
which is sometimes a mark of genius
in extreme old age. The poems tend to
prattle and to make simple jokes or
utter wise saws happily, as the poems
of gifted children, who have not yet
felt the weight of puberty, also tend to
do. Poetry for Mr. Frost is now a
game, played naturally, for fun, and
not to shine or compete. Mr. Graves is
much younger, in his middle sixties.

What worries reviewers in his case is
that, after saying that a poet who
survives his twenties is lucky to be
given five good poems a year, and
after being extremely severe in
excluding even many much admired
poems from his several collected volumes, he has now produced, in two
successive years, volumes each of
close on forty poems. Will he keep it
up, and when he is Mr. Frost's
age shall we have two or three
supplementary volumes of collected
poems to consider? And in this present volume are his standards of self-
judgment as rigorous as usual?

Mr. Graves's excellent introduction
to the Frost volume (intended originally, one gathers, not for this volume
but for a general selection of Mr.
Frost's poems) makes the claim for
Robert Frost that he is the first
American poet to be "honestly reck-
oned a master-poet by world standards," where America had previously produced "good provincial poets"
and had also produced Whitman, who
might have been a master-poet, if he
had only realized "how much more
was required of him." (Mr. Graves
leaves out of consideration Mr. Pound
and Mr. Eliot, younger men than Mr.
Frost, though Mr. Pound started publishing verse nearly ten years before
him.) Many of the qualities Mr.
Graves praises in Mr. Frost, such as
his readiness to accept the unexpected, his unwillingness to plan a
poem in advance, and his respect for
metre, his sense of the life of a poem
coming partly from "the strain of
rhythm upon metre," are qualities
which critics would also praise in Mr.
Graves.

It is, in fact, curious and interesting
to compare Mr. Frost's volume with
Mr. Graves's. There is a poem by Mr.

Frost that is at least very Gravesian in its properties, "Questioning Faces":

The winter owl banked just in time
    to pass
And save herself from breaking
    window glass.
And her wings straining suddenly
    aspread
Caught colour from the last of
    evening red
In a display of underdown and quill
To glassed-in children at the
    windowsill.

Mr. Graves would probably not have used the verb "bank," which compares the owl to an old-fashioned aeroplane. But the poem combines dry presentation and rich implicit meaning; is a parable, as many of Mr. Graves's own best poems also are.

Some of the longer poems tend to ramble rather, but even in them there are often sharp and surprising concentrations of thought. There is a fine poem about the milkweed, a plant the nectar of whose flower is, apparently, intoxicating to butterflies who exhaust themselves struggling to get at it. All this effort is merely to

Leave as their posterity one pod
With an inheritance of restless
    dream,

for future butterflies. And Mr. Frost comments wryly:

But waste was of the essence of the
    scheme.

Here, again, we have a fable with a moral and one that has never been forgotten by a poet who has never been afraid of familiar tones or topics and who has always let the grand style catch up on him rather than straining himself to catch up on it. If Mr. Frost's old age is not Yeats's, neither is it Wordsworth's: perhaps we should remember the gaiety of Hokusai, the "old man mad about painting."

Checklist of Additional Reviews

Philip Booth. "Journey out of a Dark Forest." *New York Times Book Review,* March 25, 1962, pp. 1, 44.

Charles Poore. "Books of the Times." *New York Times,* March 27, 1962, p. 35.

Booklist and Subscription Books Bulletin, 58 (May 1, 1962), 599.

Bookmark, 21 (June 1962), 256.

Vincent Miller. "The Home of Robert Frost." *National Review,* 12 (June 5, 1962), 411-12.

Robert Kimbrough. *Wisconsin Studies in Contemporary Literature,* 3 (Spring-Summer 1962), 104-107.

R. S. *Wisconsin Library Bulletin,* 58 (July-August 1962), 240.

Stanley Kunitz. "Frost, Williams, & Company." *Harper's Magazine,* 225 (October 1962), 100-102.

Appendix

Checklist of additional reviews for various editions of *Selected Poems* and *Come-In*.

Selected Poems. New York: Holt, 1923; London: Heinemann, 1923.

"Prose and Poetry." *Times Literary Supplement* [London], March 29, 1923, p. 213.

"Robert Frost." *Booklist,* 25 (March 1929), 256.

"Selected Poems, by Robert Frost." *The Dial,* 86 (May 1929), 436.

Selected Poems. London: Jonathan Cape, 1936. Introductory essays by W. H. Auden, C. Day Lewis, Paul Engle, and Edwin Muir.

John Holmes. "Robert Frost Conquers the Poetic Realm." *Boston Evening Transcript,* February 13, 1937, Sec. 6, pp. 1-2.

Desmond MacCarthy. "A Country Poet: Mr. Robert Frost's Verse." *London Sunday Times,* May 16, 1937, p. 6.

Come In and Other Poems. New York: Holt, 1943; London: Jonathan Cape, 1944. Selection and introduction by Louis Untermeyer.

Bookmark, 4 (March 1943), 10.

Adelbert M. Jakeman. "Frost, Late and Early." *Springfield Sunday Union and Republican,* April 4, 1943, Sec. 3, p. 7.

George F. Whicher. "Robert Frost's Best." *New York Herald Tribune Weekly Book Review,* April 4, 1943, p. 4.

Thomas Lyle Collins. "Meet Robert Frost." *New York Times Book Review,* April 11, 1943, p. 12.

"Untermeyer on Frost." *Time,* 41 (April 12, 1943), 100.

F. J. Bishop. "New Volume By and About Dean of American Poets." *Chicago Sun Book Week,* 1, April 18, 1943, p. 8.

Alice M. Jordan. *Horn Book,* 19 (May 1943), 172.

Mary Katherine Reely, ed. "A Selected List of Current Books." *Wisconsin Library Bulletin,* 39 (May 1943), 71.

Booklist, 39 (May 1, 1943), 351.

Pearl Strachan. "The World of Poetry." *Christian Science Monitor Weekly Magazine,* May 1, 1943, p. 10.

William A. Donaghy. *America,* 69 (June 5, 1943), 246.

Florence Bethune Sloan. "Come and Read" section, *Christian Science Monitor,* August 26, 1943, p. 4.

T[heodore] M[aynard]. *Catholic World,* 157 (August 1943), 552-53.

Alan Swallow. "A Review of Some Current Poetry." *New Mexico Quarterly Review,* 13 (Summer 1943), 218.

Index

Index

[Abercombie, Lascelles], 11-14
Academy, The, 5
A[dams], F[ranklin] P[ierce], 41
Adams, J. Donald, 198
Adams, Walter Wood, 225
Aiken, Conrad, 200
Akins, Zoë, 41
America, 133, 152, 181, 276
American Mercury, 137
American Review of Reviews, 21
Amherst Graduates' Quarterly, 149
Among Our Books, 111
*Anthology of Magazine Verse for 1915
and Year Book of American Poetry,*
41
*Anthology of Magazine Verse for 1916
and Year Book of American Poetry,*
43
Arvin, Newton, 123
Athenaeum, 1
Atlantic Monthly, 28, 149, 182, 195,
213, 235, 259

Bacon, Leonard, 185, 207
Barrett, Alfred, 152
Bascom, Elva L., 111
Bates, Esther Willard, 209
Baxter, Sylvester, 21
Benét, Stephen Vincent, 169
Benét, William Rose, 116
Best Sellers, 197
B., F., 93
Bishop, F. J., 275
Blackmur, R. P., 130
Bogan, Louise, 151, 205, 269
Booklist, 80, 111, 149, 182, 205, 219,
238, 275, 276

*Booklist and Subscription Books Bul-
letin,* 273
Bookman, 41, 62, 69, 89
Bookmark, 182, 238, 273, 275
Book-of-the-Month Club News, 149
Booth, Philip, 273
Boston Daily Globe, 205
Boston Evening Transcript, 5, 71, 93,
113, 149, 275
Boyle, Frances Alter, 185
Bradley, W. A., 43
Bradley, William Aspenwall, 41
Bragdon, Elspeth, 129
Braithwaite, William Stanley, 41, 43
B[raithwaite], W. S., 5
B[regy], K[atherine], 181
Brégy, Katherine, 205, 219
Brickell, Herschel, 80, 115, 149
Brooks, Philip, 149
Browne, George H., 36
*Bulletin of the Poetry Society of
America,* 41

Campbell, Gladys, 216
Canadian Forum, 107, 216
Carpenter, Frederick I., 110
Catholic World, 79, 149, 181, 205,
219, 276
C., B., 75
Chapbook, 39
Chicago Daily Tribune, 149
Chicago Evening Post, 24, 41
Chicago Sun Book Week, 187, 275
*Chicago Sunday Tribune Magazine of
Books,* 245
Chicago Sun-Times, 227
Christian Century, 74, 100, 141

Christian Science Monitor, 128, 209, 250, 276
Christian Science Monitor Weekly Magazine, 161, 201, 276
Churchman, 205
Church, Richard, 101
Ciardi, John, 241
Cleghorn, Sarah N., 79
Clemens, Cyril, 167
Collins, Thomas Lyle, 275
Columbus Sunday Dispatch, 127
Colum, Mary M., 170
Colum, Padraic, 43
Commonweal, 139, 195, 238, 262
Cox, Sidney, 47, 221
Crawford, John, 80
Current History, 149, 174
Current Opinion, 41

Dabbs, James McBride, 125
Daiches, David, 238
Dallas Morning News, 122
Davison, Peter, 259
Deen, Rosemary F., 262
Delineator, 149
Denver Post, 75
Deutsch, Babette, 69, 80
Dial, The, 4, 41, 43, 79, 275
Donaghy, William A., 181, 276
Doughty, LeGarde S., 139
[Douglas, Norman], 3
Dudley, Dorothy, 65
Dupee, F. W., 200

Emerson, Dorothy, 149
English Review, The, 3, 14
Enright, D. J., 263
Evanston Daily News-Index, 149

Farrar, John, 55
Feeney, Leonard, 133
Firkins, O. W., 8
Fitts, Dudley, 136
Fitzgerald, Robert, 235
Fletcher, John Gould, 39
F[lint], F. S., 3
Forgotson, E. S., 205

Fortnightly Review, 111
Forum and Century, 167
Fremantle, Anne, 195
Furioso, 225

Gannett, Lewis, 149
Garnett, Edward, 28
Gibson, Wilfrid Wilson, 41
Gregory, Horace, 132
Grigson, Geoffrey, 106
Guardian, The, 263

Hall, Edward B., 71
Hall, James Norman, 149
Harding, Walter, 245
Harper's, 35
Harper's Magazine, 273
Henderson, Alice Corbin, 41
Heuffer, Ford Madox, 41
Hicks, Granville, 83
Hillyer, Robert, 182
Holmes, John, 113, 149, 231, 250, 275
Horn Book, 275
Howells, William Dean, 35
Hudson Review, 223
Humphries, Rolfe, 134, 232
Hutchinson, Percy, 80
H., W., 249

Independent, 27, 36

Jakeman, Adelbert M., 275
Jarrell, Randall, 208
Johnston, J. H., 238
Jones, Llewellyn, 41
Jordan, Alice M., 275

K., B. M., 79
Kell, Richard, 263
Kennedy, Leo, 187, 227
Kilmer, Kenton, 197
Kimbrough, Robert, 273
Knowlton, Edgar C., 140
Kunitz, Stanley, 273

Leach, Henry G., 167
Library Journal, 185, 219, 238, 258

Literary Digest, 41
Literary Digest International Book Review, 55
Littel, Robert, 58
London Sunday Times, 149, 275
Lowell, Amy, 17

MacCarthy, Desmond, 275
Margoshes, Adam, 174
Mark Twain Quarterly, 167
Massachusetts Review, 264
M[aynard], T[heodore], 276
McDonald, Gerald, 219, 238
McMillin, Lawrence, 223
Meredith, William, 270
Mertins, Louis, 182
Michigan Alumnus, 67
Miller, Vincent, 273
M[onroe], H[arriet], 46, 78
Moore, Merrill, 147
Moore, Virginia, 101
Morley, Christopher, 149
Morton, David, 67
M., T., 149
Munro, Harold, 15

National Review, 273
Nation and Athenaeum, The, 93
Nation, The, 8, 11, 60, 76, 95, 130, 200, 232
Nethercot, Arthur H., 149
Newdick, Robert A., 146
Newdick, Robert S., 127
New England Quarterly, 110, 136, 163, 182
New Masses, 134
New Mexico Quarterly Review, 276
New Republic, 17, 43, 47, 58, 77, 83, 132, 200, 235, 253
New Statesman, 88, 263
Newsweek, 205
News-Week, 118
New Yorker, 151, 182, 205, 219, 238, 269
New York Evening Post, 41, 80
New York Herald Tribune, 149, 247
New York Herald Tribune Books, 80, 86, 149, 153, 172
New York Herald Tribune Weekly Book Review, 192, 210, 238, 275
New York Post, 115
New York Times, 149, 205, 238, 273
New York Times Book Review, 41, 80, 119, 149, 167, 170, 189, 198, 208, 221, 238, 273, 275
New York Tribune, 41
Nicholl, Louise Townsend, 111
North American Review, 80

Observer, The, 145
O'Donnell, William G., 264
Olson, Lawrence, 225
Open Shelf, 182, 205, 238
Opie, Thomas F., 205
Orton, Vrest, 163
Outlook, 41, 67
Outlook and Independent, 111

Partisan Review, 123
Payne, L. W., Jr., 122
Payne, William Morton, 4
Pierce, Frederick, E., 70
Poetry, 1, 15, 46, 65, 78, 158, 176, 205, 216, 221, 270
Poetry and Drama, 3, 15
Poore, Charles, 238, 273
Porter, Kenneth, 182
Pound, Ezra, 1, 15
Pratt Institute Library Quarterly Booklist, 182
Prescott, Orville, 205

R., E., 149
Reedy's Mirror, 41
Reely, Mary Katherine, 80, 111, 149, 182, 205, 276
Reporter, 254
Review of Reviews, 149
Ritchey, John, 161
Rittenhouse, Jessie B., 41
R., J., 128
Robie, Burton A., 258-59
Root, E. Merrill, 74, 141

Rosenthal, M. L., 254
Ross, Malcolm, 216
Rukeyser, Muriel, 158

San Francisco Chronicle, 212, 249
Saturday Review, 106
Saturday Review of Literature, 71, 111, 116, 169, 185, 207, 231, 241
Schneider, Isdor, 95
Scholastic, 149
Scott, W. T., 176
Selincourt, Basil De, 145
Sewanee Review, 146, 147
Shorer, Mark, 195
Sloan, Florence Bethune, 276
Snell, George, 212
Snow, Wilbert, 149, 172
South Atlantic Quarterly, 140
Southern Literary Messenger, 182
Southern Review, 143
Spectator, 51, 101
Spencer, Theodore, 77
Springfield Sunday Republican, 129
Springfield Sunday Union and Republican, 205, 275
Springfield Union-Republican, 80
S., R., 273
Stauffer, Donald A., 213
Stephens, James, 149
Stevenson, Adlai E., 253
Strachan, Pearl, 276
Strobel, Marion, 149
Strong, L. A. G., 93
Survey, 80
Swallow, Alan, 276

Taggard, Genevieve, 86
Theatre Arts, 205
Thomas, Edward, 14

Thompson, Lawrance, 189
Thompson, Ralph, 149
Time, 127, 154, 174, 201, 219, 228, 275
Times Literary Supplement, 1, 41, 98, 166, 179, 272, 275
Tinker, Edward L., 167

United States Quarterly Book List, 219
Untermeyer, Louis, 24, 62, 71, 111, 137, 202, 212, 275
U. S. Quarterly Book List, 205

Van Doren, Mark, 60, 76, 192, 238
Viereck, Peter, 235
Virginia Quarterly Review, 103, 157, 202
Voices, 225

Walton, Eda Lou, 119
Warren, C. Henry, 89, 111
[Wheeler, Edmund J.], 41
Whicher, George F., 177, 203, 210, 275
Whicher, Hariett F., 149
Whipple, Leon, 80
Wilbur, Richard, 247
Williams, William Carlos, 221
Wilson, James Southall, 103, 157
Wisconsin Library Bulletin, 80, 111, 149, 182, 205, 273, 276
Wisconsin Studies in Contemporary Literature, 273
World Tomorrow, 79

Yale Review, 70, 101, 125, 177, 203, 212

Zabel, Morton D., 143